Sonic Identity at the Margins

Sonic Identity at the Margins

Edited by
Jessie Fillerup and Joanna K. Love

BLOOMSBURY ACADEMIC
NEW YORK • LONDON • OXFORD • NEW DELHI • SYDNEY

BLOOMSBURY ACADEMIC
Bloomsbury Publishing Inc
1385 Broadway, New York, NY 10018, USA
50 Bedford Square, London, WC1B 3DP, UK
29 Earlsfort Terrace, Dublin 2, Ireland

BLOOMSBURY, BLOOMSBURY ACADEMIC and the Diana logo are trademarks of
Bloomsbury Publishing Plc

First published in the United States of America 2022
This paperback edition published 2023

Copyright © Jessie Fillerup and Joanna K. Love, 2022

Each chapter copyright by the contributor, 2022

For legal purposes the Acknowledgments on pp. 281–282 constitute
an extension of this copyright page.

Cover design: Louise Dugdale
Cover image © Scott P. Yates – USA TODAY NETWORK

All rights reserved. No part of this publication may be reproduced
or transmitted in any form or by any means, electronic or mechanical,
including photocopying, recording, or any information storage or
retrieval system, without prior permission in writing from the publishers.

Bloomsbury Publishing Inc does not have any control over, or responsibility for,
any third-party websites referred to or in this book. All internet addresses given in this
book were correct at the time of going to press. The author and publisher regret any
inconvenience caused if addresses have changed or sites have ceased to exist,
but can accept no responsibility for any such changes.

A catalog record for this book is available from the Library of Congress.

ISBN: HB: 978-1-5013-6878-3
PB: 978-1-5013-6882-0
ePDF: 978-1-5013-6880-6
eBook: 978-1-5013-6879-0

Typeset by Integra Software Services Pvt. Ltd.

To find out more about our authors and books visit www.bloomsbury.com
and sign up for our newsletters.

For the Department of Music at the University of Richmond

Contents

List of Illustrations ix
Contributors xii

Introduction to *Sonic Identity at the Margins*
   Joanna K. Love and Jessie Fillerup 1

Part 1 Hearing Race and Place

1 Mapping Sonic and Affective Geographies in Richmond, Virginia
   Andrew McGraw 19
2 Musical Indianism: Reassessing the Archive
   Victoria Rose Clark (Nanticoke) 43
3 Reconsidering "Rhythm" as a Cultural Marker in
   Black String Band Music *Landon Bain* 61
4 "The Year of Jubilee Is Come": Metatextual Resonance in Antislavery
   Hymn Parodies *Erin Fulton* 75
5 Accidental Alterity in Messiaen's *Quatre études de rythme*
   David Wolfson 97

Part 2 Sounding "Otherness" in Contemporary Media

6 Decolonizing Game Audio and Approaching Sound in
   Digital Storytelling *Kate Galloway* 113
7 Finding Home in the Unknown: Sounding Self-Determination
   from the Streets to the Void *Andrew J. Kluth* 135
8 Colonial Encounters, Alien Languages, and the Exotic
   Music of Denis Villeneuve's *Arrival* *Paige Zalman* 151
9 Decolonizing Disability: "Muteness," Music, and Eugenics in Screen
   Representation *James Deaville* 163
10 Hearing Borderline Personality Disorder in *Crazy Ex-Girlfriend*
   Joanna K. Love and Jessie Fillerup 185

Part 3 Performing Identity

11 Shirish Korde on Intercultural Composition
    Christopher Chandler — 205

12 Sonic Dismantling, Appropriation, and Confederate Monuments
    David Kirkland Garner — 219

13 *The Lanna Dream*: Reflections of Constructed Identities
    Waewdao Sirisook and Abbas Rasul — 235

14 American Blackness in Berlin: Race and Nationality in
    Contemporary Jazz Performance *Bertram D. Ashe* — 247

15 Remaking Traditions and Rehearing the Self:
    A Conversation with Reena Esmail *Christopher Chandler* — 263

Acknowledgments — 281
Index — 283

Illustrations

Figures

1.1 AudibleRVA map with several layers displayed. Gray dots = noise complaints; black stars = active venues; gray stars = defunct venues; black pins = ethnographic interviews; black squares = music infrastructure (music schools, stores, studios)   20
1.2 Black population density/noise complaints 2007–2019. Black population density indicated by shading   23
1.3a–d Typical noise complaint patterns before and after passage of restrictive noise ordinance. (a) Top left: June–July 2010, "scatter plot" pattern. (b) Top right: November–December 2011, complaints registered along Chamberlayne Avenue. (c) Bottom left. August–September 2012, complaints registered along Jefferson Davis Highway. (d) Bottom right. May–June 2013, complaints bordering and within the Fan (center of map)   24
1.4a–b Richmond HOLC maps (Nelson et al. 2020). Top: original HOLC map from the late 1930s. Bottom: HOLC map with poverty data from the 2000s   29
1.5 HOLC map with typical soundscape spectrograms, June 2019   30
1.6 Black population density/venues/events from AudibleRVA Calendar, as heatmap   33
1.7 AudibleRVA calendar of events by genre. October 2018–October 2019   34
6.1 *Never Alone* gameplay stills. Top: Nuna and Fox maneuver across ice floes. Bottom: Nuna and Fox work together to defeat the Polar Bear in his cave   118
6.2 *Invaders* gameplay stills   124
6.3 *Honour Water* gameplay stills. Top: the song "Gizaagi'igonan Gimaamaanan Aki." Bottom: the song "Miigwech Nibi"   127
7.1 Clipping. From left to right: Jonathan Snipes, William Hutson, and Daveed Diggs. Photo credit: Suzy Poling   138

7.2	*Splendor & Misery* cover art, featuring Cargo as an astronaut with tattered clothes and previously shackled feet	140
8.1	*Arrival* (2016), point of view shot of an alien pod from a helicopter	157
10.1	*Crazy Ex-Girlfriend*, still image of the season two theme song. The CW, episode 19, 2016	191
10.2	*Crazy Ex-Girlfriend*, still image of Trent performing the season two theme song. The CW, episode 43, 2018	192
10.3	*Crazy Ex-Girlfriend*, still image of Rebecca watching a video of herself performing. The CW, episode 37, 2017	194
10.4	*Crazy Ex-Girlfriend*, still image of the season three theme song. The CW, episode 34, 2017	196
13.1	*The Lanna Dream* (2019), Sirisook performing with a blow-up sex doll	240
13.2	*The Lanna Dream* (2019), Sirisook reproducing an exoticized pose, as if performing for tourists	241
15.1	Reena Esmail. Photo by Hannah Arista	272

Tables

4.1	Parodies in selected songsters in reverse chronological order, 1834–1852	79
5.1	*Île de feu I* schemata and form	105
5.2	*Île de feu II* schemata and form	106
7.1	*Splendor & Misery* (2016) track listing, totaling thirty-seven minutes	137
9.1	Characters with speaking or named roles in the 100 top-grossing American films of 2019, correlated with demographic data from 2018 (AII 2020: 15, 26–7; AII 2019: 4)	165
9.2	Types of disability represented in the 100 top-grossing American films of 2019 with gender distribution (AII 2020: 26–7)	165

Examples

2.1	Harvey Worthington Loomis, "The Chattering Squaw," *Lyrics of the Red Man*, Book II, op.76 (c. 1904)	44

4.1	"Better Days Coming." Music as notated in Mansfield (1848: 232), showing texts from Mansfield and Brown (1840: 29)	87
5.1	Olivier Messiaen, *Mode de valeurs et d'intensités*, mm. 48–52	98
5.2	Messiaen, *Île de feu I*, mm. 1–2. First statement of theme in right hand, top staff	103
5.3	Messiaen, *Île de feu II*, mm. 1–7. First statement of theme in left hand, bottom staff	107

Contributors

Bertram D. Ashe is Jabez A Bostwick Professor of English and American Studies at the University of Richmond, USA, and the author of *Twisted: My Dreadlock Chronicles* (2015), a nonfiction finalist for a Library of Virginia Literary Award. He teaches and writes about a post–Civil Rights Movement school of literature and culture, referred to as "post-blackness," as well as the expressive-culture triumvirate of black hair, basketball, and jazz. He is contributing coeditor, with Ilka Saal, of *Slavery and the Post-Black Imagination* (2020), and his essay, "The Trey Ellis Eighties and the Launching of an Artistic 'School,'" is forthcoming in *African American Literature in Transition, 1980–1990*.

Landon Bain is a doctoral candidate in music at the University of California, San Diego, USA. His primary research interests include US old-time music, critical race studies, and the history and cultural politics of folk revivals. His writing on these issues focuses on the racialization of sound in old-time and bluegrass music. He is also an active participant in San Diego's local old-time scene, performing on banjo and guitar.

Christopher Chandler is Assistant Professor of Music at Union College, USA, and a cofounder of the [Switch~ Ensemble]. A composer of acoustic and electroacoustic music, he teaches courses in composition, theory, and technology. His work draws on field recordings, found sound objects, and custom generative software. Awards and recognition for his music include a BMI Student Composer Award, an ASCAP/SEAMUS Commission, New Music USA Project Grants, and the Nadia Boulanger Composition Prize from the American Conservatory in Fontainebleau, France. Christopher holds degrees from the Eastman School of Music, Bowling Green State University, and the University of Richmond.

Victoria Rose Clark (Nanticoke) is a digital librarian at Répertoire international de la presse musicale. She holds a PhD in Critical and Comparative Studies in Music from the University of Virginia, USA. She studies representations of, and collaborations with, American Indians in American music. Her work has been funded by fellowships and grants from the Newberry Library, Pennsylvania State University, Indiana University, and the University of Virginia. She has presented papers at the Newberry Library, the Society for American Music, the University of Richmond, and the University of Virginia.

James Deaville teaches music in the School for Studies in Art and Culture at Carleton University, CA, with particular pedagogical and research interests in the various interfaces of music, media, and disability. He edited *Music in Television* (2010) and with Christina Baade coedited *Music and the Broadcast Experience* (2016). He has published contributions on music and disability in the *Oxford Handbook of Music and Disability Studies* (2015), *Journal of Interdisciplinary Voice Studies* (2019), and *Journal of Literary & Cultural Disability Studies* (2022). He is principal editor (with Ron Rodman and Siu-Lan Tan) for the *Oxford Handbook of Music and Advertising* (2021).

Reena Esmail is a composer who works between the worlds of Indian and Western classical music to bring communities together through the creation of equitable musical spaces. She holds degrees from The Juilliard School and the Yale School of Music, USA, and has written for Kronos Quartet, Albany Symphony, and Conspirare. A resident of Los Angeles, she is the 2020–23 Swan Family Artist in Residence with Los Angeles Master Chorale and the 2020–21 Composer in Residence with Seattle Symphony. She is the artistic director of Shastra, a nonprofit organization that promotes cross-cultural music connecting musical traditions of India and the West.

Jessie Fillerup is Associate Professor of Music at the University of Richmond, USA, and the author of *Magician of Sound: Ravel and the Aesthetics of Illusion* (2021). She has written on French music, opera, musical temporality, and magic for publications such as *Music & Letters, Cambridge Opera Journal, 19th-Century Music,* and *Music Theory Online*. Her work has been supported by numerous grants and fellowships, including the Mellon Foundation, the National Endowment for the Humanities, and the Aarhus Institute of Advanced Studies (Denmark). Her latest book project, *Enchanted: Music and Conjuring in the Long Nineteenth Century*, examines music in theatrical magic shows.

Erin Fulton is a doctoral candidate at the University of Kentucky, USA. Her dissertation examines the role of hymn-singing during informal devotion in

1840s New England. She serves as bibliographer for the Sounding Spirit Project, a digital humanities initiative improving access to Southern sacred music imprints published in 1850–1925. She is also director of a Nunn Center for Oral History project, which documents Southern Harmony singing in Western Kentucky. Her work can be read in the journal *Nota Bene* and in *Nineteenth-Century Music Criticism*, ed. Teresa Cascudo (2017). She plans to pursue a career in music librarianship.

Kate Galloway is Lecturer in Music at Rensselaer Polytechnic Institute, USA, where she teaches in the Electronic Arts, Music, and Games and Simulation Arts and Sciences programs. Her research and teaching address sonic responses to environmentalism, sound studies, digital culture, interactive media, Indigenous musical modernities, and ecological knowledge. Her monograph, *Remix, Reuse, Recycle: Music, Media Technologies, and Remediating the Environment* (under contract with Oxford University Press), examines how and why contemporary artists remix and recycle sounds, music, and texts encoded with environmental knowledge. Her work is published in *The Soundtrack*, *Ethnomusicology*, *MUSICultures*, *Tourist Studies*, *Sound Studies*, *Feminist Media Histories*, and *Popular Music*.

David Kirkland Garner is Assistant Professor of Composition and Theory at the University of South Carolina, USA, and holds degrees from Duke University, University of Michigan, and Rice University, USA. His music reconfigures past sounds—from Bach to minimalism to the banjo—into new sonic shapes and directions. He seeks to make time and history audible, particularly through an exploration of archival recordings documenting the musical traditions of the southern United States. Garner's first album, *Dark Holler*, was released in 2017 by New Focus Recordings.

Andrew J. Kluth is Visiting Assistant Professor of Music at Case Western Reserve University, USA. His interdisciplinary interests include music and philosophy. He is primarily concerned with music after 1950, and his teaching and research focus on experimentalisms, popular music, and aesthetics. His publications appear in the *Journal of Jazz Studies*, *The International Journal of New Media, Technology and the Arts*, and *DownBeat Magazine*, and he has presented research at conferences throughout the United States, UK, and Europe. As a saxophonist he has worked in the American and European scenes and has been a teaching artist for the Herbie Hancock Institute of Jazz.

Shirish Korde is Distinguished Professor of Humanities at the College of the Holy Cross, USA. He has composed for soloists, chamber ensembles, orchestras, and the theater, including five operas and an experimental 2020 Zoom opera (*Aède*). His compositions have been performed by the Minnesota, New Zealand, and Chicago Symphony orchestras, and he has received grants and awards from the National Endowment for the Arts, the Massachusetts Cultural Council, the Siemens Foundation, and the Leif Foundation, among others. His music is available on the Chandos, Mode, and Neuma labels. In 2021, the newly formed South Asian Symphony Orchestra will premiere a new work, *Oceans Rising*, in Chennai, India.

Joanna K. Love is Associate Professor of Music at the University of Richmond, USA, and the Book Reviews Editor for the *Journal of the Society for American Music (JSAM)*. She researches American and popular musics in multimedia and has written extensively on music in US brand and political advertising. Her work has appeared in volumes for Oxford University Press and Routledge, as well as journals including *JSAM* and *Music and Politics*. Her 2019 book, *Soda Goes Pop: Pepsi-Cola Advertising and Popular Music*, was supported by an AAUW fellowship. Her current project is titled *Popular Music and Political Resistance at America's Super Bowl*.

Andrew McGraw is Associate Professor of Music at the University of Richmond, USA. He received his PhD in ethnomusicology at Wesleyan University, USA, in 2005 and has published extensively on traditional and experimental music in Southeast Asia. He is the author of *Radical Traditions: Re-imagining Culture in Balinese Contemporary Music* (2013), which was supported by a Fulbright grant and a fellowship at the Cornell Society for the Humanities. He is coeditor, with Sumarsam, of *Performing Indonesia* (2016). His current work on the AudibleRVA project has grown out of a long-term project on music and ethics.

Abbas Rasul is a professional writer. He is of Indian African descent and values authentic personal and cultural artistic expression. He seeks to develop new understandings and knowledges of cultural identity and the processes that mediate difference in contemporary society. He currently writes articles and fiction to assist in the development of perspectives that celebrate and promote diversity.

Waewdao Sirisook is the director of the Lanna Wisdom School, Chiang Mai, Thailand, and a professor at Chiang Mai University. She earned a master's degree from the University of California, Los Angeles, USA. Through dance and the arts, she not only discovered her Lanna heritage, but with the many grants and prizes earned over her professional career, she has dedicated herself to piecing together forgotten fragments of her culture. Her life and work focus on issues of alienation, identity, disenfranchisement, and reformation. She is currently working on projects that promote diversity and develop a better understanding of Lanna's culture and history.

David Wolfson is a lecturer at Hunter College, USA. He is a composer, librettist, and pianist. His research interests are interdisciplinary, focusing on intersections of the psychology of music with other musical areas. He holds a PhD in Music Composition from Rutgers University, USA and lives in New York City.

Paige Zalman is currently pursuing a PhD in higher education from West Virginia University, USA. She holds an MA in musicology from the same institution, as well as a BM in music performance from the University of North Carolina Wilmington. Her original research has appeared in *American Music* and in the edited volume, *The Opioid Epidemic and U.S. Culture: Expression, Art, and Politics in an Age of Addiction*. Her research interests include musical theater, opera, popular music, gender studies in music, music and contemporary politics, and musical borrowing.

Introduction to *Sonic Identity at the Margins*

Joanna K. Love and Jessie Fillerup

Meri Sakhi Ki Avaaz (*My Sister's Voice*), a vocal and orchestral piece written in 2018 by the Los Angeles–based composer Reena Esmail, challenges audiences to hear anew the canonic "Flower Duet" from Léo Delibes's 1883 opera, *Lakmé*. Combining recorded samples from the opera with newly composed music performed by a live orchestra, Esmail turns the famous duet into a bilingual interaction between a classically trained Hindustani vocalist and a Western-trained opera singer, suggesting what the number might have sounded like had Delibes's musical style actually reflected the Indian setting of the fictional tale. *Meri Sakhi Ki Avaaz* explores the complexity and fluidity of identity in today's world: the piece exemplifies how Esmail, born in the United States to Indian parents, lives and composes between two cultures.

Esmail's piece was performed as part of a year-long festival (2018–2019) hosted by the Department of Music at the University of Richmond, Virginia, that convened dozens of composers, scholars, and performers from around the world. One of its hallmark events, the "Contested Frequencies" conference, featured an array of panel discussions, papers, and concerts encouraging the campus and the broader community to hear beyond the hegemonic structures and persistent ideologies that have shaped perceptions of marginalized music and sounds. The compositions and scholarship presented there extended and challenged foundational work on musical "othering" by employing twenty-first-century interdisciplinary perspectives and analytical tools.[1] The performance of Esmail's composition excmplified these aims in its sonic blurring of the lines between past and present, language and tradition, technology and performance, Western and non-Western, colonization and Indigeneity, self and other, immigrant and native-born. *Meri Sakhi Ki Avaaz* thus encapsulated the festival and conference's primary themes, which in turn have become the premise of this book: to analyze and interpret how marginalized identities manifest in music and sound.

Sonic Identity at the Margins features the work of academics, composers, and performers who participated in the conference, highlighting their interdisciplinary approaches to examining the ways that sonic identity has been experienced, articulated, defined, and resisted from the nineteenth century to the present. Given the myriad performative, social, cultural, and historical aspects of identity formation, the authors' methodological approaches range from personal accounts and embodied expression to archival research and hermeneutic interpretation. Their analyses of real and imagined spaces—from video games and monument sites to depictions of outer space—focus on sonic creation, performance, and reception. Drawing from the fields of musicology, ethnomusicology, dance, creative writing, composition, music theory, and media studies, the authors advocate for, challenge, and reimagine the roles played by music and sound in constructing notions of identity. The book therefore encompasses a broad array of musical experiences, including antislavery songsters, Indigenous tunes and soundscapes, noise, multimedia, popular music, jazz, and instrumental solo and symphonic works.

Sonic Identity, Now and Then

Organizers of the 2019 "Contested Frequencies" conference—the volume editors and Andrew McGraw, author of Chapter 1 and director of the year-long festival—recognized the significance of hosting the event in Richmond, Virginia. The city's complex history as the former capital of the US Confederacy and the site of Patrick Henry's famous Revolutionary War–inciting speech ("Give me liberty, or give me death!") proved a fitting location to host difficult conversations about representation, identity, selfhood, and nationhood. However, none of us could have imagined the degree to which the conference's location and predominant themes—race, privilege, redlining, Confederate statues, slavery, and colonialism—would become central to the national conversation the following year. In the summer and fall of 2020, an unprecedented reckoning with the nation's structures of bias and inequality began to unfold after Black Lives Matter protests occurred across the country, incited by a viral video capturing yet another unarmed Black man, George Floyd, being senselessly killed by a police officer.

As we were editing this volume, the city of Richmond's leaders finally undertook meaningful and symbolic actions to fight the region's legacy of white supremacy, racism, and segregation. With the support of many constituents and advocacy groups, mayor Levar Stoney accomplished in just over a month what other leaders had toiled to do for years, ordering on July 1, 2020, the removal of the imposing statues erected over a century ago to glorify Confederate "lost cause" rhetoric and manifestly enforce Jim Crow segregation along Monument Avenue, now a main artery of the city.[2] As nationwide disputes over the removal of Confederate statues and other white-supremacist symbols have again heated up, we cannot help but partially attribute Mayor Stoney's decisive action to the current affairs—including the COVID-19 pandemic—that have forced us all to pause and *listen*. This collective act of listening was perhaps best evidenced on July 4, 2020—the nation's Independence Day—when Nina Simone's 1976 performance of "I Wish I Knew How It Would Feel to Be Free" was projected onto the newly graffitied statue of the Confederate General, Robert E. Lee (pictured on this book's cover). This artistic repurposing of the statue into a public concert privileging Black voices evoked a symbolic gravity that would have been unimaginable just a few months prior.[3] Much like Esmail's *Meri Sakhi Ki Avaaz*, the visual and sonic overlaying of past and present, technology and performance, self and other, dominance and oppression displaced the canonic monument, turning it into a background for the re-hearing of Simone's well-known song. The event demonstrated how hegemonic structures might effectively be transformed through image and sound.

The other major event that has unfolded is, of course, the COVID-19 pandemic that has taken more than 3 million lives, shuttered entire industries, derailed economies, and transformed every facet of contemporary life. In the United States, the pandemic has made the country's systemic inequalities and deficiencies impossible to ignore: those most affected by the crisis are Black, Indigenous, Latinx, aged, economically disadvantaged, disabled, and women.[4] Yet one modest bright spot has been the way many lives were forced to slow down, creating a (brief) sense of global empathy that has allowed non-hegemonic voices to resonate more meaningfully within national and worldwide conversations. It seems that more than ever before, we collectively realize what civil rights activists, artists, writers, and scholars have proclaimed for decades: that ideologies of listening in the United States—what Jennifer Lynn Stoever calls "the listening ear" (2016: 13)—have been shaped and constrained by the structures of white elite masculinity. Not coincidentally, the same issues have (re)arisen within the academy, ignited most recently when the music theorist, Philip Ewell, publicly challenged the "white racial frame" and the history of white supremacy that dominates the field.[5] *Sonic Identity at the Margins* joins these important conversations, reexamining how sonic identity is formed and interpreted, and the ways in which it affects how we hear ourselves and one another.

Approaches and Themes

Identity, much like sound itself, is increasingly understood as ephemeral, fluid, and polysemic. Recent research on the intersectional and evolving natures of identity formation—projected from within and shaped by external forces—owes much to the scholars of race and gender studies, many of whom have written extensively about music's role in expressing identity.[6] Following these and other contemporary theorists (cited throughout), the authors of this book do not view identity as fixed or stable but recognize the many ways it is formed, represented, and interpreted in particular places and times. Indeed, the diverse topics and methods they examine are unified by the attention paid to expressions of marginalizing and marginalized identities, which emerge from evolving historical, cultural, social, and political contexts.

Given the pluralities that underpin identity formation and notions of marginality (defined here, more generally, as non-dominant or non-hegemonic), the chapters do not adopt a single methodological framework, nor do they seek to theorize or categorically define how marginalized sonic identities are formed or who forms them. They instead offer novel approaches to a range of musical experiences, engaging with non-canonic musics and focusing on marginalized voices, resonating through the subjects of inquiry and the identities of the contributors themselves. The authors thus heed calls by Ewell and his predecessors to (re)consider and decenter dominant structures and privileged viewpoints when creating, performing, and listening and to reassess the methods used to analyze these experiences. Accordingly, some authors in this volume, like Andrew McGraw (Chapter 1) and Victoria Rose Clark (Nanticoke) (Chapter 2), challenge the very nature and purpose of archival research and its associated methods, seeking to expand possibilities for gathering and interpreting materials. Others interrogate the relevance of distinctions by genre or musical practice, as evident in the chapters by Landon Bain (Chapter 3), Joanna K. Love and Jessie Fillerup (Chapter 10), Bertram Ashe (Chapter 14), and the interviews conducted by Christopher Chandler (Chapters 11 and 15). Many chapters confront (mis) understandings about how marginalized populations are represented; all of the chapters, both explicitly and implicitly, deal with sonic engagement as a kind of "critical performance" and "political act," as reexamined by Nina Sun Eidsheim in her recent work (2019).

The case studies featured here extend concepts and methods explored in the interdisciplinary studies of music and identity that first gained prominence in the 1990s. These works challenged assumptions about homogeneity and teleology based on location and region (cf. Straw 1991), examined how musical materials are used to discuss the "social construction, exploration and control of identity categories and their boundaries" (Stokes 1997: 23), and interrogated musical experience and identity as a "mobile" process (Frith 1996: 109). *Sonic Identity at the Margins* also builds on foundational turn-of-the-millennium research on musical exoticism, subcultural communities, borrowing, appropriation, whiteness, and othering—including work by Jonathan Bellman (1998), Ingrid Monson (1995), Georgina Born and David Hesmondhalgh (2000), Timothy D. Taylor (2007), Laurent Aubert (2007), and Ralph Locke (2009), among others. Moreover, many chapters attend to the "systems of dominance and oppression" that inform how sound is used to "mark" or distinguish, creating boundaries that separate certain communities (Taylor 2007: 1; Dyer 1997: 8; Stokes 1997: 5). Others engage with the expansive interdisciplinary literature on colonialism and its intersections with globalization (cf. Gebesmair and Smudits 2001; Bloechl 2008; Kroier 2012; White 2012; Tan 2012; Huggan 2013; Loomba 2015; Taylor 2016), in some cases modeling efforts by Linda Tuhiwai Smith ([1999] 2012), Glen Sean Coulthard (2014), and Walter D. Mignolo and Catherine E. Walsh (2018) to decolonize disciplinary tools and global histories.

Recent studies on musical identity have adopted an educational, pedagogical, or therapeutic focus (cf. Green 2011; McFerran, Derrington, and Saarikallio 2019; Stakelum 2016) or have examined specific genres or styles practiced by particular groups, regions, communities, and nations (Applegate and Potter 2002; Biddle and Vanessa 2007; Fulcher 2011; Morra 2014; MacDonald, Hargreaves, and Miell 2017). *Sonic Identity at the Margins* takes a wider view, investigating a variety of topics through methods drawn from a range of humanistic and artistic fields. For example, Waewdao Sirisook and Abbas Rasul (Chapter 13) couple Sirisook's expertise as a dancer and choreographer with the colonial histories of Thailand, while Chandler explores intercultural compositional processes in his interviews with Reena Esmail and Shirish Korde. In Chapter 14, Ashe intertwines his lived experience of Black musical traditions with a sharp observational style that uses humor and vivid language to critique cross-cultural practices. McGraw, Kate Galloway (Chapter 6), Bain (Chapter 3), and Andrew J. Kluth (Chapter 7) combine their (ethno)musicological training with approaches drawn from the digital humanities, sound studies, and critical race theory. Clark and Erin Fulton (Chapter 4) demonstrate the nuances and possibilities of archival research, while fellow musicologists James Deaville (Chapter 9), Love, and Fillerup introduce new research on media and disability studies. In Chapter 12, the composer David Kirkland Garner draws on his personal experiences and regional knowledge of "the South" to examine his recent compositions, which seek to position dominant structures against marginalized sounds. David Wolfson applies cognitive theory to musical analysis in Chapter 5 to demonstrate a new type of musical othering in Olivier Messiaen's music. Paige Zalman (Chapter 8) pairs colonial theory with hermeneutics to study the sonic representations of the alien Other in film.

Despite this book's diversity of topics and approaches, cross-disciplinary dialogues emerge across the volume as the authors explore sonic identity from one of three primary vantage points: the personal, local communities, and global perspectives. Chapters focused on the personal consider how the "self" is sonically constructed or interpreted in compositions, performances, and multimedia. Chandler, for example, highlights how Korde's and Esmail's music reflects their experiences with immigration and hybridity. Garner examines concerns about appropriation and his own racial privilege in a recent composition about the American South, and Ashe interrogates his own encounters with Black diasporic musical traditions in Germany. Deaville, Love, and Fillerup analyze how multimedia soundtracks might alternately express or misrepresent the personal experiences of characters with disabilities and mental health challenges. Wolfson investigates Messiaen's self-othering in his idiosyncratic musical style, and Kluth identifies the lasting repercussions of slavery on personal identity as expressed in experimental hip hop.

These topics intersect with the second category of identity explored here, local communities. Many of these chapters confront the historical complexities of racial relationships in the United States. For example, McGraw's study of noise and policing in Richmond, Virginia, reveals the persistence of Jim Crow redlining policies on the city's sonic production. Bain considers the effect of the music industry's segregationist practices on contemporary understandings of Black Appalachian musical traditions. Fulton demonstrates the antislavery political fervor concealed within nineteenth-century songsters, which often critiqued the hypocritical embrace of slavery among some Christians, whereas

Clark repositions the agency of First Nations communities in the United States, focusing on Indigenous contributions to the Musical Indianism movement of the nineteenth and twentieth centuries.

The colonial impulses that shaped the United States and other nations extend to the third area of inquiry—sonic identity across the globe, and even into outer space. Authors dealing with these themes seek to reinscribe the value of knowledge from native cultures. Galloway, for instance, studies video game sound design that promotes narratives of ecological cooperation between Indigenous peoples living in North America and their environments. Sirisook and Rasul reflect on the many ways that the multimedia performance, *The Lanna Dream* (2019), works to literally "undress" tourist fantasies of Sirisook's culture. Zalman demonstrates how the musical score and sound design for the science-fiction film *Arrival* (2016) offers insightful lessons on the pervasiveness of colonial ideology in media and pop culture.

Within and across these themes—the personal, local, and global—the volume's chapters connect with and complement one another, sometimes in unexpected ways. Esmail's remarks on composing the fluid nature of Indian and American intercultural identity into her pieces resonate with Ashe's reflections on the performativity of music and race in jazz performances in Germany and with Sirisook's embodied response to the effects of the Western gaze on her culture. McGraw's analysis of acoustic territories and racial segregation in Richmond speaks both to Kluth's chapter on the abiding echoes of slavery in Afrofuturist hip hop and to Garner's personal reflections on writing music about Southern monuments and white supremacy. Through analytical case studies, interviews, and personal chapters, *Sonic Identity at the Margins* bridges critical and creative work to offer interconnected, fresh perspectives on marginalized sounds and musics.

Chapter Overview

The chapters in this volume are organized into three parts according to their shared themes or approaches. Part One, "Hearing Race and Place," examines perceptions of racial identity and notions of place, both literal and figurative, interrogating histories that implicate past and modern practices alike. Chapter 1, "Mapping Sonic and Affective Geographies in Richmond Virginia," examines how sound maps might reveal and repair the lasting effects of redlining and de facto segregation in today's southern cities. Using sound and demographic data from an ongoing digital mapping project of a local music scene, McGraw demonstrates how the intersections of race and class determine the city's "acoustic politics of space," as well as the "sonic rights and resources" of its citizens. Examining who is permitted to "flourish through sound" in Richmond, he asks, "What role might sound and music play in forging new, more inclusive affective publics, enabling broader access to the common good?"

Chapter 2, "Musical Indianism: Reassessing the Archive," applies decolonial approaches to archival methods to better illuminate the roles Indigenous people played in shaping the classical "Indianist" movement in the United States. Clark revisits early twentieth-century ethnographies of First Nations communities and individuals, introducing new perspectives on sonic agency that diverge from historical discourses, which typically place nonnative composers at the center of the movement. Instead, she uses archival sources to recenter Indigenous actions in a process she calls "musical Indianism," which she defines as "the holistic study of the labor that generated [the] musical products."

In Chapter 3, Bain similarly questions the reliability of documented histories and archival materials in Appalachian old-time music. In "Reconsidering 'Rhythm' as Cultural Marker in Black String Band Music," Bain questions how essentialist and racialized notions of musical style, especially those that tie Blackness to rhythm, continue to misinform current understandings of both Black and white generational musical traditions in North Carolina. He proposes an "anti-anti-essentialist" approach that "embrac[es] more regionally rooted, historically contingent approaches to stylistic analysis and critical race theory."

A rereading of primary source documents also informs Fulton's arguments in Chapter 4, " 'The Year of Jubilee Is Come': Metatextual Resonance in Antislavery Hymn Parodies." Here she reveals new information about the abolitionist cause through hymn parodies disseminated in antislavery songsters in the United States. Her study of twelve songsters published between 1834 and 1854 shows how Black and white antislavery writers attempted to provoke sympathy for enslaved people by editing the texts of popular hymns, reflecting the experiences of the enslaved and reminding Christian believers of their moral obligations.

Part I concludes with Wolfson's discussion of Oliver Messiaen's *Île de feu I & II* (1950), where he examines musical motifs purportedly inspired by and dedicated to the people of Papua. In "Accidental Alterity in Messiaen's *Quatre études de rythme*" (Chapter 5), Wolfson parses the reasons behind the composer's exoticizing impulses, using schema theory to propose how listeners might hear juxtapositions of the piece's exoticist and proto-serialist themes. His analysis ultimately reveals why Messian's unfamiliar serial style might actually be heard as "other" instead of the Papuan themes he characterizes as such.

Part II, "Sounding 'Otherness' in Contemporary Media," considers representations of real and imagined marginalized populations in video games, recordings, television series, and films. All of the chapters in this section interrogate hegemonic power structures that shape mediated sonic perspectives, and many engage specifically with the long-term (and ongoing) effects of colonialism, slavery, and globalization. Some employ emerging theories of race and Indigeneity, while others look at entanglements among the cultural constructs of gender and disability.

Chapter 6, "Decolonizing Game Audio and Approaching Sound in Digital Storytelling," investigates how new methods of video game and sound design tell authentic stories of the native peoples living in North America and their symbiotic relationship to nature. Galloway studies a sample of Indigenous-developed and co-developed games that express their communities' lived experiences and traditions. She demonstrates how and why various games use "sound and music to resound Indigenous futures, ecological relationships and crises, and ways of knowing the land," revealing how digital technology and Indigenous ecological knowledge can coexist and flourish through mutually supportive endeavors.

Chapter 7, "Finding Home in the Unknown: Sounding Self-Determination from the Streets to the Void," theorizes how an Afrofuturist hip hop album set in outer space grapples with the long-term effects of slavery. Kluth analyzes clipping.'s 2016 album, *Splendor and Misery*, blending critical race theory with studies of noise to show how the album's avant-garde, science-fiction-themed soundtrack offers glimpses of "agency and hope in the face of nihilism and existential dread." The narrative protagonist of the album, a former slave adrift in space, finds that losing his sense of self and his spatial and temporal tethers opens a future full of possibility, free from oppressive power structures.

Another space-themed chapter, "Colonial Encounters, Alien Languages, and the Exotic Music of Denis Villeneuve's *Arrival*," discusses how Jóhann Jóhannsson's 2016 experimental film score perpetuates the fear of the space alien Other. In Chapter 8, Zalman argues that the score pits familiar musical tropes drawn from acoustic Western art music against Jóhannsson's (initially) unfamiliar, electronic, non-melodic portrayal of the alien visitors, projecting anxieties about colonial domination onto them. Her analysis demonstrates how film soundtracks—even those featuring non-human characters—continue to reinforce harmful ideologies that oppose the Western self against the unknown Other.

In Chapter 9, "Decolonizing Disability: 'Muteness,' Music, and Eugenics in Screen Representation," Deaville examines how mute characters are typically misrepresented in popular films. Drawing from scholarship in disability studies and recent statistical analyses of disability portrayed in film, Deaville demonstrates how sound and music have been used to colonize representations of nonspeaking characters, such as Ada, the protagonist in Jane Campion's film *The Piano* (1993). Linking such representations to the history of eugenics, he advocates for the decolonization and dismediation of disability in audiovisual media.

Chapter 10, coauthored by Fillerup and Love, rounds out this section by seeking links between musical portrayals of gender and mental health. "Hearing Borderline Personality Disorder in *Crazy Ex-Girlfriend*" explores how blurred musical structures and parodied genres in the acclaimed television series (that ran from 2015 to 2019) help define the title character's unstable views of self and other. We demonstrate how the show's metatextual practices and theme songs turn pop and musical theater conventions into potential symptoms of mental illness and reveal how the protagonist's performative variations on the love-crazed woman illuminate gendered stigmas that pervade popular culture in the United States.

Part III, "Performing Identity," examines how musical identity is expressed through composition and received in performance. Chandler's interviews with South Asian-American composers Shirish Korde and Reena Esmail serve as bookends for this section. These chapters suggest new ways of hearing hybrid and multinational identities by describing the composers' aims to bridge conventionally opposing traditions, including East versus West and aural versus notated. Chapter 11, "Shirish Korde on Intercultural Composition," reveals how the composer integrates his multidisciplinary backgrounds in jazz, ethnography, and composition into his music. In pieces like *Lalit–2nd Prism* (2019), for orchestra, solo cello, and tabla, Korde brings together performers with a variety of cultural backgrounds and challenges them to incorporate musical techniques from other traditions into their own skill sets.

Next, Garner grapples with his efforts to sonically deconstruct southern Confederate monuments in his piece, *Red hot sun turning over* (2019). In Chapter 12, "Sonic Dismantling, Appropriation, and Confederate Monuments,"

Garner questions and historicizes his stylistic choices, describing his intentions to "sonically dismantle" structures of white supremacy by using and remaking preexisting tunes and recordings. He positions his compositional objectives within national conversations about race, ideological conceptions of "the South," and cultural appropriation.

Sirisook and Rasul provide similar context for Sirisook's 2019 multimedia performance piece in Chapter 13, "*The Lanna Dream*: Reflections of Constructed Identities." Here, they describe how the roles of colonialism and the Western gaze influenced Sirisook's decision to feature hybridized Lanna and Western music, which accompanies her choreographic response to tourists' consumptive views of northern Thai culture. The chapter interrogates the relationship between the region's visitors and its residents, who often feel they must perform a fabricated version of Lanna culture for outsiders. Sirisook's performance gives voice to the identities of her people, exploring the precarity of their transactional relationships with tourists and their negotiations between the desire for authentic revitalization and financial security.

In Chapter 14, "American Blackness in Berlin: Race and Nationality in Contemporary Jazz Performance," Ashe reflects on hearing diasporic Black jazz traditions performed by an all-white band in Germany. As a Black American, he examines some of the genre's fundamental characteristics in this unfamiliar context, including the role of call and response, asking, "What happens to jazz performance when the music is played by and for people who, collectively, were born and raised *outside* the nation and the cultural tradition from which the music originally came?" After experiencing a Black vernacular event in a German jazz club, Ashe investigates its sources, including the musical and cultural background of one of the band's performers and the presence of Black Americans in the audience.

Chapter 15 brings the book full circle with Chandler's interview of Esmail, including a discussion of the piece *Meri Sakhi Ki Avaaz*, described at the beginning of this introduction. In "Re-Making Traditions and Re-Hearing the Self: A Conversation with Reena Esmail," the composer characterizes this and other works in which she seeks to find "resonance" between the Indian and American cultures that she inhabits. She further explains how the commissioning process sometimes involves uncomfortable cultural implications, noting that she has felt most inspired by projects that sought genuine cultural connections and resisted tokenizing impulses.

***

By studying the marginalized perspectives of sonic creation, performance, and reception from without and within, through past and present, and in future and imagined spaces, *Sonic Identity at the Margins* offers multiple entry points for learning more about the relationships between sound and identity. It contributes to proliferating conversations in academia, as well as those in (inter)national and local communities, demonstrating the possibilities that interdisciplinary scholarship and personal narrative hold for understanding sonic identity's many manifestations. By featuring a variety of topics, methods, and writing styles, we expect this book to engage not only music scholars, students, performers, and composers, but also cultural theorists and practitioners from non-musical disciplines. The analytical and performative chapters of *Sonic Identity at the Margins* use this uncertain moment in global history to draw readers into challenging topics, acknowledging that as we collectively grapple with them, we each occupy different positions of privilege due to our variously raced, gendered, sexual, able-bodied, national, classed, or educated identities. We further recognize the inevitable shortcomings in attempting to address the kinds of complex issues that one collection cannot fully unpack. And yet, in our attempts to listen backward and forward through a diversity of experiences and practices, we hope to amplify—in a literal sense—the perspectives of those less heard and to offer an encouraging answer to the question posed over two decades ago by Martin Stokes in *Ethnicity, Identity, and Music: The Musical Construction of Place*: "Does music provide any means by which the boundaries [of ethnicity and place] might be challenged in any lasting way?" (1997: 24). By centering the many marginalized identities explored in this collection, we enthusiastically answer, "Yes!"

Notes

1 See, for example, Born and Hesmondhalgh (2000), Taylor (2007), and others listed throughout this volume.
2 Notably, Dr. Julian Hayter, Associate Professor of Leadership Studies at the University of Richmond, provided attendees a narrated tour of Monument Avenue's fraught history during the "Contested Frequencies" conference. Over a century's worth of materials detailing the processes of designing, fundraising, erecting, and revealing Richmond's monuments can also be found in the online exhibits curated

by the American Civil War Museum on its "On Monument Avenue" website: https://onmonumentave.com/onlineexhibits. The Robert E. Lee statue currently remains standing due to an ongoing legal battle over the ownership of the land on which it presides, though Richmond's citizens have made it into an artistic canvas for the Black Lives Matter movement, making its presence more inclusive and reflective.
3   We give special thanks to the photographer, Scott P. Yates, and to USA TODAY NETWORK for granting us permission to reproduce this image on our cover.
4   Among the many datasets and proliferating scholarship documenting the effects of the pandemic, an October 15, 2020, report on the death rate categorized by ethnicity and region in the United States provides a sobering account of these trends ("The Color of the Coronavirus" 2020).
5   Ewell extends the concept of the "white racial frame" from Joe Feagin's work (2013).
6   See, for example, bell hooks and Patricia Hill Collins on Black bodies in popular music.

References

Applegate, C. and P. Potter, eds. (2002), *Music and German National Identity*, Chicago: University of Chicago Press.

Aubert, L. (2007), *The Music of the Other: New Challenges for Ethnomusicology in a Global Age*, trans. Carla Ribeiro, Burlington: Ashgate.

Bellman, J., ed. (1998), *The Exotic in Western Music*, Boston: Northeastern University Press.

Biddle, I. and V. Knights, eds. (2007), *Music, National Identity, and the Politics of Location: Between the Global and the Local*, New York: Routledge.

Born, G. and D. Hesmondhalgh, eds. (2000), *Western Music and Its Others: Difference, Representation, and Appropriation in Music*, Berkeley and Los Angeles: University of California Press.

Bloechl, O. A. (2008), *Native American Song at the Frontiers of Early Modern Music*, New York: Cambridge University Press.

Collins, P. H. (2004), *Black Sexual Politics: African Americans, Gender, and the New Racism*, New York: Routledge.

Coulthard, G. S. (2014), *Red Skin, White Masks: Rejecting the Colonial Politics of Recognition*, Minneapolis: University of Minnesota Press.

Dyer, R. (1997), *White*, London: Routledge.

Eidsheim, N. S. (2019), *The Race of Sound: Listening, Timbre, & Vocality in African American Music*, Durham, NC: Duke University Press.

Ewell, P. A. (2020), "Music Theory and the White Racial Frame," *Music Theory Online*, 26 (2), DOI: 10.30535/mto.26.2.4 (accessed October 1, 2020).

Feagin, J. (2013), *The White Racial Frame: Centuries of Racial Framing and Counter-Framing*, New York: Routledge.

Frith, S. (1996), "Music and Identity," in S. Hall and P. du Gay (eds.), *Questions of Cultural Identity*, 108–27, London: Sage.

Fulcher, J. F. (2011), *Oxford Handbook of the New Cultural History of Music*, Oxford: Oxford University Press.

Gebesmair, A. and A. Smudits (2001), *Global Repertoires: Popular Music within and beyond the Transnational Music Industry*, Burlington, VT: Ashgate.

Green, L. ed. (2011), *Learning, Teaching, and Musical Identity: Voices across Cultures*, Bloomington: Indiana University Press.

hooks, b. (1992), *Black Looks: Race and Representation*, Boston, MA: South End Press.

Huggan, G. (2013), *The Oxford Handbook of Postcolonial Studies*, Oxford: Oxford University Press.

Kroier, J. (2012), "Music, Global History, and Postcoloniality," *International Review of the Aesthetics and Sociology of Music*, 43 (1): 139–86.

Locke, R. (2009), *Musical Exoticism: Images and Reflections*, Cambridge: Cambridge University Press.

Loomba, A. (2015), *Colonialism/Postcolonialism*, 3rd edn, London: Routledge.

MacDonald, R., D. J. Hargreaves, and D. Miell, eds. (2017), *Handbook of Musical Identities*, Oxford: Oxford University Press.

McFerran, K., P. Derrington, and S. Saarikallio, eds. (2019), *Handbook of Music, Adolescents, and Well-Being*, Oxford: Oxford University Press.

Mignolo, W. D. and C. E. Walsh (2018), *On Decoloniality: Concepts, Analytics, Praxis*, Durham, NC: Duke University Press.

Monson, I. (1995), "The Problem with White Hipness: Race, Gender, and Cultural Conceptions in Jazz Historical Discourse," *Journal of the American Musicological Society*, 48 (3): 396–422

Morra, I. (2014), *Britishness, Popular Music, and National Identity: The Making of Modern Britain*, New York: Routledge.

"On Monument Avenue," (2020), *The American Civil War Museum*. https://onmonumentave.com/ (accessed October 1, 2020).

Smith, L. T. ([1999] 2012), *Decolonizing Methodologies: Research and Indigenous Peoples*, London: Zed Books.

Stakelum, M., ed. (2016), *Developing the Musician: Contemporary Perspectives on Teaching and Learning*, Abingdon: Routledge.

Straw, W. (1991), "Systems of Articulation, Logics of Change: Communities and Scenes in Popular Music," *Cultural Studies*, 5 (3): 368–88.

Stokes, M., ed. (1997), *Ethnicity, Identity and Music: The Musical Construction of Place*, Oxford: Berg.

Stoever, J. L. (2016), *The Sonic Color Line: Race & the Cultural Politics of Listening*. New York: New York University Press.

Tan, M. C. C. (2012), *Acoustic Interculturalism: Listening to Performance*, London and New York: Palgrave Macmillan.

Taylor, T. D. (2007), *Beyond Exoticism: Western Music and the World*, Durham: Duke University Press.

Taylor, T. D. (2016), *Music and Capitalism: A History of the Present*, Chicago: University of Chicago Press.

"The Color of the Coronavirus: COVID-19 Deaths by Race and Ethnicity in the U.S," (2020), *APM Research Lab*, October 15. https://www.apmresearchlab.org/covid/deaths-by-race (accessed October 27, 2020).

White, B. (2012), *Music and Globalization: Critical Encounters*, Bloomington: Indiana University Press.

Part One

Hearing Race and Place

1

Mapping Sonic and Affective Geographies in Richmond, Virginia

Andrew McGraw

Introduction

Richmond, the historic capital of the Confederacy, has a post-civil-war history pockmarked by racist housing policies and attempts to extend Jim Crow laws. The strategies employed include "redlining" (grading property values according to race) and using public housing projects and school district gerrymandering to further segregate populations. In the 1930s, Virginia's "racial integrity laws" prohibited interracial marriage and were used to segregate neighborhoods by disallowing people from living in an area whose residents they could not marry—policies borrowed by the Nazis when they developed their own Aryan purity laws (Campbell 2011: 144). The 1968 Fair Housing Act, which opened some areas to non-white populations, accelerated "white flight" out of the city toward the south and west, further depleting Richmond's tax base. As demonstrated through the AudibleRVA project (McGraw 2020b), a digital humanities project established at the University of Richmond, the sonic and affective aftermath of these and other racist policies are mapped onto Richmond's present-day geography.

Begun in 2013, the AudibleRVA project combines multiple ArcGIS map layers outlining relationships between sound and the affective experience of place. Layers include noise complaints and citations, music venues and events, ethnographies, an archive of music made in the city jail, and student soundscape points and research projects (Figure 1.1). At the heart of the project is the recognition that all mapping is political and that all visual representations of data tell stories reflecting particular research questions and positioned perspectives (Tufte 2001: 53; Droumeva 2017: 337).

Figure 1.1 AudibleRVA map with several layers displayed. Gray dots = noise complaints; black stars = active venues; gray stars = defunct venues; black pins = ethnographic interviews; black squares = music infrastructure (music schools, stores, studios).

In this chapter, I interpret quantitative and qualitative data from AudibleRVA to explain the acoustic politics of space in Richmond, illustrating the differential distribution of sonic rights and resources. The project's core assumption is that a society's ethical life (Keane 2015: 6) is partly expressed through the allocation of sonic "goods," including access to music-making and listening and musical infrastructure (venues, schools, stores). How does access to such sonic goods—and the right to make and be free from "noise"—express and reproduce a society's political theory and ethics? Whose sounds are muted? These questions of justice, equity, and distribution have been central themes in Western moral theory since Aristotle's *Nichomachean Ethics* (Ross 2009). My project's analytic focus does not concern normative definitions of noise, sound, or music but rather what we might call opportunities for sonic *eudaimonia*, Aristotle's term for "flourishing" and the goal of his ethics. Who in Richmond is extended the opportunity to flourish through sound, and how is sound policed to restrict flourishing?

Sound is a modality through which a public organizes itself—a means of expressing inclusion and exclusion, marking territory and constituting normative citizenship. The discontinuous topography of the AudibleRVA map layers resonates with theories of modern publics as a collection of disjunct and overlapping "affective societies" (Slaby and von Scheve 2019: 1), often with distinct sonic cultures and value systems. Within this context the AudibleRVA map leads to another question: What role might sound and music play in forging new, more inclusive affective publics, enabling broader access to the common good? This chapter focuses on the intersections of class and race in Richmond, primarily in terms of the binaries between perceived Blackness and whiteness, historically the most salient social divide in the city. Since the geographies mapped in this chapter include many other growing populations of marginalized groups (primarily Hispanic and Asian), the discussion below should be understood as only one of many possible ways to analyze the intersections of identity, class, place, and the law in Richmond.

Affect and Sound

In attempting to understand the meaning of Richmond's soundscape, I have conceived of it as an assemblage of interactions between affective and sonic fields (McGraw forthcoming). I understand a field as an enabling condition of a situation that has concrete effects by orienting phenomena around its lines of force. Fields are not inner, mental worlds accessible to one person only. They are immanent-real, not simply a property or quality of a situation. The sonic field comprises vibrating pressure differentials in a media, including vibrations below and above human-cochlear hearing and at all possible amplitudes. It encompasses all modes of vibration—music, sound, noise, silence—including vibrations within auditory systems (nerves, guts, bones) and across transductive thresholds.

The affective field is subtler. Despite considerable disciplinary schisms over the meaning of affect, I think theorists can agree that we experience more than we explicitly represent to ourselves. In my usage, affect is meaningful feeling in a situation, diffuse and discursive, below, within, and beyond language. Recent phenomenological and materialist attempts to describe the affective experience of sound in a space by enumerating all of the substance, apprehensions, discursive systems, and networks measurable within it never seem to produce a complete description. This, I argue, is because affective experience is partly conditioned by the *probability space* of a situation, which is established by presence *and* absence, possibility *and* constraint, things you can measure and things you cannot. Our affective experience of a situation emerges from a sense of what has happened, is happening, and what will (or will not) probably happen within it. In Richmond, understanding the experience of place as interactions between affective and sonic fields helps us recognize the city's "sonic color lines" (Stoever 2016: 1).

Noise

In his canonical text on noise and society, Attali says:

> It is necessary to ban subversive noise because it betokens demands for cultural autonomy, support for differences or marginality: a concern for maintaining tonalism, the primacy of melody, a distrust of new languages, codes, or instruments, a refusal of the abnormal—these characteristics are common to all regimes of that nature. They are direct translations of the political importance of cultural repression and noise control.
>
> (2003: 7)

In this section I outline how "noise," in its various guises, is associated with African American life in Richmond and is policed for its perceived link to subversive and criminal behaviors. I facilitate a music studio program in the city jail, the population of which is 92 percent African American in a city where the Black population is 50 percent. The styles of hip hop preferred by Black male residents in the program are sometimes referred to as "noise" by the overwhelmingly African American staff, who encourage participants not to produce "thug" or "street" music, but instead to create "uplifting" and "positive" tracks that concern "the struggle" or "recovery." Staff expressed concern to me that "rough" music "leaking out" of the jail would reinforce racist stereotypes associating Black men with inherent criminality.[1] As I describe below, the policing of Black "noise" extends beyond the jail walls, segregating the city's geography through discontinuous soundscapes.

Noise ordinances in American cities have long been associated with both class and race. "Street" music was a regular target of early (nineteenth-century) noise ordinances, partly as a means to legitimate the ticketed music being programmed in new concert halls (Schafer 1977: 66).[2] Noise complaints in contemporary Richmond align similarly. Figure 1.2 illustrates the AudibleRVA noise layer, which records the roughly 40,000 noise complaints registered by

Figure 1.2 Black population density/noise complaints 2007–2019. Black population density indicated by shading.

the police between 2007 and 2019.[3] This information was obtained through a Freedom of Information Act request to the Richmond police department. This map layer outlines the sonic dimensions of racialized surveillance and privilege more than it does the distribution of objective noise levels in the city. As the map confirms, the city's ordinances disproportionately affect the acoustic practices of African Americans. The panes of Figure 1.3 illustrate a marked transformation in complaint patterns in Richmond before and after 2011, when a restrictive noise ordinance was passed.[4] This controversial new ordinance defines "excessive sound" as that which "exceeds 55 dBA during nighttime hours and sound that exceeds 65 dBA during daytime hours when measured inside a structure, or sound that exceeds 65 dBA during nighttime hours and sound that exceeds 75 dBA during daytime hours when measured outside a structure, or both" (Richmond City Government 2016). For context, 65 dBA is roughly equivalent to the volume of everyday conversation. Any individual or business responsible for excessive sound may be issued a citation.[5] That only thirty-three citations resulted from the 40,153 complaints registered between 2007 and 2019 suggests that the noise ordinance functions as a proxy for other forms of racialized surveillance and punishment through uneven and targeted enforcement.[6]

Such enforcement is exemplified in Figure 1.3, where the "scatter plot" pattern of noise complaints registered prior to the passage of the ordinance indicated in panel A transforms into the highly patterned strings of complaints registered in panels B, C, and D. The complaints in A track Chamberlayne Avenue through an African American neighborhood, while those in panel B track along Jefferson Davis Highway through Black neighborhoods south of the James River. Complaints are also evident within and bordering the primarily white "Fan District" in the middle of the city, shown in panel D.

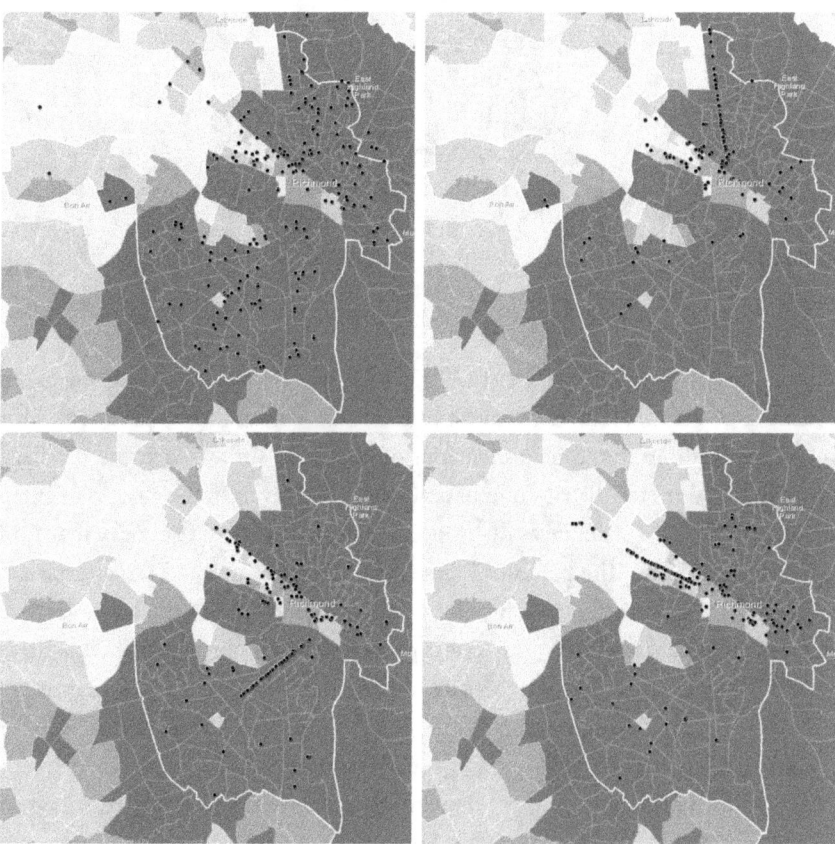

Figure 1.3a–d Typical noise complaint patterns before and after passage of restrictive noise ordinance. (a) Top left: June–July 2010, "scatter plot" pattern. (b) Top right: November–December 2011, complaints registered along Chamberlayne Avenue. (c) Bottom left. August–September 2012, complaints registered along Jefferson Davis Highway. (d) Bottom right. May–June 2013, complaints bordering and within the Fan (center of map).

Some jail residents have stated that their arrest was tied to a noise complaint. When police respond, they may run names in their database to find outstanding warrants or arrest individuals for other offenses such as minor drug possession. In this context Black "noise" becomes a proxy for punitive racialized surveillance. Given Richmond's cultural and social history, Blackness—especially Black masculinity—is strongly associated with noise. Indeed, the ordinance seems to single out this group based on stereotypes about their listening habits. Anyone playing music via a "loudspeaker" in their car must obtain a permit from the city—language that ostensibly regulates businesses such as ice-cream trucks. But in practice, the ordinance represents a means to control the widespread African American cultural practice of installing powerful car stereo systems. Based on my own observations living in a multiracial (40 percent African American) neighborhood in the city, hip hop is the primary genre played through car stereo systems, and it accounts for 90 percent of the music produced in the jail studio program.

The preference for strong bass over Western "tonalism"—evident in the genres of rap preferred by this community, and the practice of accentuating it further with powerful subwoofers—is precisely the "demand for cultural autonomy" Attali describes. Low frequencies can engulf a space with diffuse energy, making it difficult to locate their source; they can seem to come from everywhere at once. When originating from mobile audio systems playing "noisy" rap, this sonic "invasion" of a territory can prick panic in neighborhoods historically zoned as white. The fact that much urban sound exceeds the ordinance's very low threshold enables officers to instruct those who do not "know their place," to "move along" (to quote a resident of the city jail) if they are thought to be outside of their proper territories. While in many American cities, race is both an auditory construction and a bodily orientation in space (Ahmed 2007: 158), identity in Richmond, as Figure 1.3 illustrates, can be defined partly by inhabiting a certain sonic field.

The experiences of African American jail residents, as expressed to me, suggest that the string-like pattern of complaints seen in Figures 1.3c and 1.3d reflect officer "shake downs" of African Americans playing music in their cars and portable stereos. (The city police department did not respond to my requests for comment.) Preliminary data shown in the Audible RVA map layers suggests that policing noise functions as a form of sonic "stop-and-frisk" in Richmond, a practice that has been ruled unconstitutional in other states (Goldstein 2013). In this context sound becomes a means to regulate public and private space, establishing and maintaining affective boundaries between communities.

Silence, Speaking, Listening

Silence and comparative quiet have long been associated with white bourgeois personhood as expressions of dispassionate rationality, the disciplined body, and a domestic moral economy (Stoever 2016: 95). Across America, suburban sprawl during the era of white flight (most prominently between 1950 and 1990) enabled comparative sonic privacy between homes, allowing families to avoid the more intense, continuous sonic contact with others typical of city life. This sonic experience of social difference is highly attenuated in the suburb; indeed, the "Black noise" of American inner cities was sometimes cited as a reason for white flight (Stoever 2016: 189). The data on noise complaints in and around Richmond reflects the expectation and demand for greater silence in suburban areas. Between 2007 and 2019 there were 42,517 noise complaints registered in the city, which in 2017 had a population of 227,000, or .18 complaints per resident.[7] For the same period, the surrounding counties of Chesterfield (population 343,599 in 2017) and Henrico (population 327,898 in 2017) registered 194,462 complaints, or .3 complaints per resident.

In the city itself, Richmond's white neighborhoods, especially the wealthy Windsor Farms area (just left of center in Figure 1.3a), appear comparatively silent on the noise map. There are *no* reported noise complaints originating from the city's several gated communities, which are overwhelmingly wealthy white neighborhoods. As Stoever has argued, the sonic control needed to maintain silence is an assertion of privilege. To enforce silence expresses the neoliberal concept of a negative right: to be *free from* the sound of the other. Incarceration, by contrast, effectively removes an individual's sound from the broader community while exposing them to new forms of sonic oppression. To be homeless or incarcerated is to lose control over one's sonic environment. For instance, residents in the jail frequently describe the sound of the pneumatic locks on their cell doors as the facility's distinguishing sonority. As the doors automatically open each day in a pre-programmed order, the locks produce a distinctive, rhythmic "fuh-fuh-fuh" sound that residents describe as "haunting." Many report hearing it in their sleep.

The affective tone of a place is often expressed and experienced through everyday speaking and listening. To re-establish order when the residents get "rowdy," deputies in the jail will often bark the phrase, "five-minute noise level check!", which all residents must repeat in chorus before remaining completely silent for the next five minutes. I am hailed as "sir" by many inside the jail, and residents who do not know me will not speak to me unless spoken to. These forms of aural discipline and surveillance contribute to the pervasive carceral affect of the institution (McGraw forthcoming). In Richmond's public spaces, Black silence similarly signifies deference, expressing a sedimented history of Black listening-as-obedience enforced during slavery and Jim Crow. The practice of sonically acknowledging whiteness persists through oppressive forms of listening, speech, and silence. Moving to Richmond in 2006 after living in Kansas City and New England, I was struck that Black men, including those much older than I, often responded to me with an apparently obeisant, "Yes, sir." Such aural practices recall Richard Wright's 1937 essay *The Ethics of Living Jim Crow*, in which he describes "answering all of his [boss's] questions with sharp yessirs and nosirs," always being "very careful to pronounce my *sirs* distinctly, in order that he might know that I was polite, *that I knew where I was,* and that I knew that he was a white man" (Wright 2001: 5). Punishing noisy activities and imposing silence are expressions of power. In Richmond, the *lawful* breaking of silence is a privilege of whiteness.

The Privilege of Complaint

Noise complaint data is partly a representation of the ways residents enact their sonic privilege and respond to sonic injustice. An anecdote may help explain this point. I regularly take my students to NASA's acoustics lab in Langley, a ninety-minute drive to the east, where scientists have been working on developing "quiet" supersonic commercial aircraft that could fly cross-country. Existing supersonic aircraft designs produce loud sonic booms that would violate local noise ordinances along the flightpath, resulting in high penalties. Though NASA scientists have been mathematically modeling various designs that would produce less noise for years, they have recently discovered that the problem is more complex than a simple measure of total decibels. In preliminary surveys, test subjects felt that some sonic booms were more irritating than other sounds, even if they were the same volume. This finding led the NASA acousticians to develop social-psychological experiments involving members of the local Hampton Roads community. Sitting in a mock living room, participants rated, on a scale of 1 to 10, how annoying they found various sonic boom simulations and how likely they would be to complain to authorities. The scientists quickly found that subjects' ratings were correlated more strongly with race than with the sounds themselves: African American subjects were less likely to complain.

The tendency to be annoyed and to complain correlated with both whiteness and wealth. As one scientist said, "Maybe Ms. Kennedy, let's call her that, knows the sheriff, or even her local senator. She knows she'll get a hearing. But if you're African American, you're simply being a good scientist by *not* inviting the police into your neighborhood. You're acting on evidence."

By far the loudest sounds in Richmond come from the NASCAR raceway on the city's northern border, indicated in the top right quadrant of Figure 1.2. In the stands the sound level is regularly around 100 dB, up to 130 dB in the pits; races are clearly audible from my home on the other side of town, 9 kilometers away. NASCAR is strongly associated with white working class and rural populations in the United States, which makes its location in an overwhelmingly Black middle-class neighborhood in Richmond somewhat strange. Stranger still is the comparatively low number of noise complaints in the area. That these are officially sanctioned events likely leads potential complainants to assume there is no point in calling the police. The strategic placement of the raceway and the community response to it express the intersection of sound, power, and race in Richmond. Built in 1946 adjacent to neighborhoods that had been "redlined" as Black-only, the raceway has long functioned as a sonic expression of white power.

Housing

In the late 1930s the Home Owners Lending Corporation (HOLC) graded Richmond housing stock using a color-coding system: green indicated the most valuable white neighborhoods, blue the working and middle-class white neighborhoods, yellow the less desirable and sometimes ethnically mixed neighborhoods, and red the least desirable stock, intended only for African Americans (Campbell 2011: 125; Rothstein 2018: 64). The racist distribution of bank loans based on this scheme further segregated the city by race and class, disenfranchising the Black population. Such policies were reinforced in the 1950s by the construction of low-income housing intended for Black communities displaced when the construction of Interstate 95 destroyed their historic neighborhoods and business centers, primarily in the Jackson Ward area, known for decades as the "Black Wall Street" due to its high concentration of African American–owned banks and businesses. Figure 1.4a depicts the 1930s HOLC map, while Figure 1.4b shows poverty levels from the 2000s, revealing close correlations with historic redlining patterns.

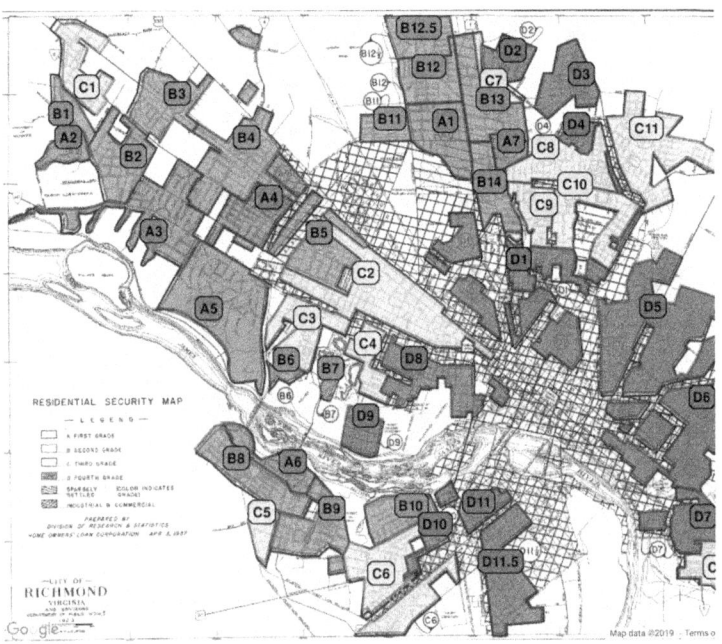

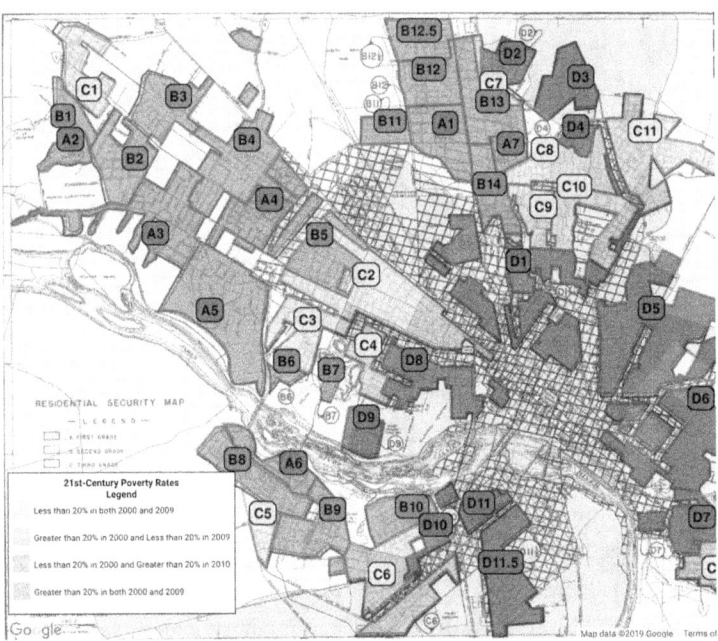

Figure 1.4a–b Richmond HOLC maps (Nelson et al. 2020). Top: original HOLC map from the late 1930s. Bottom: HOLC map with poverty data from the 2000s.

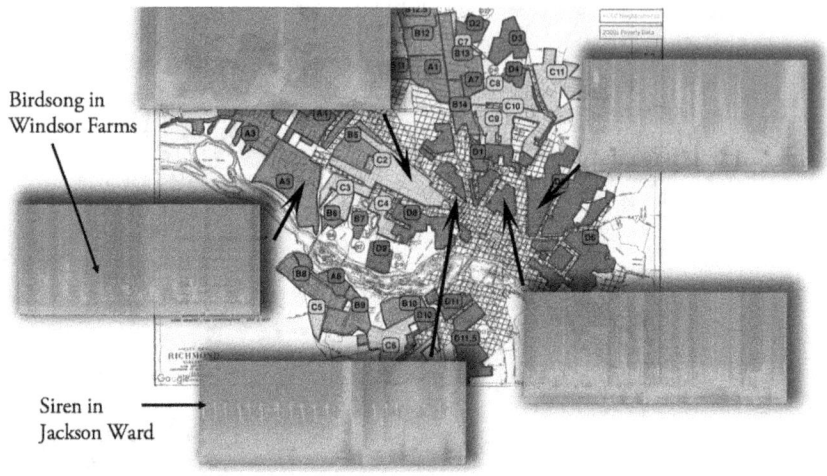

Figure 1.5 HOLC map with typical soundscape spectrograms, June 2019.

The racing of space and its economic and demographic consequences continues to manifest in sound. Today, redlined areas are louder, marked by persistent low-frequency traffic and other anthropogenic noises. Greenlined areas remain verdant spaces distinguished by comparative silence and birdsong, as the spectrograms in Figure 1.5 indicate. The HOLC grades also correlate with heat vulnerability as well: if distressed and impoverished communities are the most vulnerable to rising temperatures this century, the bird-filled trees of Windsor Farms make it the coolest place in Richmond during the summer months.

Gentrification

By 2005, mid-twentieth-century white flight from the city had run its course, and younger whites began moving back in, gentrifying Black neighborhoods. This coincided with the rapid expansion of the Virginia Commonwealth University (VCU) campus into Jackson Ward and Randolph, which are historically Black middle-class neighborhoods, and the Fan, a wealthier and whiter part of town. The strategic placement of student housing along the periphery of the campus has created a sonic frontier in which loud student lifestyles have led to an increase in noise complaints. As documented in other American cities, loud student housing can have the effect of lowering adjacent property values, enabling the further expansion of the campus (Austrian and Norton 2002: 36; Salkin and Levin 2010: 5). The VCU police department's "noise van," which began operating in 2014, monitors and measures student noise, driving by housing complexes displaying a large sign stating "Warning: Noise Detection in Progress" on the side of the vehicle. The van primarily functions as a form of managing public relations with the surrounding community, allowing the school to be seen as responding to community complaints without taking consequential actions.[8]

The demolition and new construction of campus buildings in the Jackson Ward area reflect historic patterns of white privilege, creating loud noise in Black spaces, much like the aforementioned NASCAR racetrack does. Noise complaints are also rising in historically Black neighborhoods, such as Church Hill, that are being gentrified by white "hipsters" and professionals, many of whom had been raised in outlying suburbs. This demographic change introduced white bourgeois expectations, including the demand for domestic silence, into the inner city.

Policing Music

Bars are often a crucial component in the economic sustainability of local music scenes in America because they can underwrite live music performance from the profits of selling alcohol, without bearing the costs of maintaining a full kitchen and its staff. But there are no bars in Virginia. Establishments selling mixed drinks are required to meet a $4,000 per month food sales quota, meaning the state's "bars" must exist within restaurants, which typically have high overheads and slim margins. As a result, most live music in the city is performed in the background as patrons dine, restricting the kinds of music one tends to hear. When the state issues an alcohol license, it can even include restrictions that prohibit the performance of certain kinds of music in the establishment. (The officials I interviewed at the Alcohol Board singled out hip hop.[9]) For example, a license restriction issued to the Canal Club in the predominantly African American neighborhood of Shockoe Bottom includes a dress code prohibiting "oversized t-shirts … athletic wear … 'do' rags, head bands [and] bandanas," as well as the appearance of "live bands, recording artists, DJ's and other promotional events that highlights [sic] hip hop, rap or gangster rap music" (Commonwealth of Virginia 2004). Although the ABC board responded to my request for records by claiming that several restrictions could no longer be located, a number of local venue owners reported similar restrictions being issued in the city from at least the 1980s.

Partly as a result of such policies, there are no hip hop venues in Richmond. Most live hip hop is performed in parking lots and at house parties, and these events are often shut down by police for violating noise ordinances. Richmond's restrictive dancehall ordinance further requires venues to pay for special permits, a yearly fee, and security staff if more than 10 percent of its floor space is used for dancing. Shortly after the passage of the dance hall ordinance in 2011 the two remaining legal Black dance clubs were closed down. Thus state laws and municipal ordinances render much of Richmond's young and Black musical activity illicit—and its enforcement activates officers' implicit and explicit biases, which often correlate with race.

The link between live music and dining in Richmond puts it out of reach for poorer residents of the city.[10] Hearing live music often means paying for a cover, a meal, and drinks—which, for a couple, can cost around $100. In response, the Black population has long taken advantage of the legal exceptions to alcohol policies accorded to "private clubs." Members of these clubs, which are not obligated to serve entrees or staff a kitchen, can store their own mixed drinks on site and charge fees for live music events. While these spaces are not officially open to the public, members can admit and serve alcohol to their friends. The distinction between more expensive public venues and private, often Black, clubs further segregates Richmond's sonic and affective spaces across racial lines. Most of Richmond's white residents, and many of its white musicians, have no idea that these clubs exist and are important sites for music-making in the city.

Mapping Music

The AudibleRVA map can layer archived data from the AudibleRVA music calendar, which scrapes and aggregates local digital concert listings. Still in its beta stage, this dataset includes over 3,000 distinct events ranging from October 2018 to October 2019. Analysis of this dataset and the historical print archive of local event listings reveals that public venues forced to operate as restaurants go in and out of business quite rapidly. Only a few have survived longer than a decade, and those are overwhelmingly white-male-owned—the demographic with broadest access to business loans. I could identify only four Black-owned venues operating in the city between 1990 and 2020. Figure 1.1 above represents a total of nearly 100 venues operating in the city since the early 1980s. Venue volatility is directly tied to Richmond's byzantine assemblage of sound ordinances, zoning, alcohol laws, and permits, all of which disproportionately disadvantage African American communities. The current scene as represented by the digital archive is overwhelmingly white, male, and hipster in a city where white men are, at most, 20 percent of the population. The sonic geography of African American music-making is thus disproportionately small in the digital archive when compared to Richmond's demographics.

Figure 1.6 includes data from the calendar for the period 2018–2019, represented as a heat map, indicating that the overwhelming majority of events

Figure 1.6 Black population density/venues/events from AudibleRVA Calendar, as heatmap.

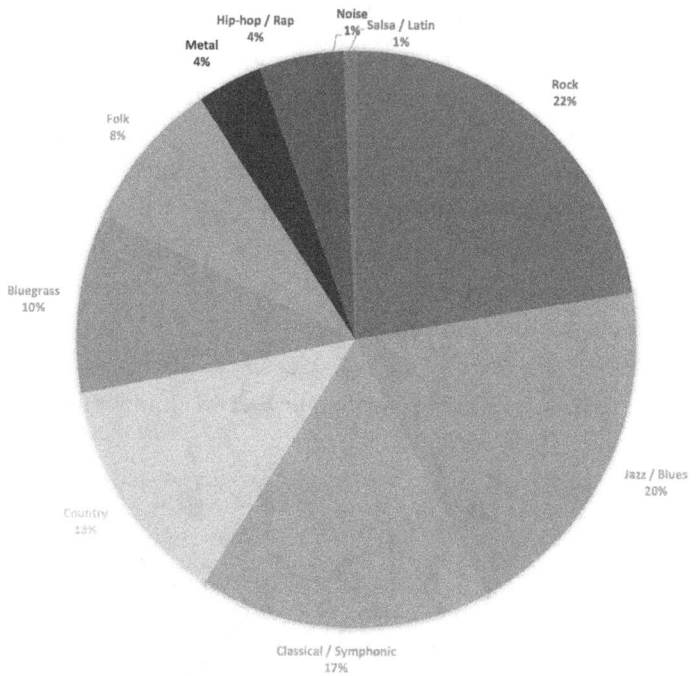

Figure 1.7 AudibleRVA calendar of events by genre. October 2018–October 2019.

take place in only a handful of venues in the city center. Figure 1.7 presents a pie chart of the relative frequency of events by self-described genre. Just as the noise layers should not be interpreted as an objective measure of environmental sound across the city, the music event layer does not objectively measure all musical activity. It does not, for example, include music-making in churches or other sacred spaces, private house concerts, or underground shows.

Overcoming Segregated Affective Publics

Acoustemology, as Steven Feld describes it, refers to "knowing with and knowing through the audible." Though Feld intended to highlight how sound mediates social relationships, the concept of acoustemology is more typically employed to describe an individual listener's (usually an academic's) subjective experience of the local soundscape (2015: 12). While acoustemologies are primarily framed through reflexive individualism, the AudibleRVA maps suggest the need for an acoustemology that focuses on *collective being* to understand how the politics of belonging emerges from the affective experience of place and sound. In most situations, affective experience is based upon what is probable or possible for *us* (not *me*) as members of particular groups in a particular space and time. A series of "sound points" or "sound walks," often included in sound mapping projects (and usually recorded by privileged college faculty and students), cannot represent this. No microphone can fully capture such affective geographies because they are phenomenological. A microphone equalizes all sounds in the environment according to decibel loudness, which is not how sounds present themselves to our biological ear or to our phenomenological experience of place. A soundscape recording in which a siren is just one of many objectively captured vibrations cannot represent the affective experience of community members who have been traumatized by police violence; for them, the siren may be the most significant sound in the environment. Blocks that appear to gentrifiers as continuous zones may be strongly striated territories for others.[11] Recordings, on their own, cannot communicate the atmosphere—the interactions between sonic and affective fields—of a place.

Sound marks the affective geographies laid down over time and place by historical patterns of oppression, opportunity, forgetting, and memory. But because sound is promiscuous and not easily contained, as Stoever has argued, "sonic color lines," like those described in this chapter, are also spaces of affective possibility and transformation. Sound's transformative potential was eventually recognized by Richmond city leaders as they struggled to respond to the aftermath of segregation and white flight. In the late 1960s and early 1970s, the white majority in city hall first attempted to respond to the political and financial implications of white flight by annexing white neighborhoods from the surrounding counties (Henrico and Chesterfield), a process deemed unconstitutional by the Supreme Court, which imposed a temporary injunction on voting in the city from 1972 to 1977 (Campbell 2011: 151). The resulting cultural and political impasse was partly addressed through artistic, and especially musical, festivals and events. James "Plunky" Branch, a foundational figure in the city's music scene, described to me how music festivals were established in "neutral" parts of town to forge new sonic geographies of shared affect across racial difference.

> The white community either through fear or through prejudice or from not knowing how to chart a course in this new setup, were not supportive of the Black majority of the city council or their agenda. So the arts council was the

organization that said, "we can get past this impasse by using our very … powerful board of directors." [They] determined through a series of studies that it would be beneficial to the city if the Black community and the white corporate community could combine on some projects. It was determined that one of the best ways for this to happen … was through the arts … [Festivals were a] way to bring not just people from far away but people from the counties, those [white] counties, to come to downtown. You won't be killed because there is a Black mayor! It's a place where we can have a good time, and it worked. [Citizens came to understand that] yes, you can have a festival, it can be in an inner city, it can be in an inner city that's even run by Black people, white people can come and not get mugged, Black people can come and not be arrested, we can actually have a good time in the same space.

In Richmond, forging shared sentiment across racial difference appears to be easier in comparatively neutral affective territories. This may be one reason why many of the city's successful festivals, such as the annual Richmond Folk Festival, are held on otherwise empty and uninhabited islands on the James River. Such spaces feel to have under-determined possibilities, where the rules for interaction, behavior, and policing seem unsettled. As described by local musicians, many of these spaces appear on the AudibleRVA map to be demographically mixed (or empty) and comparatively free of noise complaints.

In *The Human Condition*, Arendt (1998) describes how "publics" emerge in "spaces of appearance," such as a city square, where "I appear to others as others appear to me." Habermas's (2015) influential theories of the Western public proposed a similarly unitary and solidary body—a paradigm later critiqued by scholars like Michael Warner and Nancy Fraser, who prefer more complex images of counter- and subaltern publics within modern pluralistic societies. While the maps described in this chapter illustrate the segregated sonic geographies of hegemonic, counter- and subaltern-publics in Richmond, festivals such as the Richmond Folk Festival appeal to an Arendtian or Habermasian unified public. Organizers of this event hope to cultivate a space in which citizens can come together, feel like they are part of one civic body, and respond against the suburban sprawl of white flight.[12] Peterson has described such events as "civic performances," which she defines as "free public performances that are intended *for* the city [and that] aim to improve the city and its citizens through performance" (2010: 7).

In Richmond, these types of events also function as a form of white penance in lieu of concrete reparations or confrontational exchanges about slavery and its aftermath. Branch suggests that such festivals are neither mimetic nor epiphenomenal of capital P politics but function politically by affording opportunities to imagine *and enact* a unified civic body. But can we attribute such power to sound? In some ways, music is caught between the so-called discursive turn in cultural studies, which frames all experience as conditioned by language, and the more recent "affective turn," in which most experience is believed to exist below and/or beyond the grasp of language (Slaby and von Scheve 2019: 12). If music with lyrics straddles the apparent distinction between discourse and affect, music's association with collective sentiment and action is often linked to collective emotional and rhythmic entrainment, independent of discursive meaning (Szarecki 2017: 263).

Some scholars find that music's discursive ambiguity renders it incapable of coalescing social change. For instance, Born (2013) describes three kinds of "sonic publics" that emerge at events such as music festivals: (1) "solidary publics," which attempt to bring about political change, (2) "intimate publics" that forge subaltern belonging, and (3) "minimal publics," defined only by temporary copresence (Born 2013: 37–8). For Born, sonic publics cannot coalesce effective political change because of the need for explicit discourse, either in the top-down imposition of the law or the bottom-up resistance of rhetorical protest. Thus the political potential of music is reduced to symbolic struggles over the meaning of its supposed discursive content (cf. Szarecki 2017: 260), making the shared affective experience of music politically irrelevant. In contrast, Branch suggests that shared, affectively intense but discursively diffuse musical experiences in concert settings can have powerful political and social consequences. My lived experience in Richmond suggests to me that Branch may be correct. He and the local festival organizers appeal to the political potential generated when participants are caught up in a groove with others. Their perspective assumes that organized political action can be motivated and sustained by affective experience as much (or more) than by reasoned debate, a dynamic long understood by right-wing movements (Lünenborg 2019: 319).

Branch alludes to how sound both reveals affective geographies of melancholy and oppression and inspires shared spaces of safety and community. He suggests that sonic experience can help communities imagine the shift from probable futures conditioned by the history of racism to better futures, first experienced as shared affect in musical contexts. Achieving this would entail breaking out of what Fanon called the "affective ankylosis" built up from sedimented power relations (Fanon 2008: 101). If it is possible to shake oneself out of the old grooves of institutionalized racism, then the shared experience of music might invite durable political alliances and new forms of solidarity. But this would require concrete infrastructure—contexts for collective listening and changes to ordinances and policing practices—to facilitate and promote shared sonic experience across discontinuous social geographies. Hearing our environment as a space of shared possibility *and* shared risk might encourage citizens to enact the affective "beholden-ness" (Sharp 2016: 13) needed to counter the violence of racial abstraction. Listening closely to Richmond's discontinuous affective geographies may be a first step in redrawing the map.

Notes

1. This is a reasonable perspective considering the historical association of sound with Black criminality, dating back to the Fugitive Slave Act of 1850. Because it would be difficult to recognize escaped slaves from sight alone, their presumed criminality was often linked to accent, speech rhythm, and other "noisy" markers of the criminal body (Smith 2006).
2. See also Picker (2003) and Thompson (2004).
3. For comparison, there are roughly 350,000 complaints per year in New York City.
4. A month-by-month animation of the dataset can be found here: https://www.youtube.com/watch?v=uUmFiAVtL1E.
5. According to Section 11-25 of the City Code, the first noise violation counts as a Class 4 Misdemeanor, punishable by a fine of not more than $250; penalties and fines escalate for repeat offenses (Richmond City Government 2016).
6. Changes to noise ordinances in New Orleans after Katrina, interpreted as part of the attempt to gentrify the city, have had similarly racialized impacts. See Stephens (2014).
7. This also includes the 2,364 noise complaints registered by the Virginia Commonwealth Campus Police.
8. See Huang (2014). The VCU police department noise data is distinct from the records held by the city police and is represented in its own layer in the AudibleRVA map.
9. Although Prohibition was ended with the passage of the 21st Amendment in 1933, Virginia remained a "dry state" until the sale of mixed drinks was approved in 1968. The Virginia Alcoholic Beverage Control Authority (known as the "ABC") is an official arm of the state government and controls alcohol sales in the state through its 370 stores. Though grocery stores and other establishments may sell beer and

wine, the ABC has a monopoly on "hard" or "mixed" drinks. It also has its own armed enforcement officers. Its discretion to prohibit particular music genres in an establishment's license recalls earlier bans on jazz in cities such as Cleveland, which were also associated with the perceived "moral threat" of Black music more generally (see Fischlin et al. 2013: 12).

10 Richmond musician James "Plunky" Branch, who is quoted above, discusses the importance of private clubs in Richmond's Black community, beginning at 18:49 in the ethnographic interview posted here: http://ragakusuma.org/ohms-viewer/render.php?cachefile=Interview55205.xml.

11 For instance, though white residents are drawn to shows hosted at the microbreweries that have recently sprouted up in the city's historically Black neighborhoods, a comparatively smaller number of Black patrons are lured to events hosted by the Modlin Center, the city's largest arts presenter. The Modlin Center is located at the University of Richmond on the whiter, west side of town. This is even the case for free events.

12 I have served on the program committee of the Richmond Folk Festival since 2013 and have had many informal conversations with the organizers regarding the broader ethical aims of the festival.

References

Ahmed, S. (2007), "A Phenomenology of Whiteness," *Feminist Theory*, 8 (1): 149–68.

Arendt, H. (1998), *The Human Condition*, 2nd edn, Chicago: University of Chicago Press.

Aristotle (2009), *The Nichomachean Ethics*, trans. D. Ross, New York: Oxford University Press.

Attali, J. (2003), *Noise: The Political Economy of Music*, Minneapolis: University of Minnesota Press.

Austrian, Z. and J. Norton (2002), *Urban Universities and Real Estate Development*, University of Cleveland: University of Cleveland Center for Economic Development.

Born, G. (2013), "Introduction," in G. Born (ed.), *Music, Sound, and Space; Transformation of Public and Private Experience*, 1–69, Cambridge: Cambridge University Press.

Branch, J. (2018), Interview by A. McGraw, October 16. http://ragakusuma.org/ohms-viewer/render.php?cachefile=Interview55205.xml

Campbell, B. (2011), *Richmond's Unhealed History*, Richmond: Brandylane.

Commonwealth of Virginia, Department of Alcoholic Beverage Control (2004), *Wine and Beer License*. V. Danielson, Commissioner. License Number 6623. Richmond, Virginia.

Droumeva, M. (2017), "Soundmapping as Critical Cartography: Engaging Publics in Listening to the Environment," *Communications and the Public*, 2 (4): 335–51.

Fanon, F. (2008), *Black Skin, White Masks*, trans. R. Philcox, New York: Grove Press.

Feld, S. (2015), "Acoustemology," in D. Novak and M. Sakakeeny (eds.), *Keywords in Sound*, 12–21, Durham: Duke University Press.

Fischlin, D., A. Heble, and G. Lipsitz (2013), *The Fierce Urgency of Now: Improvisation, Rights, and the Ethics of Cocreation*, Durham: Duke University Press.

Goldstein, J. (2013), "Judge Rejects New York's Stop-and-Frisk Policy," *The New York Times*, August 13. https://advance.lexis.com/api/document?collection=news&id=urn:contentItem:5940-7GK1-JBG3-6344-00000-00&context=1516831 (accessed July 1, 2020).

Habermas, J. (2015), *The Structural Transformation of the Public Sphere: An Inquiry into a Category of Bourgeois Society*, Cambridge: Polity Press.

Huang, C. (2014), "Noise Police: VCU Force Now Has New Way to Monitor Decibels at Rowdy Parties," *Style Weekly*, August 14.

Keane, W. (2015), *Ethical Life: Its Natural and Social Histories*, Princeton: Princeton University Press.

Lünenborg, M. (2019), "Affective Publics," in J. Slaby and C. Von Scheve (eds.), *Affective Societies, Key Concepts*, 319–29, New York: Routledge.

McGraw, A. (2020a), "Feeling the Feels: Spinozist Ethics and Musical Feeling," *Culture, Theory, and Critique*. Forthcoming.

McGraw, A. (2020b), AudibleRVA, https://audiblerva.org/map (accessed July 17, 2020).

Nelson, R., L. Winling, R. Marciano, and N. Connolly, et al. (2020), "Mapping Inequality," in Robert K. Nelson and Edward L. Ayers (eds.), *American Panorama*. https://dsl.richmond.edu/panorama/redlining/ (accessed July 17, 2020).

Peterson, M. (2010), *Sound, Space, and the City: Civic Performance in Downtown Los Angeles*, Philadelphia: University of Pennsylvania Press.

Picker, J. (2003), *Victorian Soundscapes*, Oxford: Oxford University Press.

Richards, C. (2019), "Go-Go's Fight against Gentrification Is Just Getting Started. This Is What It Sounds Like: Thousands of Washingtonians Gathered on Tuesday to Protest—and to Dance," *Washington Post Blogs*, May 8. https://www.washingtonpost.com/lifestyle/style/go-gos-fight-against-gentrification-is-just-getting-started-this-is-what-it-sounds-like/2019/05/08/ff7772cc-71b5-11e9-9f06-5fc2ee80027a_story.html (accessed July 1, 2020).

Richmond City Government (2016), *Richmond, VA Code of Ordinances, Article II: Sound Control*. https://www.nonoise.org/lawlib/cities/ordinances/Richmond,%20Virginia.pdf (accessed July 1, 2020).

Rose, T. (1994), "A Style Nobody Can Deal With," in T. Rose and A. Ross (eds.), *Microphone Fiends: Youth Music, Youth Culture*, 71–88, New York: Routledge.

Rothstein, R. (2018), *The Color of Law: A Forgotten History of How Our Government Segregated America*, New York: Liveright.

Salkin, P. and A. Levine (2010), "Zoning for Off-Campus Fraternity and Sorority Houses," *Zoning and Planning Law Report*, 33 (11): 1–12.

Schafer, R. M. (1977), *The Soundscape: Our Sonic Environment and the Tuning of the World*, Rochester: Destiny Books.

Sharp, C. (2016), *In the Wake: On Blackness and Being*, Durham: Duke University Press.

Slaby, J. and C. Von Scheve, eds. (2019), *Affective Societies: Key Concepts*, New York: Routledge.

Smith, M. (2006), *How Race Is Made*, Chapel Hill: University of North Carolina Press.

Stephens, A. (2014), "Policing Sound: Lessons from the Crackdowns on Performers in New Orleans and New York, Next City." https://nextcity.org/daily/entry/street-musicians-arrests-crackdowns-buskers-new-orleans-new-york (accessed July 1, 2020).

Stoever, J. (2016), *The Sonic Color Line: Race and the Cultural Politics of Listening*, New York: New York University.

Szarecki, A. (2017), "Sonic Encounters and Intensive Politics: The Immanent Emergence and Structuration of Affective Publics at a Live Music Event, and beyond," *Communication and the Public*, 2 (4): 259–71.

Thompson, E. (2004), *The Soundscape of Modernity: Architectural Acoustics and the Culture of Listening in America, 1900–1933*, Cambridge: The MIT Press.

Tufte, E. (2001), *The Visual Display of Quantitative Information*, New York: Graphics Press.

Wright, R. ([1937] 2001), "The Ethics of Living Jim Crow: An Autobiographical Sketch," in P. Rothenberg (ed.), *Race, Class, and Gender in the United States: An Integrated Study*, 21–30, New York: Worth Publishers.

2

Musical Indianism: Reassessing the Archive

Victoria Rose Clark (Nanticoke)

In the early twentieth century, a group of like-minded composers tried to define America's classical music tradition by composing pieces inspired by or quoting from ethnographic transcriptions of American Indian song. Arthur Farwell, Charles Wakefield Cadman, and Arthur Nevin, among others, consulted compilations by ethnographers like Alice Fletcher and Frances Densmore when creating short piano pieces, song cycles, and even operas, often borrowing transcribed American Indian melodies verbatim, as Harvey Worthington Loomis did in "The Chattering Squaw" (1904, Example 2.1). Though these composers did not constitute a compositional school, they have been described as "the Indianists" in musicological scholarship (Browner 1997; Pisani 2008; Levy 2012), and their work has been filtered through narratives of borrowing, exoticism, and nationalism.

This chapter considers an alternative method for analyzing Indianist music, focusing on its mission of nationalism while using the labor and cultural products of Indigenous Americans. Instead of analyzing Indianist composers through conventional paradigms, I re-center the discussion on Indigenous agents through what I call the process of "musical Indianism"—a holistic study of the labor that generated the musical product and its reception, rather than a study of the composer's derivative work. My approach encompasses the encounters, translations, and relationships among Indigenous persons and their non-Indigenous collaborators, including ethnographers and composers. It also considers the institutionalization of Indianist music in boarding schools, and how this music was received by American Indians. Studying musical Indianism requires that we expand conventional notions of the archive and critically reexamine the ethnographic, compositional, and Indigenous materials within it. What follows are suggestions for rereading archival materials to demonstrate

Example 2.1 Harvey Worthington Loomis, "The Chattering Squaw," *Lyrics of the Red Man*, Book II, op.76 (c. 1904).

the importance of Indigenous voices in research on musical Indianism. Inspired by the concepts and priorities of Indigenous and decolonial studies, this chapter aims to encourage scholars of Indianist music and similar movements to adopt anticolonial approaches to historical narratives, thus avoiding arguments formulated from the perspective of colonial settlers.

As Eve Tuck and K. Wayne Yang warn, decolonization is not a metaphor: scholarship that decenters settler-colonial values from Indigenous topics is not always compatible with the politics of decolonization, particularly within institutions (Tuck and Yang 2012). I avoid using "decolonization" to discuss my own scholarship to respect the work of activists fighting for Indigenous rights outside of academia. At the same time, however, I acknowledge the work of many Indigenous studies scholars who invoke the term "decolonial" as a humanistic practice (Tuhiwai Smith [1999] 2012). Particularly, my work has benefitted from three recent studies that challenge colonial analyses of historical archives. Adria Imada's *Aloha America: Hula Circuits through the U.S. Empire* (2012) introduces the concept of "discrepant readings," which look between the lines of materials in imperial archives to find the stories of Indigenous resistance hidden in colonialist language. Margaret Bruchac's *Savage Kin: Indigenous Informants and American Anthropologists* (2018) suggests a similar method, using what she terms "reverse ethnography" to expand anthropological archives and reread Indigenous ethnographic interactions, locating histories that challenge dominant anthropological narratives. My method blends Imada and Bruchac's archival practice with theoretical concepts from Mark Rifkin's *Beyond Settler Time: Temporal Sovereignty and Indigenous Self-Determination* (2017). Rifkin describes how the agency granted to Indigenous individuals in retellings of their histories often depends upon their simultaneous existence with non-Indigenous cultural movements, or their "coeval" histories, a term borrowed from Johannes Fabian's *Time and the Other: How Anthropology Makes Its Object* (Rifkin 2017: viii). Rifkin's critique applies specifically to archival methods that seek to reread Indigenous agency in non-Native cultural movements. To avoid these same ends, I seek to prioritize approaches that challenge coeval determinations of Indigenous agency.

Below, I explore three parts of musical Indianism—ethnography, composition, and reception—through both the experiences of Indigenous interlocutors and the actions of the ethnographers and composers, which are documented in three places: the Alice Fletcher and Francis La Flesche ethnography archive, composer Thurlow Lieurance's archive, and American Indian writings. Throughout, I examine how Indigenous interlocutors, performers, and spectators participated in, resisted, and critically responded to musical Indianism. I expand the Indianist movement to prioritize the experiences of American Indians who both helped and impeded musical transcription and composition, and those who used or criticized Indianist music. This small selection of case studies demonstrates the need to delve more deeply into a wider range of archival materials when studying musical Indianism. In so doing, I suggest new methodological pathways for other historical movements and encourage archives to include more perspectives from American Indian voices.

La Flesche, Fletcher, and "wa-xo'-be"

The Osage interlocutors in Alice Fletcher and Francis La Flesche's ethnographic studies are a prime example of how Indigenous agents actively chose when to participate in and when to resist musical Indianism. Fletcher was one of the first ethnologists to be concerned primarily with transcribing American Indian song. She began her fieldwork in the 1880s after working as an agent for the Office of Indian Affairs (now called the Bureau of Indian Affairs), later writing reports on music and folklore for the Bureau of American Ethnology, the Peabody Museum, and the American Folklore Society (Mark 1988: 114). She also published large collections of music, like *A Study of Omaha Music* (1893), with her informant Francis La Flesche, who was an ethnographer in his own right. La Flesche, the grandson of a French-Canadian fur trader and the son of Omaha chief Joseph La Flesche, attended a Presbyterian reservation school and eventually earned a law degree from what is now George Washington University Law School (Mark 1982: 504). His extended family members were well educated and heavily involved in activism, particularly concerning personal finances and land rights. He began his ethnographic career publishing memoirs about his childhood and life on the Omaha reservation and in the reservation school. Fletcher originally encountered La Flesche as a translator and guide, but his independent studies of the Omaha and Osage nations became indispensable to her research. If she first regarded him as she would any other informant, by the 1910s, it seems they considered each other equal collaborators. Their correspondence reveals uncertainties in the ethnographic process that question the default assumptions of authenticity afforded to Indigenous collectors like La Flesche and highlight how informants might actively resist ethnographic fieldwork.

As early as 1910, La Flesche worked on the Osage reservation, in part to collect the songs of the *wa-xo'-be* ceremony—an initiation into a specific degree of Osage priesthood, celebrated with songs about the origins of their tribal organization and performed as a "theatrical production" (Bailey 1995: 76). La Flesche's correspondence suggests that his song analyses were often speculative, based more on his linguistic knowledge of the lyrics than on guidance from informants. In a letter from 1911, he wondered to Fletcher if the songs mentioning hawks, wolves, and buffalo "refer to the creation of animals as regarded as helpful to man, supernaturally," since those animals were associated "with the rising sun" (Fletcher and La Flesche Papers: Box 5A, hereafter F & LF: 5A). Fletcher implored La Flesche to continue studying the Osage language instead of relying on such literal translations, suggesting multiple times that he hire an interpreter. "I know that is what the Bureau of American Ethnology expects, that you deal directly with the people and not through an interpreter," she wrote on September 22, 1910, "but until your ear gets accustomed to the sound, you will need help" (F & LF: 5A).

Fletcher's letters reveal not only a linguistic misunderstanding of the *wa-xo'-be* songs, but also a lack of clarity about their musical and cultural significance. In the same correspondence from 1911, La Flesche wrote that the *wa-xo'-be* ceremony "is the queerest thing you ever saw … I cannot give you an idea of it in a short letter like this" (F & LF: 5A). By April 30 of that year, he had sent Fletcher his most recently completed transcriptions, but Fletcher, seeking to discern the social function of his work, asked for more information:

> When these songs are sung, are they sung by one man only? Do the people ever join? Do all the men who take part in performing the ceremony sing together? Do women ever sing these songs with the men? … I have not yet a clear idea just when this ceremony takes place, nor do I understand which one or which ones of the tribal groups take part in it.
>
> (F & LF: 5A)

La Flesche's correspondence signaled opposition and distrust from the Osage, suggesting that his interlocutors no longer wished to assist him. In one letter from June 10, 1912, La Flesche complained that an older tribal member had suddenly withdrawn his previous offer to cooperate: "The old man from whom I expected to get considerable material has gone back on me" (F & LF: 5A). He was relieved, however, that two other men "half promised to give me what they know" after a longtime informant, Wa-xri-ghi, had already shared the extent of his knowledge and could not remember enough to be of value (F & LF: 5A). Participation among the Osage continued to fluctuate throughout the decade. At the same time, La Flesche was attempting to record and understand Osage traditions, the federal government was heavily regulating the use of peyote in a "newer" religion, Peyotism (Swan 1988: 55; Maroukis 2012: 11). *Wa-xo'-be* practitioners were not necessarily adherents, as many Osage attested in La Flesche's correspondence, but the crackdown on Peyotism and the division among the Osage people over sharing ceremonial rites created an atmosphere of distrust. *Wa-xo'-be* practitioners resisted participating in La Flesche's work, feeling they might be spiritually punished for "selling" their ceremonies to him during a time when the government was trying to suppress Peyotism in favor of other Osage traditions.

Indeed, letters from 1917 indicate that even more interlocutors either refused to participate or reduced their involvement in La Flesche's *wa-xo'-be* collection: Pa-çi-'do-be claimed illness, Mon-in'-ka-mon-in ignored a request for help, and Zhin-ga'-ga-hi-ge specifically urged the Osages to discontinue *wa-xo'-be* rites for fear that "the devil would surely return to torment them" (F & LF: 5A). On January 6, 1917, Pe'-tre'mon-j reported to La Flesche that Wa-'thu-xa-ge and Saucy Calf, one of Fletcher's longtime informants, both died prematurely from giving away "forbidden" rituals. Wax-xhri-hi similarly believed that Ni-ka-wa-zhin-ton-ga died as a "penalty of sacrilege" (F & LF: 5A). By January 29, La Flesche wrote to Fletcher, "my work here has been disappointing, but I have learned other things which to some extent compensates for the time and patience expended. The old men have opposed me as they wish to keep up the rites but it is a hopeless situation for them" (F & LF: 5A). Despite the Osage's active opposition to a study they felt was spiritually and culturally dangerous, La Flesche published a detailed volume, "The Osage Tribe: Rite of the Wa-Xo'-Be," in 1930. His strained relationship with his interlocutors complicates his position as an Indigenous ethnographer and informant, as did the assumption that he was an authority on the music and traditions he studied.

Composers and Indigenous Authority

Early in their *wa-xo'-be* study, Fletcher and La Flesche sought out composer Charles Wakefield Cadman to help transcribe songs in the field. Cadman was an Indianist composer who worked with Fletcher and La Flesche in the early twentieth century in many capacities; for this endeavor, he acted as transcriptionist. A letter from April 8, 1911, cautioned that Cadman might be troublesome in the field: since "he has never transcribed any songs," Fletcher warned, "it will be difficult for him, so be careful and watch him" (F & LF: 5A). Fletcher's concerns were soon validated. In a letter from April 12, La Flesche asserted his Indigenous authority over Cadman, describing him as impatient and observing how he quickly dismissed "corrections." La Flesche complained, "The trouble with [Cadman] is he wants to write every little quaver of the voice that is not a note and was never meant to be as a note, and consequently he got more notes than words" (F & LF: 5A). He found Cadman "irritating with his importance," noting that when his transcriptions failed to accurately represent the vocal line, he would only write down what he heard. "I am going to write it that way," Cadman claimed. "I won't take oath to anything else."

In response, La Flesche interrogated Cadman's authority over the transcription. "You are responsible for the music, not I," La Flesche argued. "But I am responsible for the words and *I can take oath* that I hear so many words and so many musical syllables" (F & LF: 5A, emphasis added). Here, La Flesche suggests that he understood the language better than Cadman understood the music. On April 23, they continued the same fight, La Flesche exclaiming, "When I told him for the fifth time that the way he had it was wrong he said, 'I don't think you know any more about this than I do!' " (F & LF: 5A). Coolly, La Flesche countered that while he was admittedly not an expert in *wa-xo'-be*, he knew "enough about work like this to see that you are not doing it right and when the music is wrong as written by you I am not going to accept it."

If La Flesche functioned as "the resisted" in his work with the Osage, he adopted the role of "the resistor" when working with Cadman. His letters reveal that he felt he had more cultural authority over the music than Cadman, who was further removed from the music's origin. Although Cadman complied with the ethnographic transcription process, La Flesche felt an imperative to correct his errors, resisting as if he were one of the tribe, laboring to prevent an erroneous transcription. Yet La Flesche was perhaps less concerned with factual inconsistencies than with Cadman's disregard for his own Indigenous authority. This era of early American Indian ethnography often contained incorrect information due to flawed methodologies and interlocutor bias (Rhea 2016: 65–6; Bruchac 2018: 18). But La Flesche himself grappled with language translation and incomplete information from his interlocutors. His confrontation with Cadman seems rooted in his need for the composer to respect his (often flawed) expertise.

La Flesche exercised a great deal of control over Cadman's transcription process, just as his own interlocutors determined much of the *wa-xo'-be* project. But these acts of controlled participation and resistance are distinct from how composers in the Indianist movement felt about American Indians and their music. Many composers did not grant their American Indian sources or colleagues much agency and often conflated Indigeneity with musical primitivism in their appeals for Indianist nationalism. A notable example is Thurlow Lieurance, a non-Native composer who collected American Indian songs despite not being affiliated with an institution like the Bureau of American Ethnology or the American Folklore Society. His most famous piece, "By the Waters of Minnetonka" (1914), was based on a tune sung by Sitting Eagle, also known as Mortimer Dreamer, which he recorded during his 1911 fieldwork in present-day Montana. He attributed his ethnographic success to his ability to make American Indian friends and convince them to record; those transcriptions then became the basis for his own compositions. But his archival materials indicate a more complicated relationship with his interlocutors, as well as a general disregard for American Indian culture.

Unlike other ethnographers, Lieurance did not keep a detailed field journal, and the specifics of his fieldwork and interactions with interlocutors are unclear. His work is best understood by piecing together material from his archive with press statements and articles from the time. A 1919 article in *Musical America* claims that "Mr. Lieurance had secured one precious war-song of the Cheyenne. This is the medicine pipe song. Mortimer Dreamer (Sitting Eagle) knew the medicine-man and so was able to give Mr. Lieurance the songs peculiar to that profession" (Kinscella 1919: 4). This statement seems fairly innocuous and difficult to disprove without more specific details. The Library of Congress holds Lieurance's field recordings, which include a "medicine pipe song" attributed to Sitting Eagle. But according to the archivist who described the wax cylinders on the digitized recording, the container for the "medicine pipe song" included this note: "sung without permission of the medicine man by Sitting Eagle" (Digitized recording of Cylinder 20, Thurlow Lieurance Collection of Cylinder Recordings [Sound Recording], AFC 1948/129, Library of Congress).

It is not out of the realm of possibility that an interlocutor like Sitting Eagle would divulge sensitive information without permission, as Margaret Bruchac has shown with other American Indian ethnographers and archaeologists (2018: 48–83). Yet it is also impossible to know if Sitting Eagle sang a protected song, since Lieurance more than once bragged about his ability to record such songs despite tribal refusal. Lieurance admitted in an interview that the Taos Pueblo "war chief," Ventura, made him feel "about as welcome as a skunk" and that the chief dissuaded Pueblos from participating in his recording for fear of their spiritual well-being (Kinscella 1919: 4). This interview implies that Lieurance cared little about Ventura's spiritual concerns: he "secretly got some of the best singers away from the Pueblo and made about a hundred records," which apparently Ventura accepted "through kindness" once he heard Lieurance perform some of his compositions (Kinscella 1919: 4). This evidence points both to Lieurance's tenuous relationship with the truth and his disregard for tribal customs.

The manner in which Lieurance treated his interlocutors reflects his philosophical positions on American Indian music and American Indians as a "race." He often wrote about American Indian music as underdeveloped or primitive while complaining that the piano was unable to mimic the "split intervals" and "portamentos" of Indian musicality (Lieurance 1918: 14). He did not believe that Indians used harmony except accidentally and also wrote that American Indian music was a "human impulse" from "spontaneous, natural origin" (Lieurance et al. 1928: 5). That belief developed from his earlier claim that Indian musical characteristics corresponded "very closely—in fact dovetail exactly—with those just now being brought to light by scientific delvers in the background of Oriental life," a problematic belief in a shared, primitive past (Kinscella 1923: 4). He not only believed that American Indian music was underdeveloped but also that because Indians were unable to progress, they would never view music as an art. In a book of essays featuring the writings of Indianist composers, he wrote that he "never encountered [an Indian] that seemed to possess the qualities to do for his race what [Samuel] Coleridge-Taylor did for the negro." Indians are only able to understand music as perfunctory, not as a philosophical "necessary medium of life" (Lieurance et al. 1928: 5).

Yet Lieurance also believed that many American Indians actually wanted to assimilate to non-Native standards of music and civilization. In the introduction to his published volume, *Songs of the North American Indian*, he cited a chief who purportedly argued that Indians must adapt to white American culture because of their advanced agriculture: "Do you see the whites living upon the seeds while we eat flesh, that each of the wonderful seeds they sow in the earth returns to them a hundred fold? The flesh on which we subsist has four legs on which to escape while we have but two with which to pursue and capture it" (Lieurance 1920: 4). Lieurance extended similar thinking to American Indian music and culture, writing for *Etude* in 1918 that Indians, while concerned with the accuracy of their musical transcriptions, were grateful to white composers for turning their music into "idealized" songs whose beauty "implies to them the superhuman, they delight in it. It is a very grateful task indeed to play some of my own songs for the Indians—they can trace the relationship between the original theme and the idealized song" (Lieurance 1918: 13). His portrayal of Indians as underdeveloped or eager to assimilate is at odds with the strength and conviction I observe in my research, particularly from interlocutors and performers who were more in control of their actions and their musicality than Lieurance gives them credit for.

It is thus imperative to evaluate more closely how composers interpreted their Indigenous colleagues and informants. These relationships reveal the complex, fragile negotiations of race and identity in musical Indianism, compelling us to reconsider Indianist composers' intentions. Many composers believed either that American Indian music was America's only folk tradition or that it was linked to philosophical ideals of strength and nature that Americans should embody (Pisani 2008: 180; Levy 2012: 38). Some, like Lieurance, disparaged the subjects of their musical inspiration while at the same time claiming "Indianness" as a part of America's identity. This contradiction complicates the narrative that Indianist composers participated in a musical imagining or mythologizing of Native people and scenes, given how many of them exploited Indigenous labor and expressed contemptuous attitudes toward American Indian culture. Indianist music, written under the guise of care and uplift, grimly reflects the contemporaneous federal policies that violated Indigenous rights to "protect" the "Indian race." These sociopolitical movements, like American Indian boarding and reservation schools and the Dawes Act of 1887, were part of a federal paternalism that sought, under a facade of compassion and protection, to "solve the Indian problem" by encouraging assimilation and stripping away land rights. Composers did not simply imagine Indians. They actively took part in broader sociocultural politics that harmed American Indian people. That truth should be foregrounded in any study of their music and should force discussion on musical Indianism's effect on American Indians of the time.

Indigenous Reception

Indianist music was taught in boarding school classes and performed by American Indian musicians in pageants, recitals, and touring bands (Troutman 2009: 116–267). Evidence documenting performances of Indianist music can be found in boarding school newspapers, music journals, literary journals, local newspapers, and newsletters from American Indian organizations, but little has worked its way into current scholarship. These resources show that American Indians received Indianist music in the early twentieth century as audience members, performers, and critics. Contextualizing the relationships among ethnographers, composers, and informants by examining more widespread perceptions of Indianist music helps us better understand how this music affected different interest groups, as well as the complex relationship many American Indians had with it.

In 1906, the Yavapai-Apache doctor and American Indian activist, Carlos Montezuma, wrote an essay in *Tomorrow* magazine denouncing the teaching of American Indian music created from Indigenous songs in American Indian boarding schools. Montezuma begins the essay, titled "Indians Are Men, Not Freaks," with a dictionary definition of music: "A succession of sounds so modulated as to please the ear; melody or harmony: science of harmonical sounds: the art of producing harmony or melody: the written or printed score of a composition" (Montezuma 1906: 56). He uses that definition to indict American Indian music. The civilized ear, he argues, "distinguishes readily between mere noise and music," and whenever sounds do not conform to "science or harmony, there can be no melody, no pleasing sensation on the ear, no harmony and hence no music" (Montezuma 1906: 56). Non-Natives, including collectors, only display Indian musicality as if it were "the music of quacking ducks and cackling hens." He operated under the assumption that ethnographers could not collect "real" American Indian music, for it was "in no sense public property and could not be commonly used, and was guarded by the master of melody with all the jealous care of civilized authorship" (Montezuma 1906: 56). Instead of capturing the "mystic strains of savage opera or oratorios," which would "incur the ill will of the mighty mystery workers" and "call forth the wrath of the offended gods," ethnographers recorded and transcribed "a bit of weird melody—a semblance of a tune—a scale ignoring all standards and subject to myriad innovations—suggestive of melancholy and the tyranny of evil powers" (Montezuma 1906: 56-7). He rejects what were known as Indian musical characteristics: "la-la-la, pum, pum, pum, rattle, rattle, rattle, O O O; an indescribable blending of minors and semitones rising to falsetto screeches and descending through tangled skeins of sound to guttural tones" (Montezuma 1906: 57).

It is unclear if Montezuma felt that such tropes or musical characteristics were inherently unrepresentative, though elsewhere he wrote that they signify "evidence of that dark period in Indian life of which the best that can be said is that it ought to be forgotten in the march toward the more advanced life" ([Montezuma 1907] LaPier and Beck 2015: 42). He believed that American Indians were as cultivated and artistically capable as any "civilized" race and that initiatives preserving these types of songs would only further primitivist links to American Indian culture. Thus, he was upset when the federal government supported the researcher and composer Harold Loring in his efforts to record and arrange American Indian songs into orchestral works that would be performed by boarding school students. Montezuma feared that Loring's mission—to preserve American Indian song and teach American Indian students a classical form of Indigenous music—would impede racial progress: "We want no retrograde movements; we have naught but pity and charitable contempt for the so-called Arts of our people. These political helpers of the Indian (at good salaries from the Department and Bureau of Ethnology) would undo all that has been accomplished in the past twenty-five years" (Montezuma 1906: 57). Yet even though he objected to the pedagogical mission of Indianist techniques, he was even more inflamed by the primitive and crass nature of the American Indian music that was collected and composed—qualities that might be promoted and reified by musical Indianism.

Montezuma's stance on music, assimilation, and education was not shared by many of the activists in the Society of American Indians (SAI), an American Indian rights organization with which Montezuma was briefly associated. One faction of the SAI believed that upholding cultural traditions was vital to the uplift of the "Indian race," as did Arthur Parker, a Seneca anthropologist who famously feuded with Montezuma's position on music education (Patterson 2002: 59). Many SAI members even praised or collaborated with Indianist composers, like Zitkála-Šá (Gertrude Bonnin), a Dakota writer and musician who sometimes worked with Alice Fletcher and composed an Indianist opera with the composer William F. Hanson. Like Zitkála-Šá, some American Indian musicians used this type of Indian musicality to their advantage and spoke candidly about it.

One example is a forthright admission in La Flesche's correspondence. On August 28, 1918, Francis La Flesche recounted an interaction he had with an American Indian preacher on a train through the Midwest. When he told the preacher that he was Omaha, the preacher hummed an Omaha tune to see if La Flesche could identify it. La Flesche recognized it as a Fletcher transcription of a song he knew from childhood. The preacher said, "Miss Fletcher who wrote it to music is very clever, and has written it accurately. I use it frequently in my services and it always makes an 'impression' " (F & LF: 5A). By framing his use of an Omaha prayer song in quasi-theatrical terms, the preacher demonstrates his awareness of the power that he had to control how non-Natives perceived Indian musicality, leveraging it to his professional advantage.

Creek/Cherokee singer Tsianina Redfeather was also very aware of how her identity transformed Indianist music. In her memoir *Where Trails Have Led Me*, Tsianina described how she became acquainted with Cadman, with whom she collaborated for much of her early career. She refers to herself as a determined singer who worked tirelessly to prove her worth as a musician in a musical world that did not readily welcome outsiders. At first, Cadman was apparently "not all that enthusiastic over [her] singing," even stating "I don't think the girl will ever sing" (Tsianina 1968: 25). Tsianina was not discouraged, however: "I decided then and there that I would work hard and make him take back every word. In less than six months, I was ready for my first public concert with Cadman" (Tsianina 1968: 25). Having acquired a public platform on Cadman's stage, she viewed her performances of Indianist music as acts of goodwill:

> The press caught the spirit of this all-American combination [Cadman's music and Indian song] and I shall always love them for their "at one" feeling for the Indian race. They did not speak against anyone or anything regarding the Indian's problem—they just caught the spirit of the Red Man and gave the Indian all they had. They were on our side.
>
> (Tsianina 1968: 27)

Tsianina felt that her interpretation of Cadman's music had the power to garner non-Native audience's sympathy and support.

She also felt that Cadman's Indianist music, as a concept, was respectful and beneficial to the American Indian cause. Tsianina wrote that Cadman "had great difficulty in getting cooperation from the Indians in recording their music" because they thought "the white man after taking our land now wants to deprive us of our music too" (Tsianina 1968: 34). But she notes that Cadman eventually "won them over" with his famous composition, "From the Land of the Sky Blue Water":

> As long as there is a land of sky blue water, there will always be a Cadman who took this true, Indian melody from the Omaha tribe and made out of it a classic, a living thing, that embodies all the beauty and dignity of the American Indian … He literally gave a song picture of Indian emotion and revealed a nature of love and hate, joy and sorrow.
>
> (Tsianina 1968: 34)

She believed that Indianist music could "absorb the spirit" of American Indian songs and, if written sympathetically, would not detract from the melodies that "echoed in the forest long before the coming of the white man."

By contrast, other observers of musical Indianism questioned the music's relation to American Indian spirituality—that is, its connection to the natural world. Margaret Jones, a student at the Haskell Institute, then an American Indian boarding school, illustrates this way of thinking in an essay published in *The American Indian*, a periodical dedicated to news and writings from the tribes in present-day Oklahoma and published by the Society of Oklahoma Indians. In a 1929 volume, Jones narrates an imaginary dialogue with an apparition of Minnehaha, the fictional character from Henry Wadsworth Longfellow's poem, "The Song of Hiawatha." As Jones speaks, she is suddenly interrupted by a soprano singing Thurlow Lieurance's "By the Waters of Minnetonka" (1914). She explains to Minnehaha that Lieurance's song contains an Indian theme, but that his composition belongs to "the better type of popular music," as opposed to the original song (Jones 1929: 13). Minnehaha considers the music and notices similarities: "How very like the music I make in the silvery brooklets in the woodland is this imitation by the orchestra ... but here, no modest violet bends her velvet petals to kiss the cool, clear water" (Jones 1929: 13).

Jones's Minnehaha, an Indigenous folkloric persona, argues that while Lieurance's song borrows from American Indian tradition, it is a mere "imitation," lacking an important connection between music and nature. "By the Waters of Minnetonka" was widely performed in boarding schools by American Indian students and traveling bands, and it was particularly popular at graduation ceremonies, including the Haskell Institute. As a student, Jones had likely listened to and performed this song in an institutional educational setting many times and perhaps internalized both the song and the aesthetics and philosophies of musical Indianism. Through her poetic tale, we glimpse Jones's views of Indianism, which represent one of the many ways that American Indians perceived the movement. If some viewed Indianist music as an appropriate way for non-Natives to appreciate American Indian culture (as the preacher did), or as a way of respecting and furthering the cause of American Indian welfare (as Tsianina did), others, like Montezuma, believed that preserving Indian musicality through Indianist music would prevent racial progress. Jones's view represents a moderate position on the spectrum of American Indian responses to musical Indianism: critical of the musical appropriation, but astutely aware of the power and authority non-Natives had over the representation of Indian sound.

Conclusion

The archival methods featured in this chapter reveal a variety of American Indian responses to musical Indianism that challenge composer-centric narratives of the Indianist movement. By critically rereading and expanding the archive, we can analyze the voices and opinions of Indigenous informants and deconstruct how they are described in ethnographic language—an approach that separates Indigenous actions from ethnohistoric narratives of Indigeneity. Focusing on material outside the scope of commodified musical production considers the agency of Indigenous people beyond their connection to non-Native historical events and offers new avenues for exploring the far-reaching effects of the movement on American Indian communities. The many ways in which American Indians participated in ethnographic studies affected what sort of music was collected, how it was adapted by composers, and how audiences came to understand musical Indianism. And the fact that some interlocutors resisted such studies should lead us to think more critically about their veracity. Indianist compositions emerged not from authenticated or codified melodies but rather through complex negotiations of Indigenous knowledge and culture, destabilizing a composer-centric musical philosophy rooted in the authenticity and spirit of Indian music.

If Indigenous actions contributed to the successes and failures of musical Indianism, we must look more closely at the American Indian performers who worked with composers, the boarding school children who were forced to sing Indianist music as an assimilationist tactic, and the American Indian intellectuals who argued over outsiders intervening in cultural preservation. Studying musical Indianism from these perspectives reveals how conventional archival methods often view subaltern histories from dominant positions and how these methods may, for better or worse, shape the narrative scholars choose to tell. In prioritizing the experiences and epistemologies of Indigenous people in musical Indianism, and other movements with similar histories, we dig deeper into musicological questions on race, exoticism, appropriation, and labor, avoiding tidy historical conclusions.

References

Alice Cunningham Fletcher and Francis La Flesche Papers, Correspondence between Fletcher and La Flesche, 1873–1925, Series 1, Subseries 4, Box 5A, National Anthropological Archives, Smithsonian Institution, Washington, DC.

Bailey, G., ed. (1995), *The Osage and the Invisible World: From the Works of Francis La Flesche*, Norman: University of Oklahoma Press.

Browner, T. (1997), " 'Breathing the Indian Spirit': Thoughts on Musical Borrowing and the 'Indianist' Movement in American Music," *American Music*, 15 (3): 265–84.

Bruchac, M. (2018), *Savage Kin: Indigenous Informants and American Anthropologists*, Tucson: University of Arizona Press.

Fletcher, A., F. La Flesche, and J. C. Fillmore (1904), *A Study of Omaha Indian Music*, Peabody Museum of American Archaeology and Ethnology.

Imada, A. (2012), *Aloha America: Hula Circuits through the U.S. Empire*, Durham: Duke University Press Books.

Jones, M. (1929), "Minnehaha and Our Music," *The American Indian*, 3 (12): 13.

Kinscella, H. (1919), "Thurlow Lieurance's Researches in Indian Song Disclose Rich Material for Our Composers," *Musical America*, 29 (26): 3–4.

Kinscella, H. (1923), "Lieurance Traces American Indian Music to Oriental Origins," *Musical America*, 37 (24): 3–4.

LaPier, R. and D. Beck (2015), *City Indian: Native American Activism in Chicago, 1893–1934*, Lincoln: University of Nebraska Press.

Levy, B. (2012), *Frontier Figures: American Music and the Mythology of the American West*, Berkeley: University of California Press.

Lieurance, T. (1918), "Beauties in the Music of the American Indian," *The Etude*, 36 (1): 13–14.

Lieurance, T. (1920), *Songs of the North American Indian*, Philadelphia: Theodore Presser.

Lieurance, T., C. W. Cadman, and A. Nevin (1928), *Indian Music*, Philadelphia: Theodore Presser.

Loomis, H. W. (1904), "The Chattering Squaw," in *Lyrics of the Red Man*, op. 76, Newton, MA: Wa-Wan Press.

Mark, J. (1982), "Francis La Flesche: The American Indian as Anthropologist," *Isis*, 73 (4): 497–510.

Mark, J. (1988), *A Stranger in Her Native Land: Alice Fletcher and the American Indians*, Lincoln: University of Nebraska Press.

Maroukis, T. (2012), *The Peyote Road: Religious Freedom and the Native American Church*, Norman: University of Oklahoma Press.

Maroukis, T. (2013), "The Peyote Controversy and the Demise of the Society of American Indians," *American Indian Quarterly*, 37 (3): 161–80.

Montezuma, C. (1906), "Indians Are Men, Not Freaks," *Tomorrow Magazine* (December): 55–60.

Montezuma, C. (1907), "Against Indian Art Study," *The Daily News* (April 5), in *The Papers of Carlos Montezuma, 1871–1952*, J. Larner (ed.), microfilm reel 6, Scholarly Resources.

Patterson, M. (2002), " 'Real' Indian Songs: The Society of American Indians and the Use of Native American Culture as a Means of Reform," *American Indian Quarterly*, 26 (1): 44–66.

Pisani, M. (2008), *Imagining Native America in Music*, New Haven: Yale University Press.

Rhea, J. (2016), *A Field of Their Own: Women and American Indian History, 1830–1941*, Norman: University of Oklahoma Press.

Rifkin, M. (2017), *Beyond Settler Time: Temporal Sovereignty and Indigenous Self Determination*, Durham, NC: Duke University Press Books.

Smith, L. T. ([1999] 2012), *Decolonizing Methodologies: Research and Indigenous Peoples*, London: Zed Books.

Swan, D. (1988), "Early Osage Peyotism," *Plains Anthropologist*, 43 (163): 51–71.

Thurlow Lieurance Collection of Cylinder Recordings [Sound Recording], 1911–1912, Digitized Recording of Cylinder 20, AFC 1948/129, Library of Congress.

Tsianina (1968), *Where Trails Have Led Me*, Burbank, CA: Tsianina Blackstone.

Troutman, J. (2009), *Indian Blues: American Indians and the Politics of Music, 1879–1934*, Norman: University of Oklahoma Press.

Tuck, E. and K. W. Wang (2012), "Decolonization Is Not a Metaphor," *Decolonization: Indigeneity, Education & Society*, 1 (1): 1–40.

3

Reconsidering "Rhythm" as a Cultural Marker in Black String Band Music

Landon Bain

Joe Thompson (d. 2012), an acclaimed African American fiddler from North Carolina, became an influential figure in old-time and roots music toward the end of his life due to mentoring the wildly successful African American string band, the Carolina Chocolate Drops (CCD). Thompson's fiddle style and repertoire are often understood as links to an antebellum tradition of Black fiddling, one thought to differ from white fiddle styles, especially in terms of its approach to rhythm (i.e., its syncopation, drive, and percussiveness). Consider, for example, Terence McArdle (2012), who states in *The Washington Post* that Thompson's music "offered a link to an almost-vanished tradition of African-American string bands that predated the blues and even the Civil War." An obituary by Douglas Martin in *The New York Times* characterized Thompson's music in the same way as the scholar Paul Wells, calling it "something like square dance music, only more rhythmic" and gesturing toward an African American string band style that "predates the blues and influenced country music and bluegrass" (Martin 2012).

Embedded in these posthumous descriptions of Thompson's playing are the complex histories of Black music in the United States and their attendant debates about African musical and cultural retentions, racialized listening practices concerning "essence," and cultural reclamation in the face of historical whitewashing. While these topics have been examined in the broader discourse on Black expressive cultures, they have only recently been applied to string band music made by Black musicians in the rural South. Recent inquiries into rural Black music and musicians can be linked to two cultural and intellectual "moments" that began in the early 1990s: (1) increased scholarly interest in a Black string band tradition distinct from white string band playing and repertoire, and (2) the founding of the Affrilachian Poets group and subsequent propagation of "Affrilachia" as both a term and a discursive and aesthetic label.

I begin this chapter with a historical investigation of these two moments, connecting them to broader theoretical debates about essentialism, anti-essentialism, and "African retentions." Next, I examine how scholars have valued Joe Thompson's playing for its connections to early African American musicking, evoking narratives concerned, first and foremost, with continuities and origins rather than the markers of hybridity, adaptation, and individual agency discussed by the music scholar Karl Hagstrom Miller (2010: 7). I place this perspective in dialogue with a more synchronic approach focused on geographical region, historical circumstance, and musical affiliation, arguing that while these two narratives are not mutually exclusive (and, in fact, cannot be separated), a skewed focus on Africanist musical tropes in Thompson's playing reifies racialized notions of musical style. I thus suggest a third approach that I term "anti-anti-essentialism," following Paul Gilroy's definition (1993: 102), attempting to account for both perspectives. Ultimately, I argue that future scholarly work on Black musicking in old-time and bluegrass should move away from these tropes, instead embracing more regionally rooted, historically contingent approaches to stylistic analysis and critical race theory.

Affrilachia and 1990s Research on Black String Band Traditions

"Affrilachia," an influential portmanteau coined by the poet Frank X Walker (2000: 92–3), denotes a cultural-political movement that seeks to illuminate the presence and culture of African Americans in the Appalachian region. The term pushes against the socio-geographical stereotyping of Appalachia as exclusively white and poor, drawing attention to the diversity of the vast thirteen-state region (Spriggs 2011: 21). It also prompts a call to activism and cultural intervention, "render[ing] the invisible visible" (Spriggs 2011: 21). For William H. Turner, Affrilachia is a "brand," a means of adapting and augmenting a sense of identity and belonging, using "cultural tools" for reclamation (2011: 29).

While the Affrilachian movement initially focused on poetry and literature, music—especially old-time and string band music—eventually entered the discussion. Old-time music, in its contemporary usage, refers to a varied repertoire of (mostly) nineteenth-century fiddle tunes and songs closely associated with the American South, and Appalachia in particular, encompassing Western European dance musics, minstrel songs, Civil War marches, and, to quote Jeff Todd Titon, "unmistakable, though not well-documented, transformations and influences wrought by African and Native Americans" (2001: xv). Titon, who acknowledges the contributions of African and Native American musicians while lamenting adequate documentation, gestures toward a history of racial politics and erasures in old-time music.

These erasures are due in no small part to the efforts of record producers and executives like Ralph Peer, who, in the 1920s, divided the burgeoning vernacular music market into the categories of "hillbilly" (old-time string band and country music, which became associated with whites) and "race" music (predominantly gospel and blues music, which was linked to Black musicians and listeners). These lasting correlations effectively divided American traditional music along racial lines (Roy 2004: 265). Seventy years later, Charles Wolfe, writing in *Black Music Research Journal* (*BMRJ*), highlighted the pressing need for scholarly inquiry into what he called "rural black string band music," identifying several critical questions he believed would drive future research (1990: 34). He asked, "Is (was) there a black string band repertoire distinctive from the white one? Is there an identifiable black fiddle style? Have there been characteristic and distinctive black instrumental combinations? Have geographical features affected these combinations?"

In recent decades, scholars have followed Wolfe's injunction when discussing the banjo's African origins (Conway 1995, 2001; Thomas 2013), the presence of Black musicians on early old-time music recordings (Huber 2013), and the musical and racial hybridity of the old-time canon (Jamison 2015). Furthermore, a 2003 special issue of the *BMRJ*, titled "Black Musicians in Appalachia: An Introduction to Affrilachian Music," gathered scholars from various fields to provide an authoritative overview of Black music in the region. Fred J. Hay, evoking John Storm Roberts, articulated the issue's aim: to assert "Affrilachian music's presence in 'the oneness of black culture in the twentieth century' " (2003: 16). Perhaps the most influential framework for this "oneness of black culture" came from Samuel Floyd Jr. (1995: 10), who argued that continuity exists among "all the musical genres of the black cultural experience," which could be traced from the early years of chattel slavery in the United States to "the most recent music-making of black Americans." To support this claim, Floyd invokes "cultural memory," which refers, in his usage, to "nonfactual and non-referential motivations, actions, and beliefs that members of a culture seem, without direct knowledge or deliberate training, to 'know'—that feel unequivocally 'true' or 'right' when encountered, experienced, and executed" (1995: 8). Black scholars and leaders have often explored the multigenerational lessons passed through African American music and cultural memory, but this gesture toward a singular "oneness" of style can lead to essentialist assumptions of uniformity and stylistic permanence in Black music and musical Blackness.

Some of these ideas are reflected in an article by Paul F. Wells in a 2003 issue of the *BMRJ*, who argues that Black fiddlers likely played in a more syncopated, rhythmically oriented style, distinct from white fiddle styles. Wells mentions well-known archival sources to support this claim, including the reflections of Elizabeth W. Allston Pringle (1845–1921), who recalls a celebration held on the Chicora Wood Plantation. In her memoir *Chronicles of Chicora Wood* (published posthumously in 1922), Pringle reflects on "the dancing began in the piazza, a fiddle playing the gayest jigs, with two heavy sticks knocking to mark the time, and a triangle and bones rattling in the most exciting syncopated time; and all the young negroes on the plantation, and many from the other plantations belonging to papa, all dancing, dancing, dancing" (cited in Wells 2003: 139). For Wells, syncopation and specific percussion instruments, like the bones, triangle, and sticks, mark this music as distinctly African American, reflecting contemporaneous reports of slave music-making in the antebellum South (140).

Moreover, the difference between white and Black fiddling, Wells argues, encompasses both style and repertoire. Referring to the work of Eileen Southern ([1971] 1997), he observes that while many Black fiddlers played tunes that today would be considered staples of the white fiddle repertoire (such as "Soldier's Joy" and "Arkansas Traveler"), they also "played tunes that were more African in character—'Negro Jigs'—which do not conform to the standard British, Irish, American fiddle-tune mold but which may have influenced later Southern fiddling, both white and black" (Wells 2003: 144–5). Wells's phrase, "more African in character," seems to suggest that these tunes were more rhythmically adventurous and formally distinct from European fiddle traditions, but his claims, based on vague historical observations made by white observers, are difficult to substantiate. And though he marshals a diverse array of contemporary scholarship and archival sources to support his narrative, the documents he cites are temporally and geographically distinct, ranging from 1775 to the early twentieth century in areas from Virginia and North Carolina to New England. Such source disparities make it nearly impossible to argue for a unified and coherent Black string band tradition. If Wells and writers like him argue for the veracity of these reports, scholars like Ronald Radano (2003) point out the ideological formations of race created here through exaggerations of difference, suggesting that Wells's perceived distinctions of style prove to be more discursive than sonic.

The Limits of Archival Research: The Anti-Essentialist Critique

Both Radano and Dena Epstein (1977) have argued that ascertaining any concrete, stable notion of Black musical practices from such disparate texts requires a near-impossible feat of historical hermeneutics (Radano 2003: 5–6). While Radano engages many of the same source materials used by Wells, he finds that identifying forms such as the "Negro jig" or the "Congo minuet" as "uniquely 'black' might have seemed inappropriate, for the ability of whites to comprehend and engage in these practices shows that they had already been casting about in an intercultural body of musical resonance" (2003: 112). Put another way, processes of musical and cultural exchange had rendered inscrutable any clear division between Black and white musical practices, even in these racialized accounts.

Depictions of Black musicking by white observers thus index the anxiety of racial mixture in the context of eighteenth-century slavery and highlight the need to demarcate explicit notions of racial difference. Historical descriptions of Black fiddling likely establish and reinforce a sonic color line—a theoretical and analytical conceit which, in the words of Jennifer Lynn Stoever, unveils how "essentialist ideas about 'black' sound and listening offered … a method of grounding racial abjection in the body while cultivating white listening practices as critical, discerning, delicate, and above all, as the standard of citizenship and personhood" (2016: 5). The sonic color line addresses the "process of racializing sound" and how certain bodies were gradually expected to "produce, desire, and live amongst particular sounds" (2016: 7).

I contend that the work of Radano and Stoever can be unified under the banner of anti-essentialism. Broadly conceived, anti-essentialism opposes claims of immutable essence, preferring instead a social constructionist approach that reveals how these claims develop historically and how they come to appear natural and innate. For these thinkers, the notion that a Black musical essence might prevail in the African American string band tradition would likely qualify as an example of essentialist thinking (and a particularly resilient strain involving the trope of "African" rhythm). As Kofi Agawu asserts, the notion that African music can be defined foremost by "a special disposition towards rhythm"—and indeed, that African music is somehow more rhythmically advanced or sophisticated than "Western" music—is itself "an invention of Western discourse" (1995: 395). This myth ostensibly valorizes African music by celebrating its difference while still marking it as "Other." As Agawu notes, such thinking denies or downplays African music's harmonic and melodic features, which are understood to be inherently Western in this framework (1995: 385). This fetishizing of difference is a central facet of colonial logic, as it maintains but obscures hierarchical distinction.

Race and Region: Understanding "Rhythm" in Joe Thompson's Playing

It is clear that "rhythm" as a cultural and aesthetic marker of Blackness represents a contested theoretical space. Scholars and musicians link Joe Thompson's playing to descriptions of antebellum fiddling in different ways, sometimes evoking regionality but more often falling into essentialist discourses related to Hay's "oneness" of Black music and Floyd's notion of cultural memory. For example, in the article "Soul Clap: Rhythm and Resilience in Afro-Carolina Landscapes," Michelle Lanier draws explicit connections between Thompson's fiddle playing and the belief in African musical and cultural retentions:

> So.
> Even as drums are stripped away from African-descendent people,
> the rhythms aren't going anywhere.
> Violin playing gets more rhythmic!
> Banjos are played harder! We are doing more with what we have
> to work with.
>
> We are funneling all that percussive energy that we have.
> That is so much a part of African life,
> in the past, and currently ....
>
> Joe Thompson's fiddling was designed to go with the banjo.
> And so it was much more percussive than any White player around
>   there would

have been.
African American fiddling is percussive fiddling.
It's mimicking of the banjo.
The fiddle and banjo get together and the fiddle gets more percussive.
It just has to. (2018: 149–50)

Lanier's claim—that "African American fiddling is percussive fiddling"—appears to connect Thompson's style to historical descriptions of Black fiddling, and to older African traditions as well, clearly alluding to cultural memory as an instrument of Black musical and cultural continuity. But the concrete musical evidence for this claim is vague: after all, ensemble interplay between the fiddle and banjo is at the heart of old-time traditions, both Black and white, leading to more pressing questions. What musical attributes do commenters hear as "rhythmic" in Thompson's playing? And what, if anything, makes these attributes distinctly African American?

Fiddler and folklorist Allan Jabbour claims that African Americans "have a predilection for a fiddle style that has an abrasive, vigorous, and energetic quality," while banjoist Tommy Thompson (unrelated to Joe) asserts that the Thompsons are "as close as you'll get to the original string band" (Conway 1995: 13). Cecelia Conway suggests that the "moaning, rhythmic, and energetic" qualities of Thompson's playing approximate both older and more contemporary African musical practices (1995: 13–14). For Conway, a tangible reason for Thompson's "abrasive" timbre is a "heavy" bowing style learned from his father—though there is, of course, more to Thompson's sound than bow pressure (1995: 13). Indeed, Justin Robinson, one of the founding members of the CCD, notes that Thompson's fiddle style foregrounds over-the-bar syncopation and a bowing technique he characterized as the "double shuffle … this sort of forward-and-back motion that is going forward all at the same time, making these really great rhythmic kind of things that you have to really work very hard to get" (Carolina Chocolate Drops 2010). This bowing technique, combined with heavier bow pressure and cross-tunings, produces overtones that are part of Thompson's signature sound. When he played with his cousin Odell, a banjoist, the banjo would often take the lead, leaving the fiddle to function as a rhythm instrument—an inversion of these instruments' roles in traditional string band and fiddle/banjo duo playing.

These are just a few of the musical markers likened by commentators to historical descriptions of African American fiddling. But how has the Thompson family style, in particular, been preserved and passed on? The most persuasive argument is that Thompson learned his craft and repertoire through family traditions stretching back generations. Robinson notes that Thompson had been "playing since he was six or seven years old, and he learned from his father, and his father had learned from his father. So it's a long tradition among his family" (Carolina Chocolate Drops 2010). Here, Robinson describes a patrilineal musical heritage of Black fiddling and string band tradition, perhaps reaching back to the antebellum period. Accordingly, some tunes in Thompson's repertoire appear exclusive to his family, lending weight to the notion of musical lineage. For example, the tune "Donna's Got a Rambling Mind" seems particular to the Thompsons, musically and lyrically—a driving, one-part tune that, like another Thompson family signature, "Old Corn Liquor," seems inseparable from related dance traditions. Southern square dancing requires a "caller," an expert musician or dancer who hollers the dance moves, or figures, in real time. Depending on the dancers' skill level, the dance could simply be a series of figures performed repeatedly in the same way. However, as Phil Jamison notes, "Southern square dances evolved as an unwritten oral folk tradition. There is no one definitive version of any particular dance; each caller has their own version. And even during the course of a dance, due to the freeform timing, the caller has the freedom to improvise and change the choreography at will" (Jamison: 22). For the Thompsons, both Joe's expertise as a caller and the dance figures linked to the tunes they played were an integral part of their artistic practice; even when performing without dancers, space was always made for Joe to call dance figures. "Donna's Got a Rambling Mind," which is featured on the *Family Tradition* recording and performed by Joe and Odell Thompson on fiddle and clawhammer banjo, respectively, has become an exceptionally well-known Thompson tune due mainly, in recent years, to the CCD, who named their debut recording after it.

For the many of the scholars, critics, and journalists mentioned thus far, the sound of the Thompsons' playing represents *the* sound of the African American string band, a stylistic approach defined first and foremost through its "rhythmic" qualities and tonal sonorities, but also by a repertoire distinct from white string bands. This narrative has indeed proven to be a powerful corrective, both for the whitewashing of country and old-time musics and for the racist claims that Black old-time musicians learned this music by "imitating" white performers. Ultimately, notions of "rhythmic" gestures and "vigorous" bowing styles attempt to mobilize a politics of authenticity rooted in African cultural heritage to unveil the contributions of Black musicians, at times problematically linking this genre and its history to Hay's (2004) "oneness of black music." Moreover, as exemplified by Jabbour's comment that African American fiddlers have a "predilection" for this style, commentators who invoke such politics of authenticity cannot entirely escape the racial ideologies they seek to correct. The discourse around Thompson's style, then, seems to hover ambivalently between twentieth-century African American musical practices and regionality in one instance and an ephemeral and problematic conceit of racial "predilection" in the other.

Of course, regionality does play a vital role in understanding the rhythmic drive in Joe Thompson's playing. The string band music of Thompson's home— the Piedmont region in the central flatlands of North Carolina—is increasingly being recognized for its distinct styles of Southern string music. In particular, the string band style of Orange, Alamance, and other nearby counties (where the Thompsons are from) has been characterized by Mike Seeger as overtly "rugged and rhythmic" (*Old Time Banjo Styles* 1995) and often defined by a driving accompaniment and a fiddle style concerned less with flowing melodic lines than danceability. "Old Corn Liquor" is an ideal example of the Orange/Alamance county regional sound, underpinned by Joe's style of fiddling and Odell's driving clawhammer banjo playing.

In the flatlands, which were more stylistically diverse than the mountain communities further north, old-time string band music coexisted, then and now, with blues, bluegrass, and other popular music forms. The English folklorist and song collector Cecil Sharpe dismissed the folk traditions of this region precisely for their hybridity, the mingling of older and contemporary styles obscuring the musical "purity" he fetishized (Carlin 2004: 3). It is difficult, then, to argue that the Piedmont string band sound preserves anything particularly "ancient" or "unchanging"—though to be sure, the notion of folk traditions as "unchanging" and "pure" is always problematic. Instead, the Piedmont region functions as an ideal case study, revealing the fluidity and adaptability of musical traditions. Seeger notes that in the Piedmont region, this style of string band music would have been played by white and Black musicians alike, and Carlin, recalling conversations with Joe Thompson himself, states that though African and Anglo Americans had different names for the social occasions linked to this music ("frolics" and "square-dances," respectively), "there was no difference in the music or the [dance] figures" (*Family Tradition* 1999: liner notes). Thompson's playing thus highlights the complex cultural exchange of style and repertoire in the Piedmont region, signaling that along racial lines, there may have been more stylistic similarities than differences.

An Anti-Anti-essentialist and Hybrid Approach

The foregoing evidence confirms that an evaluation of Thompson's style, and the style of other African American fiddlers, should be based as much (if not more so) on regionality as on notions of race. Such an approach would allow historians and fans to move beyond reductive assessments that hover dangerously close to essentialism. Indeed, Thompson's style should be heard as a complex interplay of familial traditions, regional influences, *and* the politics of race. An overt focus on Africanist musical traits in Thompson's playing and the extrapolation of stylistically bounded notions of African American musical expression unintentionally strengthens the hegemony of whiteness in country, old-time, and bluegrass musics.

To be sure, Affrilachian discourse and the work of the scholars previously cited have carved out a space for marginalized cultures in the public, commercial, and institutional spheres by naming what was once invisible: Black and non-white peoples and cultures in the Appalachian region. The CCD and, in particular, founding member Rhiannon Giddens have been the most successful and publicly visible of the Black string band revivalists. Because CCD learned much of their initial repertoire—and, in the case of Giddens and Robinson, their fiddle style— from Joe Thompson, his sound has become perhaps the most well-known exemplar of the Black string band tradition in the United States and abroad. In performing and extending this style, Giddens has garnered significant acclaim, embarking on a successful solo career after her departure from the CCD. In 2016, she received the Steve Martin Prize for Excellence in Bluegrass and Banjo; the following year, she was awarded a MacArthur genius grant and invited as the keynote speaker for the 2017 International Bluegrass Music Association (IBMA) conference.

The revival of public interest in Black string band traditions, spurred on by the success of Giddens and the CCD, has also captured the attention of country and folk music institutions, including the IBMA and the Grand Ole Opry, who wish to signal progressive values and to highlight inclusion and diversity. But these integrationist ideals, founded as they are on notions of difference, may prove as precarious as they are powerful. The word "healing"—referring, for many commentators, to an easing of racial tensions in the United States—has been invoked to describe the CCD's practice many times, including their performance as the first Black string band at the Grand Ole Opry. Yet, as Giddens points out in her IBMA keynote address, we should be wary of uncritically celebrating this healing moment: "But I have to ask—a healing moment for whom? One or two black groups or one or two black country stars is not a substitution for recognizing the true multi-cultural history of this music. We have a lot of work to do" (Giddens 2017).

In this poignant quote, we may detect Giddens's discomfort with cultural institutions that might tokenize her work and the music of the CCD. Despite good intentions, it is clear that the eager embrace of Giddens and the CCD indeed constitutes a sort of multiculturalist fetishization of difference that is, in some respects, ultimately complicit in white supremacy. Here again, we are confronted with a colonialist logic in which hierarchies are obscured by the self-congratulatory rhetoric of diversity and inclusion. As bell hooks has observed, white supremacist thinking often makes room for Black or non-white "exceptions" (hooks 2013: 5), potentially reducing the Black string band tradition, via Giddens and the CCD, to a mere footnote in the history of white cultural expression. A handful of Black musicians cannot act as a synecdoche for such a complex and multifaceted tradition, just as this tradition cannot be reduced to a handful of racialized stylistic traits. Such thinking is part and parcel of white supremacy. Its effect, intentional or otherwise, is to keep marginalized sonic identities at the margins where they ostensibly belong.

Paul Gilroy's (1993: 102) notion of anti-anti-essentialism suggests an alternative to racialized theories of musical style. On the one hand, Gilroy opposes a radical social constructionist approach to racial identity that minimizes or dismisses the lived realities of race, but on the other, he criticizes what he describes as an Afrocentric, linear understanding of time (Gilroy 1993: 100–1, 190). In its most extreme iterations, this sort of essentialist viewpoint urges Black subjects "if not to forget the slave experience ... then to replace it at the center of our thinking with a mystical and ruthlessly positive notion of Africa that is indifferent to intraracial variation and is frozen at the point where blacks boarded the ships that would carry them into the woes and horrors of the middle passage" (Gilroy 1993: 189). Such an approach, Gilroy argues, mobilizes a highly reductive conception of African "tradition" to assert continuity between the varied musical and cultural practices of Black subjects and vague notions of an African past (191).

To counter these extremes, Gilroy proposes a focus on both "roots and routes," paying particular attention to liminality, or "flows and exchanges," and describing this theoretical turn toward cultural exchange, transformation, and diaspora as "anti-anti-essentialism" (Gilroy 1993: 102, 190). Though Carter Mathes has summarized anti-anti-essentialism as "an idea of black consciousness that is flexible and moves between the insufficient terms of 'essentialist' and 'anti-essentialist' " (2013), it seems clear to me that Gilroy wants to move beyond them, not merely between them. Following Gilroy, my intention is not to dismiss ideas about cultural memory in Black music, but to unveil racialized musical tropes and listening practices as cultural constructs in order to highlight the power dynamics at play. Future work on Black musicking in old-time, bluegrass, and country would be best served by holding these tropes at a critical distance, questioning even the most affirmative examples of this line of thinking (which characterizes much of the writing I have discussed here).

Yet while it is important to critique and historically situate claims of unchanging racial essence, there is also a pressing need for an approach to the Black string band tradition that can account for its cultural complexity and variety. Embracing hybridity would push against the historic and persistent segregation of sound and heed Giddens's call to recognize this music's "true multi-cultural history." Such an approach would bring Miller's (2010) notions of hybridity and adaptation in contact with Gilroy's anti-anti-essentialism, which "calls the very desire to be centered into question" (Gilroy 1993: 190). A renewed focus on regional diversity and historical and geographical specificity would promote an understanding of old-time music as always already hybrid.

This methodology would seek to expand the stylistic borders of Black old-time music, emphasizing a more localized, synchronic approach to stylistic development and variation. It would accentuate the importance of region and contemporaneity in the music of Joe and Odell Thompson, placing their brand of string band music in dialogue with broader musical practices in the North Carolina Piedmont. Crucially, approaching old-time, country, and bluegrass musics as an always already hybrid does not delineate bounded notions of Blackness, which only strengthen the hegemonic whiteness of these genres. Deconstructing the theoretical approaches and assumptions that uphold white power structures will require careful attention to the overlap between artificially imposed stylistic boundaries, the complex cultural flows and exchanges so quickly reduced to claims of immutable sonic difference. A focus on hybridity and "de-centering" identity facilitates the undoing of a sonic color line that has been, and continues to be, powerfully reinforced by the recording industry.

References

Agawu, K. (1995), "The Invention of 'African Rhythm,'" *Journal of the American Musicological Society*, 48 (3): 380–95.

Carlin, B. (2004), *String Bands in the North Carolina Piedmont*, Jefferson, NC: McFarland & Company, Inc.

"Carolina Chocolate Drops and a String Band Tradition" (2010), *National Public Radio (NPR)*, September 3. https://www-editor.npr.org/templates/story/story.php?storyId=129458600 (accessed July 30, 2020).

Conway, C. (1995), *African Banjo Echoes in Appalachia: A Study of Folk Traditions*, Knoxville: University of Tennessee Press.

Conway, C. (2001), "Appalachian Echoes of the African Banjo," in J. C. Inscoe (ed.), *Appalachians and Race: From Slavery to Segregation*, Lexington: University Press of Kentucky.

Epstein, D. (1977), *Sinful Tunes and Spirituals: Black Folk Music to the Civil War*, Urbana: University of Illinois Press.

Floyd Jr., S.A. (1995), *The Power of Black Music: Interpreting Its History from Africa to the United States*, New York: Oxford University Press.

Giddens, R. (2017), "Rhiannon Giddens's Keynote Address at IBMA Conference: Community and Connection," *Nonesuch Records*, October 3. www.nonesuch.com/journal/rhiannon-giddens-keynote-address-ibma-conference-community-connection-2017-10-03 (accessed April 15, 2018).

Gilroy, P. (1993), *The Black Atlantic: Modernity and Double Consciousness*, Cambridge, MA: Harvard University Press.

Hay, F. J. (2003), "Black Musicians in Appalachia: An Introduction to Affrilachian Music," *Black Music Research Journal*, 23 (1/2): 1–19.

hooks, b. (2013), *Writing beyond Race: Living Theory and Practice*, New York: Routledge.

Huber, P. (2013), "Black Hillbillies: African American Musicians on Old-Time Records, 1924–1932," in D. Pecknold (ed.), *Hidden in the Mix: The African American Presence in Country Music*, 19–81, Durham: Duke University Press.

Jamison, P. (2015), *Hoedowns, Reels, and Frolics: Roots and Branches of Southern Appalachian Dance*, Champaign: University of Illinois Press.

Lanier, M. (2018), "Soul Clap: Rhythm and Resilience in Afro-Carolina Landscapes," *Southern Cultures*, 24 (3): 144–59.

Martin, D. (2012), "Joe Thompson Dies at 93; Helped Preserve the Black String Band," *The New York Times*, March 1. https://www.nytimes.com/2012/03/02/arts/music/joe-thompson-dies-at-93-fiddler-of-string-band-legacy.html (accessed July 30, 2013).

Mathes, C. (2013), "The Sounds of Anti-Anti-Essentialism: Listening to Black Consciousness in the Classroom," *Sounding Out!*, April 15. https://soundstudiesblog.com/2013/04/15/the-sounds-of-anti-anti-essentialism/ (accessed July 30, 2020).

McArdle, T. (2012), "Joe Thompson, 93, Well-Respected Fiddler," *The Washington Post*, February 29. https://www.washingtonpost.com/entertainment/music/joe-thompson-93-well-respected-fiddler/2012/02/27/gIQAjuW1iR_story.html (accessed July 30, 2020).

Miller, K. H. (2010), *Segregating Sound: Inventing Folk and Pop Music in the Age of Jim Crow*, Durham: Duke University Press.

Old-time Banjo Styles: Taught by Mike Seeger (1995) [Film], USA: Homespun Tapes.

Radano, R. (2003), *Lying up a Nation: Race and Black Music*, Chicago: University of Chicago Press.

Roy, W. G. (2004), "'Race Records' and 'Hillbilly Music:' Institutional Origins of Racial Categories in the American Commercial Recording Industry," *Poetics*, 32 (3–4): 265-79.

Southern, E. ([1971] 1997), *The Music of Black Americans: A History*, 3rd edn, New York: Norton.

Spriggs, B. (2011), "Frank X Walker: Exemplar of Affrilachia," *Appalachian Heritage*, 39 (4): 21-5.

Stoever, J. L. (2016), *The Sonic Color Line: Race and the Cultural Politics of Listening*, New York, NY: New York University Press.

Thomas, T. (2013), "Why African Americans Put the Banjo Down," in D. Pecknold (ed.), *Hidden in the Mix: The African American Presence in Country Music*, Durham: Duke University Press, 143–70.

Thompson, J. (1999), *Family Tradition* [Compact disc], Rounder Records Corp., C 2161.

Titon, J. T. (2001), *Old-Time Kentucky Fiddle Tunes*, Lexington: The University Press of Kentucky.

Turner, W. H. (2011), "Affrilachia as Brand," *Appalachian Heritage*, 39 (4): 27–30.

Walker, F. X. (2000), *Affrilachia: Poems by Frank X Walker*, Lexington, KY: Old Cove Press.

Wells, P. F. (2003), "Fiddling as an Avenue of Black-White Musical Interchange," *Black Music Research Journal*, 23 (1/2): 135–47.

Wolfe, C. (1990), "Rural Black String Band Music," *Black Music Research Journal*, 10 (1): 32-5.

4

"The Year of Jubilee Is Come": Metatextual Resonance in Antislavery Hymn Parodies

Erin Fulton

When the American Antislavery Society wanted a songbook, it turned to pastor-musician Edwin F. Hatfield, who turned to his own knowledge of hymnody. His *Freedom's Lyre* freely adapted the shifting canon of hymns that Anglophone Protestants had sung and studied over the past century. Echoing an unacknowledged fellow hymn-editor, Hatfield explained in the preface how he "treated the hymns which have come before him as public property, which he had a right to modify and use according to his own judgment," introducing changes to them " 'wherever it appeared that the piece could thereby be improved,' or adapted to the holy cause of Emancipation" (1840: [iii]–iv, quoting Mason and Greene 1831: vii). This idea—that hymn texts could or even ought to be altered to better support a civic argument—was widespread in the antebellum United States, and Hatfield was far from the only antislavery author to employ it.

This chapter probes interconnections between mainstream hymnody and antislavery songbooks like *Freedom's Lyre*, focusing on the textual elements editors modified to rally support. I expand on previous studies of antislavery songsters, recognizing that scholars have struggled to identify known primary sources as parody. For example, Abby Love Smith identifies thirty-five instances of hymn parody in eight antislavery sources while tracing only antislavery adaptations of hymn texts. My research here encompasses a larger body of work and also considers parodies based on hymn tunes. Some of my findings therefore contradict Smith's, especially her assertion that altered hymns lost favor after 1840 (2008: 16, 18). My work further expands on Cheryl Boots's 2013 study of hymn-singing in the antislavery and Indian rights movements, which focuses on mainstream, unaltered hymns performed in activist contexts or written by Black and Indigenous authors. I also revisit antislavery songsters by Joshua McCarter Simpson and William Wells Brown, which have also been examined by scholars. Aaron McClendon, for example, persuasively argues that *Anti-Slavery Harp* owed more to religious music than to minstrelsy but fails to recognize that many of its texts directly parodize hymns (2014: 88–91). Vicki Eaklor mentions that Simpson directs some of his lyrics to be sung to hymn tunes, and her lengthier work on antislavery music briefly alludes to parodies of hymn texts (1980: 101; 1988: xxxi). Most recently, Julia Chybowski (2020) explores the interplay between Simpson's poetry and his musical sources. Overall, scholars of antislavery music have been aware of its interplay with mainstream hymnody, while still leaving the structural and semantic relationships between the two repertoires largely unexplored.

I investigate this lacuna by comparing twelve antislavery songsters published between 1834 and 1852 with repertoire found in contemporaneous hymn collections. Here, I argue that antislavery writers sought to provoke sympathy by editing with and against the grain of popular hymns. After positioning antislavery songsters within contemporaneous methods of hymn dissemination and the wider practice of parody, I provide an overview of the selected books. I then draw on specific examples to demonstrate how parodists leveraged their audience's familiarity with standard hymns, transforming recognizable repertoire into support for the antislavery cause. The chapter concludes by considering why antislavery music relied so heavily on parody to reach its intended audiences.

Hymns, Songsters, and Parodies

Discussing antislavery music requires knowledge of hymnodic convention. Since Anglophone hymnodists historically employed a limited number of poetic scansions (or meters), any hymn—i.e., a metrical text—could usually be sung to any one of a large body of tunes sharing the corresponding meter. Some tunes originated as church music; others had secular roots. Hymns most often circulated in hymnals without musical notation. Tunes were disseminated in a more specialized type of publication known as the "tunebook" and marketed primarily to choirs and music students. Antislavery songbooks represent a third publication type: the songster. These collections of anthologized lyrics—briefer and physically smaller than a typical hymnal—were meant for a particular occasion or purpose and sometimes included notated music. Depending on the intended use, songsters could be sacred or secular. Antislavery songsters included parodies of hymns that had circulated in earlier hymnal or songster repertoires, but their form and content aligned most closely with those of sacred songsters.

I refer to parody here as an artistic practice involving calculated imitations of preexisting music or text, especially in the middlebrow sphere. Employing the word so broadly is a deliberate anachronism; of the surveyed texts, only two are explicitly labeled as parodies (Clark 1848: 52; *Anti-Slavery Songs* 1849: 22). This usage conforms to contemporaneous understandings of parody as transformative but not necessarily provocative: that is, "to alter, as verses or words, and apply to a purpose different from that of the original" (Webster 1842: s.v. "parody"). Although antislavery editors employed parody with particular enthusiasm, such alterations were widespread and rarely remarked upon in eighteenth- and nineteenth-century hymn collections (Stackhouse 1997; Brewer 2015). Since worship was regarded by Protestants as a means of grace—a tool by which God edifies man—a hymn needed to evoke a particular spiritual response in the singer, leading editors to adapt them freely to their communities' circumstances.

In some cases, such as the "correction" of doctrinally questionable hymns, the parody superseded the original version. Other parodies—including the majority of antislavery types—more closely resembled the function of parody and contrafactum in sixteenth- or seventeenth-century polyphony. The parody did not replace its model but drew on it to create a distinctly new text, typically without any implication of mockery. As Chybowski notes of Simpson, editors pursued "the practice of writing new, timely, and often politically oriented lyrics for an existing popular melody ... to enhance the moral and political influences" of songs (2020). Consider this Thomas Moore lyric, first published in 1824 and anthologized in numerous hymnals:

> This world is all a fleeting show
> For man's illusion given;
> The smiles of Joy, the tears of Woe
> Deceitful shine, deceitful flow—
> There's nothing true but Heaven! (Moore [1816–1824] 1838: [361])[1]

This text soon inspired a parody titled "The Contrast":

> This world's not "all a fleeting show
> For man's illusion given";

> He that hath soothed a widow's woe,
> Or wiped an orphan's tear, doth know
> There's *something* here of heaven. (Winchell 1829: 119)

Moore's unaltered version continued to be reprinted, often in the same books and on the same page as its parody. Though they might appear contradictory, both were considered valid expressions of Christian worldviews.

Parodies could also begin from music. A minority of hymns *were* closely associated with a single tune. Both the hymn and its parody might comprise a complete song that had already circulated prior to entering the hymn repertoire. Alternatively, a hymn might be written to suit a specific tune. Smith identifies a small number of such works, calling their originals "model texts" (2008: 23). By writing new texts to familiar melodies, parodists could invoke well-known hymns without being constrained by their literary characteristics. For instance, antislavery songsters frequently reuse the tune associated with this anonymous Adventist hymn:

> You will see your Lord a-coming
> To the old church-yards,
> With a band of music
> Sounding through the air. (*Second Advent Hymns* 1842: 1)

The popularity of the OLD CHURCHYARDS tune may be due to the Hutchinson Family Singers, vocal abolitionists who had adapted the music to a secular, autobiographical song (see Gac 2007: 160–4). They include only one allusion to the original lyrics:

> We have come from the mountains
> Of the "Old Granite State" …
> *With a band of music*
> We are passing 'round the world. ([Hutchinson] 1843: 1–7, emphasis mine)

Antislavery editors were probably familiar with both. Indeed, some songs refer primarily to the Adventist hymn, while others evoke the Hutchinsons's secular version. Such variety among parodies was typical in the economy of hymn dissemination. In the preface quoted above, Hatfield explains how, by making "the most free use of his materials," he acted "in common with every other modern compiler of … devotional poetry" (1840: [iii]). Antislavery activists thus consistently adopted Christian practices; hymn parodies were as much a part of that model as were hymns themselves.

Conventional Parodies

The twelve songsters selected for this study—listed in Table 4.1—demonstrate the variety found in antislavery song.[2] They represent Massachusetts, New York, and Ohio publishers: two northeastern centers of activism and a corridor through which many enslaved people fled. Places of publication range from a utopian settlement in Hopedale, Massachusetts, to the free Black community of Zanesville, Ohio. The largest book contains 291 selections and the smallest merely 13. Most indicate appropriate music for each text by stating the conventional tune name, although four offer notated music. Compilers include prominent abolitionists and relative unknowns. I include two songsters compiled by professional musician George W. Clark, preserving part of the repertoire that he sang and taught at antislavery conventions around the country. While white buyers were the primary audience, two of the songster editors—Brown and Simpson—were Black. Simpson was also the sole contributing author to *Original Anti-Slavery Songs* (Table 4.1, 1852), while the other songsters borrow from—and parody—one another.

These songsters incorporate hymns in varying degrees. Table 4.1 summarizes their parodied content, including direct parodies of hymn texts and tunes associated prominently or exclusively with hymn-singing. Editors of later

Table 4.1 Parodies in selected songsters in reverse chronological order, 1834–1852

Collection	Total songs	Parodies	Percent parody
Garrison (1834)	32	31	97%
Chapman (1836)	154	8	5%
Hatfield (1840)	293	36	12%
Liberty and Anti-Slavery Song Book (1842)	18	16	89%
Lincoln (1843)	56	18	32%
Clark (1844)	137	57	42%
Stacy (1844)	32	28	88%
Gilmore (1846)	51	13	25%
Brown (1848)	48	18	38%
Clark (1848)	129	52	40%
Anti-Slavery Songs (1849)	59	19	32%
Simpson (1852)	13	4	31%

songsters often follow models offered by Maria Weston Chapman and William Lloyd Garrison in the 1830s; like Chapman, editors who anthologize fewer parodies usually include more unaltered hymns. In combination, the songsters embrace 304 selections and 177 individual texts based on identifiable hymnodic models. Only eight texts appear in five or more of the songsters—a smaller proportion of shared repertoire than one would encounter across typical hymnals from the same era. The selection and distribution of tunes are less varied. Hymn tunes appear in the songsters 183 times. AMERICA—used today for "My Country, 'Tis of Thee"—was the favorite, appearing eighteen times across the different songsters. There are also ninety-two instances of secular-origin tunes that were closely associated with a particular sacred text. For ambiguous melodies like these, the parody's text often indicates whether the author had a secular or sacred model in mind.

These numbers demonstrate the extensive interconnections between antislavery song and mainstream hymnody, but they cannot explain the methods or motives behind that relationship. Some parodies remain within the conventional boundaries of the hymn repertoire, essentially being hymns *about* antislavery. Karen Anton speculates that "familiarity with tunes would help people learn songs more quickly, particularly in cases in which the structure of the original text remained through the use of parody" (2010: 34). Along with these didactic advantages, allusions to conventional hymnody added respectability to the antislavery cause. Indeed, some antislavery editors even ascribed altered hymns to their original authors, surreptitiously projecting their own sentiments onto respected Christian writers and gaining the authority of an established tradition (Smith 2008: 9). George W. Stacy invoked this effect when he closed *Anti-Slavery Hymns* with a text by Scottish poet James Montgomery that endorses immediate abolition:

> The end will come; it will not wait;
> Bonds, yokes and scourges have their date;
> Slavery itself must pass away
> And be a tale of yesterday. (1844: 23, Table 4.1)

The placement of this tune at the end of the songster is significant because the last page of a hymnal was traditionally reserved for doxologies. Stacy assigned this incendiary text the most doxological melody possible—the sixteenth-century psalm tune OLD HUNDRED. While the tune and its position in the songster evoke praise to the eternal Trinity, the text asserts that slavery cannot be eternal. Paired with OLD HUNDRED, the text may have seemed more palatable to the unconvinced listener.

Whereas venerable OLD HUNDRED was multivalent, Thomas Hastings's ZION was popular in antislavery contexts because it was originally written for and closely identified with Thomas Kelly's "On the mountain's top appearing" (see Hastings and Mason 1834: 18). Kelly's hymn equates Christians amid the world to exiled Israelites, promising, "Mourning captive, God himself shall loose thy bands" (Kelly 1802: 74). Seizing on this image of release from bondage, antislavery authors created new lyrics with ZION in mind. One promises human rescue, enjoining the pious not to rest while "a bondman, in his chains, remains to weep" (*Liberty and Anti-Slavery Songster* 1842: 4–5, Table 4.1). Another asks, "Mourning brother! Who can loose that cruel band?" and answers in a later strophe, "*Love* will break th' oppressor's yoke" (Stacy 1844: 4, Table 4.1). Both parodies emulate Kelly's most famous couplet, drawing parallels between biblical exile and modern slavery, and between a beloved hymn and still-inflammatory sentiments.

Antislavery advocates often imitated typical worship practices, including their use of music. Some antislavery songs were even meant for church-sanctioned occasions, like "monthly concerts" of prayer to support social causes.[3] Antislavery meetings themselves used prayer, testimony, and other trappings of worship to make "non-church space religiously meaningful" (Smith 2008: 7). Singing fulfilled specific functions, especially at openings and closings. For that reason, many songsters included dismissions like this anonymous text's adjourning blessing:

Here we've had a cordial greeting,
And we've had a thrilling meeting,
And our labour here completing
We'll seek the next town;
From town to town we'll battle
Until slavery's beat down. (Clark 1848: 214, Table 4.1)

This parody, set to OLD CHURCHYARDS, suggests the image of an itinerant evangelist spreading the antislavery message. Another, even bolder one, written anonymously to the hymn tune SOMMERVILLE, defends Sabbath antislavery meetings with the assertion, "What's holy time? There is no time too pure … to raise the bondman from the dust" (Clark 1848: 203, Table 4.1). It concludes by stating, "For this the Sabbath's hours were given … that we therein might worship Heaven," positioning antislavery work as a moral obligation of equal weight as public worship.

Authors also capitalized on the biblical references in classic hymns. Lewis Edson's tune LENOX often appeared with the chorus "The year of jubilee is come; return, ye ransomed sinners, home,"[4] evoking the injunction in Leviticus 25:40 to free bondsmen during the jubilee celebrated every fifty years by the ancient Israelites. Protestant theologians described the Israelite jubilee as a foreshadowing of the thousand-year golden age alluded to in the New Testament book of Revelations. Many antebellum Christians—especially those associated with social reform movements, including antislavery—believed that the world would enjoy this period of perfected faith and morality prior to Christ's return to earth (see Miller 1998: 115). Antislavery activists therefore saw the jubilee as a divine decree requiring earthly labor to fulfill. Indeed, Brown's version replaces the chorus often associated with LENOX with "Come on, come on, and joined we be to make the fettered bondman free," urging listeners to hasten the jubilee year (1848: 35, Table 4.1). A Montgomery text that Hatfield paired with the same tune envisions it as already having arrived, proclaiming "Joy to the slave!—the slave is free! It is the year of Jubilee" (1840: 245, Table 4.1). These songs frame antislavery meetings as expressions of piety suffused with scriptural and Christian tradition.

Songs like these tied the antislavery message to Christian worship practices, sacred texts, and theology. Antislavery hymn parodies also associated the sacred with Black existence in a way that mainstream hymnody rarely, if ever, did. By rewriting conventional hymns to reflect Black voices—usually imagined, but occasionally authentic—these authors linked Black dignity to Christian dignity, Black experience to human experience. Jon Cruz observes a similar phenomenon: when antislavery advocates valorized spirituals, they "created a critical humanistic interest" in a musical tradition previously considered to be an "alien noise" (1999: [3]; see also 6–7). In the realm of hymnody, poet Samuel Francis Smith and composer Lowell Mason had originally written "Sister, thou wast mild and lovely" and its tune, MOUNT VERNON, to commemorate the death of a white Boston schoolgirl in 1833:

> Sister, thou wast mild and lovely,
> Gentle as the summer breeze,
> Pleasant as the air of evening
> When it floats among the trees. (Mason 1841: 209)

Clark applies the title "We Are All Children of One Parent" to a parody in *The Youth's Cabinet*, which instead depicts a living girl whose enslavement denies her that peaceful childhood:

> Sister, thou art worn and weary,
> Toiling for another's gain;
> Life with thee is dark and dreary,
> Filled with wretchedness and pain. (1844: 177, Table 4.1)

The narrator later demands that hearers do "all that lies within our power" until "our sister's griefs are o'er." By transforming a lament into a call for action, Clark contends that the exploited Black child is as much a part of the Christian family as the sainted white one. At a time when the only nationally visible repertoire depicting Black life was the minstrel song, texts like these offered an alternative musical image of Black Americans as fellow children of God.

In practice, though, Black and white congregations generally sang the same or similar hymns (Boots 2013: 82–91). As Mark Noll writes, hymn-singing was an "activity that all evangelicals shared, and … the one experience that bound them most closely together" (2004: 14). Yet that common repertoire rarely addressed the experiences of the enslaved or of Black people in general. Parodists mapped such experiences onto popular hymns, as Hatfield did with this Methodist text:

> Come on, my Partners in Distress,
> My comrades thro' the wilderness,
> Who still your Bodies feel …
> Who suffer for our Master here;
> We shall before his Face appear,
> And by his Side sit down. (Wesley 1749: 1:29–30)

Hatfield's version reimagines earthly suffering from a slave's perspective:

> Come on, my partners in distress,
> My comrades in the wilderness,
> Who groan beneath your chains …
> Though, like our Lord, we suffer here,
> We shall before his face appear
> And at his side sit down. (1840: 44, Table 4.1)

Instead of suffering *for* Christ, the speaker suffers *like* Christ. Using a hymn that already traversed racial barriers, Hatfield encourages (implicitly white) listeners to contemplate the physical and spiritual agonies that their enslaved siblings in Christ faced.

Unconventional Parodies

Simpson's text, "O come! Come away, my sable sons and daughters," emulates the structure and themes of its model with similar rigor (1852: 17, Table 4.1). Set to the German student tune KRAMBAMBULI, this text alludes to a large family of anonymous hymns that enjoin the listener to "come away" from a troublesome life to the comforts of social worship (cf. Rhinehart 1848: 86). Yet this parody is significantly less reverent than the preceding examples. Simpson structures the song as a conversation between a group of Southern slaves and the British empress (whom they address repeatedly as "Mother Victoria"). She advises the slaves to wait till "dogs and masters are asleep, then slily from your cabbins creep" and assures them that "[y]ou'll meet with many a northern friend who will his best endeavors lend." An invitation to worship becomes an invitation to Canada, the welcome issuing from Queen Victoria's mouth—a far cry from a conventional hymn.

In the preface to a collected volume of his lyrics, Simpson later described how "a spirit of poetry ... seemed to waft before my mind horrid pictures of the condition of my people, and something seemed to say, 'Write and sing about it—you can sing what would be death to speak' " (1874: [1]). Like Simpson's "O come! Come away," this statement exemplifies a second register of parody—songs that ironically contradict or radically intensify their model texts. Though born in free Ohio, Simpson spent his youth compulsorily indentured after the deaths of his free Black parents and white foster father (Osborne 2004: 380-1). Local memory, as well as allusions in his own writings, suggest that he was involved in the Underground Railroad (Siebert 1951: 214; see also Eaklor 1980: 98-101). Understandably, Simpson's lyrics promote the antislavery cause with vividness and urgency. Chybowski notes the prevalence of irony in his parodies: "Often the source material is problematic, or actually counter to the abolitionist cause. [Simpson's] intentional use of melody from these well-known songs sharpened his anti-slavery messages" (2020). Yet radical language was not confined to the front lines of the antislavery battle. Mere months after the publication of *Original Anti-Slavery Songs*, for example, one of Simpson's unconventional lyrics appeared in the Boston-based abolitionist newspaper *The Liberator* ("Poetry" 1852). White antislavery activists—especially advocates of immediate abolition—frequently deployed and disseminated this rhetoric.

Some of Simpson's most vitriolic examples highlight the hypocrisy of proslavery Christians. In a later edition of his antislavery poetry, Simpson deployed two hymns in a particularly damning indictment, jointly titled "Consistent Family Worship of Slave-Holders." This pair of songs satirizes the widespread devotional discipline of twice-daily household prayer, turning Benjamin Rhodes's "Come, let us join our God to praise" into a mockery of morning worship (cf. Benson 1822: 25). Morning hymns generally include an expression of gratitude for having lived through the night, but in Simpson's version, the family thanks God that their slaves remain under their control and have not rebelled or fled: "Our dogs have guarded well the door, and Lord—what could we ask thee more?" (1874: 100). These derisive interpretations depict Christians mapping the practice of slavery onto religious worship, rather than recognizing their own offenses toward God. Simpson specifies no tune for these songs, writing only "Any Long Meter" or "Any Short Meter"—an unusually direct allusion to the performance practice of metrical hymnody.

Similarly, *Anti-Slavery Songs* satirizes "Come saints and sinners, hear me tell," an anonymous testimonial hymn from the late eighteenth century. Each strophe of the original text ends with the words "heavenly union" (cf. Smith 1797: 52). The parody, ascribed to a "northern Methodist preacher," depicts supposedly pious slaveholders doing evil six days of the week:

> Come, saints and sinners, hear me tell
> How pious priests whip Jack and Nell,
> And women buy and children sell,
> And preach all sinners down to hell,
> And sing of heavenly union. (22, Table 4.1)

As a religious catchphrase, "union" referred to the fellowship of all believers and their mutual enjoyment of God's goodness. This parody earns its sting by indicting the duplicitous professor of religion who has the nerve to "sing a sacred song … with words of heavenly union" while denying the personhood and Christian bond of his slaves.

Other hymn parodies decry the disruptions that slavery wrought upon domestic life, particularly the "selling apart" of families. Such texts depict the practice as not only inhumane but unnatural, contravening the divinely appointed bond among family members. Stacy includes a striking, atypical text attributed to "A. B.," pairing it with a tune called WANTAGE. The lyrics frankly address the disenfranchisement of enslaved families by rape:

> I want my ravished *self*,
> My plundered manhood back;
> Deprived of this, I am but pelf
> And all but *ill* I lack.
>
> I want the wife I love,
> To call her all my own,
> My children too, each cherished dove,
> For mine and mine *alone*.
>
> I want to be secure
> Amid my humble trust,
> Against the wrongs I now endure
> From *tyranny* and *lust*. (1844: 20, Table 4.1)

The identity of the music is uncertain. A. B.'s text is in short meter, whereas WANTAGE, a popular hymn tune of eighteenth-century British origin, is in common meter (Temperley 1998: *s.v.* 901a–b). Perhaps the singer was meant to repeat the fourth and fifth syllables of the first line ("I want my ravished, ravished self," etc.), thereby adapting the text to common meter and fitting it to the old-fashioned, solemn psalm tune. The song's final lines further appropriate a contemporary, secular source: Sarah Grimké's antislavery narrative, which she wrote in "sympathy for the bleeding victims of tyranny and lust" (1839: 22).

Songsters also contain narratives about righteous slaves that operate outside the stylistic and topical margins of the hymns on which they are based. As Cruz explains, the Christianization of Black Americans became an antislavery cornerstone; even pro-slavery missionaries tacitly acknowledged that slaves were potentially precious members of Christian society (1999: 4). Soon abolitionists were touting Black faith as a vital, unspoiled expression of religion. Brown offers a striking example in "The Song of the Coffle Gang," which "is said to be sung by the Slaves, as they are chained in gangs, when parting from friends for the far-off South—children taken from parents, husbands from wives, and brothers from sisters" (1848: 29, Table 4.1 and line two in Example 4.1). Brown's gloss echoes the wording of the revival chorus O THERE WILL BE MOURNING (cf. Leavitt 1830: 90–1). The verses of that hymn list successive familial and social ties that will "part to meet no more" after death, when some will fly to heaven and others are condemned to hell. This allusion implies that slave-trading is an act of human evil that sacrilegiously disrupts natural familial ties as only the judgment of God should. "The Song of the Coffle Gang" describes "wives and husbands sold apart" but offers hope in its refrain: "There's a better day a coming."

This anonymous text has attracted scholarly attention because Brown also included it in his memoir, where he described surviving slavery in Kentucky and Missouri (1847: 51–2). Scholars debate whether "The Song of the Coffle Gang" is an "authentic" slave lyric or Brown's invention. "Songs Related to the Abolition of Slavery" discredits the authenticity of Brown's version, stating that the attribution

Example 4.1 "Better Days Coming." Music as notated in Mansfield (1848: 232), showing texts from Mansfield and Brown (1840: 29).

to slaves "was probably an artistic device, as the language of the song does not seem to match historical descriptions of songs coffle gangs were made to sing by slave traders. Songs of white abolitionists often were narrated from the slave's point of view as a method of pursuasion [*sic*]" (Library of Congress n.d.). Only one other non-fiction author contemporaneous with Brown associates a variant of this text with enslaved singers, reporting that "Rev. H. Highland Garnett, pastor of the colored Presbyterian church in New York City ... says he heard his father and grandfather sing" a version while enslaved in Maryland around 1815 (Read 1864: 365–6). Critical editors Jerome McGann and Ezra Greenspan assert that the song constituted a popular spiritual (Delany [1859–1862] 2017: n35; Brown 2008: 32n25). Though nineteenth-century sources do ascribe other songs of the same basic structure to Black singers (cf. Gough 1879: 114–15; "A Worthy Clergyman" 1866), they are not enough to support such broad assertions. In short, "Song of the Coffle Gang" likely reflects editorial intervention on Brown's part but derives from a folk hymn attested in Black communities.

Despite the interest with which scholars have examined this text, none have observed that the chorus, "There's a better day a coming," is shared with an identifiable revival hymn—or that Brown's text matches scansion with a published melody for that same hymn (Mansfield 1848: 232; cf. also "Sound the Jubilee" 1862). Example 4.1 shows this melody as it appears in *The American Vocalist*, a tunebook compiled in Maine in the late 1840s that provides its only known printing. The example juxtaposes the text found in *American Vocalist* with a verse of "The Song of the Coffle Gang," revealing how comfortably Brown's text fits with the tune, as well as its similarity to the lyrics recorded there. It is likely that Brown either heard "The Song of the Coffle Gang" sung to this melody or that he wrote the text himself as a parody of the hymn. McClendon notes that a version of the "Coffle Gang" text had appeared in Clark's *Liberty Minstrel* several years before Brown printed it (2014: 84; Table 4.1, Clark 1844: 22–3). Notably, *Liberty Minstrel* also anthologizes a second, distinct hymn of nearly identical structure. Clark—a White New Englander who lacked Brown's firsthand exposure to slave song—attributes it to "a Colored Man" (1844: 140–1). Unlike "Coffle Gang," that text is paired with a newly composed tune, and the chorus lacks any known model in the hymnodic repertoire.[5] Whether these songs were invented or transcribed, both Brown and Clark saw value in depicting slaves whose first reaction to human evil is to invoke the inexorable justice of God.

While Brown ascribed "Coffle Gang" to pious slaves, other authors drew comparisons with biblical characters, implying that the strictures under which enslaved Christians practiced their religion guaranteed them pure motives and meaningful faith. For instance, Clark pairs a Henry Wadsworth Longfellow verse, "The Slave Singing at Midnight," with BAVARIA, an adaptation of Johannes Thommen's eighteenth-century chorale tune O DU LIEBE MEINER LIEBE that circulated widely in social worship songsters. The title character recites psalms, the most universal texts of Christian worship:

> Loud he sang the psalm of David!
> He a negro and enslaved,
> Sang of Israel's glorious vic'try,
> Sang of Zion, bright and free. (Clark 1844: 190, Table 4.1)

Later strophes compare the slave's singing to the music of the Israelites after escaping Egypt and that of Paul and Silas before the earthquake cracked open their prison cell in Philippi. One biblical precedent rejoices in freedom, the other in bondage. The song concludes with the humbled narrator wondering how the slave has found the strength to praise God while under such oppression.

Biblical parallels could even encompass the figure of Jesus Christ. Several parodies evoke Matthew 25:35-6: "I was a stranger, and ye took me in … I was in prison, and ye came unto me." One example, titled "The Fugitive," is paired with BONNIE DOON—a tune usually associated, in the sacred context, with a hymn about the guiding star of Bethlehem (cf. Leavitt 1830: 172-3). The speaker here is a white householder to whom a fleeing slave has appealed for shelter:

> He owned his was a sable skin,
> That which his Maker first had given:
> But mine would be a darker sin,
> That would exclude my soul from heaven. (*Anti-Slavery Songs* 1849: 53, Table 4.1)

The speaker eventually welcomes his brother with an obeisance and concludes by hoping that "God forgave my sin" for having considered withholding aid.

Montgomery's hymn, "A poor wayfaring man of grief," already alluded to these same verses of scripture (Coles and Montgomery 1841). The narrative describes a stranger who suffers various trials, the speaker recognizing that each indignity is one endured by Jesus in the Gospels; at last, the stranger is revealed to be Christ himself. Additional strophes in an antislavery variant absorb the experiences of Black Christians—including slaves—into the narrative. In one of the added verses, the stranger, having been abused by a slave-driver, is described as "baptizing" the narrator. Later, the stranger is relegated to the gallery of a church, not permitted to sit in the desirable pews reserved for white worshippers. There the narrator, like a disciple waiting to be taught, reverently seeks the stranger's feet:

> I saw him bleeding in his chains,
> And tortured 'neath the driver's lash,
> His sweat fell fast along the plains,
> Deep dyed from many a fearful gash;
> But I in bonds remembered him,
> And strove to free each fettered limb,
> As with my tears I washed his blood,
> Me he baptized with mercy's flood …
>
> I saw him in the negro pew,
> His head hung low upon his breast,
> His locks were wet with drops of dew,
> Gathered while he for entrance pressed,
> Within those aisles, whose courts were given,
> That black and white may reach one heaven;
> And as I meekly sought his feet,
> He smiled, and made a throne my seat. (Gilmore 1846: 17–18, Table 4.1)

This parody, which equates the abuse of Black bodies to the torments suffered by Christ, is among the most striking examples in the repertoire. Slaves were regularly likened to Christ's "suffering servant" persona (cf. Isaiah 53) in mid-nineteenth-century writings. Richard Bell has argued that this imagery appealed to white readers because it presented slaves as nonthreatening victims in need of rescue (2012: 530–8). This text does not, however, occupy the same rhetorical space as an autobiographical narrative or a reformist tract. Most verses are identical to Montgomery's original; many readers who encountered the antislavery parody would have previously addressed the same words to God during worship. Rather than being a helpless object of pity, the apotheosized slave is imbued with spiritual authority. He is a more apt teacher than the pastor of his segregated congregation. He initiates the implicitly white narrator into the Christian—or perhaps antislavery—community through the sacrament of baptism. The text offers a radically literal reading of the Biblical passage that first inspired Montgomery's hymn: "Inasmuch as ye have done it unto one of the least of these my brethren, ye have done it unto me" (Matthew 25:40).

Conclusions

This chapter has demonstrated the metatextual connections between hymns and a selection of antislavery songsters, considering how activists deployed such correspondences in support of their cause. Because hymns were intimately familiar to antebellum Protestants, the prevalence of hymn parodies doubtless shaped the experience of antislavery song for informed listeners. They not only sang hymns in church on Sunday but performed them socially throughout the week and "prayed" them as a form of private devotion. Their children memorized hymns before they even began to learn scripture. The hymn repertoire therefore offered a readymade set of textual tropes that already spanned political, geographic, theological, and racial barriers.

Activists were less concerned with the mechanics of parody than the emotional effect it had on readers and listeners. For Chapman, right feeling was a precursor to right thinking: "In giving man imagination and affections, God has furnished him with the powers that enable him to follow the dictates of reason" (1836: vii, Table 4.1). Jairus Lincoln also refers to the potency of these practices in his songster, writing, "[T]here are many who have not the gift of *speech-making*, but who can, by *song-singing*, make strong appeals in behalf of the slave, to every community and every heart" (1843: [3], Table 4.1). Clark believed that singing noble sentiments would impress them on one's soul, until eventually "all the people who have hearts to feel and tongues to give utterance to their feelings may sing the language of liberty, until it shall become incorporated with their very being" (1848: [iii], Table 4.1).

These hopes regarding the persuasive power of antislavery music were supported by the accounts of fellow activists. A description of Clark singing songs with the audience at an antislavery convention in Cincinnati dwells on the emotional impact of familiar music harnessed for a new cause: "Silence reigns over the crowd—the glistening eyes—the drooping hands—the smiles mingled with tears are the tokens and results of his magic power. Hark! he calls on them to join in the [familiar] chorus, and the mighty voice rings in deafening melody" (T. B. H. 1845: 107). Having almost been carried away by that "overwhelming burst of feeling," the author speculates, "Could all the people be often brought under the power of such music as we have just heard, ten years would not pass till the nation would be free." When that project was accomplished nearly twenty-five years later, abolitionist Samuel May recalled how Chapman's songster had been "a powerful weapon in our moral warfare. My memory glows with the recollections of the fervor, and often obvious effect with which we used to sing in true accord the 14th hymn, by Miss E. M. Chandler—or the 15th, by Mr. Garrison—or the 7th, by Mrs. Follen" (1869: 260).

In their persistent appeal to feeling, these editors allied themselves with the "raw, radical expressions of sympathy for slaves" that Mary Cathryn Cain has found characteristic of pre-1850s antislavery (2006: 7). Early activists tended to commiserate explicitly with specific slaves or ex-slaves and to avow human brotherhood across color lines, educating others about the horrors of slavery with the goal of provoking individual empathy. In the emotionalized, sympathy-based framework of 1830s–1840s activism, pseudo-sacred song could assert the personhood, moral agency, and Christian fellowship of the enslaved. Hymnody was a natural resort for these enthusiasts of sentiment. Like scripture, hymnody offered a body of texts that Anglophone Protestants memorized, recited, and contemplated—texts closely intertwined with their experience of Christian society and their ethical sensibilities. Yet, unlike scripture, activists could tailor hymns to support their arguments without provoking accusations of blasphemy or deviating from normative editorial practice. Antislavery lyrics finally began to appear in conventional hymnals around 1852 (see, e.g., Banvard 1852: 566–71), an indication that the antislavery movement had penetrated mainstream public discourse. Cain argues that, as the movement became increasingly sectional and diffuse at the turn of the 1850s, activists began to reframe their condemnations of slavery through the lens of white identity. Notably, the publication of antislavery songsters tapered sharply at the same time.

Recovering the relationships between antislavery song and the mainstream hymn repertoire reveals them to have been more complex and extensive than previously believed. Antislavery authors created numerous new songs which, though rooted in that familiar canon, do not simply form a topically distinct annex within conventional hymnody. They evoked the hymn repertoire through their choice of tunes and in textual allusions; some tunes of secular origin had equally rich, sacred metatextual significance, particularly in the case of social worship music. Though some parodies are essentially conventional hymns on the topic of slavery, others contradict or intensify the language of their models to degrees that verge on sacrilege. Moreover, hymnody's very ubiquity has obscured the centrality of its influence on antislavery music. The prefaces of these songsters make no reference to the biblical allusions, wandering choruses, and ironic juxtapositions highlighted above—even though their prevalence implies that antislavery authors considered such tools efficacious and employed them deliberately. Hatfield is the only editor who mentions altered hymns at all. An allusion to a popular hymn would scarcely have been misunderstood by the literate, socially engaged, religiously active people who patronized the antislavery press. The modern scholar, however, must labor to reconstruct a metatextual fabric that was once too obvious to merit acknowledgment. To understand one repertoire, we must know the other.

Notes

1   All quotations maintain original spelling and use either page or selection numbers, according to the source's convention.
2   Although Smith (2008) considers "Father of Mercies! Send thy grace" (Hatfield 1840: 133) an emended hymn, I omit it because the alteration suggests no antislavery sentiment and is probably an unintentional corruption.
3   Garrison (1834) mentions this practice on [3]. Several of Chapman's titles also refer to monthly concerts (1836: 203, 208, 210, 212, 215), as do *Liberty and Anti-Slavery Songster*'s (1842: 14). These events also supported Christian education, temperance, and foreign missions.
4   Edson's tune was initially published in Jocelin and Doolittle (1782: 59) with the Isaac Watts text "Ye tribes of Adam join." Nonetheless, LENOX became associated with "Blow ye the trumpet, blow" and its jubilee-themed chorus beginning with Law (1791: 50); see Temperley (1998: *s.v.* 4280).
5   I have been unable to identify any texts related to this hymn apart from a secular 1844 verse recorded in Jesse H. Jones's fictionalized autobiography (Davidson 1907: 19).

References

Antislavery Songsters

Antislavery Songsters (1849), *Anti-Slavery Songs*, Salem, OH: Aaron Hinchman for I. Trescott & Co.
Brown, W. W., ed. (1848), *The Anti-Slavery Harp*, Boston: Abner Forbes.
C[hapman], M. W., ed. (1836), *Songs of the Free and Hymns of Christian Freedom*, Boston: Isaac Knapp.
Clark, G. W., ed. (1844), *The Liberty Minstrel*, New York: Piercy & Reed.
Clark, G. W., ed. (1848), *The Free Soil Minstrel*, New York: Martyn & Ely.
Garrison, W. L., ed. (1834), *A Selection of Anti-Slavery Hymns*, Boston: Garrison & Knapp.

Gilmore, H. S., ed. (1846), *A Collection of Miscellaneous Songs for the Use of the Cincinnati High School*, Cincinnati: A. S. Sparhawk.
Hatfield, E. F., ed. (1840), *Freedom's Lyre*, New York: S. W. Benedict.
Liberty and Anti-Slavery Song Book (1842), Boston: Kidder & Wright.
Lincoln, J., ed. (1843), *Anti-Slavery Melodies for the Friends of Freedom*, Hingham, MA: A. J. Wright.
Simpson, J. M. (1852), *Original Anti-Slavery Songs*, Zanesville, OH.
Stacy, G. W., ed. (1844), *Anti-Slavery Hymns*, Hopedale, MA: Community Press.

Other Sources

Anton, K. (2010), "'My Country! 'Tis of Thee, Strong Hold of Slavery': The Musical Rhetoric of the American Antislavery Movement," *Young Scholars in Writing*, 7: 30–40.
Banvard, J. (1852), *The Christian Melodist: A New Collection of Hymns for Social Religious Worship*, Boston: Gould and Lincoln.
Bell, R. (2012), "Slave Suicide, Abolition and the Problem of Resistance," *Slavery & Abolition: A Journal of Slave and Post-Slave Studies*, 33 (4): 525–49.
Benson, J., ed. (1822), *Hymns for Children and Young Persons*, New York: N. Bangs & T. Mason.
Boots, C. C. (2013), *Singing for Equality: Hymns in the American Antislavery and Indian Rights Movements, 1640–1855*, Jefferson, NC: McFarland Books.
Brewer, C. E. (2015), "Mather Byles and the History of the Boston Appendix," in *Annual Meeting of the Society for Christian Scholarship in Music*, Emory University, GA.
Brown, W. W. (1847), *Narrative of William W. Brown, a Fugitive Slave*, Boston: Anti-Slavery Office.
Brown, W. W. (2008), *William Wells Brown: A Reader*, ed. E. Greenspan, Athens, GA: University of Georgia Press.
Cain, M. C. (2006), "Rhetorics of Race and Freedom: The Expression of Women's Whiteness in Anti-Slavery Activism," *Studies in Popular Culture*, 29 (2): 1–19.
Chybowski, J. (2020), *Intertextuality in Joshua Simpson's "Original Anti-Slavery Songs" and the Expanding Abolition Movement in 1850s America*, American Musicological Society Annual Meeting, November 15, virtual.
Coles, G. and J. Montgomery (1841), *The Stranger and His Friend*, New York: Firth & Hall.
Cruz, J. (1999), *Culture on the Margins: The Black Spiritual and the Rise of American Cultural Interpretation*, Princeton: Princeton University Press.
Davidson, J. [Jesse H. Jones] (1907), *Joshua Davidson, Christian*, ed. H. H. Loud, New York: Grafton Press.
Delany, M. R. ([1859–1862] 2017), *Blake, or, The Huts of America: A Corrected Edition*, ed. J. McGann, Cambridge: Harvard University Press.

Eaklor, V. L. (1980), "The Songs of 'The Emancipation Car': Variations on an Abolitionist Theme," *Missouri Historical Society Bulletin*, 36: 92–102.

Eaklor, V. L. (1988), *American Antislavery Songs: A Collection and Analysis*, New York: Greenwood Press.

Gac, S. (2007), *Singing for Freedom: The Hutchinson Family Singers and the Nineteenth-Century Culture of Reform*, New Haven: Yale University Press.

Gough, J. B. (1879), *Autobiography of John B. Gough*, London: Morgan and Scott.

Grimké, S. M. (1839), "Narrative and Testimony of Sarah M. Grimké," in T. Weld (ed.), *American Slavery As It Is*, 22–4, New York: American Anti-Slavery Society.

Hastings, T. and L. Mason (1834), *Spiritual Songs for Social Worship*, Boston: Carter, Hendee, & Co.

[Hutchinson, J.] (1843), *The Old Granite State*, Boston: Ditson.

Jocelin, S. and A. Doolittle (1782), *The Chorister's Companion, or, Church Music Revised*, New Haven: T. & S. Green.

Kelly, T. (1802), *A Collection of Psalms and Hymns, Extracted from Various Authors*, Dublin: Thomas Kelly.

Law, A. (1791), *The Rudiments of Music, or, A Short and Easy Treatise on the Rules of Psalmody*, Cheshire, CT: William Law.

Leavitt, J. (1830), *The Christian Lyre*, New York: Jonathan Leavitt.

Library of Congress (n.d.), "Songs Related to the Abolition of Slavery," *Library of Congress*. https://www.loc.gov/item/ihas.200197383/ (accessed June 26, 2020).

Mansfield, D. H. (1848), *The American Vocalist*, Boston: C. H. Peirce.

Mason, L. (1841), *Carmina Sacra, or, Boston Collection of Church Music*, Boston: J. H. Wilkins & R. B. Carter.

Mason, L. and D. Greene (1831), *Church Psalmody*, Boston: T. R. Marvin.

May, S. J. (1869), *Some Recollections of Our Antislavery Conflict*, Boston: Fields, Osgood, & Co.

McClendon, A. D. (2014), "Sounds of Sympathy: William Wells Brown's 'Anti-Slavery Harp,' Abolition, and the Culture of Early and Antebellum American Song," *African American Review*, 47 (1): 83–100.

Miller, R. M. (1998), *Religion and the American Civil War*, Oxford: Oxford University Press.

Moore, T. ([1816–1824] 1838), "Sacred Songs," in J. W. Lake (ed.), *The Poetical Works of Thomas Moore*, 361–9, Philadelphia: J. Crissy.

Noll, M. A. (2004), "The Defining Role of Hymns in Early Evangelicalism," in R. J. Mouw and M. A. Noll (eds.), *Wonderful Words of Life: Hymns in American Protestant History and Theology*, 3–16, Grand Rapids: William B. Eerdmans.

Osborne, W. (2004), *Music in Ohio*, Kent: Kent State University Press.

"Poetry" (1852), *The Liberator*, December 10, 200.

Read, H. (1864), *The Negro Problem Solved, or, Africa as She Was, as She Is, and as She Shall Be*, New York: A. A. Constantine.

Rhinehart, W. R. (1848), *The American Church Harp: Containing a Choice Selection of Hymns and Tunes Comprising a Variety of Metres, Well Adapted to All Christian Churches, Singing Schools, and Private Families*, Germantown, OH: W. R. Rhinehart.

Second Advent Hymns (1842), Lowell, MA: M. M. George.

Siebert, W. H. (1951), *The Mysteries of Ohio's Underground Railroads*, Columbus: Long's College Book Company.

Simpson, J. M. (1874), *The Emancipation Car: Being an Original Composition of Anti-Slavery Ballads, Composed Exclusively for the Under Ground Rail Road*, Zanesville, OH: Sullivan & Brown.

Smith, A. L. (2008), "Borrowed Language and Editorial Adjustments in Hymns of the American Anti-Slavery Movement," MA thesis, Boston University, Boston.

Smith, J. (1797), *Divine Hymns. or Spiritual Songs: For the Use of Religious Assemblies and Private Christians*, Norwich, CT: John Sterry & Co.

"Sound the Jubilee," (1862), *The Revival*, November 13: 232.

Stackhouse, R. A. (1997), *The Language of the Psalms in Worship: American Revisions of Watts' Psalter*, Lanham, MD: Scarecrow Press.

T. B. H. (1845), "South-Western Anti-Slavery Convention at Cincinnati," *The Oberlin Evangelist* (July 2, 1845): 107–8.

Temperley, N. (1998), *The Hymn Tune Index: A Census of English-Language Hymn Tunes in Printed Sources from 1535 to 1820*, Oxford: Clarendon.

Webster, N. (1842), *An American Dictionary of the English Language*, New York: White & Sheffield.

Wesley, C. (1749), *Hymns and Sacred Poems in Two Volumes*, Bristol: Felix Farley.

Winchell, R. (1829), *The Baptist Songster, or, Divine Songs for Conference Meetings*, Wethersfield, CT: Deming & Francis.

"A Worthy Clergyman" (1866), *Harper's New Monthly Magazine* (February): 406.

5

Accidental Alterity in Messiaen's *Quatre études de rythme*

David Wolfson

Île de feu I and *II* are the outer movements of a suite of four short pieces for piano by Olivier Messiaen titled *Quatre études de rythme* (*Four rhythmic etudes*). The second movement, *Mode de valeurs et d'intensités*, has received a great deal of attention for being the first treatment of duration, attack, and intensity (as well as pitch) in a numerically organized fashion, thus influencing and prefiguring the so-called total serialism of Pierre Boulez and Milton Babbitt. But the two *Île de feu* pieces—dedicated "to the people of Papua" and based on themes ostensibly in the style of Papuan melodies—are worthy of attention for their apparent exoticist content amid the less-familiar sounds of Messiaen's own serialist experiments in the middle movements.

In the introduction to *Western Music and Its Others*, Georgina Born notes that there are "two basic, structural relations-of-difference to the musical other at work in musical modernism and postmodernism" (2000: 16). One is incorporation or subsumption, not too different in essence from the type of exoticism practiced in the earlier Western canon; the other is negation and nonreference, as attempted in various high-modernist aesthetics. *Île de feu I* and *II* offer a fascinating chance to observe how these two relations-of-difference interact when juxtaposed. In this chapter I bring some of the tools of the psychology of music to bear on the question of how the perception of alterity might exist for a listener of *Quatre études de rythme*. Specifically, I ask what schemata might be activated for a listener by both the "exoticist" and the proto-serialist passages, and how the two vocabularies might affect each other. Viewed through these lenses, it becomes clear how the seeming exoticism of the "primitivist" melodies—the principal materials of the *Île de feu* pieces—might, in fact, be out-"othered" by being heard in proximity to the serially organized second movement and the similarly constructed interludes in *Île de feu II*. To a typical listener, the serial music is so alien that the (supposedly) Papuan-inspired themes will be heard as more familiar than "marked" by comparison (Dyer 1997: 37).

Overview

Mode de valeurs et d'intensités and the third movement of the suite, *Neumes rythmiques*, were composed in 1949 during Messiaen's summer teaching residency at the Tanglewood Music Center in Massachusetts. Both of the *Île de feu* pieces were written in Paris the following year (Johnson 1975: 104), during the beginning of what Robert Johnson and Peter Hill call Messiaen's "experimental" period (Johnson 1975: 105–16; Hill 1995: 318). *Mode de valeurs et d'intensités* (*Mode of [rhythmic] values and intensities*) uses an invented mode of thirty-six pitches, twenty-four durations, twelve "touches" (articulations), and seven dynamic levels. Each pitch (not pitch class) is assigned a touch, duration, and dynamic level and is only used in that configuration, although the sequence is not predetermined (Messaien 2008: 12). I will not be including a formal analysis of the piece here;[1] it is enough to say that its sound was unlike anything Messiaen (or anyone else at the time) had written before. Hill notes that without melody, harmony, a discernible rhythmic grid, or a gestural sweep to latch on to, the listener encounters "an utterly new sound-world … as arid as the blips of a computerized game" (1995: 318). A typical passage illustrates this point (Example 5.1).

Example 5.1 Olivier Messiaen, *Mode de valeurs et d'intensités*, mm. 48–52.

Mode de valeurs et d'intensités would prove extremely influential among composers of the next generation: Boulez and Karlheinz Stockhausen, among others, cited the work as seminal, and Boulez used one division of Messiaen's mode as the first row for his *Structures Book I* (Griffiths 1985: 152–3; Messaien 2008: back cover note). By comparison, *Neumes rythmiques* takes as its point of departure the neumatic notation and fixed melodic formulas of medieval music. Messiaen's versions of neumatic figures are not only fixed in terms of their melodic shapes, but also in their associated rhythms, dynamics, and harmonic content. *Neumes rythmiques* is therefore based on essentially the same conceit as the *Mode de valeurs et d'intensités*, except it uses short musical formulae rather than single notes (Griffiths 1985: 151). Additionally, it sounds more "Messiaen-esque" because he constructed the neumes using his own characteristic Indian *tala*-derived rhythms and pitches from his "modes of limited transposition."[2] It thus sounds unusual to tonally trained ears, though it fits stylistically with other modern outgrowths of the European art music tradition.

Île de feu I and *II* noticeably contrast with the inner movements in their construction and much of their musical language. Each alternates a violent, modal melody, accompanied differently and in varying pitch registers but unaltered in rhythm or intervallic content, with episodes of contrasting material. Paul Griffiths calls these movements "verse-refrain" forms (1985: 155). In *Île de feu I* the episodes are freely composed and similar in sound to *Neumes rythmiques*; in *Île de feu II*, most of the episodes are "interversions," serially constructed passages bearing a distinct family resemblance to the *Mode de valeurs et d'intensités*. This is not coincidental. As Hill puts it, the *Île de feu* movements were written to give the other two pieces "a performing context," as *Île de feu II* "builds on elements from each of the other three [etudes]" (1995: 320).

Messiaen states explicitly that the *Île de feu* themes are in the same style as Papuan melodies "communicated" to him by Archbishop André Sorin.[3] He presents these fourteen melodies "without comment" in his *Traité de rythme, de couleur, et d'ornithologie*, with no information about their roles or functions; it is unclear whether the melodies were transmitted in notated form or as recordings Messaien had transcribed (1995: vol. 7, 70–1). Messiaen's themes share with their notated sources an abundance of leaps, frequent returns to a home note, irregular note lengths, and a salient angularity. While the first of the two *Île de feu* themes is much briefer than any of these examples, the second is roughly comparable in length to a few of the shorter ones.

Messiaen's Relationship to Exoticism

During his student years at the Paris Conservatoire, Messiaen discovered rhythms called *deśītālas* in a thirteenth-century Indian musical treatise. His adaptations of the principles behind these rhythms—most notably, the use of a smallest note value functioning as a rhythmic building block rather than a regular pulse or meter—began to appear in his music as early as the *Quatuor pour la fin du temps*, and were firmly entrenched in his style by the time he composed the *Quatre études de rythme*, making *Mode de valeurs et d'intensités* a notable departure (Hook 1998: 98). These rhythmic concepts, a large part of Messiaen's characteristic sound (at least as heard in *Neumes rythmiques* and the free episodes in the *Île de feu* pieces), were gleaned from an Asian culture but were adapted and transformed to obscure their origins. They are analogous to Steve Reich's use of African rhythmic concepts to challenge Western musical structure, which John Corbett distinguishes as different from "conceptual" Orientalism, as exemplified by John Cage, or "decorative" Orientalism, as exemplified by Alan Hohvaness (2000: 170–4). Ralph Locke would describe Messiaen's type of borrowing and remodeling as "transcultural composing" (2009: 229).

The free adaptation of Indian rhythmic concepts, rather than specific sounds, cut off all audible reference to Asia, becoming "Western music with a broadened material foundation" (Šimundža 1988: 69). Messiaen used these adaptations even when quoting material from a different non-European culture. His 1945 song cycle *Harawi*, which draws heavily on Peruvian folklore and melody, uses the same Indian-derived rhythmic techniques, even though he incorporates them into what would become the first of piece of his "Tristan trilogy," based on Wagnerian themes of love and death (Hill and Simeone 2005: 156–7).

There is, however, a clear exoticizing impulse in the dedication of his *Île de feu* pieces:

> Papuans are very intelligent blacks living in the great island of Oceania called New Guinea. Their philosophy is a magical world organization. Their initiations, their secret societies, their racial identification with the animals or plants they eat, lead to terrible violence. Violence that will cut off the head of the enemy! (All told, this is more horrible than our "civilized" means of destruction? ...) Papuan folklore inherited from this set of facts barbaric power, brute force, and also a magic character. Papuan songs are simple, brief and terrible—a little like the gigantic stone heads that the Polynesians of the past have left in Easter Island. Seduced by Papuan folklore, I have tried to find themes in the same style.
>
> (1995: vol. 7, 70)

Messiaen's casual essentialism, racism, and exoticism, apparent both in this paragraph and in his attempted appropriation of the Papuan melodic style, are unmistakable, if not unusual for the period. Encounters with such attitudes, perhaps in the form of program notes in addition to the titles of the pieces themselves, would inevitably complicate how audiences receive this work.

These pieces fall within the Western Art tradition and would be programmed on a concert with other virtuosic piano pieces from within that tradition. Let us then consider members of a theoretical audience who are listening to the *Quatre études* on the first half of a solo piano concert whose second half—perhaps one of the major Beethoven sonatas—is what they have really come to hear. The program notes would likely explain a great deal about the *Mode de valeurs et d'intensités* and its subsequent influence and would probably include something like Jeremy Grimshaw's summary of the outer movements:

> The Études are bookended by the closely related *Île de Feu I* and *Île de Feu II*. Both take their inspiration from Papua and New Guinea, which merged into a single entity in the same year that Messiaen commenced work on the Études. "Île de Feu," which translates as "Island of Fire," not only describes the volcanic activity of New Guinea but also suggests the spiritual "violence of the magic rites of the region."
>
> (2019)

Here Grimshaw faithfully reports the European-style exoticism implied by the titles, the loud, percussive themes, and Messiaen's own writing about the pieces. He acknowledges that the connection to the island is tenuous at best; Messiaen never traveled there, ethnomusicological information from the area was nearly nonexistent at the time, and, as Griffiths notes drily, "Papua is not within the belt of volcanic activity suggested by the common title and by the material of these pieces" (1985: 155). These pieces thus neatly fit Ralph Locke's definition of musical exoticism as the evocation of "a place, people, or social milieu that is not entirely imaginary" (2009: 47).

Listeners and Schema Theory

Because of the narrow range of programmed repertoire in the United States,[4] as well as the relative obscurity of Messiaen's work even in classical venues, we can assume his audience in our theoretical program is typical of those who listen to Western "classical" music, having heard many more live concerts of tonal than atonal or post-tonal music. They have thus heard plenty of Bach, Mozart, and Beethoven; a lot of Tchaikovsky and Prokofiev; plenty of music that includes "exoticist" appropriation and Orientalism, such as Rimsky-Korsakov's *Scheherezade*; and a smattering of post-tonal twentieth-century music (which they may have been intrigued or put off by), perhaps including a couple of pieces by Messiaen. Non-tonal music will thus sound markedly different for many classical music listeners, since most will have few or no existing schemata for it.

A schema can be defined as a set of expectations for a given type of experience that is formed by repeated exposure to similar experiences (Huron 2007: 204). Listeners form schemata for musical genres, forms, and experiences. The broader the exposure, the richer and more detailed the schemata and sub-schemata. A devoted listener to the Western classical music canon will have schemata for symphonies and sonatas; rondos, scherzos, and adagios; and music from the baroque versus the classical eras. They are also likely to possess sub-schemata for phrase structures and cadences (to choose only a few examples). Someone unfamiliar with this canon, with no schemata in place, is more likely to think that these "all sound the same."[5] But for the average classical music listener (the focus of this inquiry), the various musical vocabularies in *Quatre études de rythme* may interact differently with the schemata they have developed by listening to other tonal pieces.[6]

David Huron notes that "listeners will form a broad category of 'otherness' into which all deviant stimuli are, by default, indiscriminately assigned" (2007: 215). For a casual listener to classical music, all of the *Quatre études de rythme* will likely be categorized this way. For the more seasoned listeners we are assuming, the variety of musical materials in the piece may activate different schemata. Indeed, musical schemata can be activated not only by the music itself, but also by extramusical cues, such as venue: if a concert hall activates schemata for classical music, the sight of an orchestra will activate one group of those schemata, while the sight of a solo pianist will activate others. Program notes and titles may activate schemata similarly.

The "Papuan" themes from *Île de feu I* and *II*, which share features (to be discussed below) with themes from more familiar classical works, are likely to activate a schema for "exoticist" music based on exposure to the many examples of Orientalist appropriations in the Western art music canon.[7] The material between themes in *Île de feu I* and in *Neumes rythmiques* may activate another, which I will call "characteristic Messiaen," based on his rhythmic, gestural, and harmonic language and his use of "modes of limited transposition." The material in *Mode de valeurs et d'intensités* and in the "interversions" in *Île de feu II* may activate yet a third, "serial music"—or, for listeners without extensive experience with serial music, activate none at all.

Schema-Oriented Analyses

What might audiences experience when first listening to *Île de feu I & II* in the context of the *Quatre études de rythme*? Those primed by the program notes to expect exoticism will not be disappointed when they first hear the opening theme statement of *Île de feu I* (Example 5.2). Indeed, the theme statement initially reads as "exotic" rather than just "modern," despite the tone clusters and irregular rhythms, precisely because it shares certain features with more familiar tonal themes. To start with, it is a melody—a sequence of individual pitches in succession, close enough in register to be singable (in contrast with the angularity of "characteristic Messiaen" or the seeming randomness of *Mode de valeurs et d'intensités*). This melody also has an obvious and definite pitch center (E). It contains an antecedent and consequent structure, the consequent phrase featuring a departure from the pitch center and a return to it. While there are obviously unfamiliar elements, there is a noticeable schematic overlap with familiar "exotic" repertoire.

In my schema-oriented descriptions and analyses of the two pieces below, I remove the microscope and step back to take the broad view, asking what might actually register with listeners on a first hearing. What schemata, if any, will be activated? As mentioned above, the themes themselves will activate schemata for melody and accompaniment, phrase structure, and modal

Example 5.2 Messiaen, *Île de feu I*, mm. 1–2. First statement of theme in right hand, top staff.

melody. For brevity, I will refer to this complex of schemata below as (Papuan) Theme I in Table 5.1. Most of the episodic material in the first movement will activate a choice of two schemata. One is most likely a rudimentary schema based on the audience's prior experience with Messiaen, including his individual rhythmic vocabulary and use of resonance effects derived from modes of limited transposition, labeled as "Messiaen."[8] The other is a general, also rudimentary schema for atonal, non-normative classical music ("atonal"). Since schema switching is likely to be slower for unfamiliar schemata than for familiar ones (Huron 2007: 211), it is possible that these latter two will be lumped together on the first listening.

Île de feu I

Over the course of the nearly two-minute piece, not more than perhaps ten seconds goes by without either the instantly recognizable theme or one of its variants sounding (Table 5.1). The audience's overall impression as the reverberation of the final notes fade is likely to be that the "exotic" theme alternated with passages that "sound like Messaien." And while there are gestures that are not as characteristically Messiaen—those I have labeled "atonal" schema—they are comparatively brief and, because of their very unfamiliarity, likely will not stick in memory as well.

Then comes *Mode de valeurs et d'intensités*. As discussed above, the typical audience for classical music has not had enough exposure to serialized music to have any schemata in place to be activated by listening to this movement. For its four-minute duration, audience members will likely be experiencing the at-sea feeling of listening to music for which they have no frame of reference, simply categorizing the music as "other." In the six minutes that follow, the soundworld of *Neumes rythmiques* is slightly more familiar. Moreover, as David Huron would remind us, music that does not take advantage of familiar schemata can nonetheless create its own by including sufficient repetition and self-similarity (2007: 367). *Neumes rythmiques*, like most of Messiaen's music, does this quite successfully; indeed, the use of recurrent melodic-harmonic-rhythmic figures (the "neumes" of the title) is the raison d'être of the piece. *Mode de valeurs et d'intensités*, however, uses less-identifiable, less memorable individual pitch-dynamic-duration combinations and therefore does not create its own schema in this way.

Table 5.1 *Île de feu I* schemata and form

Bars	Schema(ta)	Comments
1–2	(Papuan) Theme	First statement of theme, loud and low, with gong effects (low clusters). Percussive, violent affect. See Example 5.2.
3–4	Atonal	Quick ascending gesture, quick descending gesture.
5–6	(Papuan) Theme, Messiaen	Second statement of theme, midrange, still loud. Imitative birdsong *obbligato* in right hand.
7–9	Messiaen	New material, still loud.
10	Messiaen	Similar resonance effects to mm. 7–9; repeated E–G# recalls theme.
11	(Papuan) Theme, Messiaen	Theme fragment, resonance and gong effect.
12–14	Atonal	Quick ascending gesture, quick descending gesture.
15–18	Atonal	Quick ascending gesture, tremolo in upper and lower registers, slower descending gesture.
20	(Papuan) Theme, Messiaen	Third statement of theme, resonance effects, gong effects, *obbligato* recalling mm. 10–11.
21–22	(Papuan) Theme	Unison octaves, very loud, thematic variation.
23–24	Atonal	Two quick ascending gestures.
25–34	(Papuan) Theme, Messaien	Thematic variant in bass, rhythmic *obbligato*. Comments on and summarize earlier material.
35	(Papuan) Theme, Messaien	Thematic fragment, midrange, birdsong, recalls mm. 5–6.
36	Atonal	"Closing fan" gesture (Messiaen's term): descending from upper register, ascending from lower register. *Piano*, then quick crescendo.
37–38	(Papuan) Theme, Messaien	Fragment from m. 35, diminished rhythm, lower register. Descending gesture, *ffff* gong effect and grace-note lead-in to E.

Île de feu II

When the first notes of *Île de feu II* finally begin, audiences hear another loud and violent modal melody (Table 5.2). The (Papuan) Theme of *Île de feu II*, seen in Example 5.3, will activate schemata similar to that of *Île de feu I*.

Table 5.2 *Île de feu II* schemata and form

Bars	Schema(ta)	Comments
1–7	(Papuan) Theme	First thematic statement midrange, resonance effects. Loud, violent affect.
8–27	Serial/none	"Interversions I–IV." Return to soundworld of *Mode de valeurs et d'intensités*.
28–34	(Papuan) Theme	Second thematic statement, driving but harmonically static accompaniment.
35–54	Serial/none	"Interversions V–VIII."
55–61	(Papuan) Theme, Messaien	Third thematic statement, resonance effects. Accompaniment, compare mm. 28–34.
62–67	Messiaen	Free episode, dynamics from *ff* to *p*.
68–69	Atonal	Tag to the free episode. Figuration and loud, regular 8th notes (interversion row pitches).
70–75	Atonal	Fast blur of notes, *pp*, crescendo.
76–85	(Papuan) Theme, serial/none	Fourth thematic statement, octaves in lowest register, loud and layered with "Interversions IX–X."
86–87	Atonal	Free episode.
88–89	(Papuan) Theme, Messaien	Last three notes of theme, midrange with resonance above.
90–91	Messaien	New material: rapid-fire sixteenth notes, theme pitches with different rhythms.
92–113	Messiaen	Similarity to passage near end of *Île de feu I*: repeated notes, especially E.
132–134	Messaien	Similar to mm. 90–91, thematic pitches disguised in left hand. G–E repeats.
135–136	Messaien	Two loud, long, high chords; near-total contrast to everything so far.
137	(Papuan) Theme	G–E again, loud, last two notes of theme.
138	Messaien	Fast, swooping gesture to low register, similar to *Île de feu I*'s ending.

This theme bears a distinct resemblance to a musical sentence, and the second (slightly varied) statement of the initial idea is even a perfect fifth above the first. The modal identity of the theme is strong enough that the final note sounds very much like a dominant scale degree. However, by the time the audience hears this, they have also heard the second and third movements of the piece, which may activate the "characteristic Messiaen" and "serial music" schemata. How might this change the audience's response to the theme of *Île de feu II*? Because of the listeners' earlier hearing of *Île de feu I*, along with the expectation aroused by the title *Île de feu II*, they will likely know (perhaps unconsciously) that this melody functions as a theme and will thus be repeated (activating formal schemata for rondos or ritornelli). After ten minutes of music for which listeners either have no schemata, or weak or newly self-reinforcing schemata, listeners actually are back on the most familiar ground they have been on in a while.

As *Île de feu II* continues, listeners are exposed to the three musical vocabularies they have heard thus far juxtaposed and intertwined: while *Île de feu II* is structured much like *Île de feu I*, the episodic material between the

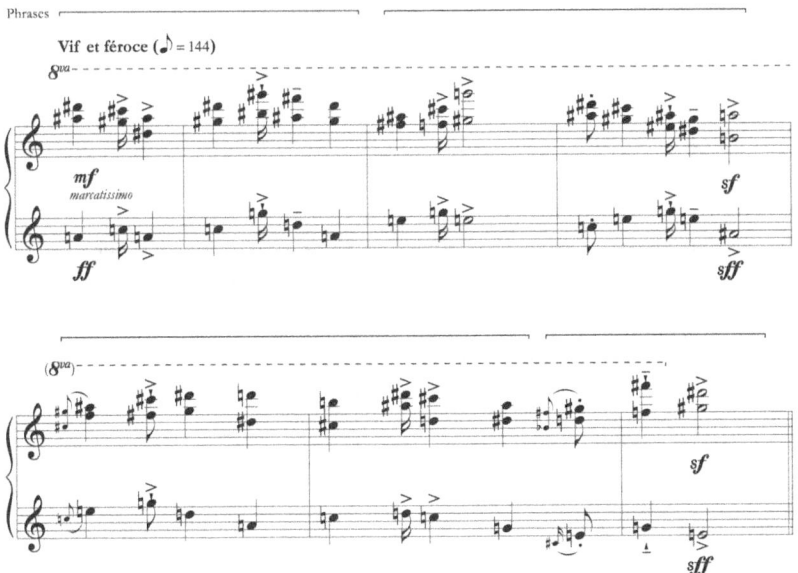

Example 5.3 Messiaen, *Île de feu II*, mm. 1-7. First statement of theme in left hand, bottom staff.

themes is primarily "Interversions," constructed in much the same way as the *Mode de valeurs et d'intensités*. There are also free episodes more in keeping with Messiaen's characteristic language, the schema for which will have been somewhat reinforced by hearing *Neumes rythmiques*. The final third of the four-and-a-half-minute etude primarily uses this language.

What might audiences think at the end of the performance? They will have heard music for which they have no schema, music for which they have only rudimentary schema, and music that, while apparently deliberately composed as an "exoticist" statement, will have activated more of their familiar schemata than any of the surrounding material. With the mantle of "other" usurped by the material in *Mode de valeurs et d'intensités* and the "Interversions" in *Île de feu II*, the "simple, brief and terrible" Papuan-inspired themes will likely have seemed redolent of a musical "home" or place of arrival. Messiaen's conception of the outer movements may indeed have been unquestioningly colonialist, in keeping with the long history of Orientalism and other practices of appropriation in European art music. But the decision to juxtapose these pieces with serial music aurally inverts this representation of alterity, shifting it onto his own experiments with serial organization and his characteristic compositional style.

Conclusion

Why Papua? It's not hard to imagine that Messiaen knew how alien *Mode de valeurs et d'intensités* would seem to his listeners, and why he might have wanted to bookend the suite with something more inviting. Perhaps Messiaen had been struck by the similarity of the melodies he had received from Archbishop Sorin to certain aspects of his own aesthetic, and had been looking for a way to use them, or perhaps he simply received the archbishop's letter the day he was considering how to finish the suite. In any case, the uncharacteristic choice to foreground the outer movements as "exotic"—through the title, stylistic appropriation, and program note—seems very much like an attempt to present a "particular, marked, [and] raced" (Dyer 1997: 38) contrast to his serial experiments, which would be perceived as safely "unmarked" by comparison. If so, the gambit backfired, as I have demonstrated in the analyses above: the choice of these ostensibly "Papuan" themes marks not only the serial experiments but Messiaen's own characteristic language, defined as the sonic "other" in the ears of a typical classical music listener.

Notes

1. Analyses can be found in the Johnson and Messiaen texts previously cited, among others.
2. Messiaen's "modes of limited transposition" are scales with enough pitch symmetry that they can be transposed fewer than eleven times without repeating the pitch collection. Both the octatonic and whole tone scales, for instance, are among these modes (although Messiaen favored less usual ones).
3. Messiaen supplies no details about the nature of or reasons for their correspondence. Sorin was Vicar Apostolic of the Archdiocese of Port Moresby, Papua New Guinea from 1946 until his death in 1959 (Lorentz 2006: 50).
4. One snapshot of this situation is given in the "Orchestra Repertoire Report" compiled by the League of American Orchestras. https://americanorchestras.org/orchestra-repertoire-report-orr-2012-2013/.
5. The same applies to any genre, of course; the claim that a given type of music "all sounds the same" is a familiar one across generational and cultural lines and can largely be attributed to missing schemata.
6. An *ecological* approach to listening foregrounds the relationship between observer and object, including between listener and cultural object (such as musical performance), specifically in terms of what affordances, or opportunities for action, the environment offers the observer (Clarke 2011: 337). Clarke's use of the term is one of many extensions of its original meaning, which is tied to the physical environment. The actions afforded by (for instance) a blatantly Orientalist appropriation might include "projection of desire onto an Other." This ecological approach could be supplementary or complementary to the schema-oriented methodology I am employing here; while both affordances and schemata are well supported in the psychological literature, their interactions are "contentious" (Cooper 2012).
7. The chances that members of this audience have a well-developed schema for traditional Papuan music are slight.
8. Griffiths uses the term "resonance" to refer to Messiaen's use of chordal structure to create orchestrational effects rather than to harmonic function (1985: 154).

References

Born, G. (2000), "Introduction," in G. Born and D. Hesmondhalgh (eds.), *Western Music and Its Others: Difference, Representation, and Appropriation in Music*, 1–58, Berkeley: University of California Press.

Clarke, E. F. (2011), "What's Going On/Music, Psychology and Ecological Theory," in M. Clayton et al. (eds.), *The Cultural Study of Music: A Critical Introduction*, 333–42, New York: Routledge.

Cooper, R. P. (2012), "Learning Action Affordances and Action Schemas," in N. M. Seel (ed.), *Encyclopedia of the Sciences of Learning*, 1758–60, Boston: Springer.

Corbett, J. (2000), "Experimental Oriental: New Music and Other Others," in G. Born and D. Hesmondhalgh (eds.), *Western Music and Its Others: Difference, Representation, and Appropriation in Music*, 163–86, Berkeley: University of California Press.

Dyer, R. (1997), *White: Essays on Race and Culture*, New York: Routledge.

Griffiths, P. (1985), *Olivier Messiaen and the Music of Time*, Ithaca: Cornell University Press.

Grimshaw, J. (n.d.), "Olivier Messiaen: *Études de rhythme* (4), for piano solo, I/32–35," *AllMusic*. https://www.allmusic.com/composition/%C3tudes-de-rhythme-4-for-piano-solo-i-32-35-mc0002358854 (accessed May 21, 2019).

Hill, P. (1995), "Piano Music II," in P. Hill (ed.), *The Messiaen Companion*, 307–51, Portland: Amadeus Press.

Hill, P. and N. Simeone (2005), *Messiaen*, New Haven: Yale University Press.

Hook, J. (1998), "Rhythm in the Music of Messiaen: An Algebraic Study and an Application in the 'Turangalila Symphony,'" *Music Theory Spectrum*, 20 (1): 97–120.

Huron, D. (2007), *Sweet Anticipation: Music and the Psychology of Expectation*, Cambridge: The MIT Press.

Johnson, R. S. (1975), *Messiaen*, Berkeley: University of California Press.

Locke, R. P. (2009), *Musical Exoticism: Images and Reflections*, Cambridge: Cambridge University Press.

Lorentz, A., "Evêque en Papouasie et archevêque de Nouméa," *Kocherschbari*, no. 54 (Winter 2006): 41–61.

Messiaen, O. (1995, 2002), *Traité de rythme, de couleur, et d'ornithologie* (1949–1992), vols. 2 and 7, Paris: Éditions musicales Alphonse Leduc.

Messiaen, O. (2008), *Quatre études de rhythme*, Paris: Éditions Durand.

"Orchestra Repertory Report 13," (2013) *League of American Orchestras*. https://americanorchestras.org/images/stories/ORR_1213/ORR13%20summary%20report.pdf (accessed December 9, 2019).

Šimundža, M. (1988), "Messiaen's Rhythmical Organisation and Classical Indian Theory of Rhythm (2)," *International Review of the Aesthetics and Sociology of Music*, 18 (1): 53–73.

Part Two

Sounding "Otherness" in Contemporary Media

6

Decolonizing Game Audio and Approaching Sound in Digital Storytelling

Kate Galloway

This chapter explores a group of video games that encourage Indigenous cultural expression and ecological awareness while combating the misrepresentation and appropriation of these communities in the mainstream game industry. Expressions of Indigenous modernity, manifested through activist play, design, code, art, and sound, indigenize cultural objects and experiences through creative acts of remaking. Indigenization is the process of making something, like a video game, but altering it to make it fit into Indigenous culture and contribute to the needs of its community. Often these objects, spaces, and cultural experiences are not typically considered aspects of Indigenous expression and participation. In the case of video game sound and sample-based compositional practices, indigenization engages inventive processes of remixing tradition, unveiling continuities among history, lived realities, and storytelling practices in the digital age. These approaches are a form of musical repatriation that challenges Western concepts of copyright and cultural ownership. Repatriation, as defined here, involves the return of cultural heritage to the community to which it belongs, facilitating reconnection and access to cultural materials, including games, stories, real and virtual soundscapes, and expressive culture reanimated through interactive and embodied acts of play.[1]

Drawing on examples from Indigenous-developed or co-developed games, I attend to the multisensory methods by which sound and music resound Indigenous futures, ecological relationships and crises, and ways of knowing the land. I focus on a game developed by E-Line Media/Upper One Games that was funded and informed by cultural consultants (the Cook Inlet Tribal Council), as well as a collection developed by game designer Elizabeth LaPensée, to survey contemporary Indigenous media research-creation practices that perform important cultural and creative work in decolonizing game sound. Specifically,

I examine *Never Alone* (2014), which follows the quest of a young Iñupiaq girl and an arctic fox; *Invaders* (2015), a remix and indigenization of the classic *Space Invaders* (1978); and *Honour Water* (2016), an Anishinaabe singing game app that draws attention to forces threatening northern waters and Traditional Ecological Knowledge (TEK). In these game environments, communities can express themselves, their traditions, and their futures on their own terms.

I begin with two questions: How can mobile computing and digital making help us explore real places, histories, and ways of knowing and being-in-the-world? How might they support the collaborative problem-solving of current issues affecting diverse communities? Ethnomusicologist Victoria Levine notes that "modernity and Indigeneity have been defined in different ways at different times, often in opposition to each other," advising that we must shift away from Eurocentric notions of modernity to recognize its alternative forms (2019: 1). We do this by approaching modernity as a process, acknowledging that tradition and technology can be simultaneously present and in play. Thus in the creative reparative spaces of Indigenous interactive digital media, such as games, Indigenous people are not treated as mere specimens of study, spectacle, and entertainment.

What unites the video games I study here, therefore, is how they invite Indigenous and non-Indigenous people not just to listen and play, but to do so attentively, and with care. These acts of listening and playing reconnect human bodies to the land and invite us to reconsider what constitutes environmental evidence, data, and knowledge to include fleshy, vibrational, and corporeal data that traces changes in how people perceive and relate to environments we know intimately. As the Métis scholar Zoe Todd points out, "[e]vidence generally precludes the flash of a school of minnows in the clear prairie lakes I intimately knew as a child, or the succulent white fish my stepdad caught for us from the Red Deer River where I was growing up" (Todd 2016; see also Todd 2017; 2014). By heeding Indigenous epistemologies of the land, including an ethics of kinship with the nonhuman, we can develop a healthier understanding of human actions on the environment, perhaps cultivating more sustainable human-environment relations and ways of being-in-the-world.

Decolonizing Game Sound

What does it look and sound like to decolonize video game narratives, gameplay, and soundscapes? "Video games are a path for passing on teachings, telling our stories, and expressing our ways of knowing," argues Anishinaabe/Métis game designer, scholar, and activist Elizabeth LaPensée (LaPensée 2014: 20; see also LaPensée 2017; Starkey 2015). Decolonizing game audio requires shifting the listening perspective, centering Indigenous voices and ways of being-in-the world while subverting existing power structures. In so doing, game designers create spaces and opportunities for these communities to tell their stories, convey their expressive culture, and participate in self-determination. By challenging how we listen to, compose, and play with diverse kinds of game sound, designers and players create physical, collaborative, creative, and virtual spaces for Indigenous voices and systems of representation to be encountered. Indeed, video games can do much more than merely avoid stereotypical images and soundscapes.

Decolonized game design moves away from gameplay mechanics and experiences that rely on spaces mapped, explored, conquered, industrialized, and claimed—processes that reinforce settler-colonial values and histories. Instead, it creates experiences rooted in human-nonhuman relationships, traditional storytelling, and transmissions of expressive culture that are similarly rooted in collaborative relationships that value stewardship, generosity, and reciprocity. Technology is not inherently in conflict with tradition and storytelling protocols. Digital communication technologies, as Thomas Hilder explains, "have themselves transformed forms of Indigenous activism" and have been adopted by Indigenous makers "to assist in cultural revival, repatriation, and transmission—processes which have helped to 'decolonize' earlier media spaces and practices" (Hilder 2017: 2; see also Dyson, Hendriks, and Grant 2006). In *Indians in Unexpected Places*, Philip Deloria writes that the custom of imagining Indigenous peoples in terms of "primitivism, technological incompetence, physical distance, and cultural difference" has remained "familiar currency in contemporary dealings with Native people" (2004: 4). Redressing this conventional narrative, Deloria describes Indigenous peoples doing things—singing opera, driving cars, acting in Hollywood—that conflict with the expectations of non-Indigenous settlers.

Never Alone, *Invaders*, and *Honour Water*, along with other Indigenous-designed games, subvert the settler-space of the North American game industry with their own stories, visuals, soundscapes, and gameplay. The makers of *Never Alone* and *Honour Water* assert, via storytelling, that instead of preserving their culture exclusively for the community, Indigenous makers must also transmit knowledge and ways of understanding to non-Indigenous people, thereby illuminating issues that plague contemporary society. Speaking of his own artistic practice and the approaches taken by many of his collaborators, Tlingit artist Nicholas Galanin explains how Indigenous multimodal art must "*open* this container of wisdom" and through it share "our language, our culture, our dance, our sovereign creative voices in the artwork that we create" (2017). Indigenous scholars have discussed the importance of stories and storytelling as discursive strategy and research method—a narrative format that best communicates the nonlinear interweaving of pasts, presents, and futures, which circle back and overlap in complex and intricate ways (King 2003; Archibald 2008; Armstrong 2013; Davis 2014; Kovach 2015, 2009).

Never Alone: Digital Storytelling, Digital Indigeneity, and Indigenous Tradition

Never Alone follows the quest of a young Iñupiaq girl and an arctic fox through the remote Arctic as they search for the source of an eternal blizzard that threatens their community.[2] Employing various kinds of digital storytelling that are developed, in part, through community outreach, the game conveys aspects of heritage and soundscapes of the lived Circumpolar North through audio (the combination of music, sound effects, and voice acting) and environmental sound. These experiences, moreover, are expressed to the communities directly affected by colonialist ideologies.

In 2012, the Cook Inlet Tribal Council (CITC), a tribal nonprofit organization based in Anchorage, Alaska, partnered with E-Line Media, a development studio that produces educational games intended to share world cultures. Together, they founded Upper One Games, the first Indigenous-owned video game company in the United States. *Never Alone* is the first title in their series of "World Games," or "social impact games," designed with a community of "cultural ambassadors" who collaboratively create gameworlds informed by their ways of knowing and being-in-the-world. Donna Haraway describes *Never Alone* as a "world game" in *Staying with the Trouble: Making Kin in the Chthulucene*, calling it a prime example of "science art worlding for living on a damaged planet" (2016: 86).

As CITC's president, Gloria O'Neill, put it, "[w]e ... wanted to be bold and be courageous, so we started thinking about how CITC could become more progressive ... How could we use technology? And we asked ourselves at the time, what is the greatest asset of our people? And we said, our culture and our stories"

(Parkinson 2014). *Never Alone*'s ambassadors are Iñupiat elders who consulted on the game throughout its development and contributed "cultural insight" videos that players can unlock during gameplay, which function as moments of cultural transmission. *Never Alone* thus represents ongoing efforts to decolonize the media industry in much the same way other digital communication technologies, as Hilder explains, have been adopted by Indigenous makers "to assist in cultural revival, repatriation, and transmission—processes which have helped to 'decolonize' earlier media spaces and practices" (2017: 2).

Upper One Games based *Never Alone*'s plot on a traditional Iñupiaq tale grounded in humanity's relationship with the nonhuman environment. The tale, "Kunuuksaayuka," was first recorded by the renowned Alaska Native storyteller Robert Nasruk Cleveland in the collection *Unipchaanich Imagluktugmiut (Stories of the Black River People*, 1980). In the *Never Alone* adaptation, the central characters are Nuna and an Arctic fox—a companion plagued by the same blizzard who represents the nonhuman community and whose skills are necessary to advance gameplay. Other revisions to the story included recasting the protagonist as a young girl to challenge existing gender representation disparities in the video game market, and giving her an animal companion to emphasize the theme of human-nonhuman relationships and facilitate cooperative play. The harsh environmental elements are represented by the Blizzard Man, a figure made of ice who forever chips away at a huge ice wall. The debris of his activity causes the blizzard plaguing Nuna's village and prevents the people from hunting. The core philosophy and game mechanics are therefore linked: throughout their quest, Nuna and the fox overcome obstacles and solve puzzles to continue their journey, unlock special content, and ultimately, locate and undo the blizzard's source. Embedded within this narrative arc are other stories, including those of the Sky People, who impart cultural knowledge in cutscene vignettes.

Indeed, Nuna and the fox solve several puzzles teaching that Sila—the Iñupiaq name for the spiritual realm between environmental phenomena and the land, moon, sun, and stars—has spirit helpers to whom humans are connected. Nuna is assisted by these spirits, including ghostly apparitions of schools of fish who jump from the water and allow her and the fox to ride on their backs (see Figure 6.1). Puzzles, like those that instruct players about Sila, illustrate one way that participatory media can express Indigenous cosmologies. By attending to these embodied experiences of gameplay, as Aubrey Anable explains, we gain a richer understanding of "how games make complex meanings across

Figure 6.1 *Never Alone* gameplay stills. Top: Nuna and Fox maneuver across ice floes. Bottom: Nuna and Fox work together to defeat the Polar Bear in his cave.

history, bodies, hardware, and code" (2018: xi). Moreover, by showing that the Arctic environment is unrelenting, these gameplay moments illustrate how players must collaborate with the more-than-human to succeed, embracing a "multinaturalism" (Ochoa Gautier 2016) that relativizes and interrogates settler colonial ideas and representations of nature, humans, nonhumans, and nonliving things.

Storytelling, whether oral or written, is a vital part of Iñupiaq culture, transmitting lessons, cultural knowledge, and values. Many of these stories include narratives of overcoming, the community often negotiating obstacles presented by the harsh northern environs. Traditional storytelling is taking on new forms in current Indigenous youth cultures, who are turning to social media, Web 2.0 formats, and video games to share and create culture. Through practices of digital repatriation—that is, restoring cultural heritage to Indigenous communities by using participatory computer-based technologies of digitization, transmission, and preservation—digital objects, like video games, challenge and rethink the long history of collaborative exchange among colonizing, colonized, and decolonizing agents. *Never Alone* is thus part of E-Line's vision to create games that share, celebrate, and extend culture, fostering game development that enables ethical, respectful, and participatory collaboration among Indigenous and non-Indigenous actors, where settler-developers leverage their privilege for positive change and meaningful inclusion. Accordingly, Indigenous artwork that examines cultural specificity and self-definition within the contexts of contemporary art practices can articulate differing worldviews, erased historical narratives, activist politics, and complex sociocultural issues that are central to the concerns of contemporary communities. In "Decolonizing the 'Web,'" Steven Loft proposes an "Indigenous media cosmology ... based in the epistemologies, histories, traditions, communication systems, art, and culture of the Aboriginal people of Turtle Island." Such a cosmology "embraces an Indigenous view of media and its attendant processes that incorporates language, culture, technology, land, spirituality, and histories encompassed in the teachings of the four directions" (2014: xvi). Games such as *Never Alone* integrate this concept, diversifying the gaming community to include those who are marginalized by a market that fails to tell their stories, portray their environments, and incorporate their soundworlds.

Lessons on cooperation with others and the environment are an essential aspect of Indigenous media cosmology and thus are mirrored in *Never Alone*'s mechanics. In their journey through the volatile Arctic landscape, Nuna and the fox encounter obstacles best navigated using special abilities specific to each character. Fox is nimble, quick, and can negotiate small, tight spaces; Nuna can carry and handle objects and tools used to open pathways for the pair to pass through. By switching strategically between characters, or by playing in co-op mode, players collaborate to solve environmental puzzles about the North. Gameplay involves conventional side-scrolling platformer mechanics: running, jumping, pushing boxes to jump to higher ledges, and using objects, like Nuna's bola—a throwing weapon made of weights on the ends of interconnected cords used to capture animals by entangling their legs—to break through ice that blocks forward progress. Though the characters are constantly running across the ice, movement feels slow and unwieldy, reflecting the players' need to participate in chase sequences or complete puzzles that require precise timing on the windy, icy terrain.

The blizzard at the center of the narrative also plays a role in the gameplay mechanics. Strong gusts of icy wind blow across the screen at apparently random intervals, requiring the player to hold a button to brace against the ground. Players try to gauge when a gust is about to blow by listening for the wind. At times, the characters might be halfway through a jump, only for the blizzard to suddenly blow them backward to their deaths. Toward the end of the game, however, players need to adapt to these same forces, precisely timing their movements so the blizzard can boost jump length. The stunning aural and visual detail of the terrain represents the Indigenous North in nuanced, multifaceted, and complex ways. *Never Alone*'s sonic geography maps the North by using sound to evoke specific places and regions. By placing emphasis on the sonic articulation of place, the game audio correlates landmarks with soundscapes, layering diegetic environmental sound and non-diegetic ambient music to aurally encode modern indigeneity into it. The game demonstrates that faithfully depicting a place and its people, avoiding culturally appropriative practices, and dismantling internalized stereotypes of the North and Indigenous cultures requires game developers to listen.

The central narrative arc thus encourages listening by telling a story of local traditional ecological knowledge (or TEK), which focuses on the living nature of weather, the vibrant matter of the environment, and the unpredictability and power of both. TEK refers to aboriginal, Indigenous, or other forms of traditional knowledges that recognize the sustainability of local resources and the means of living in balance with nature. The TEK in *Never Alone* reflects how Indigenous communities, who depend on traditional livelihoods and the tenuous balance of local ecosystems, are already facing the consequences of environmental devastation and climate change. A number of techniques portray Indigenous modernity through the game's soundscape, which blurs musical and diegetic boundaries, uses electronic music, and experiments with making and recording environmental sound.

Combining ambient music with environmental sound has particular resonance for games featuring "back-to-nature" gameplay and environmental themes. Ambient music places emphasis on tone, atmosphere, and environment over the traditional structural elements of music—form, rhythm, and melody, for example—favored by Western European styles. *Never Alone*'s ambient electronic music highlights moments of dramatic tension and suspense during gameplay, operating parallel to the diegetic soundscape to evoke a sense of topographic vastness across the expansive glacial ice fields and water bodies. In a moment of dramatic tension, cracking ice floes break under the weight of the polar bear, signaling the extradiegetic warming of the North.

As Bernie Krause has argued, a boisterous, sonically rich, varied soundscape communicates a healthy ecosystem, while a silent soundscape signals decline and disrepair. In *Voices of the Wild*, Krause reveals that more than half of his audio data comes from sites "so badly compromised by various forms of human intervention that the habitats are either altogether silent or the soundscapes can no longer be heard in any of their original forms" (2015: 29). The incessant roar of the blizzard, the repeated growls of the polar bear prepared to attack without apparent provocation, the splitting ice beneath his paws, and the relative "silence" of other forms of nonhuman life in *Never Alone* are thus sounds of alarm, indicating to the player that the gameworld environment (and, by extension, the real-world environment) is experiencing a decline in health. These sounds, which demand the player's auditory attention, warn of an environmental imbalance, requiring players to parse musical moments and soundscapes to progress through the game. Such skills are applicable outside of the gameworld as well: players can apply these modes and techniques of embodied listening to their lived experiences.

To collect sounds and design the foley for the game's audio library, sound designers and foley artists Brendan Hogan and Jamie Hunsdale made field recording trips over a period of two years. Like Nuna and the fox, they had to cope with an unpredictable environment. On their first trip the snow was too slushy to produce the crisp snow sounds of Nuna's North, and there was excess automotive noise from nearby roads. While some game sounds were directly sourced from nature, others were staged using natural materials to mimic those they were unable to record on-site. For example, to create the sound of fox paws running, walking, and trotting on snow and ice, they fit a glove with paper clips on each finger to simulate a clawed paw. To evoke collapsing icebergs and cave ice walls, they threw large frozen chunks of ice and packed snow onto pavement and recorded the impact. The wind, a soundmark that defines each moment of gameplay, was the most difficult to record, as Hogan (2014) notes:

> The challenge was to create the feeling and constant presence of wind without it masking too many other sounds with white noise, without it becoming monotonous or overbearing or indistinct. I used a lot of sounds from sound libraries as well as synthesized wind sounds, some of my own field recordings, processed versions of my breath and a "snow falling" sound I made by overlapping and filtering the sound of lightly tapping on the carpet in my home studio.

As Karen Collins explains, "the overall sonic texture of games can often create an interesting interplay between music and sound effects that blurs the distinction between the two. In many examples of games, we might question whether we are hearing sound effects, voice, ambience, or music ... Some sound effects in games are also worth considering as music rather than as nonmusical sound" (2013a: 3).[3] Accordingly, the decolonial approaches taken in *Never Alone* seek to fashion new modes of representation, along with alternative strategies and platforms for circulation that redefine and redistribute Indigenous and sonic knowledge.

Indeed, Indigenous representations in the game community are dominated by stereotypes, characterizations, and co-opted and decontextualized narratives, symbols, and cultural references. O'Neill recalls that the earliest goals of *Never Alone* during the research-creation process were to "use the tools of technology, living in a modern world, and figure out how we can share who we are with the world and at the same time connect with our young people." These tools, she adds, were not only "another way to archive our stories in a digital world" but also a way to "communicate amongst ourselves" (Scimeca 2015). As players progress through the gameworld, they thus come to understand that *Never Alone* is at once a story about a young girl trying to save her village from environmental trauma and a journey of self-determination. They also discover that neither the Circumpolar North nor Iñupiaq culture is static: the visual, ludic, and sonic design of *Never Alone* illustrates how tradition is fluid, contesting fetishized and exoticized representations of cultures and soundscapes.

Elizabeth LaPensée and Indigenous-Determined Video Game Design: *Invaders* and *Honour Water*

Elizabeth LaPensée is an Anishinaabe, Métis, and settler-Irish digital media scholar-practitioner whose expressive modes include writing, design, and art in games, comics, experimental animation, and other interactive media. She has shown her work in digital media installations at the annual imagineNATIVE festival and collaborated with Indigenous digital makers across Indian Country to create games and other interactive media that preserve and share Indigenous stories and oral histories, while also working to combat negative stereotypes of these cultures in the media. Her game design includes *Survivance* (2011), *Invaders* (2015), *Honour Water* (2016), *Thunderbird Strike* (2017) and, most recently, *When Rivers Were Trails* (2019), which notably features music by the Native American dancer and hip hop artist Supaman. *When Rivers Were Trails* is part of the Lessons of Our Land initiative, an innovative curriculum that enables Pre-K through grade twelve teachers to provide accessible tools and materials to incorporate Native American stories, lessons, and games into classroom instruction.

The mobile game *Invaders*, for iPad or iPhone, is a reinterpretation of the classic arcade game *Space Invaders*. Its narrative, game audio, and gameplay explore the histories and representations of settler colonial violence against Indigenous communities. (See the gameplay stills in Figure 6.2.) Like its predecessor, the goal of this fixed shooter is to defeat wave after wave of descending aliens vulnerable to traditional technologies of warfare, such as the bow and arrow, by controlling a horizontally moving laser. The player, partially protected by warriors on either side, tries to earn as many points (and destroy as many aliens) as possible before inevitably being killed. Each time the player's character is hit, a community member is lost, too. The alien invaders thus represent European colonial forces of the past and contemporary non-Indigenous settler industries that exploit ceded and unceded (essentially stolen) ancestral lands. Players adopt the perspective of the Indigenous person trying to evade colonization, but no matter how hard they try to escape colonial dominance, their characters are eliminated. This violence against Indigenous bodies continues today in the form of police brutality, socioeconomic suppression, and cultural marginalization and erasure—the latter stemming from assimilation strategies, including the censoring of language and expressive culture in Residential and Indian Boarding School systems in present-day Canada and the United States.

LaPensée's in-game artwork for *Invaders* was inspired by the artwork of Steven Paul Judd, a Native American (Choctaw) artist whose pieces incorporate figures from the original *Space Invaders* to depict representations of Indigenous peoples' confrontations with colonial settlers. He uses humor, playfully

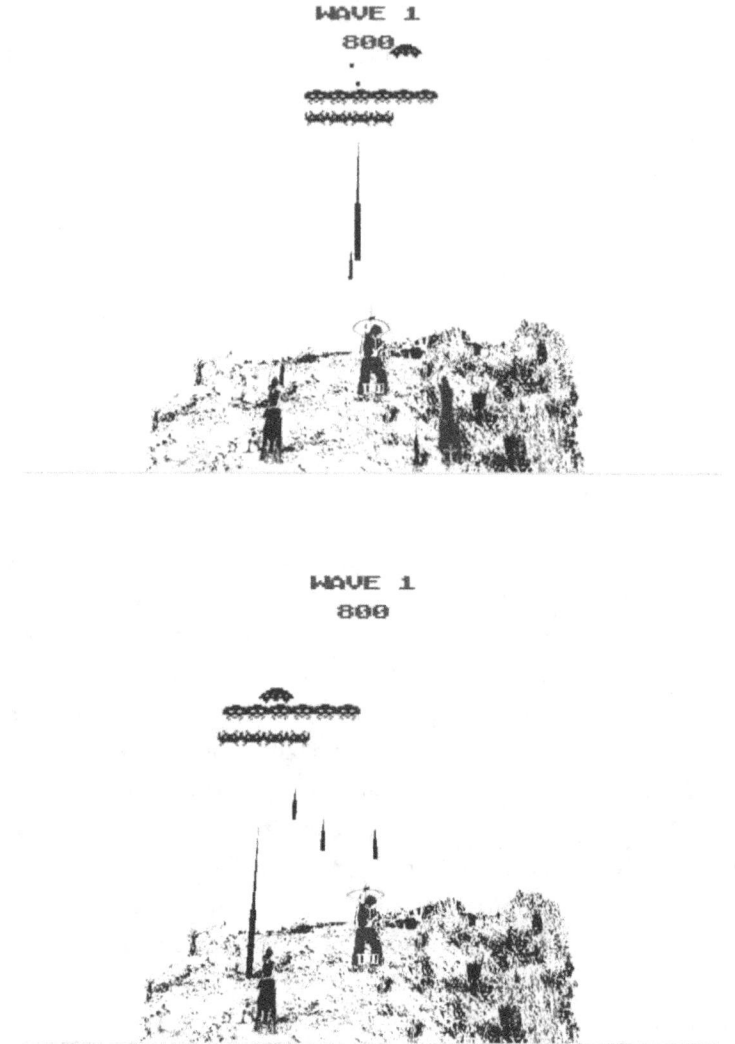

Figure 6.2 *Invaders* gameplay stills.

reinterprets preexisting images and objects, and remixes iconic images from popular culture with Indigenous cultural artifacts and stereotypes, commenting on contemporary Indigenous issues and the cultural space they occupy in the twenty-first century. LaPensée animated Judd's imagery into a playable game, collaborating on the music and sound design with the Lakota poet and musician Trevino Brings Plenty, who takes an Indigenous approach to reforming *Space Invaders*' unique soundscape. Although Trevino was born on the Cheyenne River

Sioux Reservation in South Dakota, he employs a twenty-first-century urban Indigenous perspective, challenging the dominant perspective that Indigenous creativity only comes from rural locations and reservations.

As players move the 2-D pixilated warriors left and right, shooting arrows upward at the descending alien ships, their gameplay is accompanied by a soundtrack of electronic powwow drums. The soundtrack takes drum samples—an iconic soundmark of Indigenous performance cultures from the grassland/prairie regions—and digitally remixes them to invoke Indigenous futures. It accomplishes this by remixing three specific musical features from *Space Invaders* that allow players to make audible connections between the two games. In *Invaders*, players can hear Indigenized versions of *Space Invaders*' distinctive four-note loop, uninterrupted by superimposed sound effects. Music and other sounds are activated by on-screen animation to influence player emotions, variable tempo changes correlated to changes in the on-screen narrative, as well as the player's progress.

Brings Plenty retained these iconic features while also playfully subverting and indigenizing them to create a rich sonic landscape, combining live samples with DAW plugins that merge traditional and futuristic sounds, thus decolonizing the idiom of electronic music. To create the effect, he reproduced a modified version of *Space Invaders*' iconic four-note loop, introducing an active rhythmic texture that gradually speeds up over the course of gameplay. Using an analog plugin, he produced a melodic baseline on C, B-flat, A-flat, and G that vibrates and rumbles at ninety beats per minute and then timed it to the looping sample of a hand drum recorded live. This sample, which retains a sense of live performance from audio artifacts, appears in each of the four-minute layered audio loops that shift between foreground and background. The game's densely layered soundtrack thus features interplay among the live hand drum samples, synthesized sound effects, DAW plugins, filters, "Lost in Space" pre-sets, and samples of vocality (e.g., powwow calls, warrior battle cries) treated percussively using an effect called GrossBeat. Juxtaposed against this complex network of referential samples, an ethereal sustained sequence floats on top of the thick, distorted baseline melody to present a soundworld that evokes the simultaneous presence of tradition and future.

LaPensée's *Honour Water*, a non-narrative touchscreen singing game, engages with music in another way, focusing on healing the waters and water networks that connect traditional Indigenous lands and communities. Available for free on the iPad, *Honour Water* contributes to language revitalization and transmission, featuring songs in the language of the Anishinaabeg, Anishinaabemowin.[4] The songs were approved by these communities and gifted by either Sharon Day, who coordinates Nibi Walks (Water Walks to heal the waters), the Oshkii Giizhik Singers, or elders, who provided input for placing the appropriate song selections during the singing circles and who collaborated at the Oshkii Giizhik Gathering (a weekend of Indigenous women's singing, drumming, and wellness). In this game, water teachings are interwoven with singing challenges, all accompanied by LaPensée's art.

Inspired by the Anishinaabeg gatherings that LaPensée attended at the Native American Youth and Family Center in the Pacific Northwest—a place where participants shared language, stories, food, and songs—*Honour Water* creates a similar, yet virtual, gathering space for those without access to community spaces or networks of Indigenous knowledge transmission. Due to a number of systemic and colonial societal issues, including socioeconomic, geographic, and environmental accessibility, many Indigenous women are restricted from participating in hand drum gatherings and expressions of physical community. LaPensée remediates these vital community traditions by improving accessibility and circulation among increasingly cyber-networked Indigenous youth. The water songs revised, composed, and shared by the Anishinaabekwe are also available for all people to sing, helping to widely circulate the TEK that informs how Indigenous and non-Indigenous people serve as stewards of the nonhuman environment. Indeed, this intercultural function is crucial, as toxic emissions, depletion, and pipeline spills have created a dire need for the waters to be healed.

The visuals in *Honour Water* are digitized, hand-drawn line art layered with magnified textures modified from photos of water, soil, rocks, oil, birch bark, beads, and other materials, particularly copper, which is valued by the Anishinaabe for its conductivity to transfer energy. Copper thus metaphorically transfers their culture into the game. These materials are connected to an Indigenous knowledge of the land that LaPensée personally harvested and gathered. Like the visuals, the songs in *Honour Water* convey Traditional Ecological Knowledge about the role water plays in Indigenous lifeways, the ecological crises impinging on local water systems, the scarcity of clean water, and the global water crisis affecting Indigenous and non-Indigenous, human and nonhuman beings.

Singing, here, is gameplay. Singing, recording, and sharing songs replace other games' focuses on fighting and overcoming opponents or racing to complete levels and collect items. But *Honour Water* is not without challenge. Its songs offer low-, medium-, and high-level challenges, determined by the complexity of Anishinaabemowin in the song texts, but there is no scoring system to measure accuracy or skill. Players follow scrolling texts in Anishinaabemowin and English (Figure 6.3). Playing *Honour Water* involves listening to songs and singing along,

Figure 6.3 *Honour Water* gameplay stills. Top: the song "Gizaagi'igonan Gimaamaanan Aki." Bottom: the song "Miigwech Nibi."

recorded or unrecorded. Players can choose to share their singing (and progress) by posting audio directly to social media from within the game app. The goal of this gameplay design is that through practice, Indigenous and settler players will gain comfort and confidence with singing while learning and embodying the language of the Anishinaabeg. Though Gameplay is shaped and limited by a specific branded device, games such as *Honour Water* would benefit from a more immersive gameworld space using recent VR technology. But LaPensée, who sees the multivalent advantages of presenting Indigenous ways of knowing through VR, also values community accessibility. The communities she works with and for in making these games typically have access only to the kinds of mobile and Web-based gameplay interfaces for which her games are designed.

The Vimeo site for this project includes an excerpt of gameplay footage from her game development lab drawn from the song level "Miigwech Nibi"—an expression of gratitude, thanking the waters for sustaining life (La Pensée 2016a). The example outlines a low-level challenge, which is evident in the song's repeatable phrases and beginner vocabulary. Watching and listening to this video, we can observe how the visuals correspond to images and ideas suggested by the song texts. We may also note that players are not monitored or evaluated for tone or correctness. Notably, this footage is unable to capture other integral gameplay features, like recording and sharing your own singing, pausing gameplay to conduct a close reading of the song texts, or closely examining and repeating newly encountered phrases.

LaPensée's games demonstrate what it means to design and play games for cultural survival and environmental healing. They respond to the fact that the Indigenous communities of what is now known as North America have long recognized how the waters—arteries that keep the land and its human and nonhuman communities alive—are in crisis. The Anishinaabe, like many First Nations peoples, deeply live and understand their connection to the nonhuman environment. Their traditional ancestral lands encompass the Great Lakes region, and part of their role as "water walkers" involves enacting songs and good intentions across the Great Lakes and other communities. The Anishinaabe and the culture makers who collaborated with LaPensée understand that water is vital for all life, and Traditional Ecological Knowledge about ancestral water systems can inform contemporary environmentalist policy and activism. But these same water systems are also at the center of debate in the North American resource industry, including the Idle No More movement—an ongoing protest in response to legislative abuses of Indigenous people by the

Canadian government—and, more specifically, a reaction to Bill C-45, formally known as the Jobs and Growth Act, which threatened the environment and Indigenous sovereignty. The bill, passed by the Canadian Parliament in 2012, called for the removal of protections for forests and waterways, many of which are located on ceded and unceded traditional Indigenous grounds, generating concern among Indigenous communities and environmentalists. The routes and roots of Indigenous movement across the land and by water, together with the Traditional Ecological Knowledge drawn from these waterways, are crucial to cultural vitality and resilience. Protected waterways presented a significant barrier to the energy industry, especially future oil pipeline projects, like the Enbridge Northern Gateway Pipeline, which would cross many rivers and disrupt aquatic ecosystems while moving bitumen condensate from the Athabasca tar sands to the Pacific Ocean for export. In games such as *Invaders*, *Honour Water*, *Thunderbird Strike* (2017), and *When Rivers Were Trails* (2019), LaPensée responds by creating virtual environments that promote Indigenous sovereignty, providing characters and stories to which Indigenous youth can relate, and crafting multisensory narratives of the land that offer important insights into the complex politics and land-based knowledge that should inform contemporary discussions about the global environment.

Epilogue: Listening to and Playing through Indigenous Ways of Knowing of the Land

Never Alone, *Invaders*, and *Honour Water* illustrate that participatory digital media express Indigenous ways of knowing and cosmologies "through playing with conceptualizations of time and place," as Hilder states, extending storytelling traditions and performing acts of self-determination (2017: 14). "Even when there are better representations, developers often miss the opportunity to have creative and interesting new gameplay inspired by Indigenous ways of knowing," as LaPensée argues (2016b). "I do my best to respond to these issues in my games by considering design and involving the perspectives of elders, community of Anishinaabekwewag, and youth in iterative development" (LaPensée 2016b; see also Todd 1996). Gaming technology can thus be an effective tool for sharing the language, healing, advocacy, empowerment, and Indigenous voices that continue to be marginalized or muted in our media histories.

Notes

1. For further scholarship on the repatriation of Indigenous expressive culture and recordings, as well as cultural and intellectual property issues, see Trevor Reed (2019) and Aaron Fox (2013).
2. Since some of the existing literature treats "Iñupiaq" and "Iñupiat" interchangeably, in this chapter I use Iñupiaq to refer to either individuals, the culture, or the language, while I use Iñupiat for multiple people (MacLean 2014: 109).
3. For foundational scholarship on the analysis of the function of game sound in world-building and the relationship of game sound to a player's experience of narrative and environment, see Summers (2011), Fritsch (2014), Gibbons (2016), and Collins (2013b).
4. Scholars of Indigenous cultural resilience and sustainability, including the ethnomusicologists Tara Browner (2000), Beverley Diamond (2008), Klisala Harrison (2009), Anna Hoefnagles (2012; 2004; 2002), and Janice Tulk (2006), note that women's hand drum circles continue to be an important site for language transmission, community building, and cultural resilience.

References

Anable, A. (2018), *Playing with Feelings: Video Games and Affect*, Minneapolis: University of Minnesota Press.

Archibald, J. (2008), *Indigenous Storywork: Educating the Heart, Mind, Body, and Spirit*, Vancouver, BC: University of British Columbia Press.

Armstrong, H. (2013), "Indigenizing the Curriculum: The Importance of Story," *First Nations Perspectives*, 5: 37–64.

Browner, T. (2000), "Making and Singing Pow-Wow Songs: Text, Form, and the Significance of Culture-Based Analysis," *Ethnomusicology*, 44 (2): 214–33.

Cleveland, R. (1980), *Unipchaanich Imagluktugmiut: Stories of the Black River People*, trans. R. Ramoth-Sampson and A. Newlin, Anchorage: National Bilingual Materials Development Center.

Collins, K. (2013a), "Implications of Interactivity: What Does It Mean for Sound to be 'Interactive?'," in J. Richardson, C. Gorbman, and C. Vernallis (eds.), *The Oxford Handbook of New Audiovisual Aesthetics*, 572–84, Oxford: Oxford University Press.

Collins, K. (2013b), *Playing with Sound: A Theory of Interacting with Sound and Music in Video Games*, Cambridge, MA: MIT Press.

Davis, J. (2014), "Towards a Further Understanding of What Indigenous People Have Always Known: Storytelling as the Basis of Good Pedagogy," *First Nations Perspectives*, 6: 83–96.

Deloria, P. J. (2004), *Indians in Unexpected Places*, Lawrence: University Press of Kansas.

Diamond, B. (2008), *Native American Music in Eastern North America: Experiencing Music, Expressing Culture*, Oxford: Oxford University Press.

Dyson, L., M. Hendriks, and S. Grant, eds., (2006), *Information Technology and Indigenous Peoples*, London and Melbourne: Information Science Publishing.

Fox, A. (2013), "Repatriation as Reanimation through Reciprocity," in P. Bohlman (ed.), *The Cambridge History of World Music*, 522–54, Cambridge: Cambridge University Press.

Fritsch, M. (2014), "Worlds of Music: Strategies for Creating Music-Based Experiences in Video Games," in K. Collins, B. Kapralos, and H. Tessler (eds.), *The Oxford Handbook of Interactive Audio*, 167–80, Oxford: Oxford University Press.

Galanin, Nicholas (2017), "Artist Nicholas Galanin on 'Tsu Heidei Shugaxtutaan,' " *The Contemporary Jewish Museum*. https://vimeo.com/194085564 (accessed March 23, 2017).

Gibbons, W. (2016), "Game Audio," in H. Lowood and R. Guins (eds.), *Debugging Game History: A Critical Lexicon*, 159–67, Cambridge: MIT Press.

Haraway, D. (2016), *Staying with the Trouble: Making Kin in the Chthulucene*, Durham, NC: Duke University Press.

Harrison, K. (2009), " 'Singing My Spirit of Identity': Aboriginal Music for Well-Being in a Canadian Inner City," *MUSICultures*, 36: 1–21.

Hilder, T. R. (2017), "Music, Indigeneity, Digital Media: An Introduction," in T. R. Hilder, H. Stobbart, and S. E. Tan (eds.), *Music, Indigeneity, Digital Media*, 1–27, Rochester: University of Rochester Press.

Hoefnagels, A. (2002), "Powwow Songs: Traveling Songs and Changing Protocol," *The World of Music*, 44 (1): 127–36.

Hoefnagels, A. (2004), "Northern Style Powwow Music: Musical Features and Meanings," *MUSICultures*, 31. https://journals.lib.unb.ca/index.php/MC/article/view/21605 (accessed September 1, 2020).

Hoefnagels, A. (2012), "Complementarity and Cultural Ideals: Women's Roles in Contemporary Canadian Powwows," *Women and Music: A Journal of Gender and Culture*, 16 (1): 1–22.

Hogan, B. (2014), "Guest Blog: How the Sound and Music Came Together," *Never Alone*, December 14. http://neveralonegame.com/sound-music-came-together/ (accessed September 1, 2020).

King, T. (2003), *The Truth about Stories*, Toronto: House of Anansi Press.

Kovach, M. (2009), *Indigenous Methodologies: Characteristics, Conversations, and Contexts*, Toronto: University of Toronto Press.

Kovach, M. (2015), "Emerging from the Margins: Indigenous Methodologies," in L. Brown and S. Strega (eds.), *Research as Resistance: Revisiting Critical, Indigenous, and Anti-oppressive Approaches*, 43–64, Toronto: Canadian Scholars' Press.

Krause, B. (2015), *Voices of the Wild: Animal Songs, Human Din, and the Call to Save Natural Soundscapes*, New Haven: Yale University Press.

LaPensée, E. (2016a), "Honour Water: Miigwech Nibi," *Vimeo*, October 10. https://vimeo.com/186309019 (accessed September 15, 2020).

LaPensée, E. (2014), "Indigenously-Determined Games of the Future," *kimiwan zine*, Indigenous Futurisms, 8.

LaPenseé, E. (2016b), "Mobile Game 'Honour Water' Aims to Heal the Waters through Song," *IVOH*, August 29. https://ivoh.org/news/mobile-game-honour-water-aims-heal-waters-song/ (accessed September 1, 2020).

LaPenseé, E. (2017), "Video Games Encourage Indigenous Cultural Expression," *The Conversation*, March 21. https://theconversation.com/video-games-encourage-indigenous-cultural-expression-74138 (accessed October 2, 2020).

Levine, V. (2019), "Music, Modernity, and Indigeneity: Introductory Notes," in V. Levine and D. Robinson (eds.), *Music and Modernity among First Peoples of North America*, 1–12, Middletown, CT: Wesleyan University Press.

Loft, S. (2014), "Decolonizing the 'Web,' " in S. Loft and K. Swanson (eds.), *Coded Territories: Tracing Indigenous Pathways in New Media Art*, xv–xvii, Calgary, AB: University of Calgary Press.

MacLean, E. A. (2014), *Iñupiatun Uqaluit Taniktun Sivuninit/ Iñupiaq to English Dictionary*, Fairbanks, AK: University of Alaska Press.

Parkinson, H. J. (2014), "Alaska's Indigenous Game *Never Alone* Teaches Co-Operation through Stories," *The Guardian*, September 29. https://www.theguardian.com/technology/2014/sep/29/never-alone-alaskas-indigenous-game-never-alone-teaches-cooperation-through-stories (accessed October 3, 2020).

Ochoa Gautier, A. M. (2016), "Acoustic Multinaturalism, the Value of Nature, and the Nature of Music in Ecomusicology," *boundary 2*, 43 (1): 107–41.

Reed, T. (2019), "Reclaiming Ownership of the Indigenous Voice: The Hopi Music Repatriation Project," in F. Gunderson, R. C. Lancefield, and B. Woods (eds.), *The Oxford Handbook of Musical Repatriation*, 627–54, Oxford: Oxford University Press.

Scimeca, D. (2015), "Why *Never Alone* Is So Much More than a Video Game," *The Kernal*, March 1. http://kernelmag.dailydot.com/issue-sections/features-issue-sections/11965/never-alone-alaska-native-video-game/#sthash.KHysvFBy.dpuf (accessed August 13, 2020).

Starkey, D. (2015), "*Never Alone* and the Need for American Indian Narratives in Games," *Polygon*, June 29. https://www.polygon.com/2015/6/29/8852519/never-alone-american-indian (accessed December 10, 2019).

Summers, T. (2011), "Playing the Tune: Video Game Music, Gamers, and Genre," *Act-Zeitschrift für Musik & Performance*, 2: 2–27. https://epub.uni-bayreuth.de/322/1/ACT2011_02_Summers.pdf (accessed December 10, 2019).

Todd, L. (1996), "Aboriginal Narratives in Cyberspace," in M. A. Moser and D. McLeod (eds.), *Immersed in Technology: Art and Virtual Environments*, 179–94, Cambridge, MA: MIT Press.

Todd, Z. (2014), "Fish Pluralities: Human-Animal Relations and Sites of Engagement in Paulatuuq, Arctic Canada," *Études/Inuit/Studies*, 38 (1–2): 217–38.

Todd, Z. (2016), "Indigenizing the Anthropocene: Prairie Indigenous Feminisms and Fish Co-Conspirators," *Fisher Centre for the Study of Women and Men, Hobart and William Smith Colleges*, Spring Speakers Series.

Todd, Z. (2017), "Fish, Kin and Hope: Tending to Water Violations in Amiskwaciwâskahikan and Treaty Six Territory," *Afterall: A Journal of Art, Context and Enquiry*, 43 (1): 102–7.

Tulk, J. E. (2006), "Traditional, Contest, or Something In-Between: A Case Study of Two Mi'kmaq Powwows," *MUSICultures*, 33: 15–31.

7

Finding Home in the Unknown: Sounding Self-Determination from the Streets to the Void

Andrew J. Kluth

> I'll follow the stars when the sun goes to bed,
> 'Til everything I've ever known is long dead.
> I can't go back home 'cause I want to be free,
> Someone tell the others what's become of me.
>
> —clipping., "Long Way Away (Intro)"

Indistinct and reverberating as if transmitted from far away, a lonely voice delivers these lines to open clipping.'s 2016 EP, *Splendor & Misery*. Set to melodic strains reminiscent of a spiritual, these verses evoke the dignity and sorrow of that genre's history before abruptly shifting to a fast-rapped narrative describing recent events aboard some kind of ship. Are we in the past? The future? Both? Neither? As it unfolds, this temporally liminal narrative makes apparent the record's allusions to Afrofuturism (Dery 1994: 180; Lillvis 2017: 58). It collapses time by mobilizing ancient, contemporary, and futuristic imagery and soundscapes into a strange loop of signifiers that, as Kodwo Eshun notes, are "concerned with possibilities for intervention within the dimensions of the predictive, the projected, the proleptic, the envisioned, the virtual, the anticipatory, and the future conditional" (2003: 293). What results is an indeterminate, sci-fi-tinged "counter-history" that projects the history of African American diaspora and enslavement into an expansive, speculative story of agency and hope in the face of nihilism and existential dread.

To better understand the larger context for the narrative of *Splendor & Misery*, the listener must know the history of chattel slavery in the United States, wherein for four hundred years colonizing enslavers stole and objectified Africans to be sold for labor in the Americas. The calculus of dehumanization that underpinned the terrorism and violence of the Transatlantic slave trade revolved around the idea that humans of African descent were different from those of European descent—somehow less-than, animals to be abused and exploited. These ideologies, which did not end with the formal abolition of slavery in 1863, still inform contemporary North American culture. Indeed, in the decades following the Civil War, the injustice of slavery found new manifestations in anti-Black racist policing, lynching, and Jim Crow laws enforcing segregation (as McGraw discusses in Chapter 1). These were accompanied by unfair housing practices and limited access to education and jobs for Black Americans. Despite the passage of the 1964 Civil Rights Act and the Voting Rights Act of 1965, policing informed by racial profiling, broken windows policing, and stop-and-frisk continued to advance anti-Black racism, even through the supposedly "post-racial" years of President Barack Obama's administration. Amiri Baraka (LeRoi Jones) calls this temporal hall of mirrors the "changing same" of the Black experience in the United States, finding the material and affective outcomes of enslavement in ever-new iterations of Black cultural expression ([1968] 1998). He locates a slipping relationality between the content and structure of Black music, whereby music that is emblematic of collective racial experience might take on new forms while conveying the same story. He further suggests that every new iteration of Black music in the United States reflects the persistent degradation and exploitation that "through its many changes ... [has] remained the exact replication of The Black Man In The West" ([1968] 1998: 180). This repeating logic informs the soundworld in which *Splendor & Misery*'s main character, Cargo #2331—I will refer to him as "Cargo"—must locate himself and make sense of his life.

Cargo's experience of his world is not temporally linear. Suspended animation has allowed him to travel great distances while stretching his life far beyond that of normal human experience. As such, *Splendor & Misery* is an anti-fatalist time-travel narrative much like Kurt Vonnegut's *Slaughterhouse-Five* (1969). The great insight given to Vonnegut's protagonist, Billy Pilgrim, is the recognition that time's linearity is an illusion wrought by humanity's inability to perceive its asynchronous totality. For Pilgrim, this revelation neutralizes the idea of free will and the bite of suffering by flattening ethical and moral positions in its negation of possibility and choice-making; he realizes that all things always are. Horizons are thus closed in this imagined reality, all possibilities having always already been played out, available for simultaneous experience.

Cargo, too, has come unstuck in time, but in his world no concrete aggregate reality exists. His horizons of hope, imagination, and self-determination remain open. Ethical and moral positions definitely matter, and the logic of the changing same, in spite of appearances, is not totalizing. This relationship between remembered history, experienced present, and imagined future is what clipping. explores through Cargo's engagement with sound and listening. Listening, we are shown, is a path to agency and self-determination—indeed, its role in the construction of identity constitutes how we might more fruitfully engage in political discourse, creating the self through engagement with the Other.

To better explore this world I borrow the idea that hip hop is a Black sonic technology (Akomfrah 1996; Eshun 2003: 295), employing sound as an intertextual signifying space—a sonic mix that transcends bricolage or pastiche as an epiphenomenal vector between the physical plane of acoustic space and the transcendental plane of reason (Weheliye 2005: 83). *Splendor & Misery* is structurally and thematically dense, and so, to navigate its narrative trajectory with some economy, I use four tracks—"All Black," "Wake Up," "Long Way Away," and "A Better Place"—as analytical handholds (see Table 7.1 for a complete track listing). These points of reference not only tell the story of an enslaved person alone and adrift in the blackness of space but connect that story to related ideas of the construction of self and meaning.

Table 7.1 *Splendor & Misery* (2016) track listing, totaling thirty-seven minutes

1. Long Way Away (Intro)	1:06
2. The Breach	0:56
3. All Black	6:15
4. Interlude 01 (Freestyle)	1:35
5. Wake Up	2:05
6. Long Way Away	1:31
7. Interlude 02 (Numbers)	1:04
8. True Believer	3:45
9. Long Way Away (Instrumental)	0:52
10. Air 'Em Out	3:50
11. Interlude 03 (Freestyle)	1:09
12. Break the Glass	2:22
13. Story 5	3:04
14. Baby Don't Sleep	3:07
15. A Better Place	4:26

With William Hutson and Jonathan Snipes as producers and Daveed Diggs as MC, clipping. emerged from the Los Angeles creative music scene. Its members shared many of their formative years: Diggs and Hutson grew up as friends in the San Francisco Bay area, while Hutson and Snipes were college roommates (see Figure 7.1). Invested in underground hip hop and various traditions of musical experimentalism, Hutson and Snipes began making harsh noise/power electronics remixes of rap *a capellas* for their own amusement. When Diggs heard these, he began improvising and writing bars (lyrically rhythmic hip hop verses) over their compositions, resulting in the group's first EP, *Midcity* (2013). This record set the tone for future clipping. releases that featured familiar hip hop themes of power, oppression, resistance, urban plight, desire, sex, drugs, and violence encased within thoughtful, intelligent, self-reflexive, and sometimes ironic narratives. Digg's lines are plotted against a backdrop of found sounds,

Figure 7.1 Clipping. From left to right: Jonathan Snipes, William Hutson, and Daveed Diggs. Photo credit: Suzy Poling.

harsh noise samples, ring modulators, and analog synthesizers that are just as indebted to the Euro-American avant-garde tradition as to the sampled beats, loops, and trap 808 sounds typical of hip hop. An early example of this marrying of influences is the outro of 2013's *Midcity*, which features a ten-minute phasing loop of the phrase "get money," evoking Steve Reich's 1960s minimalist tape works "It's Gonna Rain" and "Come Out."

"Noise" is an important concept for clipping. On album releases prior to *Splendor & Misery*, Daveed Diggs would announce, "It's clipping, bitch," during the opening tracks as a kind of warning shot. There is a double entendre here: "clipping" is not only the band's name but also an audio engineering term that implies waveform distortion, typically signaling that something is wrong. This play on words in the opening tracks calls attention to their intentional deployment of "noise" and polysemy, setting listener expectations by suggesting that meaning-making and one's capacity for being-in-the-world is distorted by the noise of contemporary life.

The group signed to Seattle indie label Sub Pop and, in 2014, released *CLPPNG*, a true-to-form rap record whose idiosyncratic hip hop cuts are complemented by a reading of John Cage's early 1950s electronic composition, *Williams Mix*. When these records were produced, Hutson had recently finished a PhD in Theater and Media studies at the University of California, Los Angeles, Snipes was intermittently teaching sound design in the same department, and Diggs had originated the parts of Marquis de Lafayette and Thomas Jefferson in Lin-Manuel Miranda's Broadway smash, *Hamilton*. It was while engaged in these other projects that clipping. produced their next record, *Splendor & Misery*, which was nominated for a Hugo Award for Best Dramatic Presentation, Short Form in 2017 (Heller 2017).

Building on the aesthetic of the records and mixtapes before it, *Splendor & Misery* maintains clipping.'s challenging sonic pallet and Diggs's fast-paced rapping to map the feeling of the record's urban context onto an indeterminate future. Taking its title from an unfinished science fiction manuscript of author Samuel R. Delany, the record reveals its narrative and atmospheric logic through complex, synthetic, mechanical, and sometimes violent soundscapes. As it unfolds, we learn that the protagonist is the futuristic equivalent of a "runaway slave," adrift and ostensibly alone, having been awoken from suspended animation after an accident on a cargo spaceship. Removed from a recognizable environment, he is disrupted, nameless, cultureless, reduced to an object, Cargo #2331—a familiar trope in enslavement narratives, as Baraka (Jones) reminds us: "A 'cultureless' people is a people without a memory. No history. This is the best state for slaves; to be objects, just like the rest of massa's possessions" ([1968] 1998: 182). We do not know who has enslaved Cargo, where he is being taken, or for what purpose. Enhancing the precarity of his situation, Cargo lives in fear as his captors pursue him and the lost ship. (See Figure 7.2 for visual indications of Cargo's enslavement on the album's cover art.) clipping. emplaces this narrative in a sonic world for the listener, setting found sounds (in the manner of *musique-concrète*) against ambient drones and *a capella* vocal music supplied by members of the eight-time Grammy-winning gospel sextet, Take 6. Through this aural amalgam we are pushed into an imagined interspace that is as much a memory of the future as it is the historical and socio-cultural reality of the Black diaspora in the United States.

Figure 7.2 *Splendor &Misery* cover art, featuring Cargo as an astronaut with tattered clothes and previously shackled feet.

The soundworld of *Splendor & Misery* is informed by Euro-American experimentalism and the "noise" one might expect from this tradition. As theorized in sound studies, noise disrupts, de-centers, dissolves, disembodies, or otherwise confuses order (Schafer 1998). Though potentially destructive, it can also produce transformation. Paul Hegarty suggests noise can create a space wherein perceived cognitive and ontological opposites are reevaluated: "Noise transvalues listener and subject, noise and music, hearing and listening, perception and its failure, performance and its failure, noise and its failure to be music, noise and its failure to be noise" (Hegarty 2007: 200). The anonymous group of theorists, *GegenSichKollektiv*, echoes this assessment:

> Rather than trying to reconcile knowing and feeling, noise can help us to dissociate the commensurability of experience and subjectivity in a sense that exceeds the logic of framing, by either being too much, too complex, too dense and difficult to decode, or too chaotic to be measured. One cannot have mastery over it.
>
> (2012: 194)

By frustrating a subject's previous parameters for understanding, noise can center attention and intention, inviting the listener to focus on the cognitive and embodied work of meaning-making.

Like Cargo, the noise of the album's soundworld stuns the listener into a space of confused focus that resists conceptual and temporal framing. We are confronted with sonic signifiers that evade the narrative tropes of the story, notions of "music" in general, and hip hop conventions in particular. If we engage with this soundworld despite aesthetic discomfort, its noise forces us to suspend value judgments of good or bad, right or wrong. Its sonic and epistemic alienation reflects the placeless interspace of the non-self that frustrates all positions and position-taking. The listener therefore joins Cargo adrift, laboring to apprehend this world, reaching out to make our own meaning of the situation at hand. Along with noise, *Splendor & Misery*'s swirling sonic signifiers and narratives make a pastiche of ancient, real/contemporary, and speculative/future sounds. This temporal convergence is a familiar Afrofuturist strategy, mobilizing ideas from different times to create a counter-history (Steinskog 2018: 111). The resulting confusion and disruption of linear time throughout the album challenges Cargo's understanding of the world and his place therein. Roger Savage notes that our identities are especially fragile with respect to their perceived permanence in time. The contiguity of identity depends as much on memory as on personal and social projections of possible futures (2013: 66). Thus, a breakdown in Cargo's perceived linearity of time problematizes the relationship between memory, present experience, and imagination, all of which produce and maintain notions of selfhood. Cargo must ask himself: Does the person he is now share an identity with the person he has been? What are his motivations and goals in the context of this new life?

In addition to noise and temporal perturbations, narrative asides and a literal multiplicity of voices trouble Cargo's reconstruction of identity. Diggs plays the roles of both omniscient narrator and the ship's artificial intelligence, with whom Cargo will eventually find a meaningful, emotional connection. Members of Take 6 offer interjections that repeatedly develop the phrase, "It's a long way away ...," as a fragment of a cosmic spiritual. At the record's opening, a disembodied voice (Paul Outlaw) introduces themes of enslavement and cosmic drift. This same voice later sings the bittersweet hook informed by liberation theology that punctuates the recitation of African and science fiction cosmologies in "True Believer." While the album's first two tracks acquaint us with Cargo and his situation, "All Black" presents Cargo's struggle as he apprehends it, reflecting on his past while considering his possible future.

Fittingly, "All Black" (track three, Table 7.1) involves the dissolution of self and the nihilism it might engender. A hip hop meme popularized by Jay-Z, Kanye West, Lupe Fiasco, Young Jeezy, and many others, the phrase "All Black Everything" usually alludes to a self-identification with African American pride, power, or agency. Jay-Z's "all black everything" refers to branding for his Roc Nation empire with toeholds in music, markets, and politics. Lupe Fiasco's "all black everything" imagines a utopic world without the historical oppression of African peoples that instead benefits from Black excellence. When Diggs applies the phrase to Cargo's situation, it becomes further poly-indexical, standing as much for the "all black" of the void of outer space as the existential "all black" of inner space. If anyone has a right to indulge in nihilistic ideation, it would be Cargo, whose experience rhymes with that of enslaved Africans during the Transatlantic slave trade. Protended into this futuristic cosmic narrative, Cargo bears what Cornel West called Black existential angst derived from the "lived experience of ontological wounds and emotional scars inflicted by white supremacist beliefs and images permeating U.S. society and culture" (1993: 27). The resulting threat of nihilism's loss of hope and meaning maps onto Cargo's circumstance, suggesting that without hope there can be no future, and without meaning there can be no struggle.

And yet Cargo does struggle. His struggle for agency and meaning is aided by the sound, music, and noise of *Splendor & Misery*, evoking the dual legacy of Black and Euro-American experimentalisms. Arriving from different lineages, these strategies merge and transcend their oppositional provenances to create a new synthetic whole. To make sense of this, it is helpful to consider George Lewis's characterizations of Afrological and Eurological subjectivities of musical experimentalism (1996). David Borgo has concisely summarized these ideas, noting that an Afrological perspective "implies an emphasis on personal narrative and the harmonization of one's musical personality with social environments, both actual and possible." By contrast, a Eurological perspective "implies either absolute freedom from personal narrative, culture, and conventions—an autonomy of the aesthetic object—or the need for a controlling or structuring force in the person and voice of a 'composer' " (Borgo 2002: 171). We can read a combination of these impulses in the sounds of Cargo's world, hearing "All Black" as a struggle to understand the concept of freedom somewhere between a *musique concrète* piece and a hip hop track. Low frequencies approaching the infrasonic are reminiscent of cosmic horror film soundtracks, evoking the haunted atmosphere of a spaceship's hulking mass with implications of paranormal or religious awe (Mühlhans 2017: 275–9). Hip hop's familiar signifying of Black sonic masculinity can also be heard in this sonic field (Belle 2014: 288), while disembodied electronic bleeps and bloops punctuate harsh atmospheric air sounds provided by experimental trumpet player Graham Stephenson. Though we only meet Cargo acousmatically, his enslavement narrative and the grain of Diggs's vocal timbre mobilize an African American subjectivity and history through what Nina Eidsheim has called a "phantom genealogy" of sonic Blackness (2019: 66). We are in an Afrofuturistic sonic space, but rather than a utopic and self-determinative version redolent of Sun Ra, George Clinton or, more recently, Janelle Monáe, Cargo's life and musical world is—at first hearing—unmistakably dystopic. Conflicts between the histories and power dynamics implied by the presence of Eurological and Afrological experimental strategies mix and dissolve into something new as the soundworld unfolds with Cargo's narrative. We come to realize that, despite repeated invocations of the Bible and the frequent presence of *a capella* gospel music throughout, Cargo's story is out of step with the telos of liberation theology. There is no prophesy to make sense of his plight, no messiah to save him or give meaning to his struggle. Still, as the album progresses, we learn that, somehow, hope is not entirely lost.

After a dreamlike interlude we arrive at "Wake Up" (track five, Table 7.1), in which a narration of Cargo's memories and decisions is set against frenetic electronic pulses and strains of the now-familiar "Long Way Away." In "Wake Up," we learn how Cargo's experience uncouples past from present as he mourns the familiarity of his past life. Enslavement has removed him from his familiar identity-informing personal and social structures, as well as the futures they had enabled him to imagine. Reinhart Koselleck describes these temporal metahistorical categories as the "space of experience" and the "horizon of expectation," noting how "the one is not to be had without the other" (2002: 257). In these terms, Cargo's meta-historical "horizon of expectation" has been disrupted from its relationship to the memories informing his "space of experience," leaving him in a void wherein all things can be reimagined. This is reflected in the opening lyrics of "Wake Up":

> The chance that he ever reaches any place,
> Suitable to support life in his lifetime's pretty low.
> (Get low) pretty low (get low) …
> And the chances of him of ever seeing anybody that he knows,
> Are even lower so he's making up his mind to just go.

The track subsides into the dirge-like *a capella* of "Long Way Away" (track six, Table 7.1), whose affect and lyrics explore the generational trauma described by West through the sounds of African American spirituals. Diggs confirms this reading in an interview for *UPROXX*, evoking the transcendence of pain and oppression felt by enslaved African Americans as they ran from their captors: "So much about coded slave spirituals were about leaving behind where they're at … the philosophy behind them was about transcending place. They were about home actually being in the unknown" (White 2016). The lyrical sentiment and soundworld of these tracks embrace the unknown, perhaps reflecting the hopes of those who relied on the stars for navigation while fleeing enslavement via the underground railroad. After reflecting on his loneliness, far from anything he could imagine as home, the protagonist asserts:

> There's no use in crying, no reason to wait. (… long way away …)
> We'll not again meet 'cause the distance is great. (… long way away …)
> But look to the stars when the sun is long gone. (… long way away …)
> And pray that your children do not sing this song.

Whereas African American spirituals typically presuppose the "good news" implied by Christianity's liberation theology, their symbolic tropes take on new meanings in this context. Lacking the promise of a prophesied messiah, it is up to Cargo to manifest his own future, imagined but not-yet present.

Lost among the stars, the revelations of "Wake Up" demonstrate Cargo's resolve to take action and affirm his self-determination. Almost miraculously, he is able to locate himself anew and manifest a different path for himself. This capacity for self-determination is founded on the principles of Afrofuturism that inspire the album. Consider, for example, the opening of the 1974 film, *Space Is the Place*, which begins with Sun Ra as a kind of prophet walking through a garden on what is ostensibly a far-away planet, saying:

> The music is different here. The vibrations are different. Not like planet Earth; the sound of guns, anger and frustration. There was no one to talk to on Planet Earth who would understand. We should set up a colony for black people here … see what they can do on a planet all their own without any white people there. They could drink in the beauty of this planet. It would affect their vibrations— for the better, of course. Another place in the universe up under different stars; that would be where the alter-destiny would come in.

If Sun Ra borrows from liberation theology, evoking "a better place" prophesied for a chosen people long held in captivity, his hope for freedom from the oppressor is still framed by oppressive power structures. In the remainder of *Splendor & Misery*, however, Cargo instantiates a new world no longer informed by these structures. The paralogical hope gained by traveling through the void derives from the realization that old power structures no longer define his horizon of possibilities. This inversion, which unseats nihilism's negations, is explored in a write-up about the record on Sub Pop's website:

> In a reversal of H.P. Lovecraft's concept of cosmic insignificance, the character [Cargo] finds relief in learning that humanity is of no consequence to the vast, uncaring universe. It turns out, pulling the rug out from under anthropocentrism is only horrifying to those who thought they were the center of everything to begin with.

But if all seemed to have been lost, by what process does Cargo begin to know himself in this radically open horizon of expectation? It is through his engagement with sound and listening that he comes to free himself of the received systems of valuation that have structured his notions of possibility, opening himself up for something utterly new. Cargo thus engages in a process of existential self-sounding that generates a reflexive awareness of his existence and contingent agency. The narrator describes Cargo in "All Black" as follows:

> Paranoia prone, he babbles beautifully of Babylon and enemies and foes,
> And forgoing food sustains himself on anger.
> A danger to himself and others but there are no others,
> So, the danger clear and present is presented as
> The gift of freedom wrapped in days,
> Of rapping to himself until his vocal cords collapse.

The concealing blackness of his surroundings structures his experience, forcing him to wait upon even the reverberations of his own shouts as he counts the seconds until their return. With his framing of identity gone, Cargo begins to recognize that he "is" by listening to the sound of his own voice in speech and music. While reminiscent of Descartes's famous revelation, Cargo's story is not invested in the logic of mind/body dualism, differing greatly in its cosmological and ontological assumptions. Instead, having been made a stranger to himself, Cargo labors to construct an identity by sounding the boundaries (as in to "sound the depths") of his potential being in this new world. Speech, while conventionally associated with order and knowledge in the form of *logos*, does not create order or knowledge: it must also have a listener. As Lisbeth Lipari argues, "a *logos* that speaks without listening" cannot lead to understanding and, as such, "is no *logos* at all" (2014: 5). Listening is necessarily reflexive and situates the listener in a social and ethical field, just as one cannot touch without also being touched; indeed, listening and speaking are present even when one is alone and thinking. Accordingly, Lipari asks:

> When I'm thinking silently to myself, am I speaking or listening? If I'm speaking (or listening), then who's listening (or speaking)? And along those lines, do I listen not only to words with my mind, but also to the music of the voice in my ears, and the posture and the gesture of the body with my eyes, the vibrational rhythm of others' pulsations, movements, and intonations in my body?
>
> (2014: 9)

These ethics of listening are crucial to Cargo's narrative of self-determination and illustrate how attending intentionally to sound is always a meaning- and community-building activity, even when the subject is ostensibly alone. Moreover, this attests to the reality that our worlds are ever changing and that whatever truth is, our understanding of it is always a negotiation.

Supporting Lipari, Jean-Luc Nancy's ideas attest to the primacy of listening as a clue toward understanding the process of how subjects might "be" in the world, noting that "the self" and even "truth" are never completed or foreclosed from processes of refiguration but are transitive and continually changing. Our experiences of reality are thus flexible, not concretized. Nancy suggests that if we listen to the resonance of the changing world and continually reassess our ideas of truth and self, we must recognize truth as something mutable, not "itself" in any permanent way: "[N]o longer the naked figure emerging from the cistern but the resonance of that cistern—or, if it were possible to express it thus, the echo of the naked figure in the open depths?" ([2002] 2007: 4). This revelation from the sonorous register is dependent first and foremost upon the reality of the self-reflexive self, entangled in feeling-oneself-feel. Analogous to sonar technologies, wherein the perceived distances of sonic repetition in space physically locates objects, Cargo locates his identity anew on the ship and existentially in the cosmos: "He shouts at the dark, stands back / counting the seconds before his voice returns. / All black everything." Because sound is contemporaneous with the subject as meaning, sound, and self, they all share the same form, structure, or movement, "namely *renvoi*, resonance" (Kane 2012: 446). Thus, as Cargo begins to take hold of the possibilities of his self-determination, he imaginatively protends this resonance of self into an open horizon no longer described by his previously dominating captors.

The record's closing track, "A Better Place" (track fifteen, Table 7.1), makes it clear that Cargo has accepted his hard-fought agency through the labor of new meaning-making. The sound of a triumphant organ in a major key supports the return of the spiritual-inspired melody heard in the record's opening, now joined by these words:

> If ever you find yourself beaten and broke,
> And can't feel the whip for the weight of the yoke,
> And fear that the night will not turn into day,
> Remember the darkness will show you the way.

Though still a "long way away," Cargo's alienation is being recovered. He has manifested a mode of self-determination not by dominating previously extant power dynamics but by breaking from and rejecting their power over him, recognizing the open field in which he might exercise his agency. His story reminds us that our encounters with sound and music can be profound bulwarks against nihilism's annihilation, not mere whistling in the dark to feign courage. We realize that the listening subject's self-sounding is in fact the ontological ground that enables self-determination. The music accompanying Cargo's narrative models his experience of memory, discontiguity, and imagination, pushing the listener to make a meaningful, synthetic whole of its disparate symbolic archives. In so doing, listeners are invited to identify with Cargo's process, to wager a newly meaningful future for themselves.

Hearing Cargo's story we are reminded that, even when alone, each of us comprises a community of listening and speaking. Cargo sounds himself in his solitude and thus becomes a subject capable of imagining and constructing a new understanding of himself. Moreover, connecting the idea of self-sounding discussed above to how we "be" with others asks us to reconsider the very notion of the singular self, recognizing that the idea of the "I" removed from the "we" is an abstraction that cannot truly exist (Nancy [1996] 2000: 7). As I have shown, listening is an ethical activity that engages a community of listeners and speakers. In music, as in life, listening is a necessary and foundational activity that characterizes how we interact with ourselves and others. The "we" constructed by listening constitutes our self-understanding while simultaneously building the world we share with others, mutually laboring to find home in the unknown. Listening generates political space and the possibility of offering equal standing to others in a realm of peers, "neither ruling or being ruled, but engaging with one another in joint speech and action" (Bickford 1996: 57). Cargo's narrative and the aesthetic logic of his soundworld model the complexities of our own and the struggles we may face to locate ourselves in received histories, the challenging present, and the potential becoming of the open horizon.

I write these words in the summer of 2020, when the inequitable inheritances of enslavement and anti-Black racism that characterize the lived experience of Black communities in the United States are being addressed in clearer words and actions than I have seen in my lifetime. Whatever our own relationship to this reality, it is our collective task to listen to ourselves and others, manifesting a more equitable world from that space. We can learn much from the Afrofuturist logics of *Splendor & Misery*, which challenge us to shatter the changing same's reverberating hall of mirrors and to interrupt the systemic legacies of racism, patriarchy, and homophobia in the United States. To quote Eshun, "perhaps Science Fiction is never concerned with the future, but rather with the engineering feedback between its preferred future and its becoming present" (2003: 290). In this sense, *Splendor & Misery* reorients the struggle for agency and self-determination from the context of the Black experience in the United States to the greater existential challenges of the void.

References

Baraka, A. [LeRoi Jones] ([1968] 1998), *Black Music*, New York: Da Capo Press.

Belle, C. (2014), "From Jay-Z to Dead Prez: Examining Representations of Black Masculinity in Mainstream versus Underground Hip-Hop Music," *Journal of Black Studies*, 45 (4): 287–300.

Bickford, S. (1996), *The Dissonance of Democracy: Listening, Conflict, and Citizenship*, New York: Cornell University Press.

Borgo, D. (2002), "Negotiating Freedom: Values and Practices in Contemporary Improvised Music," *Black Music Research Journal*, 22 (2): 165–88.

CLPPNG (2014), [Sound Recording] clipping., USA: Sub Pop.

Dery, M. (1994), "Black to the Future: Interviews with Samuel R. Delany, Greg Tate, and Tricia Rose," in M. Dery (ed.), *Flame Wars: The Discourse on Cyberculture*, 179–222, Durham, NC: Duke University Press.

Eidsheim, N. S. (2019), *The Race of Sound: Listening, Timbre, and Vocality in African American Music*, Durham, NC: Duke University Press.

Eshun, K. (2003), "Further Considerations of Afrofuturism," *CR: The New Centennial Review*, 3 (2): 287–302.

GegenSichKollektiv (2012), "Anti-Self: Experience-less Noise," in M. Goddard, B. Halligan and P. Hegarty (eds.), *Reverberations: The Philosophy, Aesthetics and Politics of Noise*, 193–206, New York: Continuum.

Hegarty, P. (2007), *Noise/Music: A History*, New York: Continuum.

Heller, J. (2017), "Why clipping.'s Hugo Nomination Matters for Music in Science Fiction," *Pitchfork*, April 7. https://pitchfork.com/thepitch/1483-why-clippings-hugo-nomination-matters-for-music-in-science-fiction/ (accessed July 31, 2020).

Kane, B. (2012), "Jean-Luc Nancy and the Listening Subject," *Contemporary Music Review*, 31 (5–6): 439–47.

Koselleck, R. (2002), *The Practice of Conceptual History*, trans. T. S. Presner, K. Behnke, and Jobst Welge, Stanford: Stanford University Press.

The Last Angel of History (1996), [Film] Dir. John Akomfrah, USA: Black Studio Film Collective.

Lewis, G. E. (1996), "Improvised Music after 1950: Afrological and Eurological Perspectives," *Black Music Research Journal*, 16 (1): 91–122.

Lillvis, K. (2017), *Posthuman Blackness and the Black Female Imagination*, Athens: University of Georgia Press.

Lipari, L. (2014), *Listening, Thinking, Being: Toward an Ethics of Attunement*, University Park: The Pennsylvania State University Press.

Midcity (2013), [Sound Recording] clipping., USA: Independent.

Mühlhans, J. H. (2017), "Low Frequency and Infrasound: A Critical Review of the Myths, Misbeliefs and Their Relevance to Music Perception Research," *Musicae Scientiae*, 21 (3): 267–86.

Nancy, J. ([1996] 2000), *Being Singular Plural*, trans. Robert D. Richardson and Anne E. O'Byrne, Stanford: Stanford University Press.

Nancy, J. ([2002] 2007), *Listening*, trans. Charlotte Mandell, NY: Fordham University Press.

Savage, R. W. H. (2013), "Fragile Identities, Capable Selves," *Ricoeur Studies*, 4 (2): 64–78.

Schafer, M. R. (1998), *The Book of Noise*, Wellington, NZ: Arcana Editions.

Space Is the Place (1974), [Film] Dir John Coney, USA: Harte Recordings.

Splendor & Misery (2016), [Sound Recording] clipping., USA: Sub Pop.

Steinskog, E. (2018), *Afrofuturism and Black Sound Studies: Culture, Technology, and Things to Come*, London: Palgrave Macmillan.

Sub Pop (2016), "clipping. Splendor & Misery," Sub Pop Mega Mart. https://megamart.subpop.com/releases/clipping/splendor_and_misery (accessed July 5, 2020).

Vonnegut, K. (1969), *Slaughterhouse-Five, or the Children's Crusade: A Duty-Dance with Death*, New York: Delacorte Press.

Weheliye, A. G. (2005), *Phonographies: Grooves in Sonic Afro-Modernity*, Durham, NC: Duke University Press.

West, C. (1993), *Race Matters*, New York: Vintage Books.

White, C. (2016), "Rapping in Space: How Clipping Broke the Fourth Wall and Entered the Fourth Dimension," *UPROXX*, September 16. https://uproxx.com/music/clippping-splendor-and-misery-daveed-diggs/ (accessed June 14, 2019).

8

Colonial Encounters, Alien Languages, and the Exotic Music of Denis Villeneuve's *Arrival*

Paige Zalman

In the first alien encounter scene of Denis Villeneuve's 2016 film *Arrival*, two massive extraterrestrials appear from behind a glass screen, shrouded in fog. They loom several stories above the overwhelmed human onlookers, their towering size sonically emphasized by a startlingly loud note arising from a glissando in the bass and muted brass. As the humans stare in wonder at the enormous tentacled beings, Jóhann Jóhannsson's dramatic score rises by half step and then falls by augmented second before fading to an echo and disappearing. The same gesture repeats seconds later, familiar now, but somehow just as startling. Its exotic sound is evident not only in its intervallic relationships and use of ornamentation but also in its unusual timbre, reminiscent of an erhu, a stringed instrument originating from China. This first visual encounter with the extraterrestrials is heightened by the sounds of musical alterity, inducing fear and depicting the othered celestial visitors as a source of anxiety for the human characters and the audience alike. Indeed, in this scene and throughout the film, Jóhannsson's musical score intensifies the film's broader themes, racializing the alien Other and evoking the conventional belief that unknown beings are inherently harmful. Relationships between the human characters and the extraterrestrials are thus reminiscent of earlier colonial encounters between Western colonists and othered Indigenous groups who suffered at the hands of such conquests, or of present-day immigration policies and race relations in the United States.

In this essay, I draw upon Jóhannsson's musical score from the film *Arrival* to explore the similarities between the portrayal of fictional extraterrestrials and the historical, cultural, and musical representations of colonized non-Western Others. I draw upon the work of Georgina Born, David Hesmondhalgh, Olivia Bloechl, and Woody Doane to demonstrate how the lens of postcolonial theory and theories of whiteness can examine the ways in which the film, through score and plot, engages with past and contemporary political and racialized themes of power, domination, and otherness. By analyzing Jóhannsson's score and comparing it with similarly themed films, I offer a new perspective on *Arrival*'s relevance to contemporary issues of power and race in the United States, showing how the film's portrayal of the extraterrestrial Others draws attention to, and perhaps exacerbates, racist and xenophobic anxieties.

Villeneuve's *Arrival* was based on Ted Chiang's novella, "Story of Your Life," and adapted by screenwriter Eric Heisserer. In the film, linguist Louise Banks (played by Amy Adams) and physicist Ian Donnelley (Jeremey Renner) are hired by the United States Army to discover the aliens' purpose on Earth. As Louise studies the extraterrestrials' language and attempts to teach them her own, she has unexplainable visions of raising a little girl named Hannah, diagnosed at a young age with a fatal illness. Meanwhile, other global powers, especially China, have grown distrustful of the aliens. When Louise is forced to ask about the aliens' purpose before either party can fully understand one another, the aliens respond with a phrase misinterpreted as "use weapon," and tensions escalate. The military powers respond by giving the extraterrestrials twenty-four hours to leave Earth or face an attack, but Louise, determined to prevent warfare, returns to the alien vessel to clarify their message. She discovers that the "weapon" is actually a gift—the aliens' non-linear language, allowing those who have mastered it to comprehend time out of chronological order. Louise realizes that the alien language has allowed her to glimpse her own future, including her unborn daughter. As the Chinese military prepares to attack the pods, Louise has another proleptic vision in which she meets General Shang, who thanks her for convincing him of the aliens' peaceful purpose. Having learned in her vision the dying words of the general's wife, Louise relays this message in the present timeline to Shang via satellite phone. The Chinese military backs down and the other hostile countries follow suit, allowing the aliens to depart peacefully. Louise reflects on this experience with Ian, with whom she soon makes a conscious decision to have a child, despite knowing that her visions of Hannah dying young will come true.

Because communication and language are so central to the plot of *Arrival*, Jóhannsson felt "motivated by the script and the story" to create the bulk of the score by recording and experimenting with human voices (Hall 2016). To achieve this, the composer worked with the Theater of Voices chamber choir, a group that he described as "strange" and "experimental" due to their use of extended vocal techniques (Hall 2016). These same words might describe Jóhannsson's composition for *Arrival*, whose futuristic electronic sounds and looping techniques markedly contrast with the motivically driven scores of well-known film composers like John Williams and Michael Giacchino (O'Connell 2016; Hirway 2016; Taylor 2018). Jóhannsson's disorienting ambient music transports audiences into an unearthly soundscape that emphasizes the striking alterity of the extraterrestrials and their presence on Earth. Paired with the aliens' pod vessels, enormous tentacled bodies, and curious written language, Jóhannsson further renders these uncanny visuals "exotic," evoking wonder and apprehension at once.

Although Jóhannsson's music makes up the bulk of *Arrival*'s score, the British composer Max Richter's affecting string piece, "On the Nature of Daylight," accompanies the opening and closing scenes of the film, which show Louise and Hannah in a montage of memories that vary from heart-warming to heart-breaking. To characterize Louise's bittersweet time with Hannah, Richter uses familiar classical film music techniques, introducing an evocative, repetitive melody and gradually layering others upon it, culminating in a wash of sound that is both texturally warm and emotionally sorrowful. The piece, written in B-flat minor, is slow and cyclical, reflecting the circular temporality of the film's story. When juxtaposed with Richter's sentimental string piece, which is meant to accentuate Louise's (notably human) feelings of love and grief, Jóhannsson's ethereal, non-tonal sounds and unusual timbres heighten the alien visitors' perceived foreignness.

Thus *Arrival*'s score presents a case study for examining how film music perpetuates colonialist ideologies and fear of the racialized Other. Indeed, if such ideologies were driven by a desire for "exploration and discovery," Jóhannsson's experimentalism suggests a similar approach to music, as John Corbett notes (2000: 166). If Richter's music represents "normal" human life, with its attendant joys and tragedies, Jóhannsson's accentuates the comparative "abnormality" of the extraterrestrials, whose differences make them unwelcome in this (earthly) land. Further, the stark contrast between Richter's European (white) idiom and Jóhannsson's exotic (othered) electronics demonstrates how ideologies of fear are composed in blockbuster and science-fiction films—musical idioms pitted against one another in the same way that humans and aliens are typically at odds. Socially constructed conceptions of race tend to "characterize social relationships between groups having unequal levels of power," which *Arrival* recreates in its plot and score through the analogous humans and aliens (Doane 2003: 9).

Doane notes how, throughout history, "white racial identity has been asserted and group mobilization has occurred when whites felt threatened by social changes, immigration, and challenges from subordinate groups" (2003: 8). The humans' militaristic mobilization against the extraterrestrials can be seen as a symbol of whiteness—an assertion of white supremacy in the face of foreign visitors, illustrated by the two opposing musical idioms.

Musical Alterity in Science Fiction Scores

While Jóhannsson's score might be considered innovative in its approach to timbre, functionally it emerges from a long-standing film score tradition that perpetuates colonialist ideals and fear of the Other. Scholars have noted how electronic music has been used in science fiction to exoticize extraterrestrials (Niebur 2010: 26; Prock 2014: 371). This approach can be heard in Bernard Herrmann's score for Robert Wise's 1951 film *The Day the Earth Stood Still*, which makes heavy use of the theremin, an electronic instrument that creates sound when the performer's hands move in proximity to two antennae, one controlling amplitude and the other frequency (Wierzbicki 2002: 126). The score's musical language recalls that of horror films, using low tuba and brass registers to represent alien characters as fearsome and menacing. At the first appearance of the alien Klaatu's metal robot, a sinister, legato theme in the low brass is accompanied by the mid-register wavering of the theremin as the robot exits the spaceship—an ominous sound that has become synonymous with danger in science-fiction films. The theme underscores the unnecessary violence that the military had deployed against Klaatu, accompanying the robot as it shoots lasers from its eyes, destroying all the military's tanks and artillery as the civilian crowd runs away, terrified and screaming. Though the robot and Klaatu visit Earth for a peace-keeping mission, Hermann's score suggests a colonialist interpretation: even though the human military instigated the ensuing violence, the extraterrestrial Others are represented as dangerous aggressors. If film scores sometimes function as "unheard melodies"—a type of emotional and perceptual manipulation—Hermann's music is particularly effective here, both reinforcing the plot and creating a subconscious fear of the alien Other that manipulates the audience's "sensory background" (Gorbman 1987: 12). A similar idiom appears in the horror-inspired scenes of Steven Spielberg's 1977 film, *Close Encounters of the Third Kind* (Lerner 2004: 102), particularly when alien visitors abduct the toddler, Barry. In this scene, John Williams draws upon dissonant, menacing effects, and musically extreme registers to heighten the terror that Barry's mother experiences as she tries to protect her child from aliens. Though these space visitors also turn out to be peaceful tourists, Williams's fright-invoking musical depiction exacerbates the audience's fear of apparent intruders.

More current films follow this same tactical formula. For instance, in the 2011 film *Super 8*, directed by J. J. Abrams, the alien theme in Michael Giacchino's score is the only one featuring low brass in the minor mode (Ross 2010). While the themes representing humans and their relationships evolve and intermingle in quasi-Wagnerian fashion, the alien theme is unique in its timbre, register, and function, remaining static and ominous even after the extraterrestrial character is humanized in a plot twist (Kay 2011: 30). Giacchino's approach to characterizing the alien Other recalls Gorbman's observations about the composers of Western films, who portrayed Native American characters with stereotypical tom-tom rhythms and exotic modal motifs that failed to reflect their changing narratives (2000: 235).

More recently, the 2018 film *Annihilation*, directed by Alex Garland, suggests musical exoticism with electronic synthesizers. The film follows five women as they embark on a research expedition into a curious electromagnetic field that has appeared on Earth, where other researchers have voyaged and never returned. Because most of the film is focused on human characters, the composers Geoff Barrow and Ben Salisbury avoided synthesizers until the end of the film, emphasizing what Salisbury called "a human story" by using instruments like the acoustic guitar and strings (Beta 2018). Yet during the climax of the film—when Lena, the last surviving researcher, encounters the birth of an extraterrestrial humanoid—the visuals are underscored with a loud synthesizer, its jarring alterity strikingly different from the soundscapes heard earlier in the film. As the orchestral strings transform into a synthesizer riff that sounds intended for a dance club, Lena watches as a colorful nebulous cloud morphs before her eyes into a shiny, iridescent being. Gradually the dance-like motif is replaced with grating synthesized timbres that increase in pitch and intensity as Lena tries to shoot the alien and then seeks to escape—only to find herself face to face with it in the next room. A four-note alien motive appears in the synthesizer while backwards-looped strings twinkle underneath; the alien mirrors her every movement, producing a horrifying dance-like duet across the room (Yoshida 2018). As the alien overpowers Lena, first taking on her appearance and then killing her, dissonant, wordless human voices sing, as if in mourning.

Barrow and Salisbury's approach to musical alterity for the alien—electronics, innovative looping techniques, and eerie human voices—mirrors Jóhannsson's tactics. This new type of futuristic soundscape seems to have replaced instruments like the theremin and vibraphone, long associated with space and aliens in science-fiction films. Indeed, even in films without alien encounters, ambient music and electronically manipulated scores have become more common; Hans Zimmer's score for the 2010 film *Inception* indicates how this musical practice has moved into the spotlight (Itzkoff 2010). Yet compared with the musical practices from science-fiction films in the 1950s and 1960s, these new techniques, in some ways, more effectively highlight the underlying sense of fear and anxiety. In *Arrival*, the use of electronic loops suggests that the extraterrestrials are more technologically advanced than the human characters, heightening the human fear of domination.

An Alien Soundscape

Jóhannsson's alien soundscape begins when the extraterrestrials land on Earth, as Louise and her university students watch the developments on the news. A low, unceasing drone conveys Louise's sense of fear, uncertainty, and curiosity about the alien pods, cuing the spectator to feel similarly. This ambient drone, used in several instances throughout the film, is reminiscent of the Indian tanpura, a long-necked string instrument that creates a continuous harmonic foundation to support the instrumental or vocal melody in a raga. Jóhannsson's drone likewise functions as a foundational layer for the hypnotic, repetitive melodies in the higher registers. While the low drone evokes a conventional sense of foreboding, its similarity to the Indian tanpura situates the extraterrestrials more firmly in a colonial context, bringing to mind not only exotic depictions of the Middle East but also India's colonization by Britain and other European settlers, foreshadowing the hostilities to come. But in *Arrival*, the aliens are the perceived colonizers: humans fear them because they fear their own colonization, and Jóhannsson's racializing music exacerbates these concerns.

As Louise, Ian, and their team fly in a helicopter to the site of the alien pod in Montana, ethereal music reflects the awe-inspiring sight of the strange pod towering over a foggy valley framed by mountains (Figure 8.1). Beneath it is the drone, joined by slow, wavering timbres that alternate between three pitches a minor third apart, enharmonically evoking the augmented second

Figure 8.1 *Arrival* (2016), point of view shot of an alien pod from a helicopter.

(D to B)—an interval frequently used in Western music to convey exoticism (McClary 1992: 65). Sinister string tremolos and the metallic pulsing of a cymbal contribute to the eerie alien soundscape, underscored by the persistent beating of helicopter blades, the sound of which was adjusted in rhythm and frequency to contribute seamlessly to the ethereal soundscape (Kulezic-Wilson 2020: 37). The composite effect is in equal parts unnerving, thrilling, and terrifying, at once reflecting Louise's disconcerted feelings while communicating to the audience that these visitors are indeed alien in every sense.

The military's colonialist imperatives are explicitly articulated in a short exchange between Louise and one of the commanders at the army base. After China, Russia, and several other countries make the controversial decision to give the extraterrestrials a twenty-four-hour ultimatum, the commander says to Louise, "We have to consider the idea that our visitors are prodding us to fight among ourselves until only one faction prevails." Louise, taken aback, responds, "There's no evidence of that." The commander then replies, "Sure there is—just grab a history book. The British with India, the Germans with Rwanda, they've even got a name for it in Hungary. Yeah. We're a world with no single leader. It's impossible to deal with just one of us. And with the word 'weapon' now." The historical example he evokes, in which the West functioned as the dangerous aggressor, is unintentionally ironic. The commander—like most of the human characters—projects Western colonialist imperatives onto peaceful alien beings, responding to them with fear and aggression. The humans' fear, at its core, centers on the idea of power as it pertains to race relations: if whiteness, "in all of its manifestations, is embodied racial power," the humans' assertions of dominance are born from the threat of change in racial power dynamics (Bonilla-Silva 2003: 271).

Yet not all of the humans in the film feel threatened by the aliens. In an earlier incident, when Louise tries to communicate by writing on a handheld dry erase board, one of the extraterrestrials creates a symbol in mid-air by releasing an ink-like substance from its tentacled limb. Jóhannsson's score expresses Louise's excitement at this breakthrough, layering consonant sounds on top of wordless female voices, spaced by a major third—a marked contrast to the minor third and augmented second that had prevailed in music linked to the aliens. In addition to the voices, which alternate between sounds like humming and singing (on the syllable "la"), Jóhannsson adds an uneven pulsing, producing a familiar wave effect, along with a low bass note reminiscent of the drone, though it, too, comes and goes. These layers of human voices, unfolding in different phrase lengths, suggest the muddled sounds of a crowded room, thus creating an auditory manifestation of the linguistic barrier that has finally been breached. This breakthrough is visibly thrilling for Louise, but it represents an ominous turn in the plot, as the commanders become exceedingly distrustful of the extraterrestrials. If the wordless voices reflect how both parties are still unable to fully understand one another, they also lack semantic meaning and their unintelligibility recalls Western colonists' ideas about the language of native peoples. Olivia A. Bloechl points out how Captain John Smith's writings about the New World described Native American song as "hellish notes and screeches," their strange language and music indicative of devil worship (Bloechl 2008: 52). From the commanders' perspective at the army base, the incomprehensible vocalisms in Jóhannsson's score might also evoke this same assumption that "different" and "foreign" must be synonymous with "bad." Yet at the same time, the use of human voices sonically humanizes the aliens for Louise and for the audience; the music in this scene is consonant and pleasant, reflecting Louise's optimism as the parties finally learn to communicate. In this pivotal scene, Jóhannsson's scoring becomes more sympathetic to the aliens, demonstrating that the needlessly feared Others may have good intentions after all.

During a later scene where Louise meets General Shang at a ritzy ball, Jóhannsson's otherworldly score is juxtaposed with an almost serene soundscape permeating Louise's vision of the future. As Louise and the General begin to talk, we hear a diegetic string ensemble performing the fourth movement, "Larghetto," of *Serenade for Strings in E Major*, op. 22, by Antonín Dvořák. The excerpt in the film features a violin playing a slow, legato melody, accompanied by familiar sonorities and recognizably Western timbres that constitute a dramatic change from Jóhannsson's alien music. As Dvořák's piece unfolds, guests sip cocktails wearing floor-length gowns and suits, creating an audiovisual combination that evokes Western ideals of refinement and sophistication. By associating the humans with Dvořák's art music, the comparative exoticism and dangerous uncertainty of the extraterrestrials' alien soundworld are even more apparent. Tim Summers notes similar instances of musical difference in representations of nonhuman characters in the *Star Trek* franchise: the otherness of aliens is often created musically through ominous sound effects and motivic material starkly different from the instrumentation, timbre, and intervallic relationships representing the human characters (2013: 47). In some ways, the juxtaposition of Jóhannsson's unearthly soundscape with Richter's and Dvořák's strings recalls similar techniques in the *Star Trek* scores, demonstrating how *Arrival*'s music merely uses a new idiom to expand on earlier practice. But *Arrival*'s use of Western "high art" music to represent the humans also reproduces nationalist and ethnocentrist narratives that further reinforce the exoticized scoring of the aliens.

During Louise's vision, General Shang remarks that Louise's actions were the sole reason he did not carry out his attack on the extraterrestrials: "In war," he says, "there are no winners, only widows" (Patches 2016). Scholars of postcolonial studies would disagree. Ania Loomba, for example, notes how colonialism led to a complete restructuring of learning, literature, and language, using the perceived inferiority and savagery of non-Europeans to justify their cultural and military domination (2015: 72–3). Indeed, the use of Western art music to represent the supposed cultural superiority of the humans in *Arrival* reflects the dynamics of restructuring and domination found in colonial societies. The fear of extraterrestrials, which motivates the human impetus for violence, also mirrors the United States' dealings with Syrian refugees and Mexican immigrants in recent years. But if American politics suggest no end in sight to this discrimination against perceived outsiders, Louise's actions serve as a catalyst for peace.

After Louise's words convince the General to call off his attack, all twelve alien pods take off into cloudy skies, leaving as peacefully as they arrived. The mysterious, quiet vessels move slowly, gently displacing clouds as they rise into the outer reaches of Earth's atmosphere and disappear. Their departure is the last we hear of Jóhannsson's exotic soundscape, manipulated human voices in high and low registers hovering over a serene, synthesized chord, mirroring the awe-inspiring sight of the pods' climb to the heavens. In the lowest register, a legato note rises by perfect fifth as the pods lift into the sky. The prominence of this open, consonant interval with a clear mimetic basis also reflects a return to order and everyday life for the humans—and, more significantly, it signals that these beings were not, in fact, a threat. Nonetheless, when Richter's aching "On the Nature of Daylight" returns at the film's close, accompanying a montage of scenes depicting the interwoven destinies of Louise, Ian, and Hannah, it confirms the arrival of normative human experience in the absence of the Others.

Conclusion

Jóhannsson's soundscape for *Arrival* takes its audience through a journey that begins with a fear of the racialized Other and ends with a more sympathetic sonic suggestion that perhaps we need not fear those different from us after all. Yet during such a politically, socially, and racially divisive time in the United States, media might acquire deeper, and potentially more problematic, meanings. For instance, the fates of Syrian refugees at the height of the Syrian Civil War and the asylum-seekers at the Mexican border have remained sources of controversy. The fearmongering surrounding this highly politicized rhetoric is reminiscent of—and perhaps amplified and reinscribed by—the racialized fear expressed by the human characters in *Arrival*, musically illustrated by Jóhannsson's exotic musical tropes and eerie low-register effects. The film, and Jóhannsson's scoring in particular, translates modern racial politics into sound, revealing how colonial and imperialist musical imaginings might shape our ways of engaging with other life forms as we continue our efforts to explore the far reaches of the galaxy.

References

Beta, A. (2018), "*Annihilation*: Geoff Barrow and Ben Salisbury Talk Its Haunting Score," *Rolling Stone*. https://www.rollingstone.com/music/music-features/annihilationgeoff-barrow-and-ben-salisbury-talk-its-haunting-score-197947/ (accessed July 1, 2020).

Bloechl, O. (2008), *Native American Song at the Frontiers of Early Modern Music*, New York: Cambridge University Press.

Bonilla-Silva, E. (2003), "'New Racism,' Color-Blind Racism, and the Future of Whiteness in America," in A. W. Doane and E. Bonilla-Silva (eds.), *White Out: The Continuing Significance of Racism*, 271–84, London, UK: Routledge.

Corbett, J. (2000), "Experimental Oriental: New Music and Other Others," in G. Born and D. Hesmondhalgh (eds.), *Western Music and Its Others: Difference, Representation, and Appropriation in Music*, 163–86, Berkeley: University of California Press.

Doane, A. W. (2003), "Rethinking Whiteness Studies," in A. W. Doane and E. Bonilla-Silva (eds.), *White Out: The Continuing Significance of Racism*, 3–20, London, UK: Routledge.

Gorbman, C. (1987), *Unheard Melodies: Narrative Film Music*, Bloomington: Indiana University Press.

Gorbman, C. (2000), "Scoring the Indian: Music in the Liberal Western," in G. Born and D. Hesmondhalgh (eds.), *Western Music and Its Others: Difference, Representation, and Appropriation in Music*, 234–53, Berkeley: University of California Press, 2000.

Hall, J. (2016), "Interview: *Arrival* Composer Jóhann Jóhannsson on How You Score First Contact," *Slash Film*, November 11. https://www.slashfilm.com/johannjohannsson-arrival-music/ (accessed July 1, 2020).

Hirway, H. (2016), "Song Exploder: Jóhann Jóhannsson on the Secrets of *Arrival*'s Score," *Vulture*, November 17. http://www.vulture.com/2016/11/arrival-score-johannjohannsson-song-exploder.html (accessed July 1, 2020).

Itzkoff, D. (2010), "Hans Zimmer Extracts the Secrets of the *Inception* Score," *The New York Times*, July 28. https://artsbeat.blogs.nytimes.com/2010/07/28/hans-zimmer-extracts-the-secrets-of-the-inception-score/ (accessed July 1, 2020).

Kay, D. (2011), "Score Analysis: What Makes *Super 8* Super?" *Film Score Monthly*, 16 (8): 30.

Kulezic-Wilson, D. (2020), *Sound Design Is the New Score: Theory, Aesthetics, and Erotics of the Integrated Soundtrack*, Oxford: Oxford University Press.

Lerner, N. (2004), "Nostalgia, Masculinist Discourse, and Authoritarianism in John Williams's Scores for *Star Wars* and *Close Encounters of the Third Kind*," in P. Hayward (ed.), *Off the Planet: Music, Sound, and Science Fiction Cinema*, 96–109, London: John Libbey.

Loomba, A. (2015), *Colonialism/Postcolonialism*, 3rd edn, London: Routledge.

McClary, S. (1992), *Georges Bizet: "Carmen"*, Cambridge Opera Handbooks, Cambridge: University of Cambridge Press.

Niebur, L. (2010), *Special Sound: The Creation and Legacy of the BBC Radiophonic Workshop*, Oxford: Oxford University Press.

O'Connell, S. (2016), "*Arrival* Composer Jóhann Jóhannsson: 'People Are Hungry for New Sounds,'" *The Guardian*, November 26. https://www.theguardian.com/

music/2016/nov/26/arrival-johann-johannsson-soundtrack-oscar-nominated (accessed July 1, 2020).

Patches, M. (2016), "The Mystery Line in *Arrival*, Revealed," *Thrillist*, November 13. https://www.thrillist.com/entertainment/nation/arrival-chinese-line-ending (accessed July 1, 2020).

Prock, S. (2014), "Strange Voices: Subjectivity and Gender in *Forbidden Planet*'s Soundscape of Tomorrow," *Journal of the Society for American Music*, 8 (3): 371–400.

Richter, M. (2004). *The Blue Notebooks*. Compact Disc, Brighton: Fatcat Records.

Ross, A. (2010), "The Spooky Fill," *The New Yorker*, May 17. https://www.newyorker.com/magazine/2010/05/17/the-spooky-fill (accessed July 1, 2020).

Summers, T. (2013), "*Star Trek* and the Musical Depiction of the Alien Other," *Music, Sound & The Moving Image*, 7 (1): 19–52.

Taylor, D. (2018), [Podcast], "Loop Groups," *Twenty Thousand Hertz*, August 6. https://www.20k.org/episodes/loopgroups (accessed July 1, 2020).

Wierzbicki, J. (2002), "Weird Vibrations: How the Theremin Gave Musical Voice to Hollywood's Extraterrestrial 'Others,' " *Journal of Popular Film and Television*, 30 (3): 125–35.

Yoshida, E. (2018), "Let's Talk about the Ending of *Annihilation*," *Vulture*, February 23. http://www.vulture.com/2018/02/annihilation-movie-ending-explained.html (accessed July 1, 2020).

9

Decolonizing Disability: "Muteness," Music, and Eugenics in Screen Representation

James Deaville

The concepts of colonization and decolonization have not prominently figured in the academic discourse on disability, which has historically focused on bodies and minds in the Global North.[1] However, if colonialism demarcates a "mode of domination" (Veracini 2017: 2), the academic privileging of disability in the Global North over its embodiments in the Global South can be understood as participating in the colonial enterprise (Friedner and Zoanni 2018). Moreover, throughout the world, the hegemony of the able-bodied has ever exercised control over the disabled population by marginalizing, stigmatizing, abjectifying, and ultimately discarding people with disabilities and debilities.[2] As Rachel Presley has argued, we must "approach dis/ability within the broader matrix of colonization, questioning and challenging the ways in which dominant power relations recognize, regulate, and govern our lifeways" (Presley 2019).

In this chapter, I explore what it means to colonize and decolonize disability through music and sound with particular reference to screen representations. The chapter first examines a recent attempt by the Annenberg Inclusion Initiative (AII) to establish a quantitative basis for assessing the representation of disabilities and "mental health conditions" in film and television. In dialogue with their findings, I present an alternative dataset with interpretations that extend beyond script narratives, considering the lived experiences of actors with disabilities. The roles of music and sound in "disabling" film and television narrative will figure in the essay's central section. In order to demonstrate the analytical depth required to come to terms with the sights and sounds of disability on screen, the chapter investigates the colonizing of one particular mediated disability, "muteness." I conclude by considering possible paths for analyzing and, ultimately, decolonizing disability in audiovisual media through a study of the soundtrack for Jane Campion's film, *The Piano*, drawing upon resources from the growing subfield of disability media studies.[3] Over all of these deliberations hovers the lingering specter of eugenics, which continues to cast its stigmatizing shadow over filmmakers and audiences alike, long after its disavowal by the academic community (O'Brien 2011).

Moving images and digital media are the most common sources of information about disability for the general public. The problem with these mediated sights and sounds is that by attending to disabled bodies and minds on television, film, and the internet, we are consuming and thus exercising power over the subaltern Others of disability (c.f. Lopez 2017). To express the point bluntly, the "act of looking [and listening] exerts domination on the person" (Lee 2020: 109), and that experience of superiority draws on a lifetime of exposure to disability on screen, as filtered through societal stereotypes and judgments (Mogendorff 2013). These representations then empower and enable the Western urge to colonize bodies that "are presented as strange, shameful, wrong, impaired, wounded, scarred, disabled, lacking, different or 'other' in the media" (Garrisi and Johanssen 2020: 1).

Music and sound are complicit in screen mediations of disability, giving life and meaning to moving images (Gorbman 1987: 4). In so doing, they support the believability of character representations, which is especially important for film characters whose disabilities may not be easily identified by audioviewers, as is the case with the Pottersville manic episode of George Bailey in *It's a Wonderful Life* (1946) or Jim Preston's increasing depression in *Passengers* (2016). And, as Claudia Gorbman argued in her pioneering study of film music, making characters and their situations credible is a crucial component in music's function in film (Gorbman 1987: 4; see also AII 2019).

The Annenberg Inclusion Initiative (AII) and Disability Drag/Disabled Mimicry

In late 2017, the University of Southern California Annenberg School for Communication and Journalism launched the AII to address inequality in the entertainment industries. The AII's 2020 report, titled *Inequality in 1,300 Popular Films: Examining Portrayals of Gender, Race/Ethnicity, LGBT & Disability from 2007 to 2019*, quantitatively observes major disparities between lived identity categories—such as race, ethnicity, gender, sexual orientation, and disability—and their representation in American films, as Tables 9.1 and 9.2 illustrate. The report notes that "not only were characters with disabilities rare in film, they were erased from half of the movies in the sample, and females with disabilities were missing from 77 movies. In terms of demographics, characters with disabilities also skewed male, White, and older" (AII 2020: 28). These remarks followed a more fulsome observation in the quantitative study from 2018: "Movies consistently portray few characters with disabilities, and rarely are these individuals the focus of storytelling. When characters with disabilities do appear, they are predominantly white, straight, and male. Viewers hoping for an authentic picture of individuals with disabilities will find little to watch in the top films of 2017" (AII 2018: 25).

But the phrase "authentic picture" is problematic, presuming that actors' "accurate" portrayals of disabilities validate that representation, even though they themselves have no impairments.[4] Thus unlike the report's advocacy for the self-representation of women and racialized minorities, its authors here seem to

Table 9.1 Characters with speaking or named roles in the 100 top-grossing American films of 2019, correlated with demographic data from 2018 (AII 2020: 15, 26–7; AII 2019: 4)

Identity category	On-screen prevalence (%)	Deviation from general population (2019) (%)
Women	34	−17.7
Black	15.7	+3.5
Latino	4.9	−13
Disability	2.3	−25.6

Table 9.2 Types of disability represented in the 100 top-grossing American films of 2019, with gender distribution (AII 2020: 26–7)

Type of disability/gender identity	Percentage
Physical	64.7
Cognitive	29.4
Communicative	28.9
Male	67.6
Female	32.4

promote what scholar Tobin Siebers calls "disability drag" and activist Dominick Evans designates "disabled mimicry" (Lane 2019: 38), whereby able-bodied actors pass as disabled characters.[5] The type of quantitative study represented by the AII report can be said to colonize disability, but under the guise of promoting the inclusion of *characters* with disabilities in film and television. The study's failure to account for the presence or absence of disabled bodies and minds on screen calls to mind unacceptable historical practices of misrepresenting gender and race in film and television (Dixon, Weeks, and Smith 2019).

The same misguided emphasis on "authentic and nuanced portrayals" (AII 2019) guides AII director Stacey L. Smith when she and her research team address screen representations of people with mental-health issues in a follow-up report from May 2019, called *Mental Health Conditions in Film & TV: Portrayals that Dehumanize and Stigmatize Characters*. This report again colonizes disability, this time in the form of mental health, by failing to consider the voices and bodies of the community, both in determining the strength of screen portrayals and in promoting the inequitable practice of disability drag. The researchers confuse actors portraying people with mental health conditions with equity-driven staffing and casting decisions for women and people of color. The playbook they adopt is familiar, calling for "authenticity" in disabled mimicry while claiming to be speaking on behalf of the community: "By authentically depicting the nuanced and complex way that mental health conditions intersect individuals' lives, media can introduce audiences to new ways of thinking" (AII Mental Health 2019: 29).

While such quantifications of screen representations may serve their purpose for readily observable identity characteristics, they can only measure the frequency of portrayals for disabled and LGBTQ characters, not the casting of individuals from those communities.[6] In reality, viewers interested in "an authentic picture of individuals with disabilities" will find virtually nothing in top films and media, because almost none of these roles are occupied by people with disabilities in real life. So while Shaun Murphy, the title character of CBS's *The Good Doctor*, is autistic, actor Freddie Highmore is not; Artie Abrams, from the Fox television show *Glee*, requires a wheelchair, but actor Kevin McHale does not; and Elisa Esposito, in Guillermo del Toro's 2017 film, *The Shape of Water*, does not speak, though Sally Hawkins, who portrays her, does. Indeed, an actor "faking" a disability can be the crowning achievement of one's career: witness Dustin Hoffman's Oscar-winning con of autism in *Rain Man* or Daniel Day-Lewis's Oscar-rewarded fakery of cerebral palsy in *My Left Foot*. As disabled blogger Dominick Evans comments, such depictions are "a mockery of disability, through the weird vocal intonation or accents we hear when [someone is] portraying CP or Deaf characters" (Evans 2017).

Hence the community of people with disabilities has been colonized by the Hollywood film and television industries, along with those who unquestioningly consume their products. Contrary to the AII reports' limited and limiting assessment of disability on screen, disability is indeed a ubiquitous feature of American film and television, discursively reinforcing "normalcy" in its role as "narrative prosthesis." According to David Mitchell and Sharon Snyder (2000), narrative prosthesis is the "pervasive discursive dependency on disability throughout art, literature and film" (Legassic 2015: 301), whereby a character with a disability serves to prop up the primary narrative of normativity and able-bodiedness. Thus in a film's denouement, the order that was disrupted by the flaw of disability is restored, and the eugenicist paradigm of "cure or kill" prevails for the disabled character.[7] The character in question is either rehabilitated or removed from society, as we can see in a storyline like that of Tiny Tim in Charles Dickens's *A Christmas Carol*. As disability theorist Lennart Davis explains, "Dickens does not use Tiny Tim to condemn the treatment of crippled children in Victorian society but to finesse Scrooge's awakening to charity and human kindness towards others" (Davis 2013: 120). In narrative prosthesis the disabled character is unmistakably presented as flawed or in a position of lack—a bundle of negative meanings signifying deviation, unruliness, or pathology and requiring narrative resolutions or containment. This scenario replays itself time and again in film, in characters ranging from the benign Cowardly Lion in the *Wizard of Oz* to the self-destructive Jack Maine in *A Star Is Born*.[8]

(De-)Colonizing Disability in Film and Television Studies

To confirm the thesis that Hollywood has colonized disability—and further, that misrepresentations of disability abound in screen media—I have compiled a list of films and television programs that featured one or more characters with disabilities.[9] My study has detected disability in over 1,000 English-language narrative-fiction films and television shows, organized from a meta-list encompassing all phases and genres of moving-image history from 1927 to 2020. The database for these media records is structured according to a standard relational model (RDBMS) that uses Structured Query Language (SQL) for writing and querying data. The model is under construction and is currently stored within NVivo, a data management package facilitating the classification and relational examination of unstructured multimedia data.

Despite containing over 1,000 items, the list is far from complete, and it includes some intentional exclusions: (1) documentaries, which fall outside the assessment of fictional constructions of disability; (2) independent films, due to their limited public circulation; and (3) horror films that do not overtly invoke disability, since it would have otherwise been necessary to cite almost the entire genre, which invariably involves the "engendering of fear through the embodiment of otherness" (Honisch 2019: 114). Moreover, there are films that engage with disability in ways unobserved by audiences and critics alike: thus none of the consulted listings recognize George Bailey's partial deafness and psychotic episode in *It's a Wonderful Life* as disabling conditions, even though identifying those effects might suggest that we reinterpret Frank Capra's "heartwarming" story as an American nightmare. Finally, neither the database nor the 2.5 percentage of disabled characters noted in the AII report captures the relative impact of the films or programs that have relied upon disability for their narrative power.

While various forms of physical impairment and mental illness have inhabited sound cinema at least since Tod Browning's pre-Code horror film *Freaks* (1932),[10] Barry Levinson's *Rain Man* (1988) served as a turning point for foregrounding disability. The title of a 2015 *Washington Post* review article by Justin Moyer is therefore illuminating: "Welcome Eddie Redmayne: Since *Rain Man*, Majority of Best Oscar Winners Played Sick or Disabled" (2015).[11] The performances of these male actors—women cripping up on screen have received neither the same roles nor acclamation—draw upon audiovisual tropes of disability representation that Martin Norden's classic 1994 text has provocatively designated "Noble Warrior" (29), "Obsessive Avenger" (112), and "Saintly Sage" (131). Such stereotypes conform to audience expectations, as Nicole Markotic argues, since "disabled characters on film seemingly *must* reveal a 'spiritual' attribute that makes their disability tragic because of their 'suffering' … or somehow heightens their dignity and goodness" (2016: 4–5).

Though a growing body of literature has coalesced around mediations of disability, it remains, as the editors of *The Routledge Companion to Disability and Media* note, "an emergent field" (Ellis et al. 2020: 1). That essay collection, as well as other recent studies (Ellcessor and Kirkpatrick 2017; Johanssen and Garrisi

2020), reflects the degree of scholarly engagement with the "othering" of disabled people in screen media and points to paths forward for both representation and access. Monographs by Markotic (2016) and Katie Ellis (2019), among others, advance the cross-pollination of media and disability studies beyond the issue of quantitative (under-)representation to questions of the discursive and epistemological foundations for damaged bodies and minds in audiovisual media. Through such publications the work of decolonizing disability studies is beginning to take place.

One possible theoretical framework for forging the necessary connections between disability and media studies is Mara Mills and Jonathan Stern's concept of "dismediation," which recognizes each field's co-constitutiveness: by appropriating media technologies, it "takes some measure of impairment to be a given, rather than an incontrovertible obstacle or a revolution" (2018: 366). As a decolonizing strategy for the diverse intersections of disability and media, dismediation "demands that we radically expand the methods, sites, and contexts through which disability and media are understood" (2018: 367). Concerning the linkage of disability and moving images, it would mean delving beneath the surface of appearances and engaging in interdisciplinary questions drawn from industry, policy, and history, among other fields. Mills and Sterne's dismediation encourages our attending to specific aspects of mediation, such as verbal and sonic modes of communication, in order to "pluraliz[e] the understandings of media and mediation within disability studies" (2018: 367).

In another effort to decolonize disability media studies, Ellcessor and Kirkpatrick advocate broadening the scope of investigation to encompass "media texts, audiences, industries, and technologies" (2017: 11), while Johanssen and Garrisi stress extending our perspective to encompass non-Western and non-white bodies in representation (2020: 10–11). Ellis's study of disability and Australian digital television cultures illustrates how a dismediatizing study of textuality can "give us some answers as to the meanings of the images and sounds we encounter both on and through television" (2019: 28). However, none of the chapters in these recent anthologies meaningfully attend to the sounds of the media with which they engage, privileging instead the visuality, textuality, and contextuality of the objects of their gazes. Such work maintains the colonizing ocularcentrism of film and media studies: despite the centrality of the soundtrack, music and sound do not figure to any appreciable extent, especially for disability narratives.[12]

(De-)Colonizing Disability in Film and Television through Music and Sound

As the "ultimate hidden persuader" (Cook 2000: 122), music is an especially powerful agent in mediated portrayals of disability, tasked with invisibly yet tangibly supporting the overarching narrative while also establishing disability tropes or stereotypes. In such contexts, music is a tool for the colonizing of disability in screen media, which can naturalize the score while still enacting the eugenic imperative. But music's invisibility can also offer a unique interpretive perspective on disability in the most varied audiovisual narratives, helping researchers identify (mis-)representations and attempt to counteract their pernicious work (Schrader 2014). If disabled bodies often lack visible agency in screen media (Mogk 2013), through the aural realm they possess the ability to "sound other," disclosing and/or destabilizing dominant discourses. Investigating the cinematic and televisual intersections of music and disability allows us to contest the social agendas underlying these mediated discourses, as shall become apparent through this chapter's case study of *The Piano*.

Since the publication of the landmark collection *Sounding Off: Theorizing Disability in Music* in 2006 (Lerner and Strauss), music scholars have increasingly taken up the challenge of addressing the intersections between music, disability, and media.[13] The music of audiovisual media remains an under-researched concern for those who are committed to decolonizing the soundtrack's contributions to harmful or misleading screen narratives of disability. However, as the work by scholars like Neil Lerner (2006) and William Cheng (2017) reveal, attending to details of the score can reveal to unsuspecting members of the public and the academy how music (and sound) have been complicit in colonizing disability in screen representations and how the tenacious principles of eugenics surreptitiously persist in soundtracks (see also Schrader 2014; Cowan 2020). More recently, sound-studies researchers such as Lori Kido Lopez and Matt Selway have begun to decolonize disability through projects involving listening to film and television (Lopez 2017; Selway 2019).

To explore how one might decolonize and dismediate disability in audiovisual media, I consider one particular form of disability, "muteness," for which film directors seem to have a particular penchant in recent years, especially when present in a non-d/Deaf or hearing character.[14] Though the proportion of people with "muteness" in the North American population is smaller than that of d/Deaf persons who do not speak, nonspeaking but hearing roles in film nevertheless outnumber the others by almost ten to one, according to my database (see also Heggen 2014). As the source of music most intimately tied to the body, the voice and its impairments (including voicelessness) have figured centrally in music and disability discourse—yet the research on vocality and moving images has lagged behind.[15] If we consider voice as "a physical phenomenon inflected by the matter of embodied difference" (Rangan 2015: 96), and its lack as that of "bodies … that are materially 'incommunicado' " (Mitchell and Snyder 2019: 151), then its screen absence might well create a tangible, even visceral experience for the audience. But even when considering a film that depends on the lack of physical voice, as in *The Shape of Water*, scholars may adopt "other avenues for valuing the alternative capacities of nonnormative subjects" (Mitchell and Snyder 2019: 151) while still failing to consider the material realities of the soundtrack.

In a recent essay discussing voicelessness in film during the "silent" era, Julie Brown develops a sophisticated case for the "material visualization of sound" through "voice apprehension," identifying the "various methods for materializing voice as prostheses for the absence of realistic synchronized vocal presence" (2020: 17, 31, 29).[16] Along the way, she recognizes the inappropriate ableist language of the commonly used designations "silent film" or "mute film," which are problematic for a number of reasons: "mute," in particular, implies disagency in everyday language, as in the sentence, "They stared in mute horror." Moreover, the nonspeaking person—once called "dumb"[17]—has been traditionally positioned as intellectually inferior, a stigmatization that has carried over into cinematic and televisual practice. For example, in Nicolas Winding Refn's film, *Valhalla Rising* (2009), the violent, nonspeaking Viking, One Eye, played by Mads Mikkelsen, is framed as a barbarian, but one with an innate wisdom—a cross between Norden's "saintly sage" and "obsessive avenger."

My survey of 1,000 films and television shows identified slightly over sixty of them in which nonspeaking (usually female) characters prominently figure.[18] The reasons for and the modes of such vocal disruption in screen media are manifold, ranging from disability to psychological disorder. Thus a nonspeaking character may be silent due to selective mutism—defined as "a consistent failure to speak in certain social situations where there is a natural expectation of speaking" (American Psychiatric Association 2013: 312.23 [F94.0])—or to muteness, which Michel Chion describes as "a physical condition that prevents the subject from speaking" (1999: 96). Of course, screen actors may be rendered "speechless" for other causes: they may have suffered a sudden shock, for example; may display varying degrees of vocal reduction (e.g., a soft talker or a mumbler); or may engage in the numerous alternatives to speech that Harpo Marx developed to perfection (Koestenbaum 2012).

To understand this cinematic privileging of one form of disability ("muteness") over another ("d/Deaf-muteness"), I turn to Chion's ground-breaking *The Voice in Cinema* (1999), which dedicates one chapter to cinematic nonspeaking characters.[19] Whereas silent film already had speaking but voiceless characters, the silence of the nonspeaking movie role was ironically made possible by sound film (1999: 8, 95). In describing such characters, Chion anticipates the narrative prosthesis, though disability representation was not one of his concerns:

> The mute character serves the narrative, and at the same time often plays a subservient role. Thus he's servant both to a central character and to the fiction. He's rarely the protagonist or the crux of the plot; most often he's a secondary character, marginal and tangential, but also somehow positioned intimately close to the heart of the mystery.
>
> (Chion 1999: 95–6)

Chion then explains why the hearing but nonspeaking character is so valuable for the narrative, especially when suspense is required:

> Wherever he turns up, he generates doubt; we rarely know for sure whether he cannot speak or will not speak, and what's more, we don't know how much or how little he knows ... The mute is considered the guardian of the secret, and we are accustomed to him serving in this way ... Since we cannot easily determine what he knows and does not know, the mute is often assumed to know all, or at least to be keeping to himself the knowledge.
>
> (1999: 96)

What Chion fails to mention is the role of the soundtrack in its potential to serve as a surrogate voice for the nonspeaking character (cf., Molina 1997). Rangan eloquently challenges the ocularcentrism and vococentrism of media studies when she notes how, in Leslie Thornton's films, "counterintuitive insights regarding the way that sound operates in relation to the image in cinema ... rearrange our understanding of the voice and of the horizons of humanity onto which it can open" (2015: 95). Accordingly, the soundtrack provides an invisible medium for circumventing the interlocking structures of subjugation imposed by the visual narrative. While music possesses the potential to envoice forcibly muted female characters, thereby resisting misogynist and ableist screen narratives, its polysemy can reaffirm and heighten these intersecting oppressions.

(De-)Colonizing Disability through Music and Sound in "The Piano"

Jane Campion's Oscar-winning film *The Piano* (1993) affords an opportunity to consider how music and sound can function for a nonspeaking protagonist under the eugenic paradigm. The sonic aspect of the film can be said to rest upon Rangan's call for an "expanded mode of listening" in cinema, whereby the act of listening becomes "a means of disrupting the filmgoer's habitualized modes of perception and developing a more acute auditory attunement" (2015: 111 and 113). Ironically, a film's denial of the causal and semantic modes of listening resulting from a character's voicelessness enables the "multiplication and expansion of the auditory dimension" and the "phenomenal boundlessness of sound" (Rangan 2015: 119).

Despite the scholarly attention and recognition accorded to *The Piano*, its soundtrack remains under-researched, even though Campion privileged the sonic realm. This is all the more surprising considering Mitchell and Snyder's advocacy of uncovering film's "neo-materialist modes of storytelling [that] offer other avenues for valuing the alternative capacities of nonnormative subjects" (2019: 151). Applying Rangan's expanded mode of listening to *The Piano* supplements prior research while pointing to new directions for inquiry into de/colonizing disability through music. Arguably, nowhere in the film does the auditory dimension figure more prominently than in its denouement, where we discover the eugenic imperative of cure or kill vividly on display.

A favorite of academics at conferences and in publications in the later 1990s, *The Piano* appeared at a time when feminist scholarship was questioning representations of patriarchy and violence against women in cinema; disability occupied a secondary position. The film tells the story of Ada from Scotland, who is brought to nineteenth-century New Zealand as a bride for the settler Alasdair Stewart. But there is a complication: for undisclosed reasons, she has not spoken since age six, using the piano as a voice surrogate and her daughter, Fiona, as a signing interpreter. Once established in her new surroundings, however, she becomes involved with fellow settler Baines in an affair that leads Stewart in a fit of anger to chop off one of her fingers, rendering her doubly disabled.[20] In this tale of a "saintly sage" and "heroic overcomer," the symbolic significance of his silencing act of violence is not lost on the audience, for toward the end of the film, we observe her moving to the city of Nelson with Baines, eventuating her rehabilitation as a pianist, along with her acquisition of spoken language. One could thus argue that Ada's disability serves as a narrative prosthesis for the central romantic story of forbidden love and its outcomes.

Michael Nyman, the film's music composer, envoiced Ada by blending Scottish folk stylizations and musical minimalisms, shading into the New Age sound with which Nyman is associated. Campion wanted the music to reflect Ada's emotional world (Tims 2012), so Nyman opted for lyricism rather than his trademark driving string sound. His appropriation of Scottish folk songs could be considered colonizing, to the extent that his musical settings conform to what Dylan Robinson has termed "inclusionary music," whereby, despite "an acoustic blending of musics … the fundamental tenets of Western musical genres and form remain intact, thereby reinforcing settler structural logic" (2020: 8). In justifying his "multicultural enrichment" of the musical materials (Robinson 2020: 118), Nyman asserts that the score represents a "substitute for her voice," having created "Ada's repertoire as a pianist, almost as if she had been the composer of it" (Campion, 1993: 150, cited in ap Siôn 2007: 185). Indeed, Ada is a nonspeaking settler, so on one level it makes sense that the sounds of her surrogate voice resonate with tunes from the homeland. Yet Nyman's controlling "voice-over" through his arrangements of folk songs also atemporalizes and dislocates, in other words, *colonizes* Ada and her voicelessness. This act of ventriloquizing (or channeling) Scottish-style music interpellates his late twentieth-century style into her nineteenth-century bodymind as a surrogate New Age voice.[21] Music's invisible persuasive powers certainly help to make Ada's disability believable and, in the economy of the narrative prosthesis, Nyman's score complies in the end with the ineluctable eugenic outcome. Thus it reinforces the cure narrative, which requires her return to "civilization" in the Epilogue to cultivate her soundworld, embodied as Ada resumes her piano performance (Nyman's version of "The Flowers o' the Forest" as the "Silver-Fingered Fling") and learns to speak. As Molina observes, it was almost inevitable that "all signs of damage would have to be erased, and all handicaps removed" (1997: 273).

The Piano does not end on this note, however. Just before the Epilogue, Ada decides on the voyage to Nelson to have her piano thrown overboard, and she intentionally follows it into the deep. This is where Campion, speaking in retrospect, would have liked to have ended the film, but as she remarked in a 2013 interview, "I didn't have the nerve at the time" (Evans 2013).[22] Had the film concluded with Ada drowning, suspended above her beloved piano-voice, the director (and the eugenic imperative) would have been satisfied. But the music of this scene already suggests a different ending.

The watery yet exultant strains of Nyman's original creation, "All Imperfect Things," accompany the entire underwater scene and, in their rising flow, do not admit a tragic outcome. Here again we experience Nyman "speaking" for Ada: under the ocean's surface she becomes functionally voiceless, where her lack cannot be "heard." For this scene, Campion eschews voice-over narration, allowing Nyman's liquescent lyricism to ebulliently fill the soundscape. At this crucial turning point, where Ada changes her mind and then struggles against the cords, Nyman has perhaps decoupled the traditional synchresis of image and sound—and yet, he retains control over the scene by virtue of the soundtrack's overarching emotional trajectory.[23] This voiceless underwater drama reminds us of Rangan's call for an "acute auditory attunement" (2015: 113) in order to apprehend how the dimension of sound can inflect disability meanings in audiovisual media.

Campion's Epilogue follows, its first section enacting the cure narrative with Ada's rehabilitation and reintegration into human society. Then Ada's performance of "The Flowers o' the Forest" theme fades out, and her first-person voice-over dominates the soundtrack, drawing us back to the piano's submerged resting place. Ada's closing narration over her piano playing and her practice at speaking superimposes three layers of voice, suggesting a polyphonic, multi-temporal enactment of the "movement of the film toward restoration and renewal—with the promise of a happy future" (Molina 1997: 273). A lack of underscore lends weight to the words that carry the narrative to its end, as we observe a continuous visual fade-out from Ada's inert figure to a blue screen. After the rehabilitation scene, Campion introduced a form of the alternative ending she desired—a shot of the stilling sea accompanied only by Ada's narration: "At night I think of my piano in its ocean grave, and sometimes of myself floating above it. Down there everything is so still and silent that it lulls me to sleep. It is a weird lullaby and so it is; it is mine." In the absence of music and surface sound, we become more attuned to the auditory dimension "down there," the audible evocation of the silence of the grave made even more acute by the four-second lapse in her voice-over. The film ends with Ada reciting Thomas Hood's early nineteenth-century sonnet, "Silence," whereby the symbolic silence of the "deep, deep sea" represents both Ada's nonverbal world and the stillness of the grave: "There is a silence where hath been no sound, there is a silence where no sound may be, in the cold grave, under the deep deep sea." All we are left with is Ada's voice, there is no music to break the stillness, and silence serves as a lullaby that ironically symbolizes her agency. The powerful yet invisible presence of acoustic and synthesized music has given way to the most primal human sound, voice, which—as near-death experience specialist P. M. H. Atwater suggests—"is the last faculty to leave in death" (2020: E15). Ada may be removed from human society in the end, but only on her own terms: disability is decolonized, not through music but *silence*.

The final moments of *The Piano* call to mind the aqueous close of *The Shape of Water*,[24] where nonspeaking lead character Elisa is depicted as departing the terrestrial world by means of a visual fade-out, without ever (re-)acquiring a human voice. Both films end with ambiguity in terms of the protagonists' fates. Elisa's neighbor Giles articulates this uncertainty in the rhetorical questions he poses in the final voiceover: "If I told you about her, what would I say? That they lived happily ever after? I believe they did. That they were in love? That they remained in love? I'm sure that's true." However, whichever outcome may ultimately befall Ada and Elisa, as far as human society is concerned, the disability has been removed and its problem resolved.

In the end, nonspeaking figures on screen actually tell us much about how the film and television industries regard the inclusion of disability in their products, which aim more at colonizing to secure box office receipts and awards than at representing true inclusion. Much more work needs to be undertaken to uncover the mechanisms and processes behind the screen colonization of disability and, in particular, music's complicity in constructing eugenic narratives. Once we understand the visible and invisible practices behind the harmful and hurtful (mis-)representation and stigmatization of disability in moving images, we can begin to take control by exposing them, engaging in meaningful acts of decolonization and dismediation.

Notes

1. A recent issue of *Current Anthropology* (Vol. 61, Supplement 21, 2020) explores the position of disability in the field, editors Faye Ginsburg and Rayna Rapp prefacing the issue with the question, "How do we decolonize disability?" (Ginsburg and Rapp 2020: S10).
2. For the distinction between disability and debility, see Puar (2017).
3. Among others, see Ellis et al. (2019), Ellcessor and Kirkpatrick (2017), and Garisi and Johanssen (2020).
4. For a nuanced discussion of television representations of disability, see Martin (2020).

5   The term "crip face" has also found use, but some disability studies theorists have problematized the appropriation of a term that arose from a different set of oppressions ("blackface") (c.f. Lane 2019).
6   The 2018 AII report did garner attention from the media, who regarded it as empirical proof for discriminatory practices in screen industries. Later versions have highlighted areas where progress is needed. It remains unclear whether the annual reports are directed at scriptwriters, showrunners, directors and producers, investors, or the general public.
7   This designation can be traced back to Robert Wood (1986: 73). See also Norden (1994: 107) and Garland-Thomson (2004).
8   For a recent study of cinema drawing on the concept of narrative prosthesis, see Grue (2021).
9   The study relied on curated lists about disability and moving-image representations created by and for the disability community. I thank Samantha McEwan and Chantal Lemire for their assistance.
10 See, for example, Krugman (2018), Wilde and Millett (2018), and Brodesco (2014).
11 Moyer provided a long list of other winners, observing that "fourteen of twenty-seven Best Actors tackled characters facing significant mental or physical barriers to what many consider normal life."
12 If "colonizing involves a relationship which leaves one side dependent on the other to define the world" (McCaskill 1983: 289, cited in Tagalik 2010: 8), then the ocularcentric approach of media studies would qualify as such vis-à-vis a multisensory paradigm. For a critique of the historical privileging of visuality in media studies, see Peirse (2012) and Glushneva (2017). Regarding the crucial role of the soundtrack for film (and television), see Jim Buhler's *Theories of the Soundtrack* (2019). For a nuanced, "dismediating" study of intersections between soundtrack, media, and disability, see Selway (2019).
13 The COVID-19 pandemic's effects have made this study all the more urgent, with the quarantined public consuming audiovisual media at a prodigious rate, daily experiencing the distressing sights and sounds from ICUs on the news and seeking relief in screen entertainment that often featured damaged bodies and minds.
14 The designation of "muteness" is contested by people whose vocal silence is for reasons other than impairment. The inability to speak (or muteness) may be caused by congenital deafness, injury to the vocal cords, or disease (among others), whereas the unwillingness to speak (or mutism) may result from psychological disorders like depression or trauma. The anxiety condition known as selective mutism symbolically issues a nonverbal protest.
15 See collections edited by Buhler and Lewis (2020), Feldman and Zeitlin (2019), Eidsheim and Holmes (2019), and Eidsheim and Meizel (2019).

16 Given Mitchell and Snyder's reading of *The Shape of Water*, Brown's use of the designation of "prosthesis" is more than ironic.
17 See Loman, Andrews, and Shaw (2011) for a discussion of terminology for nonspeaking individuals.
18 The study intentionally excluded films featuring characters who are d/Deaf or hearing impaired and do not speak (previously "deaf-mutes"), because the film and television industries treat them differently from nonspeaking characters.
19 Chion, as translated by Gorbman, calls them "mute," and he presumes they are male.
20 Stewart's mutilation of her surrogate voice has been invoked in a variety of interpretations, ranging from the literal punishment for her "infidelity" (DuPuis 1996: 73) to a figurative rendering of the Bluebeard play as symbolizing white colonial patriarchy (Thorham 2019).
21 In general, critics commented favorably on the score as plangent and plaintive (Greenberg 1994; Klinger 2006).
22 Campion added, "[S]he should have stayed under there... It would be more real, wouldn't it? It would be better" (Evans 2013).
23 Nyman noted that he writes "specific pieces of music for specific settings, not responses to images" (cited in ap Siôn 2007: 184).
24 The two films share other features: the protagonists are nonspeaking women, the final shots reveal them departing from human society under the cathartic sea, they end with a voice-over recitation of a poem, and sound and music perform the narrative functions normally assigned to voice.

References

Andrews, J. F., P. C. Shaw and G. Lomas (2011), "Deaf and Hard of Hearing Students," in J. M. Kauffman and D. P. Hallahan (eds.), *Handbook of Special Education*, 241–54, Hoboken: Taylor & Francis.

American Psychiatric Association (2013), *Diagnostic and Statistical Manual of Mental Disorders*, 5th edn, Washington, DC: APA Publishing.

Annenberg Inclusion Initiative (AII) (2017), "USC Annenberg Launches 'Annenberg Inclusion Initiative,'" *Annenberg Inclusion Initiative*, November 16. https://annenberg.usc.edu/research/annenberg-inclusion-initiative/usc-annenberg-launches-inclusion-initiative (accessed March 21, 2021).

Annenberg Inclusion Initiative (AII) (2018), Smith, S. L., M. Choueiti, K. Pieper, A. Case and A. Choi (eds.), "Inequality in 1,100 Popular Films: Examining Portrayals of Gender, Race/Ethnicity, LGBT & Disability from 2007 to 2017," *Annenberg Inclusion*

Initiative (AII), July. http://assets.uscannenberg.org/docs/inequality-in-1100-popular-films.pdf (accessed March 21, 2021).

Annenberg Inclusion Initiative (AII) (2019), Smith, S. L., M. Choueiti, K. Pieper, K. Yao, A. Case and A. Choi (eds.), "Inequality in 1,200 Popular Films: Examining Portrayals of Gender, Race/ Ethnicity, LGBTQ & Disability from 2007 to 2017," *Annenberg Inclusion Initiative* (AII), September. http://assets.uscannenberg.org/docs/inequality-in-1200-popular-films.pdf (accessed March 21, 2021).

Annenberg Inclusion Initiative (AII) (2020), "Inequality across 1,300 Popular Films: Examining Gender and Race/Ethnicity of Leads/Co Leads from 2007 to 2019," *Annenberg Inclusion Initiative* (AII), September. http://assets.uscannenberg.org/docs/aii-inequality_1300_popular_films_09-08-2020.pdf (accessed March 21, 2021).

ap Siôn, P. (2007), *The Music of Michael Nyman: Texts, Contexts and Intertexts*, Aldershot, UK: Ashgate Publishing Ltd.

Atwater, P. M. H. (2020), "The Three Near-Death Experiences of P.M.H. Atwater," *Narrative Inquiry in Bioethics*, 10 (1): E13–E15.

Beller, J. (2006), *The Cinematic Mode of Production: Attention Economy and the Society of the Spectacle*, Hanover, NH: Dartmouth College Press.

Brodesco, A. (2014), "Filming the Freak Show: Non-Normative Bodies on Screen," *Medicina nei secoli*, 26 (1): 291–312.

Brown, J. (2020), "Apprehending Human Voice in the 'Silent Cinema,'" in J. Buhler and H. Lewis (eds.), *Voicing the Cinema: Film Music and the Integrated Soundtrack*, 17–33, Chicago: University of Illinois Press.

Buhler, J. (2019), *Theories of the Soundtrack*, New York: Oxford University Press.

Buhler, J. and H. Lewis, eds. (2020), *Voicing the Cinema: Film Music and the Integrated Soundtrack*, Urbana: University of Illinois Press.

Cheng, W. (2017), "Staging Overcoming: Narratives of Disability and Meritocracy in Reality Singing Competitions," *Journal of the Society for American Music*, 11 (2): 184–214.

Chion, M. (1999), *The Voice in Cinema*, trans. C. Gorbman, New York: Columbia University Press.

Cook, N. (2000), *Music: A Very Short Introduction*, Oxford: Oxford University Press.

Cowan, A. W. (2020), "Listen to Yourself!: Spotify, Ancestry DNA, and the Fortunes of Race Science in the Twenty-First Century," *Sounding Out!*, March 9. https://soundstudiesblog.com/2020/03/09/listen-to-yourself-spotify-ancestry-dna-and-the-fortunes-of-race-science-in-the-twenty-first-century/ (accessed March 21, 2021).

Davis, L. J. (2013), *The Disability Studies Reader*, 4th edn, London: Taylor and Francis.

Dixon, T. L., K. R. Weeks and M. A. Smith (2019), "Media Constructions of Culture, Race, and Ethnicity," *Oxford Research Encyclopedia of Communication*, May 23. https://oxfordre.com/communication/view/10.1093/acrefore/9780190228613.001.0001/acrefore-9780190228613-e-502 (accessed March 21, 2021).

DuPuis, R. (1996), "Romanticizing Colonialism: Power and Pleasure in Jane Campion's 'The Piano,'" *The Contemporary Pacific*, 8 (1): 51–79.

Ellcessor, E. and B. Kirkpatrick, eds. (2017), *Disability Media Studies*, New York: New York University Press.

Ellis, K. (2019), *Disability and Digital Television Cultures: Representation, Access, and Reception*, London: Routledge.

Ellis, K., G. Goggin, B. Haller and R. Curtis, eds. (2020), *The Routledge Companion to Disability and Media*, New York: Routledge.

Eidsheim, N. and J. Holmes (2019), "'A Song for You': The Role of Voice in the Reification and De-Naturalization of Able-Bodiedness," *Journal of Interdisciplinary Voice Studies*, 4 (2): 131.

Eidsheim, N. and K. Meizel, eds. (2019), *The Oxford Handbook of Voice Studies*, New York: Oxford University Press.

Evans, B. (2013), "'I Didn't Have the Nerve at the Time': Director of Oscar-Winning Film *The Piano* Wishes She Had Killed Off Main Character in Final Scene," *The Daily Mail*, July 9. https://www.dailymail.co.uk/tvshowbiz/article-2358690/The-Piano-director-Jane-Campion-wishes-killed-main-character-final-scene.html (accessed March 21, 2021).

Evans, D. (2017), "Please Stop Comparing Disabled Mimicry to Blackface," *The Crip Crusader*, July 18. https://www.dominickevans.com/2017/07/please-stop-comparing-cripping-up-to-blackface/ (accessed March 21, 2021).

Feldman, M. and J. T. Zeitlin, eds. (2019), *The Voice as Something More: Essays Toward Materiality*, Chicago: University of Chicago Press.

Friedner, M. and T. Zoanni (2018), "Disability from the South: Toward a Lexicon," *Somatosphere*. http://somatosphere.net/2018/disability-from-the-south-toward-a-lexicon.html/ (accessed March 21, 2021).

Garland-Thomson, R. (2004), "The Cultural Logic of Euthanasia: 'Sad Fancyings' in Herman Melville's 'Bartleby,'" *American Literature*, 76 (4): 777–806.

Garrisi, D. and J. Johanssen (2020), "Introduction," in J. Johanssen and D. Garrisi (eds.), *Disability, Media, and Representations: Other Bodies*, 1–18, New York: Routledge.

Ginsburg, F. and R. Rapp (2020), "Disability/Anthropology: Rethinking the Parameters of the Human: An Introduction to Supplement 21," *Current Anthropology*, 61 (21): S4–S15. https://www.journals.uchicago.edu/doi/full/10.1086/705503

Glushneva, I. (2017), "Embodied Spectatorship: Phenomenological Turn in Contemporary Film Theory," MA diss., University of Kansas, Lawrence.

Gorbman, C. (1987), *Unheard Melodies: Narrative Film Music*, London: BFI Pub.

Greenberg, H. (1994), "The Piano by Jane Campion and Jan Chapman: Review," *Film Quarterly*, 47 (3): 46–50.

Grue, J. (2021), "Ablenationalists Assemble: On Disability in the Marvel Cinematic Universe," *Journal of Literary & Cultural Disability Studies*, 15 (1): 1–17.

Heggen, A. H. (2014), "The Role of Disability in *Buffy the Vampire Slayer*," PhD diss., University of New Mexico, Albuquerque.

Honisch, S. S. (2019), "Singing Tone: Disability and Pianistic Voices," *Journal of Interdisciplinary Voice Studies*, 4 (2): 247–55.

Hood, T. (1839), "Silence," in W. E. Burton and E. A. Poe (eds.), *Burton's Gentleman's Magazine and American Monthly Review*, 5 (September): 144.

Hood, T. (1823), "Silence," *London Magazine*, 8 (February): 215.

Johanssen, J. and D. Garrisi, eds. (2020), *Disability, Media, and Representations: Other Bodies*, New York: Routledge.

Klinger, B. (2006), "The Art Film, Affect and the Female Viewer: *The Piano* Revisited," *Screen*, 47 (1): 19–41.

Koestenbaum, W. (2012), *The Anatomy of Harpo Marx*, Berkeley: University of California Press.

Krugman, S. D. (2018), "Reclamation of the Disabled Body: A Textual Analysis of Browning's *Freaks* (1932) vs. Modern Media's Sideshow Generation," *Word and Text*, 8 (1): 95–110.

Lane, D. C. (2019), "Presuming Competence: An Examination of Ableism in Film and Television," Honor's diss., Florida State University, Tallahassee.

Learning for Justice (n.d.), "Social Justice Standards: Unpacking Identity," *Learning for Justice*. https://www.learningforjustice.org/professional-development/social-justice-standards-unpacking-identity (accessed March 21, 2021).

Lee, M. (2020), "Knowing North Korea through Photographs of Abled/Disabled Bodies in Western News, Disability, Media, and Representations," in J. Johanssen and D. Garrisi (eds.), *Disability, Media, and Representations: Other Bodies*, 94–113, New York: Routledge.

Legassic, C. (2015), "'The Perfect Neanderthal Man': Rondo Hatton as the Creeper and the Cultural Economy of 1940s B-Films," in M. DeGiglio-Bellemare, C. Ellbé and K. Woofter (eds.), *Recovering 1940s Horror Cinema: Traces of a Lost Decade*, 295–318, Lanham: Lexington Books.

Lerner, N. L. (2006), "The Horrors of One-Handed Pianism: Music and Disability in *The Beast with Five Fingers*," in N. W. Lerner and J. N. Straus (eds.), *Sounding Off: Theorizing Disability in Music*, 75–89, New York: Routledge.

Lerner, N. W. and J. N. Straus, eds. (2006), *Sounding Off: Theorizing Disability in Music*, New York: Routledge.

Lopez, L. K. (2017), "How to Stare at Your Television: The Ethics of Consuming Race and Disability on *Freakshow*," in E. Ellcessor and B. Kirkpatrick (eds.), *Disability Media Studies*, 107–26, New York: New York University Press.

Markotic, N. (2016), *Disability in Film and Literature*, Jefferson, NC: McFarland.

Martin, W. (2020), "Watching Disability: A Discourse Analysis of Representations of Disabled Characters in Scripted Television Programs," PhD diss., The University of Southern Mississippi, Hattiesburg.

McCaskill, D. (1983), "Native People and the Justice System," in I. Getty and A. Lussier (eds.), *As Long as the Sun Shines and the Water Flows*, 288–98, Vancouver, BC: University of British Columbia Press.

Mills, M. and J. Sterne (2018), "Afterword II: Dissemination—Three Proposals, Six Tactics," in F. Ellcessor and B. Kirkpatrick (eds.), *Disability Media Studies*, New York: New York University Press.

Mitchell, D. T. and S. L. Snyder (2000), *Narrative Prosthesis: Disability and the Dependencies of Discourse*, Ann Arbor: University of Michigan Press.

Mitchell, D. T. and S. L. Snyder (2019), "Room for (Materiality's) Maneuver: Reading the Oppositional in Guillermo del Toro's *The Shape of Water*," *JCMS: Journal of Cinema and Media Studies*, 58 (4): 150–6.

Mogendorff, K. (2013), "The Blurring of Boundaries between Research and Everyday Life: Dilemmas of Employing One's Own Experiential Knowledge in Disability Research," *Disability Studies Quarterly*, 33 (2). https://dsq-sds.org/article/view/3713/3231 (accessed March 21, 2021).

Mogk, M. E., ed. (2013), *Different Bodies: Essays on Disability in Film and Television*, Jefferson, NC: McFarland Publishing.

Molina, C. (1997), "Muteness and Mutilation: The Aesthetics of Disability in Jane Campion's *The Piano*," in D. T. Mitchell and S. L. Snyder (eds.), *The Body and Physical Difference: Discourses of Disability*, 267–82, Ann Arbor: University of Michigan Press.

Moyer, J. W. (2015), "Welcome Eddie Redmayne: Since *Rain Man*, Majority of Best Oscar Winners Played Sick or Disabled," *The Washington Post*, February 23. https://www.washingtonpost.com/news/morning-mix/wp/2015/02/23/since-rain-man-majority-of-best-actor-winners-played-sick-or-disabled/ (accessed March 21, 2021).

Norden, M. F. (1994), *The Cinema of Isolation: A History of Physical Disability in the Movies*, New Brunswick, NJ: Rutgers University Press.

O'Brien, G. (2011), "Anchors on the Ship of Progress and Weeds in the Human Garden: Objectivist Rhetoric in American Eugenic Writings," *Disability Studies Quarterly*, 31 (3). https://dsq-sds.org/article/view/1668/1603 (accessed March 21, 2021).

Peirse, A. (2012), "Ocularcentrism, Horror, and *The Lord of the Rings* Films," *Journal of Adaptation in Film & Performance*, 5 (1): 41–50.

Pope-Hennessy, U. (1971), *Edgar Allan Poe*, New York: Ardent Media.

Presley, R. (2019), "Decolonizing the Body: Indigenizing Our Approach to Disability Studies," *The Activist History Review*, October 29. https://activisthistory.com/2019/10/29/decolonizing-the-body-indigenizing-our-approach-to-disability-studies/#_ftn6 (accessed March 21, 2021).

Puar, J. (2017), *The Right to Maim: Debility, Capacity, Disability*, Durham, NC: Duke University Press.

Rangan, P. (2015), "In Defense of Voicelessness: The Matter of the Voice and the Films of Leslie Thornton," *Feminist Media Histories*, 1 (3): 95–126.

Robinson, D. (2020), *Hungry Listening: Resonant Theory for Indigenous Sound Studies*, Minneapolis: University of Minnesota Press.

Schrader, M. (2014), "The Sound of Disability: Music, the Obsessive Avenger, and Eugenics in America," in S. C. Pelkey and A. Bushard (eds.), *Anxiety Muted: American Film Music in a Suburban Age*, 168–85, New York: Oxford University Press.

Selway, M. (2019), "The Sound of the Unsound: The Role of Film Sound Design in Depicting Schizophrenia and Schizophrenic Hallucination in *The Soloist*," *Sound Studies*, 5 (2): 140–54.

Smith, B. (2019), "Seeing the Music: Portrayals of Authenticity in British Period Film Music," MA diss., University of Lapland, Rovaniemi.

Smith, S. L., M. Choueiti and K. Pieper (2017), "Media, Diversity, & Social Change Initiative," *Annenberg Inclusion Initiative* (AII), July. https://annenberg.usc.edu/sites/default/files/Dr_Stacy_L_Smith-Inequality_in_900_Popular_Films.pdf (accessed March 21, 2021).

Smith, S. L., M. Choueiti, A. Choi, K. Pieper and C. Moutier (2019), "Mental Health Conditions in Film & TV," *Annenberg Inclusion Initiative*, May. http://assets.uscannenberg.org/docs/aii-study-mental-health-media_052019.pdf (accessed March 21, 2021).

Tagalik, S. (2010), "A Framework for Indigenous School Health: Foundations in Cultural Principles," *National Collaborating Centre for Aboriginal Health* (NCCAH). https://www.nccih.ca/docs/health/RPT-FrameworkIndigenousSchoolHealth-Tagalik-EN.pdf (accessed March 21, 2021).

Thornham, S. (2019), "Beyond Bluebeard: Feminist Nostalgia and *Top of the Lake* (2013)," *Feminist Media Studies*, 19 (1): 102–17.

Tims, A. (2012), "How We Made: Michael Nyman and Jane Campion on *The Piano*," *The Guardian*, July 30. https://www.theguardian.com/film/2012/jul/30/how-we-made-the-piano (accessed March 21, 2021).

Veracini, L. (2017), "Introduction: Settler Colonialism as a Distinct Mode of Domination," in E. Cavanagh and L. Veracini (eds.), *The Routledge Handbook of the History of Settler Colonialism*, 1–8, London: Routledge.

Wilde, A. and S. Millett (2018), "Watching 'Freaks'—Young People Negotiating What It Is to Be Human," Leeds Beckett Media Research Festival, January 19. http://eprints.leedsbeckett.ac.uk/id/eprint/4667/ (accessed March 21, 2021).

Wood, R. (1986), *Hollywood from Vietnam to Reagan*, New York: Columbia University Press.

10

Hearing Borderline Personality Disorder in *Crazy Ex-Girlfriend*

Joanna K. Love and Jessie Fillerup

The Emmy and Golden Globe-winning CW television show *Crazy Ex-Girlfriend* (2015–2019) has garnered the attention of critics, media, women's magazines, and even mental health professionals for its frank satirizing of long-held social stigmas, particularly those involving women's mental health and the accompanying ideologies of gender, sex, and reproduction. Media and fan commentary have praised the use of parody and satire in the show's musical numbers, crafted by its star and creator, Rachel Bloom, co-creator and producer Aline Brosh McKenna, and songwriters Adam Schlesinger and Jack Dolgen. Part of the show's critical success stems from its harnessing of music to push a trope from opera and romantic comedies to its natural, yet rarely explored, conclusion: what if the woman crazed by love is, in fact, mentally ill?

This chapter examines how the show aurally constructs the perspective of its mentally ill lead character, Rebecca Bunch, by blurring (or rendering permeable) coded musical tropes and other structural boundaries—including televisual modes, narrative continuity, diegeses, and the distinctions between Rebecca's interior life and that of other characters. More specifically, it demonstrates how the show's unconventional use of aural structural breaches and intertextual pop parodies reflects the nature of Rebecca's borderline personality disorder, whose diagnostic criteria include unstable interpersonal relationships, impulsive behavior, dissociative symptoms, and a distorted sense of self (APA Dictionary of Psychology 2020). Many of the show's episodes feature leitmotivic underscoring—a tactic drawn from opera, musical theater, and movie musicals—that subverts conventional usage through meta-musical devices and paratextual references. Indeed, musical and textual quotations of the show's introductory theme songs (a different one for each season) function as plot developments and leitmotifs, often seeping into the episodes themselves. The show's metatextual practices and the subjects explored in its theme songs thus promote an interior, first-person perspective, turning pop and musical theater conventions into potential symptoms of mental illness.

But as Rebecca herself states in the first season's theme song, "the situation's a lot more nuanced than that." Accordingly, her musical performances of the love-crazed woman magnify the symptoms of her illness while highlighting the pervasive gendered codes and stigmas that underlay pop culture's portrayals of "appropriate" feminine behavior. If these confusing and contradictory codes challenge Rebecca's efforts to see herself clearly and seek help, they also provide a familiar entry point for viewers to see (or rather, to hear) themselves in her struggles—even for those not personally experiencing mental illness. In this chapter, we contribute to existing scholarship on disability in musicals and emerging work on *Crazy Ex-Girlfriend* (c.f., Knapp and Knapp 2019, 2020; A. Knapp 2020; Shine 2020), by showing how music offers innovative ways to understand the main character's performative identity (Altman 1987).

Hearing Rebecca's Perspective

By employing dark, anti-musical themes and meta-musical devices, *Crazy Ex-Girlfriend* (*CXG*)—like many television musicals—assumes viewers' familiarity with the genre's conventions. In many instances, the show calls for considerable knowledge of tropes common in Broadway, film, and TV musicals, as well as an extensive array of twentieth- and twenty-first-century popular musics, performers, and music videos. Although, as Jessica Shine (2020) argues, Rebecca tries on various aesthetics, styles, and vocal timbres to complicate the often one-dimensional portrayal female of characters in iconic musicals, some of the show's musical numbers also work to reveal a "greater truth," as Amy Bauer describes it—something the characters are unwilling to express to one another or, in some cases, even themselves. Typically such sentiments are communicated through intertextual allusions that evoke or critique certain genres, styles, and conventions (2016: 210). A number of Rebecca's songs function ironically in this vein, expressing vehement denials of her feelings and motivations, perhaps heard most clearly in the season two theme song ("I'm Just a Girl in Love," discussed below) and "I'm Not Sad, You're Sad" (season four, episode twelve). Indeed, music and sound in *CXG* compellingly draw the viewer into Rebecca's subject position, offering a first-person perspective on her own "greater truth," which she learns, late in the third season, is her ongoing struggle with borderline personality disorder (BPD). As a "culturally stigmatized bodily difference" (Strauss 2011: 9), her BPD effectively functions as a disability—one that is literally performed throughout the series.

The show's pilot episode establishes Rebecca's internal conflicts within minutes. A cold open shows teenage Rebecca in a summer camp performance of *South Pacific*, singing in the chorus for the number "A Wonderful Guy." Ten years later, she is working at a law firm in New York City, living the dream her mother had envisioned for her. When a colleague informs her that she is about to be promoted to partner, Rebecca finds the news strangely distressing. As she focuses on a nearby flyer for a butter campaign (featuring the phrase, "When was the last time you were truly happy?"), the murmuring sounds of office work fade, swallowed up by a high-pitched ringing that seems to emanate from inside her head. We watch her press a hand to her temple and then, in a point-of-view shot, see her co-worker's mouth moving without any sound coming out. Hastily exiting the office, Rebecca braces herself against the side of a building, repeating frantically, "This is what happy feels like." After saying a quick prayer (despite her professed atheism), she looks up to see a billboard featuring the same joy-fixated butter advertisement. An arrow attached to the billboard suddenly tips downward, its movement accompanied by woodwind trills—and unexpectedly, Rebecca's crush from summer camp turns the corner, backlit by golden rays of sunshine. As she recognizes him, we hear a voice singing "I'm in love," a three-note motive from the opening *South Pacific* number. She reacts to the voice, suggesting that she hears it, too; indeed, she hears it multiple times while talking to her crush, Josh Chan. The motive eventually merges with the scene's underscoring as Josh's words echo in Rebecca's mind.

Returning to the office, Rebecca declines the promotion at the law firm, telling the senior partner who offered it that her next job will be "where dreams live." On cue, the woodwind trills that had accompanied Josh's entrance return, launching the instrumental introduction to the show's first original number, "West Covina" (the California city where Josh lives). In a parody of the iconic "I want" song from Disney's 1991 animated film *Beauty and the Beast*, Rebecca sings with the skill and panache of a professional, her own voice sounding to her like that of a Broadway star (or better yet, a Disney princess). Throughout the show's run, this is usually how we hear her, too, reinforcing Rebecca's vocality as a fantasy, a projection, or an enhancement of reality. But in the finale of the first season, this veil of illusion (or self-delusion) falls away, twice. The first time occurs during a flashback to her childhood: having wrangled a boy into dressing up as a disgruntled prince, Rebecca launches into a song from the fictional 1995 movie *Slumbered*, wherein we learn that her singing is just average—unobjectionable for a child her age, but not predictive of the Broadway belting we hear from her as an adult. Fast-forward to the present, the finale of season one, when Rebecca dresses up to attend the wedding of Josh's sister. It soon becomes clear that we are embedded in her fantasy world when a bird lands on her window, and she speaks to it as if she were Cinderella: "Are you here to help me get ready for the ball?" (The bird responds with a subtitled, "What? No. What?") When she starts to perform the *Slumbered* song again—rhythmically off-kilter and decidedly out of tune—we realize, perhaps for the first time, that Rebecca sounds like this all the time. The sense that we have slipped for a moment outside of her self-perception is affirmed by her date for the wedding, Greg, who calls up, "Who are you talking to?"

Using song as a vehicle to express fantasies and symptoms of mental illness is a common strategy in musicals, envoicing thoughts and emotions otherwise silent or suppressed. If musicals "routinely deploy song as an enabling form of madness," as Raymond Knapp and Zelda Knapp claim, they also tend to collapse the distinction between a character's madness and a performer's theatrical gusto, which is essential to inhabiting the role effectively (2019: 210). Sondheim, aware of this potentiality, sought to maintain the marked quality of songs signaling a character's breakdown (for example, "Rose's Turn" in *Gypsy*) by "undermining the audience's effusive response to a *tour de force* performance" (2019: 212). But rarely are we drawn into the subject position of a mentally ill character, whose hearing and vision provide the lens through which the spectator experiences the show.[1]

By establishing Rebecca's first-person point of view in the pilot and reinforcing it in subsequent episodes, *CXG* questions whether certain conventions of musicals, like characters breaking into song, might be signs of mental instability. Early in the show's run, outbursts of song come from either Rebecca herself or other characters in her presence. But by the sixth episode, Greg sings "What'll It Be (Hey, West Covina)," a parody of Billy Joel's "Piano Man," while Rebecca is elsewhere, suggesting that her subject position has absorbed most of what we experience in the show. The characters are doing what Rebecca imagines they would do if she were there—a point made emphatically in episode eight of the show's last season, when Greg returns to West Covina after a long absence. Rebecca is at first unable to recognize him, complaining to a friend who has to point him out that he is a "completely different person." Indeed, he looks different to us as well: a new actor, Sean Astin, had replaced Santino Fontana in the role. Substituting one actor for another is the sort of television genre convention viewers are meant to accept without explanation, but in *CXG*, this obvious recasting underscores the prevalence of Rebecca's perceptual lens. When it fractures, the change in perspective can be jarring. Hearing her awful singing voice in the first season finale momentarily draws us outside her subject position, reminding us that much of what we see (including, perhaps, the very act of breaking into song) may be signs of Rebecca's BPD. Her songs thus convey not only her emotions and desires—the "I wants" and "greater truths" of conventional musical numbers—but also her distorted representations of herself and others.

Rebecca's BPD symptoms, and especially her unstable self-image, are similarly expressed through underscored leitmotifs drawn from two songs heard in the first season, "I Have Friends" and "You Stupid Bitch." Her performances of these songs offer poignant insights into her loneliness and self-loathing, cultivating a sense of interiority that is crucial to understanding her mental illness. "I Have Friends"—an awkward synth-pop mash-up of the Mickey Mouse Club roll call sequences and the rhythmic backing track from Toni Basil's 1981 "Mickey"—is first performed as a duet between Rebecca and a childhood version of herself. The song's hook returns in the underscore throughout the show's run, typically functioning as a sonic mechanism of Rebecca's self-denial. In a scene from season one, she struts jauntily to her new neighbor's house to deliver a flyer for a party, accompanied by the "I Have Friends" motif, a juxtaposition that might be interpreted ironically: her network of friends is so sparse that when she throws a party, she invites a neighbor who tries to close the door in her face, saying, "No solicitors." But the show's porous dramatic boundaries, coupled with Rebecca's conscientiously plucky body language, imply that the underscore emanates from Rebecca herself, externalizing doubts that stand at odds with the inspirational music playing in her head.

A more affecting example of leitmotivic interiority occurs in the third season, which traces Rebecca's sexual and romantic entanglements with Nathaniel. After ending his regular hookups with Rebecca, Nathaniel chides himself for cheating on his girlfriend with her. Rebecca claims the hookups were her mistake, too, but he responds, "No, you're good. I know you really well, Rebecca, and you're a good person." A musical cue immediately follows Nathaniel's line, the camera tracking Rebecca's pensive, longing watchfulness. Had the show's creators wanted to inject a sense of ironic distance, they might have drawn the underscore from "I'm a Good Person," a first-season song whose lyrics would have explicitly undermined Nathaniel's appraisal of her character ("I'm a good person, yes, it's true / I'm a good person, better than you"). Instead, the cue borrows the instrumental accompaniment from another first-season number, "You Stupid Bitch," which includes lines like, "You're just a lying little bitch who ruins things and wants the world to burn." In this instance, the cue is neither commenting on the breakup nor asking us to label or judge Rebecca, instead evoking her own feelings of shame and self-loathing. By turning the inside outside, the music helps us not only to observe her emotions but also, perhaps, to share in them.

Destabilizing Theme Songs

If most of *Crazy Ex-Girlfriend*'s musical numbers promote Rebecca's point of view, the show's four theme songs introduce destabilizing structural ambiguities that mirror her symptoms. Typically, TV theme music, as Rod Rodman explains, is both intradiegetic (signifying the world of the show) and extradiegetic (buffering the flow of advertisements), functioning like the frame of a painting—a transitional juncture bridging the framed image and the wall on which it hangs (2010: 57). But *CXG*'s theme songs—musical and textual frames that typically introduce, signify, and contain the story—transcend their paratextual function, leaking in surprising ways into the story world and illuminating Rebecca's distorted perceptions. Indeed, Bloom claimed that she had crafted the theme songs to reveal something about Rebecca's "psyche" (her "greater truths"), each depicting different ways of coping with her mental health (Nilles 2017).

In the season one song, which accompanies a cartoon animation, Rebecca alludes to her depression and bristles when the other characters describe her as "crazy"—a label she decries as a "sexist term." She refutes it by justifying her actions, claiming they are bold steps toward future happiness: feeling "blue," she decides to quit her high-powered New York City job and move to a bland California suburb that "just happens" to be where her former teenage crush lives. But in season one's eleventh episode, this theme song bleeds from the title sequence into the show's internal dialogue when Paula, the "best friend" character, explains Rebecca's pursuit of love to her husband, Scott. Now detached from Rebecca's perspective, the lyrics originally sung between her and a back-up chorus ("She's a crazy ex-girlfriend"—"No, I'm not") become a nearly verbatim spoken exchange between Paula and Scott that concludes with the show's logo, accompanied by the final chord of the song.² In this moment, and many others that follow, we are asked to question Rebecca's motives: though she is a brilliant lawyer and an enlightened feminist, perhaps her abrupt cross-country move, like many of her choices, are not as harmless or inconsequential as she leads everyone to believe.

The second season's theme music, which resembles a sparkly Busby Berkeley number, ultimately conveys the volatile consequences of Rebecca's psychological instability (Figure 10.1). Beginning with, "I'm just a girl in love / I can't be held responsible for my actions," the song excuses her behaviors with loaded words like "certifiably" and "crazy," offering a funny, satirical take on the show's themes of fantasy and obsession. But in the second season finale, a courtroom flashback scene quotes snippets of the theme song text, revealing that Rebecca once had an obsession with a former Harvard law professor that drove her to commit arson—a disclosure that had been foreshadowed in previous episodes (first, and most comically, when Paula remarks that Rebecca's flyer for her housewarming party looks like the house is on fire). During the flashback, Rebecca languishes outdoors at a psychiatric institution as two nurses approach her, one remarking, "What's the deal with this one?" The other responds, "She sings to herself all day. No one knows why." The first phrase of the theme song returns, played on the harp in a languid tempo as if responding musically to the nurse's question: "She's just a girl in love." While the underscore could be read ironically—a winking musical commentary heard only by the viewer—it also functions as Rebecca's

Figure 10.1 *Crazy Ex-Girlfriend*, still image of the season two theme song. The CW, episode 19, 2016.

Figure 10.2 *Crazy Ex-Girlfriend*, still image of Trent performing the season two theme song. The CW, episode 43, 2018.

vocal proxy in that moment, supplying the culturally enabled, self-deceptive line she uses to justify her behavior.[3]

By puncturing the story world with paratextual theme songs in seasons one and two, the groundwork was laid for a more surprising, structurally transgressive incident in the third season. Trent, a man whom Rebecca had recruited to pretend to be her ex-boyfriend in the first season, returns to stalk her in the third season's episode twelve. Emerging from his hiding place under her bed, Trent performs the season two theme song wearing a red Valentine-bedazzled costume, the original lyrics altered only to accommodate his gender pronouns (Figure 10.2). As paratext, this sequence has a clear function, Trent's menacing perkiness inviting us to remember what we already know: Rebecca's version of the song, despite its bubbly retro appeal, foreshadows her breakdown, leading her to commit arson and, for a time, to be institutionalized. But how might Trent's number also function as text, plausible within the story world itself?

In seasons one and two, Trent functions as a mirror for Rebecca, mimicking a few lines of her love letter song for Josh (compare "Dear Joshua Felix Chan" with "Dear Rebecca Nora Bunch") and performing the "Trent is Getting Ready Song," a riff on Rebecca's "Sexy Getting Ready Song" from the pilot. In his season three reappearance, he borrows Rebecca's phrase "love kernels" to describe his own romantic obsession. When he pops up to perform the theme song reprise, instrumental trilling comically underlines Rebecca's horrified reaction at seeing Trent while also smoothing over a disjunct visual transition, blurring the end of her scene with the beginning of the reprise. The reprise concludes with the *Crazy Ex-Girlfriend* logo dropping, followed by Trent reiterating the song's last nonsensical utterance, originally performed by Rebecca, back at her: "I said, 'Blam!'" (to which she replies, in disbelief, "I heard you!"). The functional ambiguity of the theme song's music, lyrics, and visual references evokes Rebecca's unstable perspective, indicating that Trent's musical parody is not there just for *us* to see. The polysemous qualities of the theme songs, cultivated in the first and second seasons, bear fruit in Trent's performance, which operates like a projection of Rebecca's mind—an outlandish moment of clarity in which she recognizes the self-justifications of her own obsessive fantasies.

This reading is confirmed by another destabilizing sequence that follows soon thereafter, when Trent narrates for Rebecca a montage of flashbacks depicting his off-screen activities since the end of season two. Though these images are ostensibly visual depictions of his narrative, they include a few incongruities, such as a puzzling image of howling coyotes. When Rebecca reflects back on Trent's voiceover monologue, she realizes that the pack of "coyotes" he had joined up with were smugglers, remarking to Paula, "Oh, okay—that makes a lot more sense. Got it. So those montage visuals were from my point of view." Given Rebecca's unsettled psychological state, there are no doubt many instances when the sounds and images we see unfold from her perspective, though comparatively few occasions when she possesses the mental clarity to articulate what she is experiencing. Trent's behavior, and especially his reenactment of the season two theme song, opens a window of insight onto those moments.

The unusual treatment of the theme song in season three (discussed further below) offers another surprising and structurally important incursion of paratext. This theme is first revealed in the third episode when Rebecca's anxiety manifests a childhood version of herself—a dissociative event explained by her double as evidence that she is, indeed, "crazy." The remark cues a music video where Rebecca performs what the term means under the guise of four pop personae representing country, pop, rock, and rap styles. As the song concludes, we see the music video miniaturized on Rebecca's phone, followed by a shot of

Figure 10.3 *Crazy Ex-Girlfriend*, still image of Rebecca watching a video of herself performing. The CW, episode 37, 2017.

her sitting on the toilet watching her own performance, wearing earbuds and looking confused. The logo drop confirms that "You Do/You Don't Wanna Be Crazy" is the show's latest theme song. The dramatic origins of the song only emerge in the sixth episode, in which Rebecca receives her BPD diagnosis following a suicide attempt. Locked in the bathroom, oblivious to her friends' distress at her not hearing them bang on the door, she finally emerges holding her phone and wearing the same earbuds and blue T-shirt featured in the music video sequence. The theme song's unconventional function—at once within and outside of the story, a memory of the past but set in the present—creates a sense of recursive interiority for the viewer: as we watch Rebecca watch herself, we find ourselves drawn into her subject position (Figure 10.3). Yet at the same time we maintain our position as viewers, situated outside the story world, separated from it by our own screens, apparently the show's only impermeable barrier.

This theme song unleashed considerable commentary and criticism from viewers, who summarized it as "confusing" (Harris 2017 and Carlin 2017). But confusion was precisely the point: as Rebecca's anxiety escalates, she spirals into a suicide attempt that leads her to seek clinical help. In the series finale, the show offers a final paratextual moment that confirms Bloom's aforementioned design for the show's theme songs to reflect Rebecca's psychological states. When Paula comments on Rebecca's tendency to mentally check out of conversations,

Rebecca volunteers a glimpse into her psyche, having learned through rigorous therapy the various identities she has tried to assume. She takes Paula on a tour of the costumes and music featured in the four theme songs (as well as other musical numbers), explaining how these performances have helped her to cope. The scene thus acknowledges how the theme songs migrate from their transitional intra- and extradiegetic positions into the intradiegetic story world, linking structural breaches of televisual storytelling to Rebecca's fractured sense of selfhood.

Performing "Crazy"

CXG further explores Rebecca's disability as both exteriorized performance and interior expression by juxtaposing the musical and visual iconography of multiple popular genres. These familiar musical styles represent not only how Rebecca approaches her internal battles, but also how she grapples with cultural forces that impose hegemonic ideals onto her body and mind, preventing her from seeing and defining her wants, needs, and identity. One of the most effective examples of the show's interrogation of musical (and thereby cultural) stereotyping occurs in the aforementioned season three theme, "You Do/ You Don't Want to Be Crazy," which amplifies the complexities of Rebecca's subjectivity by freighting the show's permeable structures with historically coded musical tropes.

More specifically, the theme song efficiently deploys clichéd and stigmatized pop music signifiers to illustrate how popular music (and American culture more generally) perpetuates harmful and contradictory ideologies about women, their bodies, and their mental health—the very traits that might inspire the "crazy ex-girlfriend" moniker. Using the lenses of country-tinged rage, pop fantasy, sex-crazed rock, and misogynistic rap, Rebecca plays the role of four different musical "types." Her embodiment of these roles—separately at first, then together on the same stage (Figure 10.4)—forces her and the show's viewers to confront the fact that gender and disability are performative markers of difference (Deaville 2016: 640–60; Knapp 2016: 829). The musical genres depicted onscreen further illustrate how struggling with BPD is rarely simple or linear: as we discover in the show's final seasons, the "realities" of Rebecca's mental health are multifaceted and constantly in flux—confusing indeed, for her and everyone else.

Figure 10.4 *Crazy Ex-Girlfriend*, still image of the season three theme song. The CW, episode 34, 2017.

The third theme song, as Bloom has remarked, does not give away specific details about how the season unfolds, but instead demonstrates how Rebecca has relied on external sources as she "stumbled around for anything to grab on to" in an effort to define herself (Nilles 2017). The unprecedented time and resources poured into producing the theme song signified its importance: famed music video director Joseph Kahn filmed the sequence over two days and twenty hours (Nilles 2017). Kahn found the shoot challenging, saying that its frank portrayal of the most clichéd aspects of each musical genre went "against his instincts" (Nilles 2017). But the thirty-second clip, like any effective trailer, had to use easily decipherable signifiers, and it did so successfully, according to reviewers who accurately identified each of the parodied genres (Harris 2017; Nilles 2017). Still, some were perplexed by the purpose of these clichés early in season three, having yet to learn that the theme song's intertextual references to recordings and music videos were signaling Rebecca's forthcoming BPD diagnosis.

"You Do/You Don't Wanna Be Crazy" evoked the hundreds of popular songs that have, in various ways, defined what it means to "crazy." These songs date back to some of America's earliest recorded hits, including Mamie Smith's famous 1920 tale of betrayal in "Crazy Blues." The third theme's rage-filled, country-and-western opening vignette follows this precedent, referring most obviously to Carrie Underwood's 2005 "Before He Cheats," while aurally recalling Patsy Cline's iconic 1961 version of "Crazy." Rebecca smashing an old Pontiac Trans Am windshield further acts as visual shorthand for both Underwood's iconic video and Beyoncé's bat-swinging performance for "Hold Up" from her 2016 *Lemonade* video album, in which she breaks car windows while asking her cheating husband, "What's worse, lookin' jealous or crazy / or being walked all over lately?" Like Beyoncé, Rebecca's country personae seems to conclude that she would "rather be crazy."

Music scholars have long studied how the "craziness" (or "madness") of scorned women has been characterized in nineteenth-century opera and twentieth-century media, both of which sought to contain these women in the musical score and the social norms dictating marriage, imprisonment, or death (cf. McClary 1991; Fillerup 2016). Yet Rebecca's modern portrayal of "madness" upends these conventions: the "crazy ex-girlfriend" is never fully subsumed by any of these forces, despite her own efforts to contain herself in these ways. Accordingly, the show's plot twists stem from its critical, contemporary, and non-patriarchal lens, complicating the factors that might define Rebecca's experience as a young, professionally successful, twenty-first-century woman living with mental illness. The musical numbers center the perspective of a differently abled character instead of presuming an "objective" or normative point of view, and in so doing, highlight some key characteristics of Rebecca's BPD, including the inability to control her impulses and the struggle to maintain interpersonal and romantic relationships. The country-western vignette thus supports the first-person perspective established in the series' first two seasons and demonstrates how Rebecca performatively negotiates BPD, drawing from pop cultural texts she feels are imposed upon her. In singing "Crazy is when I go off the rails," she implicitly highlights her (BPD) difference and links her loss of control to earlier romantic mishaps—like when, for example, she blamed Josh for her unhappiness and made increasingly destructive decisions in season two.

Mimicking the ease with which Taylor Swift transitioned from country star to pop diva, the next scene shifts away from twangy vocals and slide guitar to glossy pop production. In this second vignette, Rebecca's blue gown billows against a harsh, mirrored arctic landscape, connecting visually to Swift's "Wildest Dreams" video while also hearkening back to *CXG's* season two pop parody, "Love Kernels." Here Rebecca groans, "Crazy is how your lovin' makes me feel …, " and her breathy, seductive performance of pop fantasy recalls her mental state early in season two, where she finds herself swept up by the "craziness" of love. Subtle references to Beyoncé and Jay-Z's passionate 2003 "Crazy in Love" enhance the thrill of Rebecca and Josh's once-consuming relationship, which ended when the obsessive and deceptive behaviors that brought them together were revealed. The complexity of Rebecca's emotions—and the difficulty of understanding or managing them—is reflected in her mirror image, who fails to mimic her every move.

This mirror signifier carries into the other vignettes but emerges most clearly in the third one, when Rebecca appears in drag, recalling the pop-rock performances of famous front men like Mick Jagger and Robert Plant. Her shaggy wig alludes to a young Justin Bieber, while the dark colors and mirrored room around her mimic the Flock of Seagulls's iconic 1982 video, "I Ran (So Far Away)." From this exteriorized perspective, she shouts, "I like it when a girl gets crazy in bed," asserting the stereotypical male-rocker lifestyle of "sex, drugs, and rock and roll," even as her androgynous performance complicates her hypermasculine and heteronormative posturing (cf. Walser 1993 and Fast 1999). The scene also recalls *CXG*'s exploration of social norms concerning women's bodies and sexual identities, reminding us of songs that challenged the flawless sex appeal of the Pussy Cat Dolls ("The Sexy Getting Ready Song"), parodied Katy Perry's 2008 bisexual awakening in "I Kissed a Girl" ("Feeling Kinda Naughty"), and illuminated the realities of menstruation ("Period Sex"). Though brief, this mirrored scene suggests both the complexities of Rebecca's sexual exploits and the ways in which her latest actions (namely, sleeping with her ex-boyfriend's father) have left her feeling ashamed and unsatisfied.

The fourth vignette similarly explores a reflective space with the camera panning a mirrored alley and stopping at a dead end filled with trash and graffitied walls. If this scene suggests hip hop's urban roots, Rebecca's blond wig, clothing, and misogynist rap evoke the controversial lyrics and "white trash" persona on which Eminem built his career (Kajikawa 2015: 136). Her degrading language and shaming tone come with a stern warning to stay away from a "bitch who's crazy in the head," magnifying her (re)current self-loathing state and reminding us of her persistent self-flagellating anthem, "You Stupid Bitch."[4]

We witness Rebecca's "great[est] truths" when her four personae appear together onstage (Figure 10.4 above), blurring acknowledged boundaries between well-known musical styles to conflate pop culture's many definitions of "crazy." The simultaneous onscreen representation of these styles transcends performance practices and listening audiences typically divided by race, class, gender, age, and region. Rebecca's male and female archetypes are positioned as opposing pairs, debating the costs and benefits of acting "crazy": the triggered country singer contradicts the rocker's conflation of "crazy" with sexual prowess, while the disgusted rapper refutes the pop diva's praise of all-consuming love.

Their collective confusion leads to a strained, "We hope this helps," delaying a satisfying tonic resolution until the camera cuts to Rebecca's confused "What?" as she watches on her phone.

By breaking a dramatic wall, the third season theme song encourages Rebecca (and the show's viewers) to think critically about the junctures of popular culture and mental illness parodied through gendered and stereotyped musical codes. As these codes intersect with notions of performance and difference—of which the latter characterizes disability as well as parody (Hutcheon 2000: xii)—they provide a strategy for unpacking Rebecca's own (BPD) version of "crazy." The parodied archetypes thus conflate multiple identities within Rebecca's embodiment of each carefully defined genre, rendering musical performance neither inside nor outside her sense of self, her experience of reality, or the show's diegesis. Instead, the parodies foreground her difference by emphasizing the performativity of selfhood, gender, and disability, and her blurring of "labeled" musical genres function as a metaphor for the struggles with her health. If the theme song asks just how "crazy" one can be before attracting that epithet, the show itself seems to question where, on the spectrum of mental illness, can one (woman) still pass as "sane"? There are no simple answers, as the fourth season theme song suggests: the singers performing it list several of Rebecca's seemingly contradictory traits and ultimately dismiss her altogether, concluding that she's "too hard to summarize."

Novel Possibilities

Crazy Ex-Girlfriend uses musical performance to permeate the structural boundaries established by the norms of network television and the music industry—a strategy that allows viewers to experience the main character's struggles with BPD along with her, challenging prevailing gender and mental health stereotypes reinforced by popular culture. While the show's intertextual references promote internal continuity, its breach of conventional frameworks disrupts televisual flow, dramatic linearity, and genre, providing a novel foundation for the musical numbers that provide a first-person perspective on the challenges faced by women with mental illness.

If the show is groundbreaking, it occasionally falls short in its efforts to destigmatize mental health. Bloom has no training in medicine or psychiatry, nor are we made aware that she has any personal experience with BPD, although she does report her diagnosis of depression and obsessive-compulsive disorder in her memoir (Bloom 2020). Musical satires and parodies also sometimes fall into their own traps, as Sean Nye points out, when hegemonic approaches reaffirm the structures they aim to critique (2011: 156). Indeed, the performance of BPD in *Crazy Ex-Girlfriend* is twice mediated, through Bloom and her character: the show's strategies for engaging with certain stereotypes—especially its brand of sitcom-appropriate dramedy—may thus reinscribe them in unexpected ways for some viewers. Additionally, Bloom uses musics from people marginalized by class, race, and sexuality to speak from a white, upper-class, cis-gender, and largely heteronormative perspective—consider, for example, her parody of the disco hit, "It's Raining Men" ("Let's Generalize about Men"), or her re-creation of 1960s Black girl group songs in "Maybe She's Not Such a Heinous Bitch after All." Though it is somewhat satisfying that Rebecca addresses her privilege in the last few seasons, there is little musical reciprocity for her choices.

It is significant, however, that the show succeeds in prioritizing Rebecca's perspectives, since her performance of disability brings audiences closer to Raymond Knapp's call for "the kind of musical embodiment of difference that musicals demand" (2016: 829). Avoiding a patriarchal and ableist "marriage fixes all women" narrative, *CXG* emphasizes that Rebecca's disability, along with her negotiation of culturally imposed gender expectations, is ongoing, acknowledging her difference as she works to pass as "normal"—something she desperately seeks throughout the series, as seen, for example, in the season two ballad, "(Tell me I'm Okay) Patrick." Once Rebecca decides to deal head-on with her illness in season four, her musical perspectives shift again: she performs only one solo number until the twelfth episode, when two songs—"I'm Not Sad, You're Sad" and "The Darkness"—exteriorize her emotional states. In the very next episode, she seeks medication for her BPD and decides to embrace her lifelong love of musical theater, which had been disclosed in the show's very first scene and recounted by Rebecca's "dream ghost" (her therapist) in season one, who reminded her that love can be a passion for something as much as intimate feelings for someone. Accordingly, the final episode fades out just as Rebecca is about to premiere her first musical composition onstage, in real time, openly performing her difference—her "greater truth." A musical exploration of Rebecca's borderline personality disorder might have promoted voyeurism, escapism, or categorical solutions to complex problems, but *Crazy Ex-Girlfriend*'s destabilizing use of music—in its theme songs, musical numbers, and underscoring—instead cultivates something truly radical in its viewers: a sense of empathy.

Notes

1 The 2008 musical *next to normal* is one of the few to adopt such a perspective: the audience sees and hears Gabe, who died sixteen years ago, because his mother, Diana, experiences delusions and hallucinations. For a discussion of *next to normal*, see Knapp (2016: 814–35) and Knapp and Knapp (2020: 218–20).
2 Paula tellingly turns subtext into text by changing Rebecca's line, "But that's not why I'm here!" to "And that's exactly why she's here," saying out loud what Rebecca is unable to admit to herself. Rebecca corrects her own self-deception in the final episode of the show's run, "Eleven O'Clock," where she sings, "I admitted that's where Josh lived and that's what brought me here."
3 Rebecca also confirms her denial in the confessional "Eleven O'Clock" song, transforming the theme song's lyrics from "I can't to be held responsible for my actions" to "didn't want to be held responsible for my actions."
4 Each of the articles in a special 2020 roundtable about *CXG* published in *Music and the Moving Image* analyze the use of "You Stupid Bitch" throughout the series's run. See Knapp and Knapp: 5–14, A. Knapp: 27–35, and Shine: 15–26.

References

Altman, R. (1987), *The American Film Musical*, Bloomington: Indiana University Press.

American Psychological Association (2020), "Borderline Personality Disorder," *APA Dictionary of Psychology*. https://dictionary.apa.org/borderline-personality-disorder (accessed June 1, 2020).

Bauer, A. (2016), "'Give Me Something to Sing About': Intertextuality and the Audience in 'Once More, with Feeling,'" in P. Atinello, J. K. Halfyard, and V. Knights (eds.), *Music, Sound, and Silence in Buffy the Vampire Slayer*, 209–34, New York: Routledge.

Bloom, R. (2020), *I Want to Be Where the Normal People Are*, New York: Grand Central Publishing.

Carlin, S. (2017), "'Crazy Ex-Girlfriend' Season 3 Has a New Theme Song and of Course It's Deep AF," *Bustle*, October 18. https://www.bustle.com/p/the-new-crazy-ex-girlfriend-season-3-theme-song-will-make-you-think-twice-about-using-the-word-crazy-2943523 (accessed June 1, 2019).

Coleman, L. M. (2017), "Stigma: An Enigma Demystified," in L. J. Davis (ed.), *The Disability Studies Reader*, 5th edn, 145–59, New York: Routledge.

Deaville, J. (2016), "Sounds of the Mind: Music and Madness in Popular Imagination," in B. Howe, S. Jensen-Moulton, N. Lerner, and J. Straus (eds.), *The Oxford Handbook of Music and Disability Studies*, 640–60, New York: Oxford University Press.

Fast, S. (1999), "Rethinking Issues of Gender and Sexuality in Led Zeppelin: A Woman's View of Pleasure and Power in Hard Rock," *American Music*, 17 (3): 245–99.

Fillerup, J. (2016), "Lucia's Ghosts: Sonic, Gothic, and Postmodern," *Cambridge Opera Journal*, 28 (3): 313–45.

Garland-Thomson, R. (2001), *Re-shaping, Re-thinking, Re-defining: Feminist Disability Studies*, Washington, DC: Center for Women Policy Studies.

Harris, A. (2017), "Which Is the Best *Crazy Ex-Girlfriend* Opening Credits Sequence So Far?" *Slate*, October 20. http://www.slate.com/blogs/browbeat/2017/10/20/assessing_crazy_ex_girlfriend_s_three_opening_credits_sequences_video.html (accessed May 11, 2020).

Hutcheon, L. (2000), *A Theory of Parody: The Teachings of Twentieth-Century Art Forms*, Champaign: University of Illinois Press.

Kajikawa, L. (2015), *Sounding Race in Rap Songs*, Berkeley: University of California Press.

Knapp, A. (2020), "'Cruel Optimism' and Subjectivity in Crazy-Ex Girlfriend," *Music and the Moving Image*, 13 (3): 27–35.

Knapp, R. (2016), "Waitin' for the Light to Shine: Musicals and Disability," in B. Howe, S. Jensen-Moulton, N. Lerner, and J. Straus (eds.), *The Oxford Handbook of Music and Disability Studies*, 814–35, New York: Oxford University Press.

Knapp, R. and Z. Knapp (2019), "Musicals and the Envoicing of Mental Illness and Madness: From *Lady in the Dark* to *Man of La Mancha* (and Beyond)," *Journal of Interdisciplinary Voice Studies*, 4 (2): 209–23.

Knapp, R. and Z. Knapp (2020), "*Crazy Ex-Girlfriend* and the Trajectories of Mental Illness in Musicals," *Music and the Moving Image*, 13 (3): 5–14.

McClary, S. (1991), *Feminine Endings: Music, Gender, and Sexuality*, Minneapolis: University of Minnesota Press,.

Nilles, Billy. (2017), "*Crazy Ex-Girlfriend*'s Season 3 Opening Credits Sequence Is Here to Question What It Really Means to Be Crazy," *E! Online*, October 18. https://www.eonline.com/news/887667/crazy-ex-girlfriend-s-season-3-opening-credits-sequence-is-here-to-question-what-it-really-means-to-be-crazy (accessed May 7, 2020).

Nye, S. (2011), "From Punk to the Musical, *South Park*, Music and the Cartoon Format," in J. Deaville (ed.), *Music and Television*, 143–64, New York: Routledge.

Rodman, R. (2010), *Tuning In: American Narrative Television Music*, New York: Oxford University Press.

Shine, J. (2020), "'I'm on My Own Path:' Musical Development of the Musical in *Crazy Ex-Girlfriend* (2015–2019)," *Music and the Moving Image*, 13 (3): 15–26.

Straus, Joseph (2011), *Extraordinary Measures: Disability in Music*, Oxford: Oxford University Press.

Walser, R. (1993), *Running with the Devil: Power, Gender, and Madness in Heavy Metal Music*, Middletown, CT: Wesleyan University Press.

Part Three

Performing Identity

11

Shirish Korde on Intercultural Composition

Christopher Chandler

Shirish Korde, a composer of Indian descent, writes in a style that reflects an eclectic array of global influences, including Japanese, Balinese, and Indian musics, as well as Western jazz and classical styles. Korde spent his formative years in East Africa before coming to the United States in 1965, where he studied jazz, improvisation, composition, and ethnomusicology at the Berklee College of Music, New England Conservatory, and Brown University. In addition to serving on the faculty at the College of the Holy Cross in Worcester, Massachusetts, for over forty years, he has written extensively for solo, vocal, chamber, and orchestral forces. He has also penned six large-scale operas and music theater works. Korde's compositions are lauded for their highly expressive, distinct voice, which is characterized by a thoughtful embrace of the varied musical traditions he incorporates. His music has been performed by leading ensembles and orchestras around the world, including the Da Capo Chamber Players, the Polish National Radio Symphony Orchestra, the New Zealand Philharmonic, the Boston Philharmonic Orchestra, and the Chicago Symphony Orchestra.

I had the pleasure of attending the premiere of Korde's *Lalit–2nd Prism* (2019) by the Richmond Symphony at the University of Richmond's 2018–2019 Tucker-Boatwright Festival. *Lalit–2nd Prism* showcases Korde's unique compositional style by synthesizing Western and Indian classical music traditions. I was intrigued by the fact that this performance also featured a close collaboration between two virtuoso soloists: Jan Müller-Szeraws on cello and Amit Kavthekar on tabla. The pages below reflect my phone conversation with Korde after the premiere, on May 10, 2019, where we discussed his approaches to intercultural composition. During our conversation, Korde described the effects of his diverse musical training, as well as his varied approaches to his multi-genre compositions. He further chronicled the evolution of his musical identity, which is closely linked to his study of world musics and his ethically informed approaches to musical representation and borrowing. With *Lalit-2nd Prism* as a focal point, Korde illuminated his intercultural compositional and collaborative practices. Much like his music, the interview touched on a variety of subjects, demonstrating the composer's reflective and inclusive approaches.

> Christopher Chandler (CC): You draw on several diverse styles and cultures to create your music. I wonder if you could start by talking about your background, your training, and how that has informed the music you make today.
>
> Shirish Korde (SK): I came to this country to study jazz [because of] a chance encounter with Stan Getz … in the 1960s and 1970s, he was huge. I happened to be playing a piece of his that he made really famous in the 1970s called *Desafinado*, which was a bossa nova. At that time, bossa nova was huge. Anyway, he said to me, "What are you doing playing my tune?" He was kidding of course, but he said that I should really consider going to the United States to study jazz. So I came to Berklee College in Boston to study jazz with Herb Pomeroy.
>
> I was supporting myself playing jazz and I got interested in other things, especially composition. I started studying composition with some people at Boston University and also MIT, and then I went to New England Conservatory and studied with Donald Martino and Robert Cogan. They [taught me] vastly different styles. Cogan was very interested in timbre and he was, at that time, writing his book called *Sonic Design*. I also studied with Ernst Oster, who is a disciple of [Heinrich] Schenker and may have even studied with [him] in his last days. [Gunther] Schuller was of course the [conservatory] president at that time … and I took some conducting [lessons] with him. I was there for three years and also got really interested in ethnomusicology. I went to Brown after that.

After studying ethnomusicology at Brown University, Korde was hired to teach at the College of the Holy Cross, where he has been on the faculty since 1977. During this early period of his career, Korde noted that he was influenced by European composers like György Ligeti, Iannis Xenakis, and Pierre Boulez. However, as he continued to study world music traditions, particularly Japanese and Indian music, his compositional voice began to change. Elsewhere in our conversation, he commented that, "since 1985, I started really thinking through the prisms both of Indian music and the [world] music that I have studied. Before 1985, I was writing in a much more aggressive, contemporary style …

I guess would be a way of describing it." As Korde further elaborated on this early period, he described the tension he felt as he began to more intentionally incorporate cross-cultural influences into his work. He pointed out how, at the time, few people were incorporating jazz and world music traditions into the contemporary, Western-focused musical landscape that was dominated by modernism and serialism.

> CC: I'm really curious to hear you talk about that transition of moving from jazz performance to composition. You were performing at the time too?
>
> SK: Yes, I was, and in fact I am a tenor saxophone and flute player. I don't play anymore, but yes. It was a really subtle transition. Even when I was at Berklee, I was interested in exploring different scale formations, using tabla in a jazz context, and sitar in a big band context. My interest in arranging and jazz composition were always there, so I [have always been] very interested in [composition].
>
> It wasn't a huge transition, but once I started writing in a so-called "non-jazz" tradition, I shut the jazz thing off [for a while]. I tried to write non-jazz scores and realized the folly of all that at some point. I realized that it wasn't really me. I was suppressing things that I liked. It was a different time too. It was much more polarized, so academic composers were doing crazy [John] Cage-ian things or they were doing really serial stuff. There was nothing else. There was [almost] no one incorporating jazz except for [Gunther] Schuller.
>
> CC: The "third stream" approach.[1]
>
> SK: Yes, and nobody was doing world music at that time with the exception of people like Colin McPhee and Lou Harrison. There were a few people like that. But, you just didn't get grants or support from your own teachers. You would never get performances … Thank God that it's not that way anymore.
>
> CC: The diversity of styles and areas that composers work in today is something that I hear composers from older generations talk about, especially how they had to eschew various influences. I'm curious about you "realizing the folly" of the music you were writing and how you were suppressing part of your musical identity. That's an important thing to realize. You were attracted to music through the language of jazz or the language of world music and, if I'm understanding correctly, at a certain point you gravitated towards a traditional Western system but later realized that all these other [developing interests] needed to be incorporated. How did you come to that realization?

SK: Well, I mean part of it has to do it with identity, like realizing who I am. People would ask me about Indian music, [but] I knew much more about jazz than Indian music. I knew more about Boulez and European music than I knew about my own tradition. I had some teachers who would ask me things about Indian music and I was astounded that I couldn't really say anything about that. I had studied some sitar when I was very young but not seriously enough.

I also found that I wasn't really loving listening to Elliott Carter. Although I had studied his music intensely, it wasn't what I was preoccupied with when I would go home. There, I listen to [Gustav] Mahler, or jazz, or Ravi Shankar. Those styles seemed much more alive and musical to me than listening to Carter's *String Quartet No. 2*. I appreciated the mathematics of it, the complex metric modulations, and the use of all-interval sets, but it didn't do it for me. So, on the one hand, I was discovering things about myself and also finding that, as much as I respected [Milton] Babbitt and Carter, I wasn't really getting drawn into [their styles].

I came to the realization that I needed to revisit who I am and where I come from. I went to Brown especially because of that. Bonnie Wade was at Brown at that time and her area of expertise was Indian music. I took a lot of lessons in tabla.

Korde's time at Brown provided an important period of self-reflection, where he could investigate several non-Western music traditions that would help to shape his future compositional work. At one point in our conversation, he described how his study of Indian, Japanese shakuhachi, and Balinese music centered on transcription and analysis. Regarding this practice, he said, "I started transcribing the music and studying it from a more analytical perspective. I noticed there were huge disparities between theory—like treatises on Indian classical music—and practice. I was interested in what I was learning from practitioners." He connected this type of study to his earlier transcriptions of improvisations by jazz musicians, like John Coltrane, which was a common practice in that tradition. Korde pointed to two pieces he composed after studying at Brown that signaled turning points in the development of his globally-interconnected compositional voice: *Tenderness of Cranes* (1985) is a work he wrote for solo flute that is influenced by Zen philosophy and shakuhachi music, and *Rasa* (1991) is an opera that, as Korde put it, blended "a lot of different musics—from world musics, to Indian, to electronic, to angular and tonal at the same time." He began this last work around 1989 and reflected on it, noting, "from that point on, the music changed quite a bit I would say."

In many of Korde's works, Indian ragas serve as the foundation for melodic and harmonic material. Ragas are intrinsically linked to the improvisational practices of Indian classical music, which feature a primary melodic instrument that performs the raga and additional instruments that provide a drone and rhythmic accompaniment. Ragas have some similarity with the Western idea of a scale, since both are collections of pitches used throughout a composition or improvisation. But as the sitar virtuoso Ravi Shankar explains:

> Ragas are precise melody forms. A raga is not a mere scale. Nor is it a mode. Each raga has its own ascending and descending movement, ... usage of microtones, and stresses on particular notes. With the tambura, the drone instrument in the background, the soloist does a free improvisation known as *alap*, after which he starts the theme based on a rhythmic framework known as *tala*. He can choose from many talas, such as *tintal*, a rhythmic cycle of sixteen beats or *jhaptal*, having ten beats.
>
> (quoted in Bakan 2012: 127)

The concept of a raga therefore extends beyond the characteristic melodic patterns and ornamentations of a Western scale, and also includes associations with times of the day, seasons, and moods. Curious to learn more about how Korde incorporated ragas and materials from other musical traditions into his work, I asked him about issues of representation in his compositional practice. This moved our conversation to the particulars of *Lalit–2nd Prism*.

CC: I'm gathering that you're familiar with these cultures and have become aware of their values through your study of ethnomusicology. As you have deepened your practice of incorporating world music into your own, how do you avoid doing things that don't musically align with the values of each culture?

SK: I'm interested in making sure that the tradition that I'm influenced by is represented to its best potential, which in my case is both traditions. For example, if you take [*Lalit–2nd Prism*], it's a great compliment to me when somebody in the audience who doesn't know anything about Western music comes up and says, "Wow, I really loved the way in which you dealt with rag Lalit, that was really interesting." There were some people like that in the audience in Richmond. I also appreciate the fact that other people came up and said, "That was really neat the way you orchestrated a particular section," or "the way that you voiced certain harmonies," or "the way in which you used timbre in that section." They're not really getting the Indian music raga concept at all, but that's okay too. If I can get somebody who knows both to say, "That was really interesting the way you used Lalit, and I like the way you emphasized the A-flat minor rather than the E augmented triad, which is really the tonic," it is [exceptionally] great.

I'm trying to represent each of those [traditions] with as much integrity as I can. In situations where I don't think I can get it—where [for instance] I cannot get a percussionist to do what a tabla player does—I [will] use a tabla player. If I can, I [will] use the percussionist and vice versa. If I [could] find a sitar player who [could] play the notes that I wrote for Jan [Müller-Szeraws, the cellist], then I would. I'm using the cello because I don't know any Indian classical musicians who can play cello the way Jan can play it. It would be a completely different piece if I wrote it for hand drumming and [notated all of] the rhythms. [These changes] would have resulted in a completely different structure.

I guess those are my limitations within the integrity of the [Indian] tradition. Now I'm moving into a more abstract world, where, in some of my current pieces, you may not even recognize the Indian sound—it's not that obvious.

CC: I remember people coming up to you after the concert saying, "I could hear the rag and how you were treating it." I was not attending to that in my own experience of the concert. I remember saying something afterward about the virtuosity of Amit, the tabla player, which was really incredible. How important is it for people in the audience to take away different aspects of the cultural traditions you're bringing together? For instance, you're saying in the [current pieces] you're working on, the rag might not be as apparent.

SK: If I use fragments of ragas, I don't mean them to actually express what an Indian classical musician would try to express in a raga. In this particular case, I had been obsessed with rag Lalit for five years, and I just wanted to try to capture that, not as an improvisation but as a composition. It really got me thinking a lot about the morphology of the notes. I questioned: How do you resolve things? How far can you go with stretching the raga without losing its essence? The rag doesn't modulate in my piece, but there are a lot of places that I use clusters and various other techniques that could obscure it. I was trying to test [that] out. I wanted to actually harmonize the raga using techniques that I've learned from Ligeti or someone else, in a very subtle way. But [I didn't want] an Indian listener to be put off by that [and I hoped that they] would find it enchanting or still hear the structure of Lalit. That was sort of my pre-compositional challenge, I guess: How far can

I stretch this without changing it? I think I actually could've gone further now, in retrospect.

When I asked Korde about balancing the boundaries between styles and how he thought he could have gone further, he just laughed and said it was difficult to say. He added, "I don't know where that line is because there are no models to look for." Indeed, with relatively few artists creating cross-cultural compositions like Korde, he must rely upon his informed knowledge about these musical traditions and his collaborations with expert musicians from these traditions to confront issues of integrity and representation. This especially applies to situations where the blending of styles and traditions is intentionally audible and salient for the listener. As Korde noted, there are also times where he uses materials from non-Western traditions, like ragas or rhythmic cycles, but does not necessarily intend for those aspects to be at the forefront of the listening experience. Instead, these materials become background, structural features that support the compositional process. Korde went on to describe how sometimes aspects of these supporting materials can even be brought out by the musicians without him directly asking them to do so.

SK: There are some characteristic [motivic] gestures in rag Lalit, for example the descending C, B-flat, A pattern of pitches in [*Lalit–2nd Prism*]. [This pattern of pitches] can be elaborated on, but essentially, it's this descending [motive] over a long phrase. What's interesting is [that] when the orchestra hears that, they start interpreting it. They figure out what the main notes are. I didn't tell [the conductor] Steven Smith that. I don't tell [the musicians], "Make sure you bring out the C, B-flat, A." But they hear that in the music and they start doing it, reinforcing the pre-compositional design. In just two rehearsals, they picked that up.

CC: That's fascinating. So you're saying that something you've built into the piece that is inherent, [like] in the rag that you're using, [is picked up on by] the musicians without any sort of direction.

SK: Right, because it would have taken much longer to really point that out in every phrase. But they picked that up from the way the cellist was playing and the way it's notated, and so on. They figured that out and it really enhances [the motivic] structure that is so important in that raga.

Everybody plays the rag Lalit differently and even the same performer would probably improvise a completely different solo ... every time they play it. But these basic cells [like the descending C, B-flat, A motive] are very important to that raga. The way in which you elaborate on them can vary, but you can't lose track of the main cell underneath it. If you lose track—even Indian performers will sometimes lose it—you lose the essence of the raga.

You were asking me about the line.[2] That, to me, was an important line. With *Lalit–2nd Prism*, the raga did determine what I would and would not do with it.

As Korde has already indicated, *Lalit–2nd Prism* is grounded in an Indian rag of the same name. Although the work is notated, it distills the essence of improvised North Indian classical music (or Hindustani) raga performances across three uninterrupted movements. The subtitle, *2nd Prism*, differentiates it from an earlier incarnation for only cello and tabla, which he composed specifically for Jan Müller-Szeraws. This practice of recomposition for new forces with reimagined musical materials—what Korde calls "prisms"—is common across his compositional output. Our conversation turned to address the work's lineage and the process of reworking the duo into the orchestral version. Korde discusses how he treats the orchestra as an extension of the soloists and uses its vast timbral palette to accentuate and elaborate on the soloists' materials.

> CC: We've been circling around *Lalit–2nd Prism* and using it as an example of some of the techniques you use. I wonder if we can go further into it. I know that for this piece in particular it's taken on a couple of manifestations. It first started as a solo cello and tabla work, right?
>
> SK: Yes, and then [it was] a trio with the vibraphone essentially replacing the drone and adding in some other things to it too. Then [it became] this larger work. For the duo and its relationship to this larger piece, if you took the whole orchestra out and just played the cello, it's about 70 percent [the same]. The cello part does not change that much, but everything around it changes dramatically to the extent that the cellist feels it [is] a completely different piece [when the orchestra is added], which it does! He was a little bit bothered by it because he had much more freedom in the duo. [He wasn't] bothered in a bad way, but said, "that's a completely different piece." I said to him, "It is! You [now] have a large group of instruments to keep together, somehow."
>
> CC: What's the timeline between that original duo version, the trio, and then this orchestral version?
>
> SK: I think it's about five years or so.

CC: When you were composing the original version, did you give [the performers] a completed score? Or did you rely on them while you were writing? How did you navigate that collaborative phase?

SK: For this piece, the score I gave Jan was completely done. We played around with it and fixed a few things that were awkward: [we] shifted registers and added in a tabla solo where he needed a couple of measures to recoup after a virtuosic [passage]. Other times I have worked [with the performer] as I'm writing the piece, like with the violin concerto I wrote for Joanna Kurkowicz, who is a Boston-based violinist. I showed her sketches [along the way], and that's really helpful. Amit [the tabla player for *Lalit–2nd Prism*] was recommended by another tabla player I was working with, and he has been very interested in doing the piece the way I want it done. So it's been great to have him.

CC: Tell me more about that process of reworking the duo into *Lalit–2nd Prism*. Obviously, you said that the cello part hasn't changed that much from the duo to the orchestral version. When you approach a project like that, what's your process? I know you've done this with other pieces that include "prism" versions.

SK: When I was first writing the duo part, I actually built a [different] version that I tested out for Indian flute player, harp, and percussion. The Indian flute player, a bansuri player, was an improviser, and I would just give him some cells.[3] For that, I made large sketches, trying out various harmonic combinations, even transposing the ragas using the rotational technique [Igor] Stravinsky used to generate [harmonies].

So I tried out many things with that group and made all kinds of recordings. I used some of those sketches as a point of departure to create the harmonic sequences for the cello version. For the cello and tabla version, I tried to make a purely melodic composition.

CC: That's one of the striking things about it. You've got one of the most vocal of all Western instruments—the cello—and also the tabla, which from my understanding provides a good format for Hindustani music. Then you add the orchestra, which is full of so many harmonic and orchestrational possibilities and so many timbral intricacies—sonic qualities that are not often considered or privileged in Indian music.

SK: You're right.

CC: Can you talk a bit about your approach to using the orchestra with these soloists? What were you concerned with?

SK: I was really looking at the orchestra as an extension of the cello. For example, there's a section in there where the cello and the tabla are playing pizzicato, so I tried to find timbres that could really match those [sounds]. I combined groups of instruments that could make sense and not block [the soloists]. I was also trying not to make the orchestral part too complicated, knowing that there wasn't that much time for rehearsal.

I'm influenced in my orchestration by a kind of pre-spectral view of timbre. So I'm thinking of Kaija Saariaho and Ligeti, you know, [composers] like that, because I think the drone technique is like having the overtones series present throughout. I was thinking of properties that move from simple to complex and moving from sine-wave-like structures to more noise-like structures, and vice versa. Then within that, I was thinking about very dry attacks versus the very resonant attacks within the vibraphone, etc. I don't know if [these techniques] come through or not.

CC: I think some of those things came through very nicely. One thing I'm curious about is how you're trying to merge these two worlds in this piece. You have the rag, which serves as the foundation [for] the piece, you have the rhythmic interplay of the two solo instruments, and you've got—if I understand right—some rhythmic cycles, or talas, expressed by the tabla player?

SK: Yes, that's right. I stayed with the simple raga with the sixteen beats.

CC: So the Indian influences and your Western training both come to the surface in this piece. I wonder if you have any thoughts about preserving the cultural traditions of the musics from which you draw, as you transform it with your own creative impulses?

SK: I think about the music as a reflection of who I am. I speak multiple languages, I eat multiple cuisines, and I just think ... that's what I do. On one hand, English is the language that I've chosen to [write] in. I do know the other Indian languages, but I've chosen to live in this country, so my audience is primarily a Western audience. But, since I do embody these cultures in the sense that I grew up in these two cultures simultaneously, [my work] is a reflection of that.

I am not that self-conscious about this being Indian or that being Western when I'm writing music. It's kind of like when people speak: I'm sure you've heard Indians speaking to each other, and sometimes you'll hear a phrase in English, and a phrase in Hindi, and then [another] phrase in English. It happens all the time. I think other people do that too ... On one hand, I want to represent the cultures really accurately, and on the other hand, I just see them as musical synthesis.

Korde expresses confidence in his compositional choices. As indicated in his discussion of the experimental version of *Lalit* that he created with the

Indian bansuri player, he collaborates closely with musicians from the various traditions that he draws upon. He complements this practice with his formal musical training and academic study of multiple musical traditions, which has produced a musical fluency that allows him to draw on numerous styles with relative comfort. His personal experiences also contribute to his ability to communicate between and across disparate cultural experiences.

> CC: You made an interesting point about being someone that embodies, or could be perceived as embodying, Indian music because of who you are. You recounted a story earlier about how your teachers had asked you about Indian music and you didn't know much about it—you could talk more about jazz. I wonder if you could tell me about any personal experiences [you've had] with people misrepresenting or misperceiving who you are as an individual because of the way that you look, or what they may [have] assumed about the way that you write music because [of your] Indian heritage.
>
> SK: There are "lost in translation" moments that happen. [Once] a tabla player turned to me and said, "Do I come in when the black instrument is playing?" … [laughs] … He meant the bass clarinet.
>
> The dialogue that happens as a piece is [rehearsed] is very interesting. Sometimes [things are] lost in translation, but then there's a sort of a "coming together." For example, when we first rehearsed with the [Richmond] Symphony Orchestra, there was an uptightness about the feel of the piece. Generally, I tend to hear symphonic ensembles playing behind the beat, and so they have to get used to this idea that they need to be on top … or ahead of it. Once that happens, [the orchestral players] relax with the feel of the pulse. It's not as uptight. It's really a great change when it happens; it's really beautiful. But it's difficult to articulate the "coming together." [The result is] neither Western nor Indian in the traditional sense, because in India you can't find an orchestra that will play like that. You won't find Indian musicians who will be able to match exactly what the cellist and the orchestra are doing. Tabla players tend to, in general, play their own thing in the chamber context. Having worked with Amit, coaching him in the chamber music sense first, and then in the orchestral sense, it's very rewarding. You get something that's not really [one or the other]; it's something beyond. It's a very nice energy.
>
> I have to say that there also have been disasters … [laughs] …
>
> That's why I'm happy to have a group of people I can call on to do projects like the one in Richmond. They were so nice to let me bring Jan

and Amit. I'm sure there are tabla players in Richmond that we could have hired, but it would not have been the same experience. It's a real crapshoot. It's sort of a specialized thing, I guess. I think Reena [Esmail] is finding that too. I don't think she could just hire an Indian singer. She's worked with Saili [Oak] and Lucy [Fitz Gibbon] and I think that's why [the performance] worked so well.[4]

CC: Yes, the collaboration process and the deep relationships that form from it can really make something quite special and make those performances feel unique and rewarding.

SK: I'm sure you find that in whatever style of music you're writing. If you get to know the performers, and [they] get to know exactly what it is that you're writing and like [it], and you like how they're playing, then it's a great thing. It happened in jazz with Duke Ellington's and Miles Davis's groups. It also [happened] with Phillip Glass's ensembles, Steve Reich's ensembles, and the Bang on a Can people. It's the same thing ... people have to embody the music and ... being able to work with them directly is the only real way to do it.

Despite the fact that the COVID-19 pandemic has upended musical performances in the time since my conversation with Korde, the composer has remained busy with several significant premieres and large-scale projects on the horizon. In November 2019, his new song cycle, *The Conference of the Birds* (2019), was premiered by the soprano Lucy Fitz Gibbon and the Boston Musica Viva at the Tsai Center at Boston University. The composition, which features multimedia and video projections, is based on a medieval poem by the same name written by the Sufi poet Farid ud-Din Attar. Korde also wrote the music for a theater work called *Aède of the Ocean and Land* (2020), which draws on South Asian and Western traditions. The production, directed by Elli Papakonstantinou, premiered in September 2020 and was presented live over the internet, with artists performing simultaneously from ten different time zones in five countries. Two of his larger projects have been postponed to late 2021 and 2022—an opera workshop for the tenor David Lomelí and the Dallas Opera, and a new orchestral piece for the South Asian Symphony Orchestra. The latter piece deals with themes of water and climate change and will contain a final movement that features a soprano singing a text written by the Indian poet, Rabindranath Tagore. Korde has not slowed the pace of his work despite the pause on international travel and in-person performances, and he remains committed to composing music that seeks out connections across global cultures and traditions.

Notes

1. Schuller was an American composer and horn player who was an important figure in the Boston music scene. He pioneered a musical genre he called "third stream," which fused jazz and classical music and incorporated improvisation as a central tenet.
2. Korde is referring to our earlier discussion of the boundaries that maintain the integrity of the musical traditions he incorporates into his compositions.
3. Cells are fragments of musical ideas or combinations of pitches with which the performer can freely sequence and improvise.
4. My interview with Esmail about *Meri Sakhi Ki Avaaz*, performed during the same concert as *Lalit–2nd Prism*, appears in Chapter 15.

Reference

Bakan, M. (2012), *World Music: Traditions and Transformations*, New York: McGraw Hill.

12

Sonic Dismantling, Appropriation, and Confederate Monuments

David Kirkland Garner

I am a white man from the southern United States who writes music about the region's history, racism, and power structures.[1] I am haunted by the way the South is romanticized in American culture, including a nostalgic yearning for the "Old South," its apparently simple living, forgotten Appalachian hollers, and "authentic" folkways standing in stark conflict with the realities of slavery, the Civil War, and white supremacy.[2] In many of my compositions, I try to tell stories using archival sources and sounds that pull apart the South's histories and myths. In *Red hot sun turning over: on Southern monuments, myths, and histories* (*RHSTO*)—a large-scale composition calling for the removal of Confederate monuments that premiered in 2019—I had to revise my approach to quotation, question my use of historical sources, and investigate the complex histories of appropriation in classical music.

The banjo served as my gateway into the sonic geographies of the American South. I fell in love with the instrument's sound, techniques, and cultural history in audio recordings, appreciating how its plucked, reverberant timbre is often thought to epitomize this region. I also became intrigued by the romanticized aspects of the instrument's origins and cultural history. Greil Marcus's *The Old, Weird America* (2011) and Harry Smith's 1952 compilation album, *Anthology of American Folk Music*, helped to shape my artistic conviction to write music about and around Southern ideas, objects, and sounds. But as I wrote more music drawing on these themes, I realized that the goal of making art from history comes with a profound responsibility to understand the deeply ingrained racism in America's past and present.

I am finishing this chapter in the summer of 2020, a time when political, social, and cultural institutions are being tested by COVID-19 and challenged by Black

Lives Matter and related social justice movements. Confederate monuments have been falling faster than ever before. Iconic statues of Jefferson Davis, the one-time president of the Confederacy, and of Confederate general J. E. B. Stuart, have been triumphantly removed in Richmond, Virginia, the former Confederate capital. Unfortunately, the city's Robert E. Lee statue remains in place for now, though it has been repurposed for anti-racist art that projects images of Black historical figures, including Harriet Tubman and Frederick Douglass. It feels like we are experiencing a watershed moment, with changes happening weekly, making an essay like this seem immediately dated. But I hope that the questions I raise here and the art we create together will, in their small ways, contribute to the groundswell of efforts to shift existing power structures.

Red hot sun turning over

The book that became the mantra for my piece *RHSTO* is Jenny Odell's *How to Do Nothing: Resisting the Attention Economy* (2019). Here she introduces the idea of "manifest dismantling" as process of undoing, which she describes as the opposite of "manifest destiny" (190). Her ideas made me realize that while we may ignore damaged structures—whether ideas, systems, monuments, or sonic geographies—in the hope that they will recede into the background, the dismantling process itself might reveal and address new problems.

In March 2019, I premiered *RHSTO*, an eighty-minute piece for mezzo-soprano, wind ensemble, and wind quintet, set to historical film with audio. The piece comprised sixteen movements in four categories: *Monuments*, *Pedestals*, *Arias*, and *Interludes*. In it, I explored the complex history of the South, including debates about the dismantling of Confederate monuments in public spaces. I spent a year researching and thinking about how I could work with these histories ethically and responsibly, struggling with questions of appropriation and exploitation. I still have not answered these questions, and though I did my best to address them thoughtfully in *RHSTO*, I realize that grappling with them will be a lifelong project.

I began composing *RHSTO* by focusing on ideas of whiteness and memory, aiming to create a large-scale work that tears down monuments by drawing on a myriad of historical sources. I approached this dismantling in four ways. The *Monuments* movements create aural representations of Southern history and Confederate monuments through sonification or turning data into sound. Three of the four movements sonify data on the number of Confederate monuments and memorials dedicated in the United States each year between 1861 and 2018, each using a different musical method. For example, in *Monument (Short Winds)*, each measure of music represents one year, and the wind instruments repeat chords that correspond to the number of Confederate memorials dedicated that year. Thus as the measures and years pass by, the audience hears and *feels* each dedication with the attack of each chord.

I incorporated musical quotations and other references throughout the piece. In three Monument movements and the final Aria, I quoted extensively from the opening to Anton Bruckner's Third Symphony and (in a less obvious manner) the opening chord progression from his First Symphony. I borrowed and reworked Bruckner's music for several reasons. It represented the hegemony of the European (and specifically Austro-German) tradition, striking me as monumental in form, sound, and use of repetition. Its harmonic language, written during the years of the American Civil War, anticipated late Romanticism. Hitler and the Third Reich adopted his music to aurally represent German power and superiority, demonstrating how reception and appropriation can shape the meaning of any music. In *RHSTO*, the opening and closing movements feature a fanfare from Bruckner's Third Symphony that was also used by the Nazis in their *Tag der deutschen Kunst* on June 30, 1937 (Gilliam 1994: 558). The last *Monument (Distress)* thus speaks to similar human atrocities, layering Confederate monument data, heard in the drums, with sonifications of the number of African Americans lynched in the South between 1882 and 1968, heard in the fast woodwind arpeggiations.

The four *Pedestal* movements reinterpret and warp preexisting Civil War-era band music, using techniques like time-stretching and granularization to comment on how we remember (and misremember) histories. For example, in *Pedestal (Woodman, spare that tree)*, the ensemble performs a time-stretched version of the original nineteenth-century tune of the same name. Music that normally lasts about thirty seconds has been stretched to nearly six minutes, wherein the original tune can barely be discerned as the harmonies weave slowly behind it, creating a blurred, fuzzy shadow.

The *Aria* movements examine the relationship between nostalgia and trauma, exuding a sense of warmth and restoration in a critical context by exploring how tragic events can inspire beautiful art. All four movements draw on popular songs from the Civil War era, such as Stephen Foster's "Beautiful Dreamer." Though he only traveled below the Mason-Dixon Line once, Foster wrote countless blackface minstrel tunes depicting racist scenes and characters from the South, leading some to surmise that "Southern nostalgia was, in part, invented by a Yankee who spent almost no time in the South, long before the South was even something to be nostalgic about" (Friedman 2014). The *Aria* movements thus comment, in part, on monuments like the former statue of Foster in Pittsburgh's Schenley Plaza, who once sat above a (likely enslaved) African American banjo player. (The statue was removed in 2018, over one hundred years after it had been erected.)

The four *Interlude* movements (to which I will return below) are written for wind quintet and audio playback. Five wind instruments play against and on top of field recordings of Black prisoners recorded in 1939. This artistic choice—to use actual Black voices in my music—pushed me to examine my own relationship to appropriation and its various manifestations in classical music. How might I write music about racism, whiteness, and (Confederate) Southern history without contributing to the legacy of white men who have stolen and appropriated from marginalized groups? What distinguishes quotation and allusion from more problematic practices of appropriation? Who is allowed to use which materials, and in what contexts? How can today's composers navigate sonic, political, and cultural geographies to make music in dialogue with those marginalized by society? How does a classically trained composer, especially a white male composer from the South, interact with and respect the cultures outside of his own while engaging narratives that embrace the fraught history of Western music?

I composed *RHSTO* in response to the tragic events of the "Unite the Right Rally" in Charlottesville, Virginia, on August 12, 2017, which followed on the heels of heated debates over Confederate monuments and a race-motivated massacre at Charleston's African Methodist Episcopal Church on July 17, 2015. In writing a concert-length work that reflected on these events, I found myself exploring Southern history in greater depth, including my own family's background and naming practices. I learned that my middle name, Kirkland—shared with my grandfather, great uncle, two cousins, father, and my own son—came from a Confederate general under whom my great-grandfather had served while fighting for the Confederacy in the North Carolina infantry. This discovery prompted me to write an opinion piece, published in the Columbia, South Carolina newspaper, *The State*, in which I described my family's past and my reasons for writing *RHSTO*. I argued that "we desperately need to make art with, about, and around Confederate monuments and the history of white supremacy to confront and expose the South's dark, yet still present, past" (Garner 2019b). Moreover, I pointed out the failure of legislation to remove or contextualize Confederate moments and the need to "change the public discourse" through the most powerful and effective means possible: "artistic expression and experience."

My research into Confederate monuments led me to other readings and discussions on the Civil War, social justice, racism, and Southern history. Two sources introduced me to the debate over Confederate statues from the perspective of white men who wanted them removed: Mitch Landrieu's short autobiographical book about his work to remove the Robert E. Lee statue in New Orleans (2018) and John Biewen's podcast *Scene on Radio: Seeing White* (2017). Beiwen's work stood out to me because of his questions about historical concepts of "whiteness," where he revisits questions that critical race scholars have long-investigated:

> Where did this idea of a white race come from? God? Nature? Or is it manmade? And if somebody manufactured the idea, why, for what purpose? How has the meaning of "white" changed over the centuries, and how does it function now? The stories that we carry around about whiteness and what it means—stories we may not even know we're carrying, but we are, all of us—are those stories true?

Other influential sources included Nell Irvin Painter's *The History of White People* (2011) and Ibram X. Kendi's *Stamped from the Beginning* (2017), the latter of which provides invaluable lessons on racism and anti-racism.[3] Through manifest dismantling, we can subject Southern history, culture, myths, and monuments to necessary scrutiny and reassessment. I am attempting to do my part through the medium of concert music in *RHSTO* and other works and believe, moreover, that this process might be applied generally to the field of classical music.

Appropriation and Classical Music's White Racial Frame

Classical music itself needs some dismantling to allow new voices into spaces and styles traditionally dominated by white men. Just as Western sovereignties have exploited the labor and commodity goods of colonized societies, Western composers have, for much of classical music's history, taken from other cultures with reckless abandon, stealing rhythms, melodies, harmonies, dances, timbres, and stories, often to fit within colonialist or Orientalist contexts (cf. Said 1978; Born and Hesmondhalgh 2000).

The dominance of white men in the discourses and institutions of Western art music is clearly reflected in the history of the Pulitzer Prize for Music. Of the seventy-two recipients between 1943 and 2012, only four have been women: Ellen Taffe Zwilich (1983), Shalumit Ran (1990), Melinda Wagner (1999), and Jennifer Higdon (2010). Three have gone to Black composers (all men): George Walker (1996), Wynton Marsalis (1997), and Ornette Coleman (2007). Notably, no prize was awarded in 1965, even though the jury recommended Duke Ellington as the recipient.[4] In recent years, however, the Pulitzer jury has shifted its focus, both in terms of who receives the award and what kinds of music are honored. Since 2013, the prize has been awarded to only one white man, John Luther Adams (2014). Four women have since been recipients, including one Asian woman: Caroline Shaw (2013), Julia Wolfe (2015), Du Yun (2017), and Ellen Reid (2019). Three Black artists have also been awarded: Henry Threadgill (2016), the hip hop artist Kendrick Lamar (2018), and Anthony Davis (2020), for his opera *The Central Park Five*. This shift in recognizing achievement has been a dramatic and encouraging sign that power imbalances in music are slowly being rectified.

Recently, Philip A. Ewell has written about the structural and institutional "white racial frame" that governs the field of music theory, positing that "only through a deframing and reframing of this white racial frame will we begin to see positive racial changes" in the discipline (2020). While he has been praised in many quarters, he was also sharply criticized by several contributors to a special issue of the *Journal of Schenkerian Studies* (Flaherty 2020). If Ewell's timely work may lead to structural changes in university music theory curricula, it has also prompted me to think about what deframing and reframing mean for composers. As musicians and academics challenge the dominance of white men and their power structures, how can white male composers deal with the long-held traditions of appropriation in classical music? How will these traditions change, and how should they? I think one obvious answer is to provide more opportunities for marginalized people in all areas of music-making. But another, more complicated solution involves disentangling the ethics of borrowing and appropriation, which exist on a continuum. While it is easy to hear a borrowed melody and judge its level of appropriation, for example, it is far more difficult to label borrowed textures, timbres, and conceptions of musical form.

In 1998, the composer, performer, and professor Ziproyn wrote a controversial essay titled "Who Listens If You Care?", advocating an approach to music composition that draws on Marxist philosophy and seeks to incorporate every possible musical genre, style, idea, or melody available. On the surface, this approach might seem like a heart-warming (if naively color-blind) idea of music as a global language without borders or limitations. Ziporyn challenges the tenets of Milton Babbitt's famous 1958 essay "Who Cares If You Listen?", seeking to escape from the constraints of high modernism. But his notion of a theoretically all-inclusive mode of composition seems increasingly problematic, since it perpetuates the long history of European white male composers helping themselves to musical ideas from across the globe.

My own compositional philosophies align more with those of composer Alex Temple, who pushed against Ziporyn's vision and provided a framework for understanding appropriation and equity on a case-by-case basis. Temple wrestles with the practice of appropriation in classical music by noting how many white composers "draw influence, inspiration or sonic materials from other musical worlds—gamelan music, for example, or hip-hop" (Temple 2014). She adds, "I don't think that's exploitative or disrespectful in and of itself; to my mind, it really depends on how you do it," identifying three questions to distinguish problematic from acceptable uses: "What is the power relationship between the composer and the source? Is the composer reinforcing existing cultural hierarchies? How well does the composer understand the source?" (2014).

Temple's theoretical approach was tested by a recent Twitter debate that rocked the composition world. In October 2019, Tanya Tagaq, a Canadian Inuit throat singer and experimental vocalist, called out composer Caroline Shaw and the vocal group, Roomful of Teeth, for appropriating Inuit songs without properly crediting them. Shaw, the youngest winner of the Pulitzer Prize for Music, wrote *Partita for 8 Voices* specifically for Roomful of Teeth, a group whose mission, as conceived by founder and director Brad Wells, was to learn and incorporate extended vocal techniques from traditions around the world. In 2010, Roomful of Teeth apparently learned techniques of Inuit throat singing from two Indigenous performers, which Shaw featured in her award-winning composition (Roomful of Teeth 2019).

Tagaq tweeted the following with a link to a YouTube video of Shaw's *Partita*: "This is appropriation. The third movement (at about 12 min) is entirely based on Inuit throat singing. Specifically the Love Song. No Inuit are named as composers, no Inuit hired. This won the @PulitzerPrizes @roomfulofteeth" (Tagaq 2019). Shaw, Wells, and Roomful of Teeth responded with a promise to improve and to rectify their mistakes (Shaw 2019). But

Wells had once proved skeptical of views like Tagaq's, as he remarked in a 2016 interview with Dan Ruccia:

> The question of cultural appropriation assumes that the powerful culture is the only one that is involved in the exchange, but in fact these exchanges are happening constantly. There's an arrogance in our role, thinking of ourselves as the powerful culture and handpicking little things to use to our profit. These exchanges happen everywhere all the time, and you can't stop them. They can enrich everybody.
>
> (Ruccia 2016)

As a composer, I understand where Wells is coming from. He seems to be pointing out the fluidities and nuances that characterize the global exchange of ideas, cultures, sounds, music, instruments, and performance techniques. But there is also a colonialist arrogance to Wells's statement, as there is in Ziporyn's approach, that ignores one of Temple's guiding questions on appropriation: Is the composer reinforcing existing cultural hierarchies? In this case, I think the answer is *yes*. After the Twitter exchange between Tagaq, Shaw, and Wells, Tanya Kalmanovitch tweeted "Update: @roomfulofteeth has amended their Twitter bio. They no longer self-identify as 'throat-singers' and 'yodelers,' but as a band 'dedicated to the full palette of human expression,'" thus indicating a reappraisal of Wells's thinking (Kalmanovitch 2019).

To me, Shaw's incorporation of an Inuit throat song into "Courante" without acknowledging its origin is a clear example of appropriation. In the Twitter exchange, it became apparent that Shaw and Wells did not understand their source well enough to know that the techniques they incorporated were considered songs or that Inuit throat singers do not distinguish between performing and composing the way much of the Western musical tradition does. The power dynamic played out in the usual fashion: white musicians learned of a musical tradition foreign to their culture and classical training and incorporated aspects of it into their work without recognizing the fuller implications of their borrowing.

Questioning My Approach

While it is sometimes hard to define the boundary lines of appropriation, I hope to provide a framework for respectful and intentional *making* in my own work. In *RHSTO*, I borrow (via "manifest dismantling") a great deal of music written by white men and incorporate it into narratives both deeply connected to and distant from their original sources. I feel little concern about using these texts because deconstructing music made by other white men seems an uncontroversial act: there is no power imbalance between me and the source. I also feel that it is important for me both to pull apart these sonic monuments and to point to their fraught histories by dismantling them. The works I incorporate into the *Interlude* movements similarly add to *RHSTO*'s meditation on Confederate monuments by reflecting on Reconstruction, Jim Crow laws, the mass incarceration of African Americans in the South, and the whitewashing of these histories. But the borrowed material in these movements—recordings of the voices of Black people incarcerated in the South during the Jim Crow era—differs starkly from my use of Bruckner. I do not intend to dismantle these sources, but to bring their stories to light, though I must admit that the power differential at play means that my use of them might be contested.

The recordings I used were made by John and Ruby Lomax during their 1939 Southern Mosaic trip (a collection housed at the Library of Congress and accessible online), during which they documented hundreds of hours of folk songs from Texas to Virginia, often featuring Black singers and performers. Many of their recordings of Black musicians were made in coercive circumstances; in the state penitentiaries in Arkansas, Texas, and Florida, for example, Lomax was known to have bribed prison officers to force inmates to perform (Stewart 2016: 112).

The recordings I incorporated into *RHSTO* were made at the Cummins State Farm in Arkansas and the Raiford Penitentiary in Florida. After the Civil War, the prison systems in the South continued many of the traditions of forced labor and slavery, albeit under new names and institutions, such as the "state farm" system and the convict leasing programs (Blackmon 2009; Mancini 1996). In one of many chilling examples, the first governor-appointed superintendent of the Goree State Farm in Texas (one of the other prison camps in which the Lomaxes recorded on their 1939 trip) was T. J. Goree, who had once served as a Captain in the Confederate Army (Texas Department of Criminal Justice 2004). Prisoners were treated with unimaginably brutal cruelty. Lomax provided a glimpse of these horrors in his field notes, relaying that the wife of the Cummins State Farm captain in Arkansas "complained that she was kept busy repairing the right armhole of his shirts, which tore loose when he flogged the boys in the field when they slackened work" (Lomax 1939). And indeed, these practices of incarceration, control, and labor, forged in slavery, continue to the present day (Alexander 2012).

Music and performance remain an important part of life for incarcerated Black Americans, though their songs and performing techniques have changed over time (Harbert 2010). In the early twentieth century, "the main use of music was to speed and ease the harsh work," encouraged by guards who "knew from their own agrarian experience that inmates could work harder and longer when singing" (Harbert 2010: 66–7). Collectors like the Lomaxes traveled to prisons in search of "pure" and "authentic" songs, untouched by the outside world, but by the late 1930s, John Lomax was bemoaning their disappearance, citing radio and increased access to education as the primary causes. Lomax likely benefitted the most from the early "discovery" and exploitation of influential Black musicians such as Huddie William Ledbetter (Stewart 2016: 91–119; Lomax 1939).

In *Interludes*, I use the Lomax's field recordings as a backdrop for the wind quintet music to comment on this long history of appropriation and erasure. By having these recordings uncomfortably coexist with European classical instruments, which play quantized and pitch-adjusted music drawn from transcriptions of the recordings, I seek to draw attention to the erasure, theft, and militaristic policing of the men whose voices were captured, perhaps demonstrating through sound how white supremacy both co-opts and attempts to drown out Black voices. Although I recognize that my use of these voices potentially reaffirms power imbalances and hierarchies, my intent is to call out the white power structures that dominate Southern (and American) culture. I chose to employ the actual recordings in my piece, as opposed to recreating them, to comment on these histories and to make visceral connections to past voices. But in trying to disrupt white supremacy, I worry that I have unintentionally reinforced it, following in the long tradition of appropriation and exploitation. The pressing need to explain my compositional intentions has thus led me to create a companion website for *RHSTO* that provides extensive writing, reflection, research, links, bibliographies, and context (Garner 2019a).

Now that thousands of hours of field recordings from the early to mid-twentieth century have been disseminated on the internet or released into the public domain, I wonder what composers might do with them and what they can teach us. Although many were made in unethical contexts, some were not, and until recently most have remained on reel-to-reel tapes or other outmoded formats in the storage facilities of archives and museums. I have used them to give forgotten voices another chance to be heard and to highlight moments of particular beauty that might otherwise never be heard again. Embedded in every crackly field recording is a wealth of knowledge, experience, history, and humanity from which we can learn.

In addition to questions of appropriation, I have also grappled with the fact that my identity as a white Southerner intersects in complex ways with Black Southern culture. When considering another of Temple's test questions, I feel that I do understand my sources and their histories, albeit with inherent limitations. Although I fear reinforcing cultural hierarchies, I aim to show through sound the tangled roots of Southern cultural and historical legacies. Consider, for example, the typical house in Appalachia: it is small, made of wood, and has a front porch. Folklorist Henry Glassie shows that while its architectural design seems to be Irish, the wood construction was introduced by Dutch immigrants, and the front porch was Nigerian in origin (2013). The region's culinary history similarly illuminates these tangled roots. The journalist and food critic Julia Moskin notes, "So far, no one has managed to draw a clear line between white food and Black food in the South. Many of the cooking traditions and techniques that define Southern food were invented and executed by African-Americans, whether they were cooking for their own families or for white families that enslaved or employed them" (Moskin 2018).

The history of the banjo—my gateway into Southern music and history—exemplifies the complex legacies of Southern culture. Laurent Dubois (2016) traces the instrument's development through slave songs, blackface minstrelsy, jazz, white popular culture, and the forgotten hills of Appalachia. While the banjo has been wielded by Black and white musicians alike, it now looms in the popular imagination as a paradoxical symbol of America and the South—both historical-political concepts fundamentally built upon the white appropriation of Black music and culture. The banjo is, in other words, "America's African instrument." The sonic geography of the South was mapped by Black voices, hands, and feet, but it is white participation in this culture that has been documented and disseminated in the historically segregated genres labeled "country" and "bluegrass" (Miller 2010).[5]

Learning to Dismantle

I am continuing to interrogate my compositional choices. The "tangled roots" of Southernness, as well as my own privileged family history, still lead me to question how one might sonically mark the South without appropriating Black culture. I know that composing or writing about the South must include Black voices, but how can a white Southerner include these voices without reinscribing long-standing historical and social problems: Is such a feat even possible? While I feel confident that I have free reign to mash, mush, and dismantle Bruckner, is it similarly appropriate for me to comment on injustice and cultural appropriation by incorporating the field recordings of Black prisoners in my own works? In my efforts to bring attention to these men, am I actually just perpetuating oppressive structures? Is it ethical to draw on these recordings to remember the terrible circumstances of their creation and to celebrate the beauty of their music? I identify with the Southern culture in which I was raised and yet also acknowledge that almost everything about this culture—its food, music, language, and dance—resonates with Blackness.

As I struggle with these questions, I attempt to remain humble, working to understand Southern histories—especially those not written by white, male thinkers—and striving to be antiracist in my efforts to change public policies. While I understand my artwork may not seem to have a direct effect, I hope it can contribute to the larger project of antiracism within my community. My work thus follows the example of the sculptor Richard Hunt, as explained in an interview with the prominent African American composer, T. J. Anderson. Recalling a conversation they once had about riots, Anderson remarked that he would be in the front row among the rioters. Hunt responded, "Oh no, I would be in my studio creating sculpture about the march" (Anderson 2011).

It is thus in the power of art that many, like myself, can most clearly project their activism. By dismantling historical sounds, harmonies, melodies, and textures, I hope to contribute, in my way, to the projects of Black Lives Matter protesters, such as the image of Harriet Tubman projected onto the Robert E. Lee statue on Richmond's Monument Avenue this past summer—an artistic statement that visually dismantles the white supremacist structure by relegating it to the background (*Richmond Times-Dispatch* 2020). Indeed, Tubman's image is clear and bright on the graffitied statue's pedestal, the bronze figure of Lee mounted on his horse fallen into shadow. Above her likeness are her words: "Slavery is the next thing to hell." The horse's flank becomes a surface to display the letters *BLM*, affirming that Black lives indeed matter and that, perhaps, the Civil War's end might finally be in sight.

Notes

1 I am grateful to Dan Ruccia for his help with this chapter. Dan is a composer, writer, and performer who wrote program notes for *Red hot sun turning over*. This chapter began as a dialogue between us, created with a great amount of insight and feedback from him. I also want to thank Matthew Somoroff for his editing help on this chapter.
2 The term "the South" is itself ambiguous, multifaceted, and wrapped up in these histories. It can be known as a region "south of the Mason-Dixon line, the Ohio River, and the 36° 30' parallel ... historically set apart from other sections of the country by a complex of factors: a long growing season, its staple crop patterns, the plantation system, Black agricultural labor, whether slave or free" (*Encyclopedia Britannica* 2020). The term also conjures Lost Cause narratives and white supremacist ideas, like the phrase "the South will rise again."
3 For my complete list of books and resources, see the *RHSTO* website (Garner 2019a).
4 Ellington eventually received a posthumous citation in 1999. Scott Joplin received the same in 1976.
5 Over fifty years ago, historian Bill Malone wrote about the influence of Black musicians on the origins of country music but undersold the real magnitude of their contributions (1968). More recently, scholars have written about divergences between Black and white Southern music and the complex politics of Southern sonic geographies, including their intersections with class (Mann 2008).

References

Alexander, M. (2012), *The New Jim Crow: Mass Incarceration in the Age of Colorblindness*, New York: The New Press.
Anderson, T. J. (2011), "T. J. Anderson: Any Man or Woman in a Bath Tub Can Give You a Tune," *YouTube*, January 4. https://www.youtube.com/watch?v=aAJbu4H-VB8&feature=emb_logo (accessed November 30, 2020).
Babbitt, M. (1958), "Who Cares If You Listen," *High Fidelity*, 8 (2) February, 38–40, 126–7.
Biewen, J. (2017), [Podcast], "Seeing White," *Scene on Radio*, Parts 1–14. https://www.sceneonradio.org/seeing-white/ (accessed July 30, 2020).
Blackmon, D. A. (2009), *Slavery by Another Name: The Re-Enslavement of Black Americans from the Civil War to World War II*, New York: Anchor Books.
Born, G. and D. Hesmondhalgh (2000), *Western Music and Its Others: Difference, Representation, and Appropriation in Music*, Berkeley and Los Angeles: University of California Press.

Dubois, L. (2016), *The Banjo: America's African Instrument*, Cambridge, MA: Harvard University Press.

Ewell, P. A. (2020), "Music Theory and the White Racial Frame," *Music Theory Online*, 26 (2). https://mtosmt.org/issues/mto.20.26.2/mto.20.26.2.ewell.html (accessed November 30, 2020).

Flaherty, C. (2020), "Whose Music Theory?" *Inside Higher Education*, August 7. https://www.insidehighered.com/news/2020/08/07/music-theory-journal-criticized-symposium-supposed-white-supremacist-theorist (accessed November 30, 2020).

Friedman, M. (2014), "Can't Escape Stephen Foster," *The New Yorker*, March 10. https://www.newyorker.com/culture/culture-desk/cant-escape-stephen-foster (accessed November 30, 2020).

Garner, D. K. (2019a), "Red hot sun turning over," *Davidkirklandgarner.com*. https://www.davidkirklandgarner.com/redhotsun (accessed January 8, 2020).

Garner, D. K. (2019b), "USC Music Teacher Reflects on Confederate Monuments with New Composition," *The State Newspaper*, March 28. https://www.thestate.com/opinion/op-ed/article228526659.html (accessed July 1, 2020).

Gilliam, B. (1994), "The Annexation of Anton Bruckner: Nazi Revisionism and the Politics of Appropriation," *The Musical Quarterly*, 78 (3): 584–604.

Glassie, H. (2013), "Settlement and Revival: Two Tales of Ireland in the South," *YouTube*, May 4. https://www.youtube.com/watch?v=gbQxBX_fPXc (accessed July 1, 2020).

Harbert, B. (2010), "I'll Keep on Living after I Die: Musical Manipulation and Transcendence at Louisiana State Penitentiary," *International Journal of Community Music*, 3 (1): 65–76.

Kalmanovitch, T. (@kalmanovitch) (2019), "Update: @roomfulofteeth Has Amended Their Twitter Bio," *Twitter*, October 22, 2:27 AM. https://twitter.com/kalmanovitch/status/1186529383659556865 (accessed July 1, 2020).

Kendi, I. X. (2017), *Stamped from the Beginning*, New York: Nation Books.

Landrieu, M. (2018), *In the Shadow of Statues: A White Southerner Confronts History*, New York, NY: Viking Penguin.

Lomax, J. A. (1939), "1939 Southern Recording Trip Fieldnotes," *American Folklife Center*, AFC 1939/001: fn0001, Library of Congress, Washington, DC. https://www.loc.gov/item/lomaxbib000855/ (accessed December 1, 2020).

Malone, B. (2010), *Country Music USA*, 3rd edn, Austin: University of Texas Press.

Mancini, M. J. (1996), *One Dies, Get Another: Convict Leading in the American South, 1886–1928*, Columbia, SC: University of South Carolina Press.

Mann, G. (2008), "Why Does Country Music Sound White? Race and the Voice of Nostalgia," *Ethnic and Racial Studies*, 31 (1): 73–100.

Marcus, G. (2011), *The Old, Weird America*, New York: Picador Press.

Miller, K. H. (2010), *Segregating Sound: Inventing Folk and Pop Music in the Age of Jim Crow*, Durham, NC: Duke University Press.

Moskin, J. (2018), "Is It Southern Food, or Soul Food?" *The New York Times*, August 7. https://www.nytimes.com/2018/08/07/dining/is-it-southern-food-or-soul-food.html (accessed July 1, 2020).

Odell, J. (2019), *How to Do Nothing: Resisting the Attention Economy*, Brooklyn, NY: Melville House.

Painter, N. I. (2011), *The History of White People*, New York: Norton.

"Photos: Scenes from Monument Avenue on Saturday," *Richmond Times-Dispatch*, June 20, 2020. https://richmond.com/news/local/photos-scenes-from-monument-avenue-on-saturday/collection_e67b820e-130b-514b-96be-eefd6c979db4.html#1 (accessed November 30, 2020).

Roomful of Teeth (@roomfulofteeth) (2019), "A Message from Brad and Caroline," *Twitter*, October 22, 10:18 PM. https://twitter.com/roomfulofteeth/status/1186829222771412992 (accessed November 30, 2020).

Ruccia, D. (2016), "Roomful of Teeth Sings the Sounds of the World," *Indy Weekly*, April 27. https://indyweek.com/music/features/roomful-teeth-sings-sounds-world/ (accessed July 1, 2020).

Said, E. W. (1978), *Orientalism*, New York: Pantheon Books.

Shaw, C. (@caroshawmusic) (2019), "I Apologize for My Delay in Responding to this Thread and Bringing These Issues to Light," *Twitter*, October 17, 6:02 PM. https://twitter.com/caroshawmusic/status/1184952944938012672 (accessed July 1, 2020).

"The South," (2020), *Encyclopedia Britannica*, September 30. https://www.britannica.com/place/the-South-region (accessed November 30, 2020).

Smith, H. E. (1952, 1997), *Anthology of American Folk Music*, [CD] Washington, DC: Smithsonian Folkways Recordings.

Stewart, C. A. (2016), *Long Past Slavery: Representing Race in the Federal Writers' Project*, Chapel Hill: University of North Carolina Press.

Tagaq, T. (@tagaq) (2019), "This Is Appropriation," *Twitter*, October 16, 11:01AM. https://twitter.com/tagaq/status/1184484467274080256 (accessed July 1, 2020).

Temple, A. (2014), "The Appropriation Problem," *New Music Box*, January 23. https://nmbx.newmusicusa.org/the-appropriation-problem/ (accessed July 1, 2020).

Texas Department of Criminal Justice (2004), Nashville, TN: Turner Publishing.

Ziporyn, E. (1998), "Who Listens If You Care?" in W. O. Strunk and R. P. Morgan (eds.), *Source Readings in Music History*, 41–8, New York: W. W. Norton & Company.

13

The Lanna Dream: Reflections of Constructed Identities

Waewdao Sirisook and Abbas Rasul

This chapter uses two lenses to examine The Lanna Dream (2019), a performance piece by the dancer, choreographer, and cultural advocate Waewdao Sirisook. Abbas Rasul opens the essay with historical and cultural context essential to understanding Sirisook's critique of the tourist's gaze in the Lanna region of Thailand. Sirisook then describes growing up in this region, linking her experience of cultural and linguistic suppression to the movements, music, and props she features in The Lanna Dream. Rasul closes the chapter by interpreting Sirisook's piece in light of the performativity that has come to characterize a newly revitalized but precarious Lanna culture.

The Tourist's Gaze in Lanna Culture (Abbas Rasul)

Visitors to the Lanna region are bombarded with brochures advertising its authentic, exotic nature, offering tours to tiger petting zoos and visits to hill tribe villages (Trupp 2014: 346–9). Yet contemporary Lanna culture involves many contradictions: mountain villagers perform ancient rituals as students rally for democracy; traditional wooden homes abut modern condominiums; animist belief systems coexist with modern universities and hospitals. Authentic Lanna culture is far more complex than the vision promoted by taxi drivers and the Tourism Authority of Thailand. But despite its diversity, representations of Lanna identity focus on locals dressed in classical attire performing on the grounds of historic temples, accompanied by re-envisioned traditional Lanna music seldom heard elsewhere. Selective exoticized images, presented through national and international performances, caricature the culture as unaffected by the trappings of modernity, thus reinforcing outsiders' expectations of a simple, naive culture.

Since its conception, the Lanna region has absorbed and adapted to the many surrounding influences that later became particular to Lanna identity (McGraw 2007: 127). These influences include customs and traditions from India, craftsmanship and architecture from the Mon kingdom to the east, dance traditions from the Burmese to the northwest, and elements of language from the Ayutthaya kingdom (which later became the Siamese) to the south. In the mid-nineteenth and twentieth centuries, the influence of Western colonial powers within the region destabilized long-established cultural dynamics, and their values permeated the southeast Asian continent, especially India and China. Notably, the Siamese imposed the *Siwilai* ("civilizing") policy, a strategy of cultural alignment with Western powers (Winichakul 2011: 27). *Siwilai* challenged the very root of Lanna identity: historical texts were burned, dress codes altered, musical traditions lost, the roles of women realigned, and the Lanna language restricted. The policy was so successful that by the 1980s, many of the Lanna people had lost contact with their history and heritage (Farrell 2009; Kemasingki and Tananchai 2017). From the mid-twentieth century, interest grew in minority or marginalized cultures—even, and perhaps especially, through the lens of tourism—and the Lanna kingdom gained an opportunity to revitalize its identity, rediscover its traditions, and reassemble the pieces of what remained from its past. Throughout this process, however, its people adopted new traditions and customs, always adjusting to surrounding forces. The authenticity of the culture has therefore rested in its ability to adapt to a changing world.

Waewdao Sirisook's performance of *The Lanna Dream* reflects the Lanna individual's quest to survive while under the potentially destructive power of the outsider's gaze. The many threats and possibilities afforded from the encounters with outside influences have led to a vibrant yet enigmatic culture. The complexities of these contemporary dynamics inspired Sirisook to explore colonial and tourist influences upon the Lanna culture, the costs of these relationships, and the effects that these encounters have had on the perceived authenticity of today's cultural performances.

Rediscovering My Identity (Waewdao Sirisook)

The Lanna Dream performance reflects my twenty-five years of experience in the Lanna region's performing arts scene. During those years I traveled extensively, performing in numerous shows for the Thai government and international organizations, participating in local rituals and ceremonies, and providing training to underserved youth and local and international university students. These experiences led me to discover that the Lanna region's arts and culture had undergone drastic changes in order to maintain its appeal to cultural outsiders, and it gave me a deeper understanding of the culture's relationship with nonresidents, which has always been fraught.

The journey that Lanna culture has undertaken to once again be recognized for its unique history is significant in its own right. It is strange to think about how much it has changed over the past thirty to forty years. Though I came from Chiang Rai, and later Chiang Mai, I had no knowledge of these cities' importance to Lanna culture. To the central Thai population, we were labeled "Laotian," and it was implied that we had bad breath (from consuming fermented tea leaves) and were part of the "Maew"—a pejorative term denoting the North's purportedly barbaric, uncivilized cultures, whose people were rumored to eat live animals. Although our *Pah Sin* skirts—unique to Lanna culture and handcrafted with details representing our heritage—have been a part of the Lanna identity for centuries, our clothing was labeled as that of slaves, unrefined, and without finesse. Until recently, every part of our culture had been denigrated and every action criticized, including the food we ate, the language we spoke, and the way we smiled.

My early education did not teach me about Lanna culture—neither its heritage nor the term itself. To speak the Lanna dialect at school was forbidden: only Central Thai was permitted. Information about Lanna culture was not mentioned in national educational textbooks, and teachers encouraged us to hide our heritage. When traveling to Bangkok with my secondary school, we were told by the school principal not to speak our dialect in public, but to instead "civilize" ourselves, which created a sense of apprehension among most of the students. We were the suburban lower class—people with a low social standing in Thailand—and were grouped with immigrants and laborers. I was embarrassed to speak because I felt low class, invisible, and not worthy to be among the cosmopolitan school children. As we stepped off the bus, we were unaware of the kingdom that Lanna had once been or of its history, so we abandoned our culture and language and adopted those of central Thailand.

My university experience was similar. In my first year in the undergraduate program at Chiang Mai University (CMU), a professor from Bangkok commented on my nasal voice—a reference to the Lanna dialect—in front of other professors, saying that as a "village girl" I was not as delicate or sophisticated as a "palace girl." After completing my master's degree at the University of California, Los Angeles, I returned to teach in the Fine Arts department at CMU, alongside that same professor (much to her surprise). She still uses me as an example of "a village girl made good." These interactions resonate with the colonialist influences and perspectives that persist in living memory, demonstrating that there is still much to resolve from Lanna's period of subjugation.

My education and development in dance and performance taught me the value of my heritage and helped me to regain my identity. Lanna arts helped me grasp the history to which I belonged and to rediscover my sense of self. I am no longer ashamed to speak the Lanna language. In fact, I have gained a sense of power through it: being underestimated is advantageous for us. Many outsiders simply lack a knowledge or understanding of the region's cultural wealth—the beauty and playfulness in its perspectives and the unique elements within its language. The more Lanna culture differs from others, the more it stands out.

For the past thirty to forty years, Lanna arts and culture have been thrust into the limelight, mostly to promote the cultural richness and diversity of Thailand. Despite its history of cultural suppression, the Thai government now heavily promotes Lanna culture with romanticized headlines, such as "Beauty of the North," "Roses of the North," or "The Spell of the North." Due to an increased interest in the region's cultural tourism, the Lanna people have been presented with an opportunity to reclaim their heritage, rediscover their past, and reestablish their identities. With the cultural activist Ajarn Vithi Panichaphant at the helm, I was proud to be involved in rediscovering the region's history. However, I soon learned that this renewed popularity also affected the revitalization efforts: those who sought to realize the economic potential of this growing tourist market created unfounded cultural representations that deviated significantly from the academic research that had been carried out over the past forty years. The people's need to survive and secure a future thus became focused on satisfying the desires and expectations of tourist outsiders.

Lanna culture has become popular for both national and international onlookers—those who romanticize its apparent authenticity and seek to escape the trappings of their own cultures, becoming absorbed by a world of dreams and fantasy. My performance piece, *The Lanna Dream*, reflects these desires, with each sequence crafted, choreographed, and threaded together to depict Lanna culture's true identity and its survival over time. I created *The Lanna Dream* as an individual: it comes from my small, insignificant voice. Yet it is authentic, informed by history, my education, and my desire to speak out and show the realities of being a part of this culture. The performance is a representation of Lanna culture's way of life, as well as its history, need to adapt, and desire to exist, all shared through music, dance, and a little humor.

The Performance: Contemporary Visual and Sonic Representations

The Lanna Dream begins with a projected series of photographs depicting performances of stylized and manufactured images of the region that are marketed to global audiences. These photographs, taken on historically important sites, feature ornate structures with women often taking center stage. Dancers wear traditional attire and elaborate jewelry to further highlight the iconography that is a part of Lanna's identity, while exoticizing its culture for foreign audiences. (For an excerpt of the performance, see Sirisook (2020).)

Although the musicians in these shows typically play traditional instruments featuring musical forms, sounds, and structures that are unfamiliar to outsiders, *The Lanna Dream* slide show takes a different approach: it features a cover of Rod Stewart's "Da Ya Think I'm Sexy?" performed by Torpong Samerjai on traditional instruments, including the *khlui* (a Thai bamboo flute), the *salaw* and *sueng* (two Lanna string instruments), the *klong poang pong* (a two-sided drum, also from the Lanna region), and the *ching* and *chap* (two hand cymbals). This musical fusion represents the contemporary dynamics of Lanna society, bringing its styles and culture into dialogue with those of Siam and the West.

Waew Chan (Little Waew): The Blow-up Doll

The next part of the performance includes a blow-up sex doll that I introduce to the audience. With the doll attached to my body, I have it imitate the movements performed by dancers for foreign audiences. The doll is dressed in the traditional attire of the Lanna *Tai Yoan* and wears a hairpiece wrapped into a bun and pinned with flowers, a necklace with a traditional design, a *Pah Sin* covering the legs, and a special wrap worn only for important events on the upper half of the body (Figure 13.1). Each movement is femininized and influenced by Thailand's beauty queen contestants. The doll's ventriloquist "performance" represents the roles that Lanna women are expected to project both onstage and off: to promote

Figure 13.1 *The Lanna Dream* (2019), Sirisook performing with a blow-up sex doll.

their culture by enticing the outsider's attention through the values of grace and femininity (Subhimaros 2006).

When I address the audience, I ask a series of questions about their knowledge of Lanna culture. This not only crosses the boundary between viewer and viewed but also challenges preconceptions about the audience's place, assigning them an active role in the conventionally passive dynamic between spectator and performer. I further expose the relationships between the performer and audience members by highlighting the exoticized characterizations of Lanna performers. I demonstrate moderated speech and interactions, revealing how melodious remarks spoken in an unfamiliar language might conceal offensive meanings. I also enact a series of poses that reproduce the demeanor required to take pictures with tourists—affable, visually pleasing, and composed behaviors that ensure customers' expectations of civility and propriety are met, exposing the degree to which performers' actions have become constrained by viewers' tastes (Figure 13.2).

Figure 13.2 *The Lanna Dream* (2019), Sirisook reproducing an exoticized pose, as if performing for tourists.

I use a popular Lanna song to accompany this section of *The Lanna Dream*. Written in the 1970s by Jaran Manopetch, "Long Mae Ping" had become symbolic of the Lanna revival, embellishing existing stereotypes by romanticizing its geography and its women. The lyrics tell the story of two fictionalized female characters who, much like Giacomo Puccini's Asian female protagonist in *Madama Butterfly*, commit suicide after being betrayed by foreigners. This song was the first to be performed in the Lanna language since the period of central Thai cultural and governmental subjugation (Winichakul 2011; Fairfield 2017), and it gained a large following after its release, standing at the forefront of renewed interest in Lanna history and remaining culturally relevant to this day. My performance incorporates three different versions of "Long Mae Ping" that employ Western techniques and styles, including rock, pop, and contemporary fusion, which allow the song to take on various meanings. If the song is a symbol of Lanna revival, the use of Western musical styles suggests how our culture has been reworked for consumption by international audiences.

The Hidden Lanna Revealed

A final version of "Long Mae Ping," played in a reimagining of the Lanna classical style, accompanies the piece's concluding section. This symbolic adaptation of the region's classical composition uses a traditional instrument, the *pin pia*, which had once been an integral part of Lanna performance practice but was marginalized in favor of the Siamese *piphat* ensemble during the *Siwilai* process (McGraw 2007: 140; Winichakul 2011). Knowing this history, I stand alone onstage, stripped of any costuming and jewelry, and perform a dance routine using improvised and traditional Lanna dance movements. This dance is free from fixed choreography, thus breaking the boundaries placed upon Lanna expression and highlighting the culture that is concealed from outsiders to protect it from their influences.

My unrestrained movements further deviate from the staged, two-dimensional, frontal dances used in the reenvisioning of traditional Lanna choreography for seated audiences, and are instead grounded in the relationship between the human body and nature—elements that are highly valued within the Lanna culture. My routine is free from the static and restrictive styles of traditional Thai dances and also uninhibited by the values and expectations of Western audiences. My movements symbolize freedom from the restrictions imposed by the gaze, rejecting the manufactured identities, politics, and impositions of surrounding cultural value systems. I embody Lanna culture, my motions adopting the ethos of *pithi* (grace), which underpins bodily movements in traditional, local dance routines. Thus, I conclude the performance by contrasting the projected, cultivated identity of the Lanna people imposed by outsiders' desires with an authentic, freeform dance reflecting the authentic values of the culture concealed from their gaze.

Contemporary Representations of Identity (Abbas Rasul)

As mentioned above, leaders such as Jaran Manopetch and Ajarn Vithi Panichaphant initiated and championed the Lanna cultural revitalization movement. Manopetch released the first song to be written and performed in the Lanna language since the colonial period ("Long Mae Ping"), and Ajarn Panichaphant initiated the Lanna Fine Arts department at Chiang Mai University. But the reformation process itself was not free from complication. Tourism's influences, coupled with a desire for financial stability, led to deviations from or adaptations of the traditions and customs displayed in performances. The image promoted to outsiders is that of an exoticized, premodern culture (McGraw 2007: 133)—an image designed to suit the needs of a foreign audience.

The chance to rebuild thus came at the cost of authentic cultural revival. Lanna performances have become reflexive: viewers might assume they represent Lanna culture, but in fact they emulate the viewers' own values, becoming a mediating force between the outsider and the Lanna people. Accordingly, this selective, idealized representation of Lanna classical and historical culture—its mysticism, deities, and festivals—are a strategy for fulfilling audience desires. The blow-up doll that Sirisook dresses up to project an exoticized vision of Lanna women reflects how the people often perform according to such preconceived notions (Trupp 2014: 362). Projections of contemporary Lanna identity have to strike a delicate balance between the viewer's expectations and accurate cultural representations.

Lanna performances are spectacular affairs featuring vibrant colors, ornate clothing, glittering jewelry, special lighting, delicate movements, and mysterious and enchanting music. Its clear structures and uncomplicated characters create narratives that bridge the distance between other languages and cultures, aiming to captivate the viewer and inspire a sense of familiarity. Thus, in *The Lanna Dream*, the use of traditional Lanna instruments and Western melodies evoke a distant, unknown culture that seems strangely familiar. In this way, the performance simultaneously reflects the values of viewer and performer, their desires intertwined in a common wish to experience this culture and this place.

Of course, the successful crossing of cultural and linguistic boundaries has come at a cost. By redacting its own history to suit viewers' tastes and sensibilities, Lanna culture seems locked in the past: members of its "hill tribes" are relegated to stages where the outsider can observe their ostensibly authentic lifestyles unaffected by modern, post-industrial life—experiences that are indeed manufactured. Villagers perform dance routines, dress in garments reflective of their cultural histories, and pose for photographs in front of premodern homes. But after the performance is over, they replace their tribal clothing with T-shirts and jeans, and their mobile phones reappear (Trupp 2014: 362). Some villagers admit that deviating from these constructed interactions and visibly updating their living standards would lead to a loss of income. As a result, many are disconnected from modern Lanna society but are also unable to fully claim Thai national identity, finding themselves confined within the physical and conceptual boundaries of the village, where they adopt a subservient disposition toward tourists. If the outsiders' gaze has enabled the revitalization of Lanna culture, it has also become a potential threat to the security of its future. The same tourists who stay in condominiums with high-speed internet also expect authentic Lanna culture to remain suspended in time. Performativity thus lies at the center of this culture with outsiders having retained power over the Lanna people's modes of expression. And yet an identity distinct from this fabricated authenticity persists—in the language, the matrilineal heritage, and the visible yet overlooked traces that can still be heard in marketplaces and interpersonal exchanges.

Securing a future at the cost of authentic expression has led to a fragile dependency that centers the audience's gaze—a problem that only grows as global interconnectivity increases. How, then, can spectators experience a more authentic representation of Lanna culture? For Sirisook, authenticity exists within the Lanna people themselves, who navigate today's challenges by creating new opportunities, combining traditional and contemporary modes of expression, and adapting to the changing nature of the gaze, which might be internal (Thai), regional (e.g., Chinese), or Western. Sirisook's final dance thus reflects cultural authenticity by blending the classical techniques of Lanna dance with modern improvised movements, as well as the representative music of Manopetch performed with a solo *pin pia*. She combines past and present cultural elements into a performance expressing the ever-adapting Lanna culture through her use of dance, movement, and uninhibited expression.

The current era presents a precarious compromise between expressive authenticity and cultural endurance. In some ways, this tension is specific to Lanna culture. The opportunities presented by cultural tourism have afforded the Lanna people the possibility to revitalize—to stand on stage and be seen. Compromised expressions may seem a small cost to pay for the chance to be recognized. Indeed, projecting a cultural image built on the values and desires of the spectator is a particularly creative approach toward securing a future. But this compromise could have far-reaching effects: as globalization increases, exoticized cultures will continue to vie for the outsider's attention. The Lanna people have sought to safeguard their own identities within the personal sphere—in their homes, marketplaces, weddings, and other ceremonies in small villages. Yet Lanna cultural development and expression are potentially being limited by the gaze, reducing its culture to actors playing a role, their dissimulations exposed in Sirisook's performance. Yet despite the costs of this revitalization, the Lanna people have rebuilt their society, customs, and traditions, to once again stand on the global stage. They dance for the viewer's attention with hope that the auditorium door will not be closed, nor the limelight fade, so that attention will not wander from a culture that is, once again, (re)discovering itself.

References

Fairfield, B. (2017), "The Participatory We-Self: Ethnicity and Music in Northern Thailand," PhD diss., University of Hawaii at Mānoa.

Farrell, J. A. (2009), "The Lanna Deception," *Chiang Mai Citylife*, November 27. www.chiangmaicitylife.com/citylife-articles/the-lanna-deception. (accessed May 14, 2021).

Kemasingki, P. and T. Tananchai (2017), "What Is Lanna? How Lanna Became the Identity and Brand It Is Today," *Chiang Mai Citylife*, May 1. www.chiangmaicitylife.com/clg/our-city/history/what-is-lanna-how-lanna-became-the-identity-and-brand-it-is-today/ (accessed May 14, 2021).

McGraw, A. (2007), "The Pia's Subtle Sustain: Contemporary Ethnic Identity and the Revitalization of the Lanna 'Heart Harp,'" *Asian Music*, 38 (2): 115–42.

Sirisook, W. (2020), "Lanna Dream: Second Variation Excerpt," *YouTube*, May 6. https://www.youtube.com/watch?v=yGVO1Om8W2E (accessed May 14, 2021).

Subhimaros, P. (2006), "Flower of the Nation: Gendered Representations of Thailand beyond the Borders," Conference Proceedings, Thinking Gender—the NEXT Generation, University of Leeds, June 21–22.

Trupp, A. (2014), "Ethnic Tourism in Northern Thailand: Viewpoints of the Akha and the Karen," in K. Husa, A. Trupp, and H. Wohlschlägel (eds.), *Southeast Asian Mobility Transitions: Issues, and Trends in Tourism and Migration*, 346–76, Vienna: Department of Geography and Regional Research, University of Vienna.

Winichakul, T. (2011), "Siam's Colonial Conditions and the Birth of Thai History," in V. Grabowsky (ed.), *Southeast Asian Historiography: Unraveling the Myths*, 23–45, Terwiel, Bangkok: Rivers Books.

14

American Blackness in Berlin: Race and Nationality in Contemporary Jazz Performance

Bertram D. Ashe

one

It was a Wednesday night at b-flat, a jazz club in Berlin, Germany. I was taking in everything that I could. I'd sometimes sit back-center at Berlin jazz clubs or, if it was a hot, crowded, smoke-filled late-night jam session at a place like Das Edelweiss I'd stand anywhere I could stand—elbowing for space and gasping for air. At Sunday afternoon jam sessions at the Werkstatt der Kulturen I'd be looking for a spot in the shade. But mostly, when I could manage it, I'd sit at the edge. Far left or far right. About a fourth of the way back from the stage. That Wednesday I backed up to the wall at the right of the stage, so I had an excellent vantage point: I could see everything happening, onstage and off.

My chair was like every other chair in b-flat, but in my mind I sat elevated, as high as a tennis linesman, with pinpoint perfect sightlines, able to survey every cubic inch of the space: stage, audience, servers, club vibe. All of it. If a man softly sighed—I wanted to hear it; if a woman sniffed—I'd be aware of it. I stayed critically and consciously aware of all that happened within the venue's four-wall space: who's on stage doing what with whom—and when; who comes through the door and with whom—wearing what; who leaves, and the expression on their faces when they do leave (satisfaction? unhappiness? a glow? some grief?). Gender, race, age, personal style—or lack thereof. Who's into the music, and who isn't, and what "into it" seems to mean. Who's *moving* to the music. Who isn't. Who reacts, and who doesn't. It's all filtered through my perception, of course, but still, as I sat in the club, I wanted to inhale as much sound, sight, and sensory information as possible.

It's like this: Anything that happens within the four walls of the event-space is part of the Black vernacular experience. And it all filters through me, through my own experiential, critical eyes, ears, and brain. After all, while it's true that the music is coming from the stage, as Guthrie P. Ramsey points out in *Race Music*, "growing numbers of music scholars now argue quite profitably that music is a dynamic social text, a meaningful cultural practice, a cultural transaction, and a politically charged, gendered, signifying discourse" (18). Black vernacular group creation, then, insists that there is not only rhythmic improvisation and call and response occurring *on*stage, between musicians, but also an equally important "call" sent *from* the stage to the audience, the audience's "response" informing that stage performance. It's circular, not just call-and-response, but call-and-recall, an energy feedback loop that lasts as long as the event lasts.

That inherent circularity is an elemental part of the Black vernacular tradition. At many Black American cultural events, whether the performer is on a stage or in a pulpit, there's no announcement or invitation for the audience to respond to the performer's call: the Black collective *enters the space* with an always already cultural expectation that they will actively (and often verbally) respond to the minister or performer or musician. During conventional concert hall performances of Western art music there simply is no such expectation. If invited to clap along, or to engage in "audience participation," the audience will, indeed, participate. But often the expectation is to sit quietly and watch and listen to what's happening onstage; in many cases, uninvited verbal and gestural audience response is actively frowned upon, even policed.

two

I walked into b-flat that evening with a question on my mind: What does it mean to view a jazz performance in Berlin, Germany, as a fluid, dynamic, Black American vernacular event, given the music's history and origins? I sat at the edge of the audience, observing a total of twenty-three jazz performances during a two-month stay in Berlin, between May 1 and June 30, 2018. At the majority of those performances, though certainly not all, my wife and I were either the only, or two of very few, Black bodies—onstage and off—in jazz clubs, at jazz concerts, or at jam sessions. As someone who enjoys attending jazz performances, both to study *what's onstage* and to observe the *audience experiencing* what's onstage, I was acutely aware that, often enough, I was witnessing the performance of a Black American art form with precious few Blacks, or Americans, in the space. I adopted the sort of approach E. Taylor Atkins describes in *Jazz Planet*, focusing on "how much could be learned simply by focusing on jazz audience and no-name musicians instead of 'geniuses,' or by contextualizing jazz within the broader processes of modernism and cultural 'massification'" (2003: xii). It seemed to me that just by paying attention to my surroundings, carefully watching and listening to the totality of the space, I might learn something. And yet I knew full well it would be subjective as hell—there would be no "objective" understanding of "what jazz performance means" in any literal, locked-down sense. And I didn't want or need that. In the same way jazz itself is an unpredictable art form whose performance is singular, and cannot be exactly reproduced beyond a particular evening (or beyond a particular moment during that evening), I hoped my observation at a specific jazz performance could form some sense of what jazz performance in Europe might entail.

There has been—as there should be—a contested and ongoing conversation about what jazz "is," but when it comes to the public performance of jazz as a Black vernacular traditional cultural practice, call and response and improvisation are at the music's core. So what happens to jazz performance when the music is played by and for people who, collectively, were born and raised *outside* the nation and the cultural tradition from which the music originally came? What does it mean to play a Black music not only with nobody Black in the room but with an overwhelmingly German presence? Does nationality and acculturation make a difference to those playing and listening? What role might the audience play, as putative Black vernacular "responders," to the inevitable Black vernacular "call" from the stage?

To get some answers to these questions, I interviewed, that same summer, fifteen Berlin-based jazz musicians about contemporary jazz performance in the city. Some were German, some were American, some were neither. Male, female, Black, white, Asian, bi-racial, Afro-German, queer, younger, older—this cross-section of Berlin jazz musicians had much to say on "American Blackness in Berlin." Since I cannot quote them all, I'll focus here on that one visit to b-flat, in the Mitte section of Berlin.

three

It was my wife Valerie, actually, who spotted the title of the show and the name of the band—"Fake Noise"—on the club's calendar one night while we attended a jam session at b-flat, so we returned to catch the performance on Thursday, May 31, exactly the mid-point of our two-month visit to Berlin. Here's the way the club date was advertised on the club's website (b-flat 2018):

> Don't believe everything you hear. Fake Noise is full of alternative notes …The band tells a story through their music, screaming and wailing, dragging the audience in, swallowing them whole, and then spitting them out. Was any of it true? Maybe, but does it matter?
>
> Fake Noise is a Berlin-based quartet that sounds like a punk metal band lost in a jazz school. Growing up together in a small transatlantic village mostly populated by moose, bears, and feral saxophones, the band members have had almost 100 years cumulatively to develop their reality-bending sounds, providing light in the darkest timeline.
>
> Standing out front and actively melting the audience's faces with fire and fury are Canadian/Belgian alto saxophonist Peter Van Huffel (Gorilla Mask, Scrambling EX, Kronix) and Canadian/German tenor saxophonist Jonathan Lindhorst (Limerence Quartet, Turtleboy, Innocent When You Dream). Shaking the foundations of time and space itself is the ground-breaking hard-hitting duo of Norwegian electric bassist Dan Peter Sundland (Orter Eparg, RRR, Home Stretch) and German drummer Oliver Steidle (Der Rote Bereich, Killing Popes). By combining their powers, Fake Noise flings the audience into an enormous washing machine of justice and music.

With my deep and long-lasting appreciation for puns and wordplay, I remain amazed and astonished—actually, baffled is more to the point—that it took me so long to understand what I was getting into when I walked into the gig. "Fake Noise," I eventually realized (four full days after the club date) puns wonderfully on former President Donald Trump's favorite admonition, "Fake News." When I talked to Lindhorst later about the title of the show/band, he snorted and responded, "Glad *some*body got it" (2018).

four

As the first set started there were eight people in the room, including us. B-flat is a mid-sized club so it did feel a bit sparse in there. We were, as an audience, a little spread out. But an audience is still an audience, no matter how few the people. I sat with Val at the edge of the collective, backing up to the wall at the right of the stage, and it was, as I expected, an excellent vantage point: I could see everything happening, on- and offstage. Also as expected, Fake Noise ripped into their first set as if they were playing in front of a packed house.

The music was intricate and powerful. It was clearly rehearsed, with sheet music propped up on stands, conveying a sense of intentional preparation. There were intense, dual-saxophone runs and precise starts and stops of the sort that couldn't have been achieved without rehearsal. The music itself was quirky and deliciously discordant with suddenly employed shifts and odd time signatures. The solos began and ended abruptly; notes were sprayed all over the scale. Only by the fourth tune did it occur to me that no one in the audience was applauding solos, but that made sense: the music was just that difficult and complicated—and satisfying.

I had briefly visited Berlin's jazz scene five years earlier, but this time around I had my ringer with me, my secret weapon, Valerie Ashe, who represents the Black vernacular tradition more than even she realizes, far more than I could ever dream of, given my own relatively inhibited, West Coast, suburbia-raised self. Val likes her gospel music down home; she likes her greens with fatback. She makes gumbo that rivals my mother's gumbo—and my grandmother's gumbo—and quite frankly that's not something I ever thought I'd be able to say, about anybody. She grew up in the Black church, hearing traditional, improvisational, rhythmic, signifyin(g) "calls" from a preacher to a Black congregation and back again since before she could talk. Quick-witted and warm, her deep Southern immersion into the Black collective, combined with her military-kid, raised-around-the-world upbringing, allows her to be dropped into nearly any social situation and feel at home.

No surprise: we integrated b-flat on that last day of May. A jazz performance is, like any other Black vernacular occasion, meant to be a communal event. Those of us at b-flat that night were a jazz collective, having made our way from disparate parts of Berlin (and, in Val's and my case, of the world) to come to this club, on this night, to hear this band play this music. The "call" of the music, the "response" of the audience, the environment, the space—and, perhaps, some intoxicants as well—will, under ideal circumstances, combine to provide everyone in the room, onstage and off, with something of a transcendent experience. In the Black vernacular tradition, with just the right song, or sets of songs, just the right rhythmic groove, just the right combination of tension and release, tension and release, you'll have Black attendees having a collective experience, a certain dance-floor transcendence—at "da club," on a Saturday night—that is culturally interchangeable with the religious transcendence that takes place mere hours later, in "da sanctuary," on a Sunday morning. But just as successful improvisation needs an aesthetic frame, and signifyin(g) can't achieve "repetition with a signal difference" (Gates 1988: 66) without a source, so can fluid, circular, transcendent call and response occur only if there's a "call"—even one greeted with a paltry, tepid, virtually nonexistent "response."

five

Watching four white/European guys play jazz, from a Black vernacular standpoint, is something like watching an all-white team play basketball. The rules are the same, of course, and the goal is the same: put the ball in the hoop; prevent the opposition from putting the ball in the hoop. The game isn't a different *game* based on the race or cultural aptitude of the players. But *style* does differ on the court—and on the bandstand. True, it's not like style, in and of itself, will get you any extra points, but in the same way spectators feel compelled to attend basketball games for their own set of complicated cultural reasons, jazz aficionados similarly come to attend to—and to witness—jazz music. Now, no team "wins" at a jazz concert, but arriving, in person, to engage with and respond to animated, physical expression, whether ten bodies on a court or four bodies on a bandstand, is something an audience member (or fan) chooses to do. And depending on the bodies onstage, the feel is different. Not bad. Not "wrong." Different. European audience members might well love jazz music, but that love and appreciation flow through their own acculturation— how can it not? So the question is: what are Europeans experiencing when they attend a jazz concert?

Sharon F. Patton, in *African American Art*, constructed a tight primitivist syllogism that roughly works this way. *Major premise*: "Jazz ... took its harmonic, melodic and rhythmic elements mainly from African music" (1998: 111). *Minor premise*: "The celebration of African-American culture in dance and jazz was an antidote to what was perceived to be the sterility of modern, technology-dominated Western modernist society" (1998: 111). Ergo, her *conclusion*:

> "Primitivism," the cultural crucible for modernism, was for European and white American audiences available in American Negro culture, which was regarded as a subculture to mainstream America. Despite the fact that African Americans had lived in North America from the seventeenth century, there was

a widespread belief that Africa pervaded Negro culture. As African descendants the American Negro was the modern primitive.

(Patton 1998: 111)

To see this theory in practice, take, for example, Herman Hesse's *Steppenwolf*, first published in 1927 but still germane nearly a hundred years later, where the narrator remarks, "Compared with Bach and Mozart and real music ... This [jazz] music was at least sincere, unabashedly primitive and childishly happy. There was something of the Negro in it, and something of the American, who with all his strength seems so boyishly fresh and childlike to us Europeans" (2002: 37–8). But Europeans can be attracted to music from Black American culture and still struggle, at the practical, experiential level, to open themselves up to Black vernacular cultural modes of expression. Henry Louis Gates, Jr., clarified something important about this tradition: "What distinguishes this body of work is its in-group and, at times, secretive, defensive, and aggressive character: it is not, generally speaking, produced for circulation beyond the Black group itself" (2004: 3). I thought about Gates's words while watching the audience watch Fake Noise that night.

No question, there was a version of Black vernacular "play" coming from the stage and circulating among the performers. Patterns of improvisational call-and-response were moving from player to player, from individual to audience, from group to audience. But that's where the dynamic vernacular interaction pretty much stopped cold: the reality is that all the majority of the audience did was "watch."

I feel like that narrator from *Steppenwolf*, Harry Haller, is a good way to think about Europeans' relationship with their bodies. After all, jazz was dance music in the 1920s, but though Haller hears the music and tries to move to it, he is too inhibited, too much inside his head to lose himself in the dance:

> Hermine had me lead, adapting herself as softly and lightly as the leaf of a flower, and with her, too, I now experienced all these delights that now advanced and now took wing. She, too, now exhaled the perfume of woman and love, and her dancing, too, sang with intimate tenderness the lovely and enchanting song of sex. *And yet I could not respond to all this* with warmth and freedom. *I could not entirely forget myself* in abandon.

(2002: 124–5, emphasis mine)

The jazz audience at b-flat that night in Berlin was similar to the audience at other Berlin jazz clubs I had visited, like the Kunstfabrik-Schlot, or the

A-Trane, or other venues like the Zig Zag or Peppi Guggenheim. There was no demonstrative "response" to the "call" from the stage (save applause after songs, of course), because, culturally, many Germans are simply not that demonstrative. As I scanned the audience at b-flat, most members of the audience sat stock still, wordlessly and motionlessly facing the stage. There were, surely, some random smiles, some modest, occasional head-bobbing, but however much individual audience members were, presumably, enjoying the music, that enjoyment was *locked inside their bodies*, unable to present to the world the pleasure the music was providing them.

Now, even though I'm focusing on jazz in Berlin, I have witnessed, over the course of forty years of attending jazz performances in the United States, a similar phenomenon: at Ragattabar, a jazz club in Boston, or Blues Alley, a jazz club in Washington, DC, or the Village Vanguard in New York City, or Yoshi's in Oakland, California, or the Lighthouse, in Los Angeles. All had mostly white audiences, seemingly middle class, and of a certain mature age. And in each case there was, as in Germany, a distinct lack of verbal and bodily engagement among attendees. The exceptions, in my experience, were at places like Snug Harbor in New Orleans, or the Green Mill in Chicago—unsurprising, given how these cities were critical to jazz and blues development. In both of those instances a sizable Black contingent of jazz fans rallied a response that reflected Black vernacular expectations. And yet, even at the clubs largely attended by white jazz fans, I felt an American cultural sensibility in the room. My sense is that there is, indeed, a slight difference between Americans, of any race, attending a jazz performance in the United States, and Germans, attending a jazz performance in Germany.

It's in the subtleties. My preference, not surprisingly, is a boisterous, lively, and energetic jazz audience, particularly when there is obvious and irresistible swinging power and improvisational prowess coming off the stage. It's disappointing to sit among a polite, quiet jazz audience, on either side of the Atlantic. My body always responds, whenever called by the music, with head-bobbing and finger-snapping movement, and I always maintain an awareness of who's joining me—and who isn't—in whichever jazz audience I find myself. And it does appear, from my own subjective perspective, that American jazz audiences are slightly more demonstrative than Central European audiences. There are, alas, no loud exhortations to "play that horn!" or anything like that. But American audiences do seem more physically involved, from my vantage point, than most stolid German audiences.

six

That night in b-flat, Jonathan Lindhorst was the most colorful personality of the quartet. Upbeat, gregarious, and lively, he was clearly having fun up there. Although each of the songs played that evening was instrumental, often Lindhorst's song titles marked them as political: "The Rise of the Grumbletonians" and "Natural Kakistocracy" were my favorites. ("Kakistocracy," if you're wondering, means "rule by the worst"—and yes, he's referring to who you think he is.)

Jazz is, of course, inherently political, just as playing any form of music in public is, in some context, a political act. But Val and I had stumbled, that night, on a performance that was explicitly political, as the online advertisement insisted: "By combining their powers, Fake Noise flings the audience into an enormous washing machine of justice and music." There was hyper-political *intent* onstage that moved well beyond the implicit. There we were, sitting in a club in Berlin; no Americans on stage, very few Americans off stage, enjoying the delicious irony that the target of political ridicule and mockery was not only a sitting American president, but a demonstrably racist American president, which made the vessel for that scorn—a participatory American art form launched by Black Americans—all the more politically rich. Many jazz players might well argue that they're just playing music they love, that their performance isn't political at all. "But this supposed aesthetic detachment from base politics," retorts Atkins, in *Jazz Planet*, "has too often obscured the relationship between jazz's ubiquity, colonialism, nationalist politics, and American military, economic, and cultural hegemony ... We must also recognize the ways in which various nations' jazz cultures deployed the music to assert a defiant transnational imaginary that refused to concede to (white) American dominance" (2003: xix). Clearly, Lindhorst does.

I've already admitted that I didn't at first get the pun that linked "Fake Noise" and "Fake News." But that night, in the moment, as I responded to the music from the stage, I was aware of the political nature of the titles and Lindhorst's onstage explanation of them. I could tell that the titles were markedly different from, say, "Blues to You" or countless other more familiar jazz titles. Lindhorst's titles were closer to those of Charles Mingus, like "Fables of Faubus" (1959), which was about 1950s and 1960s-era Arkansas segregationist Governor Orval Faubus, or Mingus's 1962 song, "Oh Lord Don't Let Them Drop That Atomic Bomb on Me." I could also sense that the sounds of the songs themselves were meant to drive home the titles they bore: music and titles did not operate independently. But what I *cannot* say I understood during the performance was that it did, indeed, "assert a defiant transnational imaginary," as Atkins put it; that the "refusal to concede to (white) American dominance" was an intentional, in the moment push-back. I didn't realize I was listening to the strategic deployment of a Black American art form—from non-Americans, onstage, in Germany—against Donald J. Trump, who was then president of the United States of America.

When I asked Lindhorst, days after the club date, about the political nature of Fake Noise's performance and his approach to infusing politics into his music, he said:

> There's no right or wrong way to do this. There's a way to covey things that are overtly political in music, for sure. If you look at the music of Carla Bley and the Charlie Haden Liberation Orchestra, where they're doing, like, weird disjointed versions of the "The Star-Spangled Banner" or they've got this Mexican, kind of like revolutionary vibe and it kind of goes free ... Or like Mingus ... That sounds like politics. It very much obviously does. I love that kind of music. I believe art should have content. This is my position; lots of people have different positions. And it doesn't mean I don't enjoy something that doesn't have that kind of content, but I believe my music should have content ...
>
> I love music that has an effect on people. I love protest music, I love Joni Mitchell, and as I said before, I'm very aware of the inherent Black anger in some of that music from the sixties ... I see that stuff. And this is the only way I know how to contribute to this conversation, in a way, without alienating people all the time. So it's just something I think is important to bring up.

Though Lindhorst's political expression perfectly contextualizes what I saw at b-flat that evening, I am fascinated by the phrase "without alienating people all the time." That's a reference to the knife-edge tension that informs the difficulty of infusing politics into, say, instrumental jazz music. In other words, the price I paid for not understanding the key pun signaled by the name of the group itself was that the musicians' explicit political target *did not register*, for me, during the performance. That came later. The fact that the pun wasn't repeated onstage (recall Lindhorst's response to my own dawning comprehension: "Glad *some*body got it") offers an example of the tension between art and politics. Too obvious a gesture toward politics seems to lessen the potency of the art itself, yet art that is completely devoid of politics seems too close to art-for-arts-sake pablum. That tension, perhaps, explains how such an explicitly political evening of jazz never came close to a demonstrative, fist-in-the-air "protest" concert.

seven

By the start of the second set there were seventeen people in the room—including another Black couple!—and Fake Noise's compelling, time-shifting jazz complications continued. The most vivid, group-creation moment came near the end of the second set. During that last song Val yelled out "All right!", responding to a moment during a relatively quiet bass solo. I loved it. I don't know if Dan Peter Sundland, the bass player, was surprised or startled to hear it—he certainly wasn't visibly altered in any way—but there were so few people in the club that there's no way it wasn't heard by everyone in the space.

Could we call that moment an eruption of traditional American Blackness—in Berlin? If there were four white guys onstage playing tight, time-twisting jazz, was Val's "all right!" something like a traditionally Black basketball player briefly checking into the game to "play" with them?[1] An even more interesting moment took place during the encore. Jonathan announced "Elg," the encore song, as having been unrehearsed, but it was a somewhat startling departure from the songs that preceded it: even though it was as byzantine and thorny as the rest of the tunes Fake Noise played, I could somehow instantly hear the African polyrhythms undergirding the song; my head easily snapped to the beat in ways that had been a bit more difficult for the earlier tunes; I smiled in rhythmic recognition. And suddenly, Val, in the midst of the song, nudged me and began to jokingly pantomime that swim move the Ike-ettes used to employ onstage during the pinnacle of a frantic Ike and Tina Turner Revue performance, when Tina, taking a break from singing, would position herself next to the three Ike-ettes and they'd all get down. Valerie, in that moment, sent a call back to the bandstand—and sideways, to me—as she executed a nifty bit of vertical and horizontal signifyin(g) on a memorable Ike and Tina dance move, and I laughed and nodded in response and appreciation. The groove was propulsive—and Black: "Elg," joyously executed by Fake Noise, actually prompted a surreptitious Black dance move! At *this* performance?! *Did* Val and I have a "secretive, defensive ... in-group" moment, prompted by the music itself? Or did our "response" to the polyrhythmic "call" coming from Fake Noise's "Elg" signal a brief transcendent moment that was perhaps experienced, more or less, by all twenty-one people present, onstage and off? I would never have guessed that such a multilayered cultural moment would occur while listening to the music in sets one and two.

eight

On a Friday afternoon, about a week later, I sat down with Jonathan Lindhorst at the Café Oberholtz, at Rosenthaler Platz, in Mitte (May 8, 2018). As a throat-clearing gesture, I asked him if he agreed with Wynton Marsalis's three-part characterization of jazz: based in the blues, swings, and includes improvisation? (2001: 167). I also wondered, where did his music fit into Wynton's definition? I knew what the Blackness-quotient at b-flat looked and felt like from where *I* sat, but what did the Blackness-quotient feel like onstage? Jonathan replied, flatly:

> The inherent Blackness of jazz is something you cannot disregard if you care about the music. But, at the same time, I do disagree with Wynton's statement because of jazz's ability to change and grow and mutate. And as it grew and became more inclusive in a way and spread out to becoming more like a world music, it becomes very blurry. It's like, does jazz have to swing? Well, does Latin jazz swing? No. In a way, maybe, but, like, if you're listening to Stan Getz's bossa nova records, is it still jazz? It gets classified as jazz, but it's very much *not* Black music, you know? Now, especially in Europe, European musicians have a very different relationship to this music. I mean, I came up playing up in Canada, and then I went to New York for three years, I lived in Bed Stuy [the Bedford-Stuyvesant neighborhood in Brooklyn], and I was studying with Antonio Hart, whose views on jazz are very much in line with Wynton's.
>
> Actually, Antonio forced me to confront social identity politics within jazz: He made me go to church. And I was raised atheist. There's an Anglican background in my family, so I've been to some Anglican services growing up with my grandmother, and I went to a couple of Roman Catholic services with my friends once in a while, but I've never been religious and I felt a little out of place and uncomfortable in that situation. He made me go to Emmanuel [Baptist Church], in Clinton Hill [in Brooklyn]. It's a big one. It's on Lafayette and it's a real gospel church. I walked in the room and I was like the only white guy there, just about. And it was fun and the music was awesome and the way they approached spirituality was very inspiring and very cool. He made me write about my experience and I thought about it and, see, his perspective—the thing he was kind of trying to push—it felt like, was, "This is where jazz comes from. And this is the community thing. And you have to get with this, somehow, if you're going to play jazz *for real*—if you're *really* going to play jazz, you have to get *this*."

It was really tough for me, because there was really nothing like that where I come from … This specific American gospel black thing was … it was awesome, but … I could not feel like a part of it. I'm not … I'm not … I wasn't raised with this … You know, my attitude was like, I love jazz. I love this music. And I respect this music. I respect the story. And I understand where it comes from. But … I—can't—play … *that*. I can't play *that experience*. I can only play my own experience, right? Like, I can only communicate … For me, art?—if it's going to be good?—it has to come from a place of honesty. For me to pre*tend*—

"Wait," I interrupted him. "Was he *asking* you to pretend?" And here I kind of loved Jonathan's affectionate, instantaneous protection of his former teacher, Antonio Hart. "Err, he was kind of, I mean, he wouldn't—err, ah … It's … " He fumbled his words, uncharacteristically. He didn't want to betray his beloved teacher, but he didn't want to betray the truth, either. Here's what he ended up saying:

He didn't say it outright, but the energy and the vibe, was a little bit like, "If you're not doing this, you're not doing jazz." And he took a, kind of like a, a really strict approach on that …. And by the way, I love Antonio. He was one of the best teachers I ever had. [His teaching] forced me to get a real core part of my playing together. And after having conversations with Antonio I kind of came to the conclusion that, well, for jazz to be jazz it does have to meet [Wynton's] criteria. And so sometimes I play jazz—and sometimes I don't. A lot of times I play music that does *not* meet that criteria—it comes out of jazz, it's influenced by jazz—but, it's not swinging, you know, it's not blues-based, it has no connection to the African American experience at all. Maybe it's just not jazz!

And I'm okay with that. Like, I'm fine with what we played with the Fake Noise band. You want to say that's not jazz? Fine. That's cool. Even though Peter Van Huffel, the other saxophone player, worships [jazz musicians like] Albert Ayler and Ornette Coleman and guys like that.

Look, I've been doing this since I was ten years old. There's never been anything else in my life that I actively wanted to do as much as what I'm doing right now. Twenty-five years later, I still do it and I think that's the greatest achievement of my life. I know a lot of talented guys who quit music and became dentists and lawyers and engineers and whatever. So, I'm like, "Well—sorry!"

And at this point he kind of laughed to himself. "It's like, *I'm here*, you know? I'm here, I can't change who I am and what my life was and where I'm coming out of … All I can say is I love this music. *I love this music*."

nine

And there it was: "*I love this music.*" White, Canadian, and figuratively grabbed by the scruff of his neck and the back of his pants and thrown by his teacher, Antonio Hart, fully clothed into the deep end of the Black cultural pool without so much as an admonition to "kick your legs"—yet he seems to have drippingly emerged from that pool, dried off, and retained a sense of Black cultural understanding nevertheless. When I watched him play at b-flat there very much was *some* version of American Blackness in Berlin embedded in the performance, however difficult it might be to pinpoint just how that Blackness manifested itself. It came from his playing, of course, but maybe also his lively stage presence; perhaps it was the tilt of his porkpie hat or his occasional use of the word "cats" to describe his bandmates. These gestures might sound stereotypical, but as all familiar cultural gestures do, they emerged, over time, from a particular source. However common they might seem in the present day, these signs emerged from Black America, as did so much of American culture. Jazz, like most forms of musical performance, has a visual element that augments and informs the sound emanating from the stage. So I did, indeed, feel a subtle Black American extra-musical vibe in b-flat that late May evening, even though I had no knowledge of Jonathan's background and his experience with Black culture. My interest was piqued solely by Fake Noise's performance in general and his own performance in particular, and by my and Valerie's "response" to the totality of the performative "call": the music, the audience, the band's interaction with each other and the audience's reaction to the stage. It was only after I sat down to chat with Jonathan days later that all was revealed.

And yet the Blackness at b-flat wasn't terribly obvious, either. I had to snap my own Black vernacular cultural experience onto this musical event, and while it fit, it didn't fit snugly. Jazz is, indeed, a Black American art form: Guthrie Ramsey, Antonio Hart, and others of their ilk are correct that in order to play the music deeply and well one needs some form of Black cultural immersion. The performance of jazz music is not the mere playing of notes; it's the ability to move people to engage with those on the stage, the ability to "call" and get a visible and/or audible "response." Meaning, stresses Ramsey,

> is always contingent and extremely fluid; it is never essential to a musical figuration. Real people negotiate and eventually agree on what cultural expressions such as

a musical gesture mean. They collectively decide what associations are conjured by a well-placed blue note, a familiar harmonic pattern, the soulful, virtuoso sweep of a jazz solo run, a social dancer's imaginative twist on an old dance step, or the raspy grain of a church mother's vocal declamation on a Sunday morning.

(2003: 25–6)

"Real people," in b-flat that night, referred to an eager crowd that did appreciate some Fake Noise. It was a cultural moment, a Black vernacular event, and everyone in the space participated in that event, whether the players and the audience knew it consciously or not. And yes, Sharon Patton's primitivist syllogism remained a Western cultural it-factor: that German audience was there, in all likelihood, at least in part to immerse themselves in some form of American Blackness. And yes, it's true that that audience, from my observation, "*could not respond* to all this ... warmth and freedom" emanating from the bandstand; they "*could not entirely forget*" themselves in abandon, if at all (2002: 124–5). And no, there wasn't anywhere close to a Black, down-home, intimate, group-laden, vocal and/or physical response to the music on the part of the largely German audience of jazz fans in attendance; the only observable, demonstrable audience response to any "call" from the stage came from my wife Valerie—and whatever I could muster up myself. But in the end, after all, intangible, contested, persistent cultural "Blackness" was indeed in the space, nevertheless.

ten

It was a Wednesday night at b-flat, a jazz club in Berlin, Germany. I took in everything that I could: the stage, the musicians, the audience, peering through European history, through Western culture, through an African American vernacular tradition, through a jazz lineage, all the while struggling to remain coherent and focused and alert as a Fake Noise jazz swirl pulsated from the stage.

And as the band walked offstage together after finishing their encore, I distinctly recall watching a grinning Jonathan Lindhorst, as if he were, indeed, feeling the effect of that transcendent moment, utter to the other members of Fake Noise one word: "Jazz!"—letting the raspy word linger in his mouth, making those last two letters agreeably hiss, like a snake. And then they were gone, offstage and out of view.

Note

1   The Black vernacular tradition is a cultural mode, rather than a genetic or racial one. Black people are not a monolith, and not all people of African descent are raised to be rhythmically adept at improvisational call and response, although clearly the vast majority are. I refer to Black folk who were, indeed, acculturated in the American Black vernacular as "traditional" African Americans.

References

Atkins, E. T. (2003), "Towards a Global History of Jazz," in E. T. Atkins (ed.), *Jazz Planet*, xi–xxvii, Jackson: University of Mississippi Press.

b-flat: Acoustic Music & Jazz Club, 10178 Berlin-Mitte, Dircksenstr. 40. http://www.b-flat-berlin.de (accessed May 20, 2021).

Gates, Jr., H. L. (1988), *The Signifying Monkey: A Theory of African-American Literary Criticism*, New York: Oxford University Press.

Gates, Jr., H. L. (2004), "The Vernacular Tradition," in *The Norton Anthology of African American Literature*, 2nd edn., New York: W. W. Norton & Company.

Hesse, H. (2002), *Steppenwolf*, New York: Picador.

Lindhorst, J. (2018), Interview with B. Ashe, Café Oberholtz, Rosenthaler Str. 72A, 10119 Berlin, Germany, June 8.

Marsalis, W. (2001), *Jazz in the Bittersweet Blues of Life*, Boston: Da Capo Press.

Ramsey, G. P. (2003), *Race Music: Black Cultures from Bebop to Hip-Hop*, Berkeley: University of California Press.

Patton, S. F. (1998), *African-American Art*, New York: Oxford University Press.

15

Remaking Traditions and Rehearing the Self: A Conversation with Reena Esmail

Christopher Chandler

The Indian-American composer Reena Esmail writes music that brings together Western and Indian classical music traditions, performers, and audiences. Her music reveals a distinctive voice that thoughtfully integrates elements of these seemingly disparate soundworlds. With an ascendant career in the United States, the Los Angeles–based composer is sought after for her cross-cultural approach, with commissions from the Albany Symphony, Los Angeles Master Chorale, Chicago Sinfonietta, Kronos Quartet, and Imani Winds, to name just a few. Esmail's arrival at this place in her career comes after undergraduate and graduate degrees in composition from The Julliard School and Yale University, and over a decade of studying Indian classical music idioms and incorporating them into her creative practice. Though firmly grounded in Western musical traditions, Esmail's work for solo, chamber, choral, and orchestral forces often finds common ground with Indian musical practices through collaborations with Indian musicians.

I sat down for a phone interview with Esmail on June 5, 2019, following a performance of her work at the University of Richmond's 2018–19 Tucker-Boatwright Festival. Our conversation touched on her musical background, intercultural collaborative and compositional practices, and the creative motivations behind *Meri Sakhi ki Avaaz (My Sister's Voice*—2018) and *She Will Transform You* (2019), two symphonic-vocal works performed at the festival by the Richmond Symphony Orchestra and Chorus and members of the University of Richmond's Department of Music.

Our interview began with a discussion of her early musical education and the path that led her to blend Western and Indian classical music traditions. Born in Chicago and raised in Los Angeles, Esmail described how her earliest musical experiences included private lessons on guitar, violin, and, most seriously, piano, before she started to focus on composition in her late teens. She connected this foundation in Western classical music to the cultural background of her parents, particularly her mother. Both ethnically Indian, her father was raised in Pakistan and her mother in Kenya. Her mother's family came from a part of India called Goa, where Western instruments and traditions are embedded in the culture, stemming from the region's long history as a colony of Portugal. Reflecting on her mother's closer connection to Western music, Esmail noted that it was no surprise her mother sought out lessons for her on Western instruments when she first expressed interest in music. Esmail began studying Indian classical music later in life, first at Yale and then during a Fulbright in India. This transformative period opened musical doors, deepened her connection to her family's rich lineage, and instilled a new awareness of how others perceive her cultural identity.

> Christopher Chandler (CC): I wonder if you could highlight any formative moments that happened during that journey [of beginning to learn Indian classical music], whether in the classroom at Yale or, perhaps, on your Fulbright?
>
> Reena Esmail (RE): It wasn't until I was twenty-six that I started studying Indian classical music at Yale. They had hired a professor from New Delhi to come over and teach us. She didn't know anything about Western music so what we were getting truly was Indian music through an Indian musician's lens. It was not being taught to us in a musicological way. When I started to study with her, I realized this [was] healing a very deep part of me and bringing things together for me.
>
> I think people come to Indian music for different reasons. Certainly, there are many people not of Indian origin who are just drawn to the music. For me, it was actually the cultural identity first and the idea that I spent my entire life as a vast, vast minority racially in Western classical music. You have your home [culture] and then you have the American culture that you practice outside the home. I grew up mostly with white kids in the heart of Los Angeles. Those two worlds were very disparate for me growing up. The older I got, the more I thought, well ... I want to make music with people who share my culture. It wasn't until I started meeting other Indian women who did music that this part of me started opening up. Even in the early 2000s, I started meeting Indian classical musicians, but just felt that, for whatever the reason, I didn't actually have a chance to get in there and really learn and have more than social interactions where we would make music together. I was very much an outsider.

There were definitely moments where, once I started learning the music, I suddenly felt like I was learning what it would have been like to be a version of myself that had grown up in India or had just had that musical culture. It was a missing part of me that I really felt was there. So a lot of my life has been being both this insider and this outsider. In Western music, I'm certainly an insider in the fact that I've been to all these programs and have the same education as a lot of other composers working today. But then I also have this whole other set of knowledge that pretty much no one else who is doing the work that I do has.

Being in India was amazing because I wasn't a minority for the first time in my life. I was just another Indian girl making music in India. For the very first time, I didn't experience what it was like to fight, to have to say, "People like me, people who look like me, also can make really great music."

Maybe the worst part was the reverse culture shock, where when I first came back to America, I was suddenly aware of the very subconscious discrimination that was happening that I had never even been able to detect before, because I didn't have any other way to know the world.

CC: Could you talk more about that reverse culture shock? What were some of the things that you noticed that you didn't latch on to until traveling to India?

RE: Well, there were a few things. Being in India was interesting because my teachers there, and even my other Indian musical teachers after that time, had an attitude that [was supportive and encouraging]. "Oh, well, we don't know what you've been doing before, but you've found the music of your culture. Great! Come and study. You are going to understand this." If I didn't know something, they would say, "Oh, you are definitely going to get this. This is fine." Because I looked like someone who should be able to understand. Then, I kind of went back and realized that there were so many teachers in my life who were just sure that I would never understand something. When you speak to someone in a way where you are expecting them to understand, the chances of them understanding are actually greater than when you speak to them in a way that assumes they won't.

On the other hand, when teaching, I would suddenly be aware of underhanded skepticism like, "Am I really the person who can teach Western music theory to these students?" The height [came] when I was emceeing [an] event. I was wearing a sari at an Indian *a capella* event, and afterwards I went to the music library to pick up a book on music bibliography that [was reserved for our] doctoral course. So I go in wearing this sari, and the person at the desk is treating me like I don't know what's going on. I'm a doctoral student at the School of Music; she just didn't know what to do with me. I look back at it now and think how annoying encounters like that were, but at that time, it was a deeply disorienting to question myself. "Do I deserve to be here? Am I not as good as anyone else? Am I not qualified?" It creates those issues.

As Esmail noted, the process of immersing herself in the tradition of Indian classical music came with both a newfound sense of belonging and of being adrift. The duality of being at once an insider and an outsider in two distinct cultures and traditions highlights the tensions experienced by the second-generation immigrant, who outwardly embodies one culture but has been raised in another. This theme is featured in Esmail's two symphonic-vocal works performed at the Tucker-Boatwright festival. Before discussing these specific pieces, we first explored her creative processes, aspirations, and boundaries as she sought to fuse Western and Indian musical traditions.

> CC: I wonder if we can begin to go into your music from a general perspective. As you started to absorb the music of a new culture, what was the process like when you started to put pen to paper? How did you approach trying to incorporate it into your music?
>
> RE: It was in some ways very easy and in other ways very difficult. The thing about Indian classical music and Hindustani classical music[1] is that it is very [distant from how] it is practiced from Western classical music ... I feel like everyone comes into Indian classical music from a Western perspective thinking, "Oh, they don't have notation. I'm going to teach them to notate! I'll create a notation system." And of course, once you get far enough in, you realize exactly why they don't have a notation system, because it is just not in the musical aesthetics. It really locks things in in a way that defies the logic of Hindustani classical music. But then, of course, there has to be some notation for Western musicians, so this is one thing that I really grappled with.
>
> I think of Hindustani music as having a kind of subtle mellifluous melody that comes from this improvised tradition. Hindustani music [also] has this amazing sense of rhythm and meter at all possible levels. From the smallest level to the largest level, there are layers that I think maybe aren't as explicit in Western classical music as they are in Hindustani classical music. These things, I realized, were not mutually exclusive. You can have Western meter and then go further into it in a Hindustani way. You can have a basic melody and then improvise on or ornament it in a Hindustani way.

So, over the years, I think I've been experimenting with different elements of Hindustani and Western music coming together. I [ask], "What is it like to have this type of Indian singing with this type of Western form?" It started as these dichotomies, [with me thinking], "Let me just try this with this, and that with that." And eventually, it has turned into this pidgin language for me where I am seeking both things at the same time. I am also constantly trying to learn new things on the Western side and on the Hindustani side, letting that entire dual musical world inform everything that I write.

CC: The way that I hear you framing it, it's almost like you have a constant Venn diagram of what's overlapping, what's shared and what's not. I think you put it really well, when you were here [for the festival], when you talked about the horizontal nature of Hindustani music and the vertical nature of Western classical music. That resonated a lot with me, and the fact that there is not much counterpoint in Hindustani music, or at least it is conceived in a different way.

RE: Yes. That's absolutely true. It's also because of the notation system in Western music and the lack of notation in Hindustani music that different things are possible. And then, it's just a matter of figuring out who is in room. Are there actual Hindustani musicians on the stage? And if so, what do they need in order to do what they do but still function within a Western system and vice versa. So it's a question of whether the music [is] being played by Western musicians or whether it's an actual collaboration between people, which to me is the most interesting thing.

CC: I think [your consideration of who is in the room] is a really important point. Can you speak more about that aspect of communicating with musicians from different backgrounds?

RE: When I notate, I think, "Who needs to read this?" If I'm notating for a Hindustani musician, I sometimes give them a cue list that says, "Do this here; do that there." If they look at anything that has too much information, it is going to be overwhelming. Whereas if a conductor is looking at a score [and doesn't] have enough information—for instance in my *Clarinet Concerto* (2017), [I wrote] long beam-lines through the staff when people needed to improvise—the conductor [would be] terrified until the first rehearsal. So it's a matter of who needs to see what to be comfortable, and I think it goes into a bigger issue of what language you need to speak for people to understand. There are multiple languages that will get you to the same place of understanding, and you can speak them simultaneously as long as you know how to interweave the languages with one another.

CC: That is a lovely way of putting it. I was reading the program notes for [your pieces on the festival] earlier, and you say that you were using certain rags. [A rag is a collection of pitches improvised with specific melodic patterns and ornamentations to evoke extramusical qualities, like seasons or moods.] I'm not nearly as well steeped in Indian classical music as you, [so] I did not hear those things coming through. I just heard really beautiful, luscious harmonies and detailed orchestration. How important is it for you to have those aspects resonate with the culture [for which] they are intended? How do you, from a compositional standpoint, make sure that those things are coming across to those audiences?

RE: That is deeply important to me, because I don't want to be a person who writes music for Westerners to get a taste of Indian classical music. [Also] if it is going the other way, where Indian audiences [only] get a taste of Western classical music, then I'm not doing my job.

It is hard to write something that is truly bilingual, but it is not for my lack of trying. I have basically spent the last decade trying to do that. I think if an Indian musician were to listen to it, generally they can hear, "Oh, this is in this rag," because their ears are tuned to hear those things. On the other hand, they have a hard time picking up on the rhythm, because rhythm is much more explicit in Hindustani music than it is in Western music. Where [Western musicians] would listen to a Mozart symphony and immediately hear it in 4/4, that would be very hard for Indian musicians to hear. They might feel like, "Oh, this is completely rhythm-less." I think, perhaps, if you were [an Indian musician] who knew those rags you might think, "Oh, this is totally Rageshree. I get what this is." From a Western perspective, you might think, "Oh, I see how this is orchestrated, I see how the winds come in here, I see how the text is set." My hope is that whatever the background of the person is, they will actually be able to hear those things first.

CC: Would you say that when you are writing you are aware of these musical signifiers, gestures, or other aspects that are inherent to Hindustani and Western traditions, and that you intentionally use them [in ways] that audiences could potentially hear?

RE: I absolutely think about that. I think about my audience a lot when I write because I'm someone who cares really deeply about communicating things through my music and who I'm communicating with. I especially think about the Indian audiences, because I was trained in Western music, so that is something that is easier [for me] to push the envelope. But I would also say that I push the Indian envelope too. That is something that I also feel Shirish Korde does very well: we are not afraid of pushing the Indian musicians outside of their comfort zones.[2] They are not performing straight

Indian classical music and we just surround them [with Western music]; they are also taking a step outside [their tradition] as well. Someone may be singing in a rag and then [it] might modulate, but it will be there for long enough [to] reestablish the tonal center and [Indian audiences] know it is still that rag. There might be points where the crossover is so intense that [the audience] might not understand it. But even that is a choice where I might say, "I want this to be a certain rag for a while for people to pick up on, and then maybe I want it to go somewhere else where the Indian audience might not necessarily be able to pick up on it, and that's okay."

CC: When you are sitting at your desk and working on a new piece or thinking about how these worlds can coexist and complement one another, what are the boundaries for you? Or, to put it another way, how do you avoid tokenizing something that you are immersed in?

RE: There is one factor, which is that if I'm putting any element of Hindustani music in it, I will always run it by a Hindustani musician to make sure that I'm not bastardizing something. For me, my knowledge of Western classical music is deep enough that I trust myself on the Western side to make those calls. Obviously, the true solution would be if I had been dually trained in both from the time I was a kid and [could] perform Hindustani music at the level of Saili Oak, then I would be totally fine.

But when I don't know, I always make sure to ask at least one person, "Does this feel okay to you?" In a way, it's almost easier when you put an actual Hindustani musician in the piece, because they will never do anything to bastardize their own tradition. If you create a situation that works for them, and they are purveying their tradition through your piece, then I think it takes care of those issues.

When [the piece is] just for Western musicians, I think it's important to be honest about where you are at any given time. For instance, *She Will Transform You* (2019) is only for Western musicians, but it does use Indian ragas. In this case, it's not supposed to be a Hindustani performance of Rageshree. The basis is Rageshree, and I do some other things with it [like] change keys et cetera, but you can hear the melody. So I just try to be honest about where I am.

There are early pieces where I don't use certain rags right. The Westerners can't hear it. They are fine with it, and the piece becomes its own thing. But I don't want Hindustani musicians to think that I don't know what those rags are. What I'll do, instead of changing the piece, I'll put a note in there to say, "Look, this one movement of the string quartet it says it's Jog. I didn't quite get this part of Jog at that time. So, if you hear it, don't worry. I know what it actually is now."

Cross-cultural collaborative practices lie at the heart of Esmail's creative process, highlighting her dual insider and outsider musical identity. She revealed how, when working with Indian musicians during the composition stage, the collaborative process can potentially check tokenization or exotification as she seeks to avoid problematic outcomes when blending traditions. Elsewhere in our conversation, she also elaborated on working with Western musicians during the rehearsal stage. Esmail described one situation when working on her *String Quartet* (2013) where she would sing phrases to the musicians, have them play it back, coach them, and then record their interpretation to create a style guide for future performances. This collaborative process mirrors Hindustani oral traditions and shows Esmail taking on an insider musical identity, where she assumes a more authoritative position and helps shape the performance practices necessary to realize her cross-cultural work (Figure 15.1).

Esmail's collaborative approach not only serves these functional purposes but also provides an important outlet for musical experimentation and community building. Nowhere is this more evident than in Esmail's relationship with one of her most significant collaborators, Hindustani vocalist Saili Oak. Their musical connection spans several years, during which they have worked together as teacher and student, as composer and performer, and as advocates for their respective musical traditions. They currently serve as co-artistic directors for Shastra, an organization they founded to facilitate cross-cultural exchange through workshops, symposia, and concert series. In our discussion about her relationship with Oak, Esmail touched on their history, the symphonic-vocal work *Meri Sakhi ki Avaaz (My Sister's Voice)* that she wrote for Oak, and how collaborative music-making is a way to engage in intercultural dialogue and build lasting connections.

> CC: Can you talk a bit about your relationship with Saili: how it developed and your collaborative process?
>
> RE: My relationship with Saili started when I was her student. I had been studying with Lakshmi Shankar for a while. When she passed away, I was looking for another teacher and, at that point, Saili was living in Los Angeles. I took lessons for a couple of years, we had really a great time, and then I began thinking, "What more can we do? I'm a composer. I should bring her my work." She also wanted to do a project where she could cross a little into Western classical music.
>
> I don't know if this would have worked for anyone else, but Saili and I are very similar people in terms of our relationship to our own musical

traditions. We are deeply trained in our traditions and are in similar places in our careers. But we are also open to hearing how our tradition reads in other traditions. When you know someone [well] and talk to them enough … we could suddenly think of ideas that were crazy and could only happen in two separate brains that had two separate trainings.

[For] three years, we [held] workshops where Western composers learned how to work with Indian musicians. Essentially, the way that I was learning to work with Saili, I was also teaching [to] younger composers. We spent many weekends together, talking through ideas with our students, and bouncing ideas off one another. And finally, I got this chance to write a piece for [Saili] with orchestra. In some ways, *Meri Sakhi ki Avaaz (My Sister's Voice)* became an encyclopedia of all [of] the crazy ideas that we ever had. Ideas that I wouldn't have even known that I could try …

At the same time, I care deeply about Saili as a person. She is a very close friend of mine. I was just at her wedding last week. So I [thought], "What can I give to Saili as someone who is in my professional position as a composer and someone who works with a lot of ensembles? Instead of putting her up there on the stage alone with an orchestra, why don't I actually give her a partner? Why don't I give her a Western musician, who she can begin to build a relationship with?"

She wouldn't just be a soloist but would start to really make deep relationships with other musicians, and specifically with Western singers who were in a similar [musical] place.

The first person happened to be Lucy Fitz Gibbon, who sang this piece in Richmond and also [at the premiere with the Albany Symphony]. Today is Lucy's birthday. Saili wrote [a] big post about her on Facebook, and they truly have built a deep relationship because they worked on this piece together.

I think what that looks like, as a composer, is creat[ing] environments where you decide not only who is on the stage, but also how those people interact with one another. So you can make them compete against each other, you can make them best one another, you can do any number of things, but you can also make them depend on one another. *Meri Sakhi ki Avaaz* asks the singers to depend on and learn from one another. This happens in ways that are musically explicit towards the end, where the Western singer starts to sing a bit of Indian music and vice versa. But [it] also [happens] in really practical ways, like how they are situated on the stage. In the premiere, if Saili lost her place, Lucy would be there for her.

There are times when Saili is improvising and she has to cue Lucy back in because Lucy doesn't know what she is going to do. So I know what the best [qualities are] in these two singers. I know how to have them show their best to one another and use that best not to show [one] another up, but actually guide each other.

CC: That is such a lovely image. You are not only developing a fusion between these two cultural traditions, but you are also doing so through the lens of deepening a connection between two people.

RE: Exactly.

Figure 15.1 Reena Esmail. Photo by Hannah Arista.

Themes of intercultural connection, insider and outsider duality, and self-discovery figure prominently in Esmail's *Meri Sakhi ki Avaaz (My Sister's Voice)* and *She Will Transform You*, the latter a work for orchestra and choir commissioned by the University of Richmond and the Richmond Symphony Orchestra and Chorus for the Tucker-Boatwright Festival. *Meri Sakhi ki Avaaz* examines sisterhood between two cultures, embodied by the Hindustani and Western vocal soloists. Containing equal parts English and Hindi languages, the succinct texts for each of the three movements reflect a broad view of sisterhood that includes, as Esmail describes in her program note, "what [it] looks like when expanded beyond a single family or a single culture—when two women, from two different musical cultures create space for one another's voices to be heard." *She Will Transform You* is cast in a single movement for a Western orchestra and choir and explores notions of belonging and distance through a text that centers on an immigrant mother and her child's relationship to their homeland and adopted country.

Our discussion of *Meri Sakhi ki Avaaz* focused on the first two movements. Esmail described the inspiration for the first movement, where she reimagines what French composer Léo Delibes's "Flower Duet" from *Lakmé* (1883) would have sounded like if its musical style had reflected its fictional Indian location. Esmail then explained how the second movement's harmonic systems take advantage of each vocalist's unique training to create an interdependent musical relationship. For *She Will Transform You*, Esmail elaborated on the poem's resonance with her own personal experiences as an Indian-American working with first- and second-generation immigrant children. She further discussed the connection between the work's thematic foundation and her harmonic language, which draws on an Indian raga.

CC: For *Meri Sakhi ki Avaaz* and *She Will Transform You*, I get the sense that these are both really personal pieces for you, but in different ways.

RE: They are, yes.

CC: From having read the program notes, hearing it in concert, and hearing you talk about it, *Meri Sakhi ki Avaaz* seems like it was an arrival at a place that you have been working toward for a while. It begins with this vocal duet that reimagines the "Flower Duet" from Léo Delibes's opera, *Lakmé*. It starts with a recording that gradually fades out to reveal a musical landscape incorporating pieces of text in different languages. Can you speak about this movement and why you chose to start with this reimagined music?

RE: I find that if my music references anything in the Western tradition not only musically, but culturally in terms of what it means, that "Flower Duet" is actually an amazing place to start. This comes from an opera called *Lakmé*, which is a Frenchification of the name "Lakshmi." In one scene, there are two Indian women sitting by a river and singing this song. [This "Flower Duet"] is just what a person who lived in France and who had probably never been to India imagined that to [sound like].

Imagine you are in an art gallery and looking at a Renoir painting. You see it as this really distant kind of static thing, and suddenly, what if that painting came off the wall and became a ballet and there were real people there? Suddenly you are engaging with the [real] culture of that painting as opposed to just seeing it [at a] distance. That's why I wanted that recording to be very static [and] unchanging, and then for the orchestra to come in and for you to imagine what it would be like if an Indian singer was literally singing that duet. What would it sound like? And so, that's where I thought I would start, moving from this place of exoticism to actual engagement with the culture.

CC: I really love how interconnected it all is, not only the resonance with the opera, but also the way the figuration in the recording crossfades with the figuration in the winds at the opening. This blending of two worlds also occurs in the second movement where you use harmonic systems from both traditions and modulate between them. Can you describe [how] you blended these?

RE: There are a few things at play, and it goes back to what we were talking about earlier: can things be understood through a Hindustani lens and [also] through a Western lens? There is a section at the beginning where they both sing the same phrase, but the Hindustani singer sings it in her style and the Western singer sings it in hers, so you hear those juxtaposed as two versions of this [same] phrase.

Once it gets into the part with meter, there is no tabla in the Western orchestra. With the tabla, there are so many sounds that you can make on it, and for the Hindustani singer to know where she is, I tried to recreate those sounds in the orchestra. For example, beats ten to fourteen is a high sound that doesn't have the low bass in it, so the winds do this high thing to show her that she is in that part of the rhythmic cycle. And then, beats fourteen to sixteen come back down to the next rhythmic cycle, and [she can hear] it pushing towards that end.

[The Hindustani singer] also knows that she is going to start [either] with a note that the Western singer has given her, or [one that] is in some way related, and she is going to start improvising from beat five until beat sixteen. When she gets to beat sixteen, she stops and holds one note. Then, the key changes under her and then the whole cycle happens again in a different key.

Western music values modulation, so how can you do that in a way that makes sense to a Hindustani musician? There needs to be someone else in there helping her and guiding her and that is the Western singer. So the Western singer starts what we call the *avartan*, which is the rhythmic cycle. She will sing from beats one to five and, basically, set up the key. By the time the Hindustani singer comes in, she knows what the key is. She'll start improvising, get to the end, [and] hold that note, [which] will become something different. But it is not her responsibility to change the key because [she] is not trained to do that. The Western singer will then take over on the next beat one and help establish the new key.

That's kind of how it works. For me, that was a break-through moment where I used both of their talents and their perceptive abilities [to help] them understand what was going on.

CC: It's a lovely way to build that interdependence that we have been talking about into the piece itself.

RE: Exactly.

CC: *Meri Sakhi ki Avaaz* is still a fairly recent piece for you, written in 2018, and *She Will Transform You* is obviously the newest that we have here, hot off the press.

RE: Yes!

CC: I love the poem ["Homeland"] that is the foundation for the work. How do you know the poet and what was your working relationship with her like?

RE: Yes, Neelanjana Banerjee is her name. Honestly, [composing this piece] is one of the hardest things that I have ever done. For [this] festival, think about how stressful it is to be a woman, who is a brown woman, who has to go beyond how her own culture is perceived in the West by writing a piece for mostly Western musicians, or for all Western musicians. How do I even handle this?

The University of Richmond had thought this through so carefully, and this was one of these situations where I wasn't being approached to be a random person who checked a box. You guys had given me an abstract and had thought this through, and I thought, "Okay, if they are going to be this thoughtful, I also better be very thoughtful." The last thing I wanted to do was to use some poem that says the right words, and then I realize it is some kind of colonial person and then it's a fiasco.

When the Los Angeles Master Chorale was doing my oratorio, *This Love Between Us* (2016), in November, that was around the time where I was working on this piece, and I had a really hard time finding a text. Initially, I wanted to use poems by people like Rupi Kaur and Nayyirah Waheed. Those people are women of color, who are very famous, but it's almost impossible to get the rights for any of those poems, and I tried. I actually had two other texts before this one that didn't get used. During the week of the oratorio performances, I was talking to the tabla player who was the soloist for this performance, and [his wife happened to be] a Bengali poet.

I talked to her and said I was specifically looking for things that were about the immigrant experience or what home means, what culture means. She gave me a bunch of choices and ["Homeland"] was the one that stood out to me. Neela [Neelanjana Banerjee], like me, is someone who was raised in the United States but is someone who has a really deep connection to her own culture. Who she is in her career is also who I am in [mine]. We are trying to do similar things, as you can tell from reading the text, right? So it really resonated with me, and the text was actually very long, which she cut down for me.

> Homeland: why do you elude me, tease me?
> There, my ancestors don't know me.
> Here my neighbors say "go back home" to me.
>
> When will you let me name you, claim you?
>
> But now, it is no longer about me—
> for this newborn child, I have a plea:
> Homeland, let this sweet child be,
>
> never torture her like you've done [to] me.
> Let her always find her way—surface streets and highways,
> underpasses and bikepaths, and she will transform you
>
> from concept to community, from skid row to safe haven.
> With each milestone, let her dismantle your distance,
> until one day, she arrives here
> —palm tree shadow, desert dust in her eyes—
> and smiles, and knows, she's home.
>
> —Neelanjana Banerjee, "Homeland"

CC: It's an extremely topical piece, and the way that you set the text is elegant. I don't know if I'm reading into it too much, but I also get the sense that *She*

Will Transform You is very personal to you because it describes someone who experiences what you were relaying earlier in our conversation. Is this piece about you?

RE: You know, it is not necessarily autobiographical, even though in many ways it totally is. It's more that, I go all around the country when I'm working with many different groups. I always do things with children and at schools, and a lot of times, I request to do things with children who are from immigrant backgrounds, from first and second generations. You just see the way that they have to think about things is so multidimensional …

When I was growing up, my friends would talk about their parents' experience growing up, and then I would talk about my parents' experience[s] and it was completely different. I haven't even been to the two countries where my own parents grew up. They are both ethnically Indian, but my mother grew up in Kenya and my dad grew up in Pakistan …. When I see these immigrant kids, I feel such a deep resonance with them. Because I [recognize] the thing that made it so hard for me to exist as a child, [pressures] that made me feel like I had to conform, and that made me feel like there was so much of my culture that I couldn't share until I was in my mid-twenties. I see them grappling with that now. I want to send the message that "Those things that are so hard for you now are going to be your greatest assets when you get older. Please don't forget that they exist. Do what you have to do to be okay, but please remember that is what's actually going help you and help our nation." That was what I was thinking of when writing the piece.

CC: What about in terms of the music? Conceptually, you have described how this piece might be received. How did you approach the process of composing out these ideas? What is grounding it here?

RE: For my work that doesn't involve Indian musicians, it doesn't have to sound explicitly Indian. In this case, I think the Indian sound of it is a little bit less than there is in *Meri Sakhi ki Avaaz*. I'm not going to expect people who are encountering Indian music for the first time to be purveyors of that tradition. That's not fair.

The Indian basis for it is this rag called Rageshree. The main tune [for the text], "Homeland, let this sweet child be / Never torture her as you've done me," is centered on one key [with a] melody that begins on what feels like the V. Whenever it centers on this key, that is complete Rageshree. So my idea was that Rageshree is a very deeply grounded rag that sounds like a major key in the West, but has properties in Indian music.

What I wanted to do was to explore how close, or far, [you] can get to Rageshree. There is a sense of resonance when you get to Rageshree, and a lot of times that happens with the high violin harmonics. The idea is that I'm resonating with this culture, I'm resonating with who I am, and then [the piece] pulls away into a different key. Suddenly there is no longer resonance, there is a little bit more dissonance. The idea is that when things are deeply resonant, [it] feels static and stable, and when [they are not it] feels like you are searching for something. That is what I was trying to explore in the piece.

As our conversation came to a close, we stepped back from discussing Esmail's individual compositions to the commissioning process, given the fact that she composed a new work for the Tucker-Boatwright Festival. She commented on the importance of how and why composers are approached to write a new piece, particularly for those that come from traditionally underrepresented backgrounds in the Western classical canon. She described how thoughtful conversations early on can help develop lasting relationships, avoiding the perpetuation of "tokenism" that can accompany commissioning efforts.

CC: I imagine when you are approached for commission, whether it's in the academic or orchestral world, you might have some that you don't want to touch. I wonder if you could speak to that issue of being approached to write something that you don't feel comfortable with or you feel like they are approaching you in the wrong way. What about that process informs your decision-making?

RE: I'll start by saying why I really wanted to write this commission, which is that the approach to me was so thoughtful. You can imagine there is a continuum of how I'm approached, where on the best side people are saying, "You are a person who works with this culture that maybe we don't have that much experience in, but we would love to have a window into that culture and into what it means to have your experience. We would love for our audience to have that too." And that's kind of the best possible situation where people approach it with curiosity and by asking a lot of questions.

I knew right away [that I wanted to participate], by how thoughtful the ask was, how many people were involved, and how deeply everyone had thought about it. I remember right at the beginning I had this conference call with five people, [who were] all involved in various ways and ask[ed] really thoughtful questions. When I'm composing things it's not like, "Okay, pay me this much and I'll just turn out a minute of music." I'm giving part of my soul to the commissioner, and so if I'm doing that, I want to feel that my soul is being engaged in the deepest way.

On the other hand, there is this movement nowadays of people wanting to hire composers because they feel guilty that their organizations look too white, too male, or whatever. I don't want to be the poster child for something like that—for something that's not deeply thoughtful. Because tokenism is wonderful on the front end, like you get a lot of gigs or whatever, but on the back end you get booted out and no one wants to deal with you again. Basically, you get a little more than if you were hired in the first place, but who really cares?

When I'm working with people, I think, "Is this a long working relationship I want to cultivate?" So much of with working with Richmond Symphony and with you guys is starting to opening up these windows of what would be possible. Here are all these things we could do, and let's continue to talk to each other and see where things align. Even the fact that you and I are doing an interview months after this [festival] is a testimony to the fact that you guys really wanted to have a relationship, and that meant the world to me.

There are a lot of times when people don't. But just wanting to continue to have the conversation, I think is what creates a world that is not tokenized. In the same way that I have a deep working relationship with Saili that allows me to grow over decades, I also look for those with my commissioners.

CC: I was just going to say, it seems like out of everything we talked about today, relationships are at the center of everything that you do.

RE: They are.

In the time since our conversation, Esmail has been appointed as the Los Angeles Master Chorale's 2020–23 Swan Family Artist-in-Residence and the Seattle Symphony's 2021–22 Composer-in-Residence. Both of those residencies involve significant new commissions, including a violin concerto for the legendary Hindustani violinist Kala Ramnath. Additionally, she has a number of commissions for smaller works over the next few years, for groups like the Santa Fe Desert Chorale and Conspirare, as well as pieces for individual performers like the violinist Simone Porter, the cellist Arlen Hlusko, the trombonist Brittany Lasch, and the trumpeter Mary Bowden. Beyond new commissions, she became co-chair of New Music USA's executive board in June 2020 where she continues her advocacy work for the contemporary music community.

The COVID-19 pandemic has, of course, significantly affected large ensemble performances around the world. Given the sizable forces involved for *She Will*

Transform You, Esmail has created a reduction of the piece for choir and solo flute. Prior to the pandemic, *Meri Sakhi ki Avaaz* was slated to be performed by the Dayton Philharmonic, the South Dakota Symphony Orchestra, the New West Symphony, and at the University of Puget Sound. These performances will be rescheduled, and the Berkeley Symphony will be making a recording of the work. Despite the challenges associated with music-making during the pandemic, Esmail's work remains thematically well suited for the current moment. The music's simultaneously inward- and outward-looking nature underscores our increasing global interconnectedness through cross-cultural relationships, collaborations, and reimagined traditions.

Notes

1. Indian classical music has two distinct traditions: Hindustani (associated with regions of Northern India) and Carnatic (associated with Southern India). Esmail's training is in the Hindustani tradition—the implied tradition when she uses the phrase "Indian classical music."
2. My interview with Korde, in which he too reflects on intercultural collaboration, appears in Chapter 11.

Acknowledgments

This book grew from a conference titled "Contested Frequencies" that took place among a series of music events held during the 2018–2019 school year at the University of Richmond (UR). The conference was generously funded by the university's annual Tucker-Boatwright Festival and co-sponsored by the School of Arts and Sciences and the Department of Music. We are indebted to the colleagues, administrators, students, and staff who made the conference run smoothly, as well as the international scholars, artists, and local community members who participated and attended. In particular, we thank our departmental colleague, Andrew McGraw, for imagining and coordinating such a fascinating series of performances, workshops, courses, and scholarly panels. We appreciate his suggestion to create this volume, along with his participation as a contributor and his advice throughout the book's various stages. Linda Fairtile, UR's head music librarian, also offered her indispensable expertise, initially facilitating the conference programming and later helping us to locate integral materials and sources during the COVID-19 pandemic. We are also grateful to our other department colleagues for their wholehearted support throughout the festival, the conference, and the editing and publication processes—especially our chair, Jeffrey Riehl, and administrative assistant, Linda Smalley.

    A special thank you goes to Arts and Sciences Dean, Patrice Rankine, for delivering memorable and insightful opening remarks at the 2019 conference and for offering continued support and enthusiasm for this project. Summer Research Fellowship Funding from the university's Faculty Research Committee has kept our publication schedule on track for the past three summers, and we are appreciative of our colleagues on the fellowship committee for recognizing the importance and timeliness of this volume. While working on this project, Jessie Fillerup held a fellowship at the Aarhus Institute of Advanced Studies (AIAS), which was co-funded by the Aarhus University Research Foundation and the European Union's Seventh Framework for research, grant number 609033. AIAS allowed her the flexibility and freedom to incorporate work on this volume into her fellowship activities, and she is particularly grateful to the

AIAS directors, Morten Kyndrup and Søren Keiding, for guarding the time and talents of the AIAS fellows.

We are honored to feature Scott P. Yates's photograph on this cover, and we thank him and the USA TODAY NETWORK for agreeing to license it. We are most indebted to the wonderful people at Bloomsbury Press, especially our editors Leah Babb-Rosenfeld and Rachel Moore, who have been encouraging, enthusiastic, and knowledgeable throughout the process. They have attended to our project with keen insight, generosity, flexibility, and patience. As always, we sincerely thank our families—parents, siblings, spouses, children, and friends who have become family—for their love and understanding. Not least, we thank our amazing contributors, who produced outstanding and insightful new scholarship, persevering despite the unforeseen challenges of personal, political, and social turmoil during the pandemic. It is truly a privilege to feature your important work here.

Index

ableism 167, 171, 172 See also disability, decolonizing
Abrams, J. J. 155
accessibility 8, 20, 113, 123, 126, 128, 136, 228
acoustemology 34–5
Aède of the Ocean and Land (theater production) 216
affective geographies 21–2 See also AudibleRVA
Affrilachian movement 62–4, 70 See also Black string band music
African American Art (Patton) 252–3
African Methodist Episcopal Church (Charleston, SC) 222
Afrofuturism 7, 9, 135, 141–2, 143, 145, 148 See also *Splendor & Misery* (clipping.)
Agawu, Kofi 66
agency 7–9, 62, 92, 142–3, 170–1, 175–6; of Indigenous people 45, 49, 57 See also self-determination
alien: soundscape of the 6, 9–10, 156–60 See also alterity; *Arrival* (Villeneuve)
"All Black" (clipping.) 137, 142–3, 145–6
"All Imperfect Things" (Nyman) 175
alterity 5, 6, 9–10, 97–8, 102, 104, 108, 137; in films with disability portrayal 164, 168, 169, 170; in science fiction scores 151, 154–6 See also *Quatre études de rythme*
ambient music 120–1, 140, 153, 156
"America" (hymn tune) 80
American Civil War 13n2, 221–2, 230 See also Confederate statues
The American Indian (newspaper) 56
The American Vocalist (Mansfield) 87, 88
Anable, Aubrey 117–18
Anderson, T. J. 230
Anishinaabe people 114, 115, 122–9; Anishinaabemowin (Anishinaabe language) 126–9

Annenberg Inclusion Initiative (AII, University of Southern California) 163, 164–7, 168, 177n6
Annihilation (Garland) 155–6
Anthology of American Folk Music (Smith) 219
anti-anti-essentialism 8, 62, 70–3
anti-essentialism 65–6
anti-slavery: American Antislavery Society 75; *Anti-Slavery Harp* (Brown) 76; *Anti-Slavery Hymns* (Stacy) 80–1; *Anti-Slavery Songs* (songster) 85, 89 See also hymn parodies, antislavery; slavery
Anton, Karen 80
appropriation 56, 101, 108, 113, 174, 177n5, 198, 200; *Red hot sun turning over* (Garner) 5, 6, 11, 222, 223–9, 230
ArcGIS mapping 19–20 See also AudibleRVA
archival research: limits of 6, 8, 65–6; rereading of materials 4, 8, 43–5, 57
Arendt, Hannah 36
Arista, Hannah 272
Aristotle 20
Arrival (Villeneuve) 7, 9–10, 151–60; alterity in science fiction scores 151, 154–6
Ashe, Valerie 249, 251, 255, 257, 260, 261
assimilation 51, 52, 57, 123
Astin, Sean 189
Atkins, E. Taylor 249, 255, 256
Attali, Jacques 22, 25
Attar, Farid ud-Din 216
Atwater, P. M. H. 176
AudibleRVA 7–8, 19–38; affect and sound 21–2; complaint, privilege of 27–8; gentrification 30–1; housing 28–30; mapping music 32–4; noise 22–5; policing music 31–2; segregated affective publics, overcoming 34–8, 39n12; silence, speaking, and listening 26–7

audience, role of 240, 248, 249, 251, 253–4, 261
Australia 169
authenticity 68–9, 87–8, 165–7, 228; in *The Lanna Dream* (Sirisook) 11, 235–6, 238–9, 242, 243–5
Ayler, Albert 259

Babbitt, Milton 97, 225
Banerjee, Neelanjana 275–6
Baraka, Amiri (LeRoi Jones) 136, 139–40
Barrow, Geoff 155–6
Bauer, Amy 186
"Bavaria" (hymn tune) 89
"Beautiful Dreamer" (Foster) 221–2
Beauty and the Beast (1991 film) 187
"Before He Cheats" (Underwood) 196–7
Bell, Richard 90
Berkeley, Busby 191
Berlin, Germany *See* Blackness, American, in Berlin jazz performance
"Better Days Coming" (hymn) 87, 88
"A Better Place" (clipping.) 137, 146
Beyoncé 197–8
b-flat (jazz club) *See* Blackness, American, in Berlin jazz performance
Bieber, Justin 198
Biewen, John 223
Bill C-45 (Jobs and Growth Act, Canada) 129
Blackness 21, 25; African Americans, in Richmond, VA 22–5; Black composers 224; Black excellence 142; Black Lives Matter (BLM) 2, 13n2, 219–20, 230; Black masculinity 25; Black-owned music venues 32–3; sonic Blackness 137, 143; of Southern culture 230 *See also* Afrofuturism; AudibleRVA
Blackness, American, in Berlin jazz performance 5–6, 11, 247–61; audience participation in the Black Vernacular Tradition 248, 249, 251, 253–4, 257, 260–1, 262n1; politics of 255–6
Black string band music 6, 8, 61–73; Affrilachia and 1990s research on Black string band traditions 62–5;

anti-anti-essentialist and hybrid approach 70–3; anti-essentialist critique 65–6; race and region in Joe Thompson's playing 66–70; rhythm as a cultural marker, reconsidering 248, 261n1
Bley, Carla 256
Bloechl, Olivia A. 158
Bloom, Rachel 185, 190, 194–5, 196, 199–200 *See also Crazy Ex-Girlfriend*
boarding and reservation schools 43, 52, 53, 54, 56, 57, 123
"Bonnie Doon" (hymn tune) 89
Boots, Cheryl 75
Borderline Personality Disorder (BPD) *See Crazy Ex-Girlfriend*
Borgo, David 143
Born, Georgina 37, 97
Boston Musica Viva 216
Boulez, Pierre 97, 99
Bowden, Mary 279
Branch, James "Plunky" 35–6, 37, 39n10
Brings Plenty, Trevino 124–5
Brown, Julie 171
Brown University 207–8
Brown, William Wells 76, 79, 82, 86–9
Browning, Tod 168
Bruchac, Margaret 45, 50
Bruckner, Anton 221, 227
Bureau of American Ethnology 46–7, 54
"By the Waters of Minnetonka" (Lieurance) 49–50, 56

Cadman, Charles Wakefield 48–9, 55
Cage, John 100, 139
Cain, Mary Cathryn 92
Campion, Jane 10, 163–4, 170, 173–6, 178nn20–4
Canada 7, 9, 84, 128–9, 225–6
Capra, Frank 168
Carlin, Bob 69
Carolina Chocolate Drops (CCD) 61, 67, 68, 70–1
Carter, Elliott 208
cells (music) 213, 217n3
"changing same" 136
Chapman, Maria Weston 80, 91–2, 93n3
Charlie Haden Liberation Orchestra 256

"The Chattering Squaw" (Loomis) 43, 44
Cheng, William 170
Cheyenne people 50
Chiang, Ted 152
Chiang Mai University (CMU) 237–8, 243
Chicora Wood Plantation 64
Chion, Michel 171–2, 178n19
Choctaw people 123–4
Christ, Jesus 89–90
Christianization, of Black Americans 86–9
A Christmas Carol (Dickens) 167
Chronicles of Chicora Wood (Pringle) 64
Chybowski, Julia 76, 77, 84
Circumpolar North 116–22
civic performances 36
Civil Rights Act (1964) 136
Clarinet Concerto (Esmail) 267
Clark, George W. 79, 81–2, 83, 88, 89, 91
class 21, 22–3, 26, 28, 231n5 *See also* AudibleRVA
Cleveland, Robert Nasruk 117
Cline, Patsy 196
clipping. (band): *CLPPNG* 139; *Midcity* 138–9 *See also Splendor & Misery*
Close Encounters of the Third Kind (Spielberg) 154–5
coeval histories 45
Cogan, Robert 206
cognitive theory 6
Coleman, Ornette 259
College of the Holy Cross 205, 206
Collins, Karen 122
colonialism 5–6, 108, 123–4, 223, 226, 236, 238, 275; colonialist logic 66, 71, 116, 119, 174; postcolonial theory 151–2, 159; settler colonial violence 123–4. *See also Arrival* (Villeneuve); decolonization; globalization; race
Coltrane, John 208
"Come, let us join our God to praise" (Rhodes) 85
"Come Out" (Reich) 139
"Come saints and sinners, hear me tell" (hymn) 85
Confederate statues 2–3, 7, 10–11, 13n2 *See also Red hot sun turning over*
The Conference of the Birds (Korde) 216

"Consistent Family Worship of Slave-Holders" (Simpson) 85
"The Contrast" (Winchell) 77–8
Conway, Cecelia 67
Cook Inlet Tribal Council (CITC) 116–22
Corbett, John 100, 153
cosmologies 117, 119, 129, 142, 146
counter-history 135, 141–2
country music 229, 231n5
COVID-19 pandemic 3, 13n4, 177n13, 216, 219, 279–80
"craziness" 190, 195–9; "Crazy" (Cline) 196; "Crazy Blues" (Smith) 196; "Crazy in Love" (Beyoncé and Jay-Z) 197–8
Crazy Ex-Girlfriend (CXG) (TV show) 6, 10, 185–200; first person perspective 186–90, 201n1; "I Have Friends" (song) 189; "I'm a Good Person" (song) 190; "I'm Just a Girl in Love" (song) 186, 191–2; "I'm Not Sad, You're Sad" (song) 186, 200; "Love Kernels" (song) 193, 197; " (Tell me I'm Okay) Patrick" (song) 200; performing "crazy" 195–9; "Sexy Getting Ready Song" (song) 193, 198; theme songs, as destabilizing 190–5, 201nn2–3; "Trent is Getting Ready Song" (song) 193; "West Covina" (song) 187; "What'll It Be (Hey, West Covina) " (song) 188–9; "You Do/You Don't Wanna Be Crazy" (song) 193–9; "You Stupid Bitch" (song) 189–90, 198, 201n4
Creek/Cherokee people 55
criminality 22–5, 38n1
critical race theory 6, 8, 62
cross-cultural composition *See* Esmail, Reena; Korde, Shirish
Cruz, Jon 82, 86
cultural autonomy 22, 25
cultural memory 63–4, 66–7, 72
cultural retentions 61, 66–7
cultural survival 128–9
cultural transmission 115, 117, 119, 125–6, 130n4
Cummins State Farm 227–8

The CW (TV station) See Crazy
    Ex-Girlfriend

Dakota people 54
Dallas Opera 216
Davis, Jefferson 220
Davis, Lennart 167
Dawes Act (1887) 52
Day-Lewis, Daniel 166
Day, Sharon 126
"Da Ya Think I'm Sexy? " (Stewart) 239
The Day the Earth Stood Still (Wise) 154
d/Deafness 170–1, 178n18 *See also*
    disability, decolonizing; muteness
decolonization 10, 44–5, 114–16, 117
    See also colonialism; disability,
    decolonizing; video game audio,
    decolonizing
Delany, Samuel R. 139
Delibes, Léo 1, 273–4
Deloria, Philip 115
del Toro, Guillermo 166, 171, 176, 178n16, 24
Desafinado (Getz) 206
Descartes, René 146
Dickens, Charles 167
diegesis 120, 121, 158–9, 185, 199;
    extra-diegetic sound 121, 190, 195;
    intra-diegetic sound 190, 195
Diggs, Daveed 138, 139, 142–3, 144
digital humanities 6; affective ankylosis
    37–8; ArcGIS mapping 19–20;
    digital storytelling 116–22
disability *See Crazy Ex-Girlfriend*; d/
    Deafness; mental illness; muteness
disability, decolonizing 6, 10, 163–76;
    Annenberg Inclusion Initiative
    (AII) 163, 164–7, 168, 177n6; drag/
    mimicry of disabled characters
    165–7, 177n5; in film and television
    studies 167–9, 177n9; in music and
    sound of film and television 170–2,
    178n18; in *The Piano* (Campion)
    163–4, 173–6
discrepant readings 45
dismediation 10, 169, 170, 176
Doane, Woody 154
Dolgen, Jack 185

"Donna's Got a Rambling Mind" (tune) 68
Douglass, Frederick 220
drag: disabled characters, mimicry of
    165–7, 177n5; gender 198
Dubois, Laurent 229
Dvořák, Antonín 158–9

Eaklor, Vicki 76
ecological awareness: climate change 216;
    Traditional Ecological Knowledge
    (TEK) 9, 114, 120, 125–9 *See also*
    video game audio, decolonizing
Das Edelweiss (jazz club) 247
Edson, Lewis 82, 93n4
education, music in boarding and
    reservation schools 43, 52, 53, 54,
    56, 57, 123
Eidsheim, Nina Sun 5, 143
electronic music: in science fiction scores
    153–6 *See also* video game audio,
    decolonizing
E-Line Media 113, 116–22
Ellcessor, Elizabeth 168
Ellington, Duke 224, 231n4
Ellis, Katie 168–9
Eminem 198
empathy 200
Enbridge Northern Gateway Pipeline 129
environmental sound 116, 120–1
Epstein, Dena 65
Eshun, Kodwo 135, 148
Esmail, Reena 1, 3, 5–6, 10–11, 216,
    217n4, 263–80; *Clarinet Concerto*
    267; on collaborative process
    270–2; on commissioning process
    278–9; on creative process 266–9;
    early musical education 263–6;
    *Meri Sakhi Ki Avaaz (My Sister's
    Voice)* 1, 3, 11, 263, 270–1, 273–5,
    277, 280; *She Will Transform You*
    263, 269, 273, 275–8, 279–80;
    String Quartet 270; *This Love
    Between Us* 276
essentialism 61, 64–6, 70, 71, 100–1;
    anti-anti-essentialism 62, 70–3;
    anti-essentialism 65–6
The Ethics of Living Jim Crow (Wright) 27
Etude (journal) 51

eugenic narratives, in film 10, 164, 167, 170, 173, 174, 176, 177n7 *See also* disability, decolonizing
Evans, Dominick 166, 167
Ewell, Philip A. 3–4, 13n5, 224
exoticism 5, 9, 270, 274, 275; in *Arrival* (Villeneuve) 153; in *The Lanna Dream* (Sirisook) 235–6, 240, 243; in *Quatre études de rythme* (Messiaen) 97, 100–1, 102, 103, 104, 108
experimentalism 143, 152–3 *See also Splendor & Misery* (clipping.)
exploitation 52, 83, 123, 136, 220, 223, 225, 228

Fabian, Johannes 45
Fair Housing Act (1968) 19
Fake Noise (band) 249–52, 253, 255–6, 257, 259, 260–1
Family Tradition (Thompson) 68
Fanon, Frantz 37
Faubus, Orval 255
Feld, Steven 34–5
feminism 173–6, 191
Fiasco, Lupe 142
field recordings 50, 121–2, 222, 227–30
film 145; alterity in 154–6; Annenberg Inclusion Initiative (AII) 163, 164–7, 168, 177n6; soundtrack, invisibility of 170, 172, 174–6 *See also Arrival* (Villeneuve); disability, decolonizing
First Symphony (Bruckner) 221
Fitz Gibbon, Lucy 216, 271–2
Fletcher, Alice 45, 46–8, 54
Flock of Seagulls 198
"Flower Duet" (Delibes) 1, 273–4
Floyd, George 2, 66
Floyd, Samuel, Jr. 63–4
Fontana, Santino 189
Foster, Stephen 221–2
Fraser, Nancy 36
Freaks (Browning) 168
Freedom of Information Act (1967) 23
Freedom's Lyre (Hatfield) 75
"From the Land of the Sky Blue Water" (Cadman) 55
"The Fugitive" (hymn) 89

Galanin, Nicholas 116
Garland, Alex 155–6
Garnett, H. Highland 88
Garrisi, Diana 168
Garrison, William Lloyd 80, 93n3
Gates, Henry Louis, Jr. 253
GegenSichKollektiv (anonymous group of theorists) 141
gender 10; Annenberg Inclusion Initiative (AII) 163, 164–7, 168, 177n6; codes and stigmas 186, 199; drag 198; feminism 173–6, 191; misogyny 172, 190, 195, 198; patriarchy 173, 178n20; presumption of male default 178n19; pronouns 192; representation disparities in the video game market 117 *See also* men; women
generational trauma 144
gentrification 30–1, 35, 38n6, 39n11 *See also* AudibleRVA
geographies, sonic 7–8, 219, 229, 231n5 *See also* AudibleRVA
Getz, Stan 206, 257
Giacchino, Michael 155
Giddens, Rhiannon 70–1, 72
Gilmore, H. S. 90
Gilroy, Paul 62, 71–2
"Gizaagi'igonan Gimaamaanan Aki" (Anishinaabemowin song) 127
Glassie, Henry 229
Glee (TV show) 166
globalization 5; global vantage point 7 *See also* colonialism
"The Good Doctor" (TV show) 166
Gorbman, Claudia 155, 164, 178n19
Goree, T. J.: Goree State Farm 227–8
Grand Ole Opry 70–1
Greenspan, Ezra 88
Griffiths, Paul 99, 101, 109n8
Grimké, Sarah 86
Grimshaw, Jeremy 101

Habermas, Jürgen 36
Hamilton (Miranda) 139
Hanson, William F. 54
Haraway, Donna 116
Harawi (Messiaen) 100

Hart, Antonio 258-9, 260
Haskell Institute 56
Hastings, Thomas 81
Hatfield, Edwin F. 75, 78, 82, 83, 92-3
Hawkins, Sally 166
Hay, Fred J. 63, 66, 69
healing 71-2
Hegarty, Paul 141
Heisserer, Eric 152
hermeneutics 6, 65
Herrmann, Bernard 154
Hesse, Herman 253
heteronormativity 198, 200
Highmore, Freddie 166
Hilder, Thomas 115, 117, 129
Hill, Peter 98, 99
hillbilly music 63
Hlusko, Arlen 279
Hoffman, Dustin 166
Hogan, Brendan 121-2
Hohvaness, Alan 100
"Hold Up" (Beyoncé) 197
Home Owners Lending Corporation (HOLC) 28-30
"Homeland" (Banerjee) 275-6
Honour Water (LaPensée) 114, 115-16, 123, 125-9
Hood, Thomas 175
hooks, bell 71
housing 19, 28-30 *See also* AudibleRVA
Hugo Award 139
Hunsdale, Jamie 121-2
Hunt, Richard 230
Huron, David 102 104
Hutchinson Family Singers 78
Hutson, William 138, 139
hybridity 6, 10, 11, 63, 69-70, 72-3
hymnals 76
hymn parodies, antislavery 6-7, 8, 75-93; conventional parodies 79-83, 93n3; hymnodic convention and songsters 76-8; unconventional parodies 84-90; usefulness of parody 91-3

"I Kissed a Girl" (Perry) 198
"I Ran (So Far Away)" (Flock of Seagulls) 198

"I Wish I Knew How It Would Feel to Be Free" (Simone) 3
identity 229; brand 62, 72; contiguity of 141-2; cultural 264-5; "de-centering" of 73; definitions of 4-7; in *The Lanna Dream* (Sirisook) 236-9, 242-5; listening and 137; lived identity categories 164-7; musical 5-6, 207-8, 270; national 244; performative 186; various identities 194-5, 199; white 92, 154 *See also* Blackness; disability; gender; Indian (Hindustani) music; Indigenous peoples; men; performativity; race; self; sonic identity; "the South"; whiteness; women
Idle No More movement 128-9
Île de feu I (Messiaen) 8-9, 97-8, 99, 100-1, 102, 103, 104-5 *See also Quatre études de rythme*
Île de feu II (Messiaen) 8-9, 97-8, 99, 100-1, 102-3, 105-8 *See also Quatre études de rythme*
Imada, Adria 45
imagineNATIVE festival 123
imitation 56, 68, 77; drag/mimicry of disabled characters 165-7, 177n5 *See also* hymn parodies
Inception (film) 156
inclusionary music 174
Indian (Hindustani) music 280n1; ragas 209-12, 268-9, 277-8; rhythms and pitches 99, 100, 156, 266-9 *See also* Esmail, Reena; Korde, Shirish
"the Indianists." *See* Musical Indianism
Indigeneity 1, 9, 49, 57, 114, 120; digital 116-22
Indigenization 113, 125
Indigenous peoples 7, 225-6; boarding and reservation schools 43, 52, 53, 54, 56, 57, 123; characters in Western films 155; imagineNATIVE festival 123; Indian rights movement 75; modernity, Indigenous 113, 114, 120; Montezuma 53-4; musicians 63; Native American Youth and Family Center 126; Office of Indian Affairs (now Bureau of Indian

Affairs) 46; song 158; Traditional Ecological Knowledge (TEK) 9, 114, 120, 125–9 *See also* Musical Indianism; video game audio, decolonizing; individual tribes
integrity, of cross-cultural compositions 210, 211–12, 217n2
interiority 189, 194, 195
International Bluegrass Music Association (IBMA) 70–1
intertextuality 137, 185, 186, 196, 199
interversions 99, 103, 108
Inuit people, Canadian 225–6
Iñupiat (Iñupiaq) people 114, 116–22, 130n2
Invaders (LaPensée) 114, 123–5, 129
invisibility 62, 70; of film music 170, 172, 174–6
It's a Wonderful Life (Capra) 164, 168
"It's Gonna Rain" (Reich) 139

Jabbour, Allan 67, 69
Jagger, Mick 198
Jamison, Phil 68
Jay-Z 142, 197–8
jazz 10, 11, 205–7, 249, 255, 256 *See also* Blackness, American, in Berlin jazz performance
Jim Crow laws 6, 19, 27, 227
Joel, Billy 188
Jóhannsson, Jóhann *See Arrival* (Villeneuve)
Johanssen, Jacob 169
Johnson, Robert 98, 109n1
Jones, LeRoi (Amiri Baraka) 136, 139–40
Jones, Margaret 56
Journal of Schenkerian Studies (journal) 224
jubilee 82, 93 n4
Judd, Steven Paul 123–4

Kahn, Joseph 196
Kalmanovitch, Tanya 226
Kaur, Rupi 276
Kavthekar, Amit 205, 210, 213, 215–16
Kelly, Thomas 81
Kendi, Ibram X. 223
Kirkpatrick, Bill 168

Knapp, Raymond 188, 200, 201n1
Knapp, Zelda 188, 201n1
Korde, Shirish 5, 6, 10, 205–16, 268; *The Conference of the Birds* (Korde) 216; *Lalit-2nd Prism* (Korde) 205–6, 209–16; *Rasa* (Korde) 208; *Tenderness of Cranes* (Korde) 208
Koselleck, Reinhart 144
"Krambambuli" (hymn text) 84
Krause, Bernie 121
"Kunuuksaayuka" (Iñupiaq tale) 117 *See also Never Alone* (video game)
Kurkowicz, Joanna 213

labor, Indigenous 43 *See also* Musical Indianism
La Flesche, Francis 45, 46–9, 54
La Flesche, Joseph 46
Lakmé (Delibes) 1, 273–4
Lakota people 124–5
Lalit-2nd Prism (Korde) 10, 205–6, 209–16
Landrieu, Mitch 223
language: barriers and communication 152, 158; revitalization and transmission 125–9
Lanier, Michelle 66–7
The Lanna Dream (Sirisook) 7, 11, 235–45; Lanna identity, contemporary representations of 242–5; performance and representation 239–42; personal identity, rediscovering 236–9; tourist gaze 235–6
LaPensée, Elizabeth 113, 122–9; *Honour Water* 114, 115–16, 123, 125–9; *Invaders* 114, 123–5, 129
Lasch, Brittany 279
Ledbetter, Huddie William 228
Lee, Robert E. 3, 13n2, 220, 223, 230
leitmotifs 185–6, 189–90
Lemonade (Beyoncé) 197
"Lenox" (Edson) 82, 93n4
Lerner, Neil 170
Lessons of Our Land initiative 123
Levine, Victoria 114
Levinson, Barry 166, 168
Leviticus 25:40 82
Lewis, George 143

liberation theology 142, 143, 144–5
The Liberator (newspaper) 84
Liberty Minstrel (Clark) 88, 93n5
Library of Congress 50
Lieurance, Thurlow 45, 49–52, 56
Ligeti, György 206, 210, 214
liminality 72, 135
Lincoln, Jairus 91
Lindhorst, Jonathan 250, 255–6, 257, 258–9, 260, 261
Lipari, Lisbeth 146
listening 3, 26–7; ecological approach 109n6; expanded mode of 173; to film and television 170, 173; as path to self-determination 137, 146–8; schema theory and 101–3, 109nn5–7; shifting perspective of 114–15, 129 *See also Arrival* (Villeneuve); *Crazy Ex-Girlfriend*
Locke, Ralph 100, 101
Loft, Steven 119
logos 146
Lomax, John and Ruby 227–8
Lomelí, David 216
Longfellow, Henry Wadsworth 56, 89
"Long Mae Ping" (Manopetch) 241–3, 244
"Long Way Away" (clipping.) 135, 137, 142, 144–5
Loomba, Ania 159
Loomis, Harvey Worthington 43, 44
Lopez, Lori Kido 170
Loring, Harold 54

MacArthur genius grant 70
Madama Butterfly (Puccini) 241
manifest dismantling 220, 223, 227, 230. *See also Red hot sun turning over*
Manopetch, Jaran 241–3, 244
Mansfield, Daniel Hale 87, 88
Marcus, Greil 219
marginality, definition of 4
Markotic, Nicole 168, 169
Marsalis, Wynton 258, 259
Martin, Douglas 61
Martino, Donald 206
Marx, Harpo 172
Marxism 224–5
Mason, Lowell 82–3

Mathes, Carter 72
May, Samuel 91–2
McArdle, Terence 61
McClendon, Aaron 76, 88
McGann, Jerome 88
McHale, Kevin 166
McKenna, Aline Brosh 185
memory 141–2, 144; cultural 63–4, 66–7, 72; nostalgia 221–2; whiteness and 220–3 *See also* Confederate statues
men: Black masculinity 25; as default presumed gender 178n19; male-rocker lifestyle 198; misogyny 172, 190, 195, 198; patriarchy 173, 178n20; sonic masculinity 143; white male owned music venues 32–3; white men against confederate statues 223; white men in classical music 223–4 *See also Red hot sun turning over*
mental illness: in film 164, 166, 168; *Mental Health Conditions in Film & TV: Portrayals that Dehumanize and Stigmatize Characters* (AII report) 166 *See also Crazy Ex-Girlfriend*
Meri Sakhi Ki Avaaz (My Sister's Voice) (Esmail) 1, 3, 11, 263, 270–1, 273–5, 277, 280
Messiaen, Olivier *See Quatre études de rythme*
metatextuality 10, 91–3, 185–6 *See also Crazy Ex-Girlfriend*; hymn parodies, antislavery
Métis people 114, 115, 122
Mexican asylum-seekers 159–60
Midcity (clipping.) 138–9
"Miigwech Nibi" (Anishinaabemowin song) 127, 128
Mikkelsen, Mads 171
Miller, Karl Hagstrom 62, 72
Mills, Mara 169
Mingus, Charles 255, 256
Minnehaha (fictional character) 56
Miranda, Lin-Manuel 139
misogyny 172, 190, 195, 198
Mitchell, David 167, 173, 178n16
Mitchell, Joni 256

Mode de valeurs et d'intensités (Messiaen) 97, 98-9, 100, 101, 103, 104, 108 *See also Quatre études de rythme*
modernism 103, 207, 225
modernity, Indigenous 113, 114, 120
modes of limited transposition 99, 102, 104, 109n2
Molina, Caroline 174
Montezuma, Carlos 53-4
Montgomery, James 80-1, 82, 89-90
Moore, Thomas 77-8
Mortimer Dreamer (Sitting Eagle) 49-50
Moskin, Julia 229
"Mount Vernon" (hymn tune) 82-3
Moyer, Justin 168, 177n11
Müller-Szeraws, Jan 205, 210, 212-13, 215
multinaturalism 118-19
Musical America (magazine) 50
Musical Indianism 7, 8, 43-57; archival materials, rereading of 43-5, 57; composition and Indigenous authority 48-52; ethnography 46-8; reception, Indigenous 52-7
musical infrastructure 20, 31-4, 38n9, 39nn10-12
musical lineage 68
musicals: *Hamilton* 139; *next to normal* 201n1; *South Pacific* 187 *See also Crazy Ex-Girlfriend*
musicking 62, 65
muteness 10, 163, 170-2, 177n14, 178n19; in *The Piano* 173-6 *See also* disability, decolonizing
My Left Foot (film) 166

Nancy, Jean-Luc 146-7
narrative prosthesis 167, 172, 174, 177n7
NASA acoustics lab 27
NASCAR 28, 31
nationalism 43, 49, 52, 159, 244
Native Americans *See* Indigenous peoples
Nazis 19, 221
"Negro jig" 64-5
Neumes rythmiques (Messiaen) 98, 99, 102, 104, 108 *See also Quatre études de rythme*
Never Alone (video game) 114, 115-22, 129
New Age sound 174

The New York Times (newspaper) 61
Nibi Walks 126
Nichomachean Ethics (Aristotle) 20
nihilism 142-3, 145, 147
"Noble Warrior" 168
noise 6, 20, 22-5, 38n1, 38n8, 139, 141; complaints 20, 23, 27-8, 38n3, 38nn5-7 *See also* AudibleRVA
Noll, Mark 83
Norden, Martin 168
normativity 20-1, 167
North Carolina Piedmont region 69-70, 72
NVivo (data management package) 168
Nye, Sean 200
Nyman, Michael 174-6, 178n21, 23

"O come! Come away, my sable sons and daughters" (Simpson) 84
"O du liebe meiner liebe" (Thommen) 89
"O there will be mourning" (hymn) 86
Oak, Saili 216, 269, 270-2
Obama, Barack 136
"Obsessive Avenger" 168, 171
ocularcentrism 169, 172, 177n12
Odell, Jenny 220
The Old, Weird America (Marcus) 219
"Old Churchyards" (hymn tune) 78, 81
"Old Corn Liquor" (tune) 68, 69
"Old Hundred" (hymn tune) 80-1
Omaha people 46, 54, 55
O'Neill, Gloria 116-17, 122
"On the mountain's top appearing" (Kelly) 81
"On the Nature of Daylight" (Richter) 153, 159, 160
Orientalism 100, 102, 108, 109n6, 223
Original Anti-Slavery Songs (Simpson) 79, 84
Osage people *See* Musical Indianism
"The Osage Tribe: Rite of the Wa-Xo'-Be" (La Flesche) 48
Oshkii Giizhik Singers 126
Oster, Ernst 206
Otherness *See* alterity

Painter, Nell Irvin 223
Panichaphant, Ajarn Vithi 238, 242-3
Papakonstantinou, Elli 216

Papuan-inspired melodies and themes 8–9, 97–8, 99, 100–1, 102–8, 109n7 *See also* Quatre études de rythme
paratextuality 185, 190, 192, 193–5
Paris Conservatoire 98, 100
Parker, Arthur 54
parody 185, 192–3, 195–9, 200; definition of 77; usefulness of 90–3 *See also* Crazy Ex-Girlfriend; hymn parodies, antislavery
Partita for 8 Voices (Shaw) 225–6
Passengers (film) 164
patriarchy 173, 178n20
Patton, Sharon F. 252–3, 261
Peer, Ralph 63
performativity 7, 11, 186, 187, 195–9, 235, 244 *See also* identity; *The Lanna Dream* (Sirisook)
Perry, Katy 198
Peruvian folklore and melody 100
Peterson, Marina 36
Peyotism 47
The Piano (Campion) 10, 163–4, 170, 173–6, 178nn20–4
"Piano Man" (Joel) 188
Plant, Robert 198
policing 6, 22–5, 31–2, 35, 248 *See also* AudibleRVA
political acts 5, 255–6
polysemy 4, 139, 172, 193
Pomeroy, Herb 206
"A poor wayfaring man of grief" (Montgomery) 89
Porter, Simone 279
postcolonial theory 151–2, 159
Presley, Rachel 163
primitivism 49, 51, 53–4, 97, 115, 252–3, 261
Pringle, Elizabeth W. Allston 64
privilege 26, 27–8, 31, 119, 200
probability space 21–2
prosthesis: narrative 167, 172, 174, 177n7; voice as 171, 178n16
public domain 228–9
Puccini, Giacomo 241
Pueblo people 50
Pulitzer Prize for Music 224, 225–6
Pussy Cat Dolls 198

Quatre études de rythme (Four rhythmic etudes) (Messiaen) 8–9, 97–109; exoticism Messiaen's relationship to 97, 100–1; listeners and schema theory 101–3, 109nn5–7; schema-oriented analyses 103–8. *See also* Papuan-inspired melodies and themes
Quatuor pour la fin du temps (Messiaen) 100

race: Annenberg Inclusion Initiative (AII) 163, 164–7, 168, 177n6; blackface minstrel tunes 222; critical race theory 6, 8, 62; difference, exaggeration and fetishization of 65, 66, 71; Jim Crow laws 6, 19, 27, 227; Orientalism 100, 102, 108, 109n6, 223; primitivism 49, 51, 53–4, 97, 115, 252–3, 261; "race music" 63, 248; "racial integrity laws" 19; redlining 6, 19, 28–30; relationships 6–7; segregated affective publics 34–8; sonic color line 22, 35, 65, 73; surveillance 23–5 *See also* alterity; appropriation; AudibleRVA; Blackness; Black string band music; colonialism; Confederate statues; exoticism; globalization; Indigenous peoples; *Red hot sun turning over*; slavery; whiteness
Radano, Ronald 65
Raiford Penitentiary 227–8
Rain Man (Levinson) 166, 168
Ramnath, Kala 279
Ramsey, Guthrie P. 248, 260–1
Rangan, Pooja 172, 173, 175
Rasa (Korde) 208
Rasul, Abbas 5, 7, 11, 235–6, 242–5
Red hot sun turning over: on Southern monuments, myths, and histories (RHSTO) (Garner) 10–11, 219–30; appropriation and white racial frame 223–6; creation of 220–3; learning to dismantle 230
redlining 6, 19, 28–30
Refn, Nicolas Winding 171
regionality 69–70, 72

Reich, Steve 100, 139
repatriation 113, 119
resonance 109n8, 147
reverse ethnography 45
Rhodes, Benjamin 85
Richmond, VA 2–3, 6; Jackson Ward ("Black Wall Street") 28, 30–1; Richmond Folk Festival 36, 39n12; Richmond Symphony Orchestra 205, 215–16, 263, 273, 279 See also AudibleRVA; Confederate statues
Richter, Max 153, 159, 160
Rifkin, Mark 45
Rimsky-Korsakov, Nikolai 102
Roberts, John Storm 63
Robinson, Dylan 174
Robinson, Justin 67, 68
Roc Nation 142
Rodman, Rod 190
Roomful of Teeth (vocal ensemble) 225–6
Ruccia, Dan 226

Saariaho, Kaija 214
"Saintly Sage" 168, 171, 173
Salisbury, Ben 155–6
Samerjai, Torpong 239
Savage, Roger 141–2
Scheherezade (Rimsky-Korsakov) 102
schema theory: listeners and 101–3, 109nn5–7; schema-oriented analyses 103–8 See also Quatre études de rythme
Schlesinger, Adam 185
Schuller, Gunther 206, 207, 217n1
science fiction 135, 139, 148; musical alterity in 154–6 See also Arrival (Villeneuve); Splendor & Misery (clipping.)
Scottish folk songs 174
Second Advent Hymns (songster) 78
Seeger, Mike 69
self 6, 10; dissolution of 142–3; distorted sense of 185, 189, 195 See also identity
self-denial 189, 190–2, 201nn2–3
self-determination 137–8, 145, 146–8 See also agency

self-sounding 145–6, 148
Selway, Matt 170
Seneca people 54
sensory background 154–5
Serenade for Strings in E Major (Dvořák) 158–9
serialism 9, 97–8, 103, 104, 107, 108, 207
sexual orientation: Annenberg Inclusion Initiative (AII) 163, 164–7, 168, 177n6; heteronormativity 198, 200
Shankar, Lakshmi 270
Shankar, Ravi 209
The Shape of Water (del Toro) 166, 171, 176, 178n16, 24
Sharpe, Cecil 69
Shastra 270
Shaw, Caroline 225–6
She Will Transform You (Esmail) 263, 269, 273, 275–8, 279–80
Shine, Jessica 186
Siebers, Tobin 166
Sila (spiritual realm) 117
silence 26–7; "Silence" (Hood) 175; "silent film" 171, 172 See also AudibleRVA; disability, decolonizing; muteness
Simone, Nina 3
Simpson, Joshua McCarter 76, 79, 84–5
Sirisook, Waewdao 5, 7, 11 See also The Lanna Dream
"Sister, thou wast mild and lovely" (Smith and Mason) 82–3
Sitting Eagle (Mortimer Dreamer) 49–50
Siwilai ("civilizing") policy 236, 242
Slaughterhouse Five (Vonnegut) 136
slavery 6, 135–6; Fugitive Slave Act (1850) 38n1; "The Slave Singing at Midnight" (Longfellow) 89 See also anti-slavery; hymn parodies, antislavery; Red hot sun turning over; Splendor & Misery (clipping.)
Smith, Abby Love 75, 78, 93n2
Smith, Harry 219
Smith, John 158
Smith, Mamie 196
Smith, Samuel Francis 82–3
Smith, Stacey L. 166
Smith, Steven 211
Snipes, Jonathan 138

Snyder, Sharon 167, 173, 178n16
social constructionist approach 5, 65–6, 71, 153–4
Society of American Indians (SAI) 54
Society of Oklahoma Indians 56
"Sommerville" (hymn tune) 81
Sondheim, Stephen 188
"The Song of Hiawatha" (Longfellow) 56
"The Song of the Coffle Gang" (hymn parody) 86–9
Songs of the North American Indian (Lieurance) 51
songsters 76–83 *See also* hymn parodies, antislavery
sonic Blackness 137, 143
sonic color line 22, 35, 65, 73
sonic eudaimonia 20
sonic fields 21–2
sonic "goods" 20 *See also* AudibleRVA
sonic identity: approaches and themes 4–7; chapter overview 7–12; now and then 2–4 *See also* identity
sonic masculinity 143
sonic publics 37
sonic signifiers 141–2, 143, 195–6, 198, 251–2, 257, 268
sonic technology, Black 137
Sorin, André 99, 108, 109n3
sound 6, 20–1, 35; affect and 21–2; sound effects 121–2; soundmark 122; soundscapes 20, 113–16, 120–2, 124–5, 156–60
"the South" (Southern United States) 6, 10–11, 219, 227–8, 231n2 *See also* *Red hot sun turning over*
South Asian Symphony Orchestra 216
South Pacific (musical) 187
Southern, Eileen 64
Space Invaders (video game) 114, 123–5 *See also Invaders* (LaPensée)
Space Is the Place (film) 145
Spielberg, Steven 154–5
Splendor & Misery (clipping.) 6, 9, 135–48; "All Black" 137, 142–3, 145–6; background information about 135–40; "A Better Place" 137, 146; "Long Way Away" 135, 137, 142, 144–5; "True Believer" 142; "Wake Up" 137, 144–5
Stacy, George W. 80–1, 85–6
A Star Is Born (film) 167
Star Trek (franchise) 159
The State (newspaper) 222–3
Steidle, Oliver 250
Stephenson, Graham 143
Steppenwolf (Hesse) 253
stereotypes 164, 195, 198–9, 200 *See also* tropes
Stern, Jonathan 169
Stewart, Rod 239
stigmatization 10, 163–4, 166, 171, 176, 185–7, 195, 199
Stockhausen, Karlheinz 99
Stoever, Jennifer Lynn 3, 26, 65
Stoney, Levar 3
"Story of Your Life" (Chiang) 152
storytelling, digital 116–22
String Quartet (Esmail) 270
String Quartet No. 2 (Carter) 208
Structured Query Language (SQL) 168
Structures Book I (Boulez) 99
Stuart, J. E. B. 220
A Study of Omaha Music (Fletcher and La Flesche) 46
Sub Pop 139, 145
Summers, Tim 159
Sundland, Dan Peter 250, 257
Sun Ra 145
Supaman 123
Super 8 (Abrams) 155
Swift, Taylor 197
Syrian Civil War, refugees 159–60

Tagaq, Tanya 225–6
Tagore, Rabindranath 216
Take 6 (vocal ensemble) 140, 142
Tanglewood Music Center 98
television, decolonizing disability in 166 *See also Crazy Ex-Girlfriend*
Temple, Alex 225–6, 229
Tenderness of Cranes (Korde) 208
Thailand *See The Lanna Dream* (Sirisook)
Theater of Voices chamber choir 152–3
theremin 154, 156
"third stream" approach 207, 217n1

Third Symphony (Bruckner) 221
This Love Between Us (Esmail) 276
Thommen, Johannes 89
Thompson, Joe 61, 62, 66–70, 72
Thompson, Odell 67, 68, 69, 72
Thompson, Tommy 67
Thornton, Leslie 172
time, non-linearity of 136–7, 141–2, 152
Titon, Jeff Todd 63
Tlingit people 116
Todd, Zoe 114
tokenization 11, 71, 270, 278–9
Tomorrow (magazine) 53–4
Tourism Authority of Thailand 235–6
tourist gaze 7, 11, 235–6 *See also The Lanna Dream* (Sirisook)
tradition: as fluid 122; remixing of, Indigenous 113, 116–22, 125
Traditional Ecological Knowledge (TEK) 9, 114, 120, 125–9
Traité de rythme, de couleur, et d'ornithologie (Messiaen) 99
transcription and analysis 208
transcultural composing 100
"Tristan trilogy" (Messiaen) 100
tropes 91, 141, 144, 168, 170; musical 9, 53, 62, 72, 160, 185–6, 195 *See also* stereotypes
"True Believer" (clipping.) 142
Trump, Donald 250, 255–6
Tsianina Redfeather 55
Tubman, Harriet 220, 230
Tuck, Eve 44
tunebooks, hymn 76
Turner, Ike and Tina 257
Turner, William H. 62

Underground Railroad 84
Underwood, Carrie 196–7
union, heavenly 85
Unipchaanich Imagluktugmiut (Stories of the Black River People) (Cleveland) 117
"Unite the Right Rally" (Charlottesville, Virginia) 222
University of California, Los Angeles 139
University of Richmond: "Contested Frequencies" conference 1–2, 12n2;

Tucker Boatwright Festival 205, 263, 266, 273, 275, 278–9 *See also* AudibleRVA
University of Southern California, Annenberg Inclusion Initiative (AII) 163, 164–7, 168, 177n6
Upper One Games 113, 116–22
UPROXX (website) 144

Valhalla Rising (Refn) 171
Van Huffel, Peter 250, 259
ventriloquization 174, 239–40
Ventura (Pueblo chief) 50
"verse-refrain" forms 99
Victoria, Queen of England 84
video game audio, decolonizing 7, 9, 113–29; "back-to-nature" gameplay 121; decolonizing game sound 114–16, 117; gender disparities in the video game market 117; *Honour Water* 114, 115–16, 123, 125–9; *Invaders* 114, 123–5, 129; LaPensée and Indigenous-determined game design 122–9; *Never Alone* 114, 115–22, 129
Villeneuve, Denis *See Arrival*
violence 139; in science fiction 154, 159; settler-colonial 123–4; against women 173–4, 178n20 *See also* slavery
Virginia Alcoholic Beverage Control Authority ("ABC") 31–2, 38n9
Virginia Commonwealth University (VCU) 30–1, 38n8
vococentrism 172
voice 26–7, 152–3, 171; Rebecca's vocality in *Crazy Ex-Girlfriend* 187–8, 189; self-sounding 145–6, 148; voice apprehension 171 *See also* muteness; *Splendor & Misery* (clipping.)
void 9, 142; self-sounding in the 145–6, 148 *See also Splendor & Misery* (clipping.)
Vonnegut, Kurt 136
Voting Rights Act (1965) 136

Wade, Bonnie 208
Waheed, Nayyirah 276

"Wake Up" (clipping.) 137, 144–5
Walker, Frank X. 62
"Wantage" (hymn tune) 86
Warner, Michael 36
Washington Post (newspaper) 61, 168, 177n11
wa-xo'-be ceremony 46–9
Wa-xri-ghi (Osage informant) 47
"We Are All Children of One Parent" (Clark) 83
Wells, Brad 225–6
Wells, Paul F. 61, 64–5
Werkstatt der Kulturen (jazz club) 247
Wesley, Charles 83
West, Cornel 142, 144
When Rivers Were Trails (LaPensée) 123, 129
Where Trails Have Led Me (Tsianina) 55
whiteness 70, 72, 84, 89, 90, 252, 260; abolitionist songs 88; in hymnody 82–3; identity 92, 154; memory and 220–3; penance 36–7; privilege 26, 27–8, 31; theories of 151–2, 157–8, 223; white fiddle repertoire 64; white flight 19, 26, 35; white musicians 32; white-owned music venues 32–3; white racial frame 3–4, 13n5, 223–6; white supremacy 71, 154, 222–3, 228, 231n2; whitewashing 61, 68, 227; white working class 28 *See also* AudibleRVA; Blackness, American; in Berlin jazz performance; *Red hot sun turning over*
"Wildest Dreams" (Swift) 197
Williams, John 154–5
Williams Mix (Cage) 139
Wise, Robert 154
Wizard of Oz (film) 167
Wolfe, Charles 63
women: Annenberg Inclusion Initiative (AII) 163, 164–7, 168, 177n6; of color 264–5, 275–6; composers 224; disabled, in film 10, 168, 171, 172, 173–4, 178n20, 24; feminism 173–6, 191; hand drum circles 125, 126, 130n4; misogyny 172, 190, 195, 198; representations of 238–42, 243; violence against 173–4, 178n20 *See also Crazy Ex-Girlfriend*; Esmail, Reena; *The Lanna Dream* (Sirisook)
"world games" 116–22
Wright, Richard 27

Yang, K. Wayne 44
Yavapai-Apache people 53–4
youth 82–3, 84, 119, 126, 129, 237
The Youth's Cabinet (Clark) 83

Zimmer, Hans 156
"Zion" (Hastings) 81
Ziporyn, Evan 224–5, 226
Zitkála-Šá (Gertrude Bonnin) 54

www.ingramcontent.com/pod-product-compliance
Lightning Source LLC
Chambersburg PA
CBHW070750020526
44115CB00032B/1612